RELIGION AND THE TRANSFORMATIONS OF CAPITALISM

'This impressive collection of essays is undoubtedly a major contribution to the re-establishment of the sociology of religion on a genuinely comparative and historical basis . . . I am filled with admiration for Roberts' industry, enthusiasm and clear sighted grasp of a complex field'. Harvie Ferguson, University of Glasgow.

Religion and the Transformations of Capitalism addresses from a socio-scientific standpoint the interaction of religions and forms of contemporary capitalism. The book is divided into three parts: Part I offers a series of readings of the 'classics' re-interpreted in the light of contemporary scholarship of the type Weber himself conducted; Part II contains rather different discussions of the active connections between resurgent capitalism and new religious movements in developed societies; Part III deals with aspects of 'globalization' and 'post-modernity' and their inter-relation with religious transformations.

Discussion of the global socio-cultural and economic matrix and its religious dimensions has grown in importance since the collapse of Marxist socialism and the resurgence of religious, national and ethnic identities. The collection draws upon the research and experience of scholars whose first hand acquaintance with diverse yet representative settings allows the reader to explore a wide range of interactions between economic systems and their socio-cultural contexts. This outstanding collection will be an invaluable resource for students of religious studies, comparative religions and sociological theory.

Richard Roberts is Professor of Divinity and Director of the Institute for Religion and the Human Sciences, University of St Andrews. He will shortly take up a Chair in Religious Studies at Lancaster University.

Contributors: Peter Beyer; Alan Black; David Bromley; Simon Coleman; Anne Eyre; David Gellner; James Grayson; Rosalind Hackett; Nikos Kokosalakis; Helmut Loiskandl; David Martin; Paul Morris; Julian Pas; Stephen Sharot; William Swatos Jr; Ivan Varga.

RELIGION AND THE TRANSFORMATIONS OF CAPITALISM

Comparative approaches

Edited by Richard H. Roberts

London and New York

First published 1995
by Routledge
11 New Fetter Lane, London EC4P 4EE

Simultaneously published in the USA and Canada
by Routledge
29 West 35th Street, New York, NY 10001

Typeset in Times by LaserScript, Mitcham, Surrey
Printed and bound in Great Britain by
Mackays of Chatham PLC, Chatham, Kent

British Library Cataloguing in Publication Data
A catalogue record for this book is available from the British Library

Library of Congress Cataloging in Publication Data
A catalogue record for this book has been requested

ISBN 0–415–11917–0

CONTENTS

v

Part II The new handmaid?
Religion and the empowerment of capitalism

Part III Religion and modernity/post-modernity
– capitalism and cultures East and West

CONTRIBUTORS

Peter Beyer is a lecturer in the Department for the Study of Religion, University of Toronto. His current research interests include the ecological involvement of Canadian mainline Christian churches, and the historical development and current state of a global religious system. He is the author of *Religion and Globalization* (1994).

Alan W. Black is an Associate Professor of Sociology at the University of New England, Armidale, Australia. From 1993 to 1995 he served as President of the Australian Association for the Study of Religions. He is currently an executive member of the International Sociological Association Research Committee on the Sociology of Religion. His recent books include *Religion in Australia: Sociological Perspectives* and *Australian Farmers' Attitudes to Rural Environmental Issues*. He has a forthcoming volume entitled *The Quest for Church Union*.

David G. Bromley is currently Professor of Sociology at Virginia Common-wealth University in Richmond and the University of Virginia in Charlottesville. He is currently editor of the *Journal for the Scientific Study of Religion* and is past-president of the Association for the Sociology of Religion. He writes in the area of religion, with a particular interest in contemporary religious movements. His most recent books include *The Anticult Movement: An International Perspective* and *The Handbook of Cults and Sects in America* (1993).

Simon M. Coleman is a lecturer in anthropology in the University of Durham, England. Previously, he has been a research fellow at both St John's and Churchill Colleges, Cambridge. His main research interests include the globalization of evangelical Christianity, religion and the media, and (in combination with an art historian) pilgrimage ritual and narrative. He has carried out fieldwork in Uppsala, Sweden, since 1986, and in Walsingham, Norfolk, since 1993.

Anne Eyre has a PhD in the Sociology of Religion from the University of Liverpool. She lectured for two years in Malaysia which stimulated her research interests in the Far East. She currently lectures in Theology and Society at Westminster College, Oxford and is an active member of the International

Society for the Sociology of Religion and the British Sociological Association's Sociology of Religion Study Group.

David N. Gellner studied politics, philosophy and economics at Oxford, followed by an MPhil in Indian Religion. His doctoral research has been published in *Monk, Householder, and Tantric Priest: Newar Buddhism and its hierarchy of ritual* (1992), in numerous articles, and will also appear in a multi-authored volume co-edited with Declan Quigley, *Contested Hierarchies: A collaborative ethnography of caste among the Newars of the Kathmandu Valley, Nepal* (forthcoming). He has been a junior research fellow at St John's College, Oxford, and British Academy Postdoctoral Fellow at Wolfson College and the Institute of Social and Cultural Anthropology, Oxford. He is now lecturer in social anthropology at Brunel University, London.

James Huntley Grayson, Senior Lecturer in Modern Korean Studies, in the Director of the Centre for Korean Studies at the University of Sheffield. Trained in anthropology and systematic theology, Dr Grayson served as a Methodist missionary in Korea from 1971 to 1987. His most recent book is *Korea: A Religious History* (1989).

Rosemary I.J. Hackett is a specialist in African religions. After a training in religious studies in Birmingham, Dr Hackett taught and researched for eight years in Nigeria before taking posts in the Center for African Studies at the University of Tennessee. Most of Dr Hackett's publications have been in the area of new religious movements in Africa, with a particular focus on the newer breed of Christian revivalist movement. She is editor of *New Religious Movements in Nigeria* (1987).

Nikos Kokosalakis has been senior lecturer at Liverpool University where he took early retirement recently as honorary senior fellow. He holds degrees from Athens and Geneva and a PhD from Liverpool University. He served as Secretary and President of the Research Committee on Sociology of Religion of the International Sociological Association, has written *Ethnic Identity and Religion* (1982), has contributed to various books, and has published over thirty articles in national and international professional journals.

Helmut Loiskandl is Professor of Comparative Sociology at Tokiwa University in Mito, Japan. He has taught in Europe, America and Australia. He is interested in social change in the area of migration, the interrelation of ethnic identifi- cation and religion with theoretical issues on the border of philosophy and sociology. One of his more recent publications is a translation of and introduction to Georg Simmel's *Schopenhauer and Nietzsche*.

David Martin is Honorary Professor in the Department of Religious Studies, Lancaster University, Emeritus Professor of Sociology at the LSE, London University, and International Research Associate of the Institute for the Study of Economic Culture, Boston University. He was until recently Scurlock Professor at Southern Methodist University, Dallas, and visiting appointments have been as F.D. Maurice Lecturer, King's College, London University (1991) and Sarum Lecturer, Oxford University (1994–5). His most recent book is *Tongues of Fire* (1990) and a further book on evangelical advance in Latin America is to appear co-authored with his wife, Bernice.

Paul Morris is Professor of Religious Studies at Victoria University of Wellington, New Zealand. He has recently completed a manuscript on the life and work of the German Jewish philosopher, Franz Rosenzweig. His publications include papers on religion and politics, Jewish biblical interpretation, comparative philosophy of religion, modern Jewish thought and theories of religion. His current research projects include a study of religion and colonialism.

Julian F. Pas was born and raised in Belgium. After theological studies at the University of Louvain, he spent over 6 years in Taiwan. In 1967 he went to Canada to undertake a PhD in Religious Studies (with a focus on Chinese religions). From 1969–94 he taught Religious Studies, especially China, at the University of Saskatchewan, Saskatoon. Publications include: as editor, *Turning of the Tide. Religion in China Today* (1989); translated from the French (with Norman Girandory) *Taoist Meditation* (1993); *Visions of Sukhavati Shantao's Commentary on the Kuan wu-liang-shou-Foching* (forthcoming). From 1987–93 he was editor of *Journal of Chinese Religions*. He is also the author of many articles on Chinese religions: Buddhism, Taoism and popular religion.

Richard H. Roberts is Professor of Divinity and Director of the Institute for Religion and the Human Sciences at the University of St Andrews. He is author of *Hope and its Hieroglyph: a Critical Decipherment of Ernst Bloch 'Principle of Hope'* (1989) and *A Theology on its Way? Essays on Karl Barth* (1992), and co-editor with James Good of *The Recovery of Rhetoric: Persuasive Discourse and Disciplinarity in the Human Sciences* (1993). Professor Roberts will shortly take up a Chair in Religious Studies at Lancaster University where he will specialise in the interdisciplinary study of contemporary religion in socio-cultural context. At present he is completing *Religion and the Resurgence of Capitalism*.

Stephen Sharot is Professor of Sociology in the Department of Behavioural Sciences, Ben-Gurion University of the Negev, Beersheva, Israel. His publications include *Messianism, Mysticism, and Magic: A Sociological Analysis of Jewish Religious Movements* (University of North Carolina Press, 1982) and as co-author *Ethnicity, Religion, and Class in Israeli Society* (CUP, 1991). He is Editor of the journal *Israel Social Science Research*. His current research includes a comparative study of relationships between elite and folk religions in the world religions, and a comparison of Judaism in modern Israel and the diaspora.

William H. Swatos Jr, has recently completed a second consecutive term as Editor of *Sociology of Religion: A Quarterly Review*, the official journal of the Association for the Sociology of Religion, and is now Editor-in-Chief of the forthcoming volume, *Religion and the Social Sciences: An Encyclopedia*, to be published in 1997. His recent works include the edited collections *Twentieth-Century World Religious Movements in Neo-Weberian Perspective* (1992), *A Future for Religion? New Paradigms for Social Analysis* (1993), *The Rapture of Politics: The Christian Right as the United States Approaches the Year 2000* (1994), and *Politics and Religion in Central and Eastern Europe* (1994).

Ivan Varga is Professor of Sociology at Queen's University, Kingston, Ontario, Canada. He is Honourary President of the Sociology of Religion Research Committee of the International Sociological Association and Scientific Adviser to the Institute of Sociology, Hungarian Academy of Science. His present research interests focus on religion and postmodernity, religion and modernization processes, with special emphasis on East-Central Europe. His recent publications include 'The modernization that failed', in B. Berman and P. Dutkiewicz (eds), *Crisis and Change in Eastern Europe and Africa* (1993). 'Churches, politics and society in post-communist East-Central Europe', in W. Swatos (ed.), *Politics and Religion in Central and Eastern Europe* (1994). 'Religion et société civile en Europe de l'Est: Le cas Hongrois', in P. Michel (ed.), *Religion à l'Est* (1992). 'Zivilgesellschaft und Zivilreligion in Osteuropa' [Civil society and civil religion in Eastern Europe], in *EPD Dokumentation* (1988). 'The politicisation of the transcendent', in J.M. Bak and G. Benecke (eds), in *Religion and Rural Revolt*, 1984.

PREFACE AND ACKNOWLEDGEMENTS

This collection of essays largely (but not exclusively) originated from the Conference 'Religion and the Resurgence of Capitalism' that I coordinated in the Department of Religious Studies in association with the Centre for the Study of Cultural Values. Owing to circumstances beyond my control the publication of these papers has been delayed. I am grateful first of all for the patience and forbearance shown by contributors.

My time as M.B. Reckitt Research Fellow at the University of Lancaster (1989–91) was a most rewarding experience. Collaboration with John Clayton, Paul Heelas, John Milbank and Paul Morris, amongst many others, and inter-action with the outstanding Department of Sociology, made Lancaster the ideal setting for an ambitious project. Adrian Cunningham and Patrick Sherry as successive Chairs provided consistent support throughout. My debts at Lancaster are many and heartfelt – my appreciation is here expressed to friends and colleagues with intellectual vision and the courage to tackle major issues in the context of a first class research environment.

I should also like to acknowledge and register my gratitude to the Christendom Trust who funded the Reckitt Research Fellowship and endorsed a project which brought together an extremely diverse (and at times pointedly conflictual) group at a memorable conference. Thus the opening session of the event, a remarkable con-frontation between Professors Michael Novak and Charles Davis, and moderated (although this is scarcely an apposite word) by Professor A. H. Halsey, plunged all participants into sharp but informed disagreements concerning the future of the global economy and its ethical, religious and theological factors. The present volume represents the socio-scientific contributions to the conference; the ethical and theo-logical contributions will appear (all being well) in a second collection.

At Lancaster I received invaluable and diverse help from Henry Lupton whose pioneering expertise with a database accelerated every aspect of the project. Wendy Francis and Janice Parkes unstintingly provided such secretarial help as they could under the intense pressure generated by a busy and successful Department.

Richard H. Roberts
St Andrews
February, 1994

xi

INTRODUCTION

Religion and capitalism – a new convergence?

Richard H. Roberts

The present collection of essays draws upon the research and experience of scholars whose first hand acquaintance with diverse yet representative settings allows the reader to explore a wide range of interactions between economic systems and their socio-cultural contexts. The editor's purpose in this introduction is to draw out and relate the major themes of the contributors, and to locate them in three areas of central concern to contemporary discussion of the global socio-cultural and economic matrix and its religious dimensions. These three thematic strands in the religion/capitalism problematic are as follows: first, revisions of Weber's comparative-historical sociology of religion; second, the impact of 'resurgent capitalism' and its assimilative and creative power with regard to religion and religiosity in the new synergies of various forms of 'prosperity religion' which may lend substance to claims to speak of a 'new spirit of capitalism'; and third, the emergent importance of the 'globalization' process and new configurations in the relation of modern and post-modern factors, not least since the collapse of Marxism and of the former Eastern bloc.

The religion/capitalism matrix is now in a state of relative flux, and the essays in this collection provide a representative (but not exhaustive) sample of interpreted evidence drawn from a complex situation in which new trends are emerging that are as yet not satisfactorily theorized. Thus the transformations in East–Central Europe since 1989-90[1], the relationship between religion, economic development and contemporary business and management practice (especially with regard to Japan and globalized Japanese and Japanese-influenced corporate activity worldwide),[2] and the meaning and theoretical significance of the concept of 'globalization' as a means of representing the world system in an era of post-modernity, all continue to be matters of lively debate. These have important consequences for the comprehension of religion as a substantive factor in the evolution of global and local world systems.

At a basic level the very word 'capitalism' is itself both value-charged and problematic – yet unavoidable in contemporary discussion. Thus in business ethics circles in the United States cautious exception is taken to the term 'capitalism', whereas 'free market economy' or 'democratic capitalism' are the preferred designations.[3] Other expressions such as the 'global economy' or the 'world economic system' are favoured by others; yet, properly qualified, the term 'capitalism' links contemporary debate to a longstanding tradition. Moreover, it accurately reflects the self-conscious policy of what amounted to a re-discovery and re-assertion of classical political economy in the policies of the New Right and of successive Conservative and Republican administrations in the Reagan–Thatcher era. Thus whilst 'capitalism' is employed in this volume in its generally accepted senses, its precise meaning is subject to contextual variation as and when used by contributors.

Whilst as argued above there are central themes capable of facilitating the coherent analysis of the contemporary religion/capitalism matrix, it is also important to recognize the sheer diversity and complexity, and both the local and global aspects of each empirical situation. Thus the third part of this volume extends the theoretical and empirical analyses of the first and second parts into a more illustrative review that proceeds from consideration of the newly emergent Eastern Europe, the Far East and Australia. In the remainder of this introduction we review and relate together the contents of the three divisions of the volume.

The classical arguments concerning the relationship between religion and capitalism have long been dominated by Max Weber's so-called 'Protestant ethic' thesis and his account of the de-mystification (*Entzauberung*) of the modern world in the face of the instrumental rationality of modernity. The discussion of this set of arguments has been very extensive, yet despite many apparent near deaths through a thousand qualifications, recent work,[4] not least some of that represented in the first part of this volume, is evidence of the extraordinary resilience of Weber's theses. This book brings together chapters which suggest that in an era of resurgent capitalism there is a mutual and dynamic relation between religion and economic processes, involving in some contexts the growth of new forms of religiosity in the context of economic activity and wealth creation itself.

It is against Marx's (and Engel's) immensely influential and reductive account of religion (and the other items in the cultural 'superstructure' or *Überbau*) that Max Weber (1864-1920) may be said where reacted, at least in part. Whereas Marx proposed an interpretative framework in which religion was understood in terms of alienation and epiphenomenal displacement, Weber's methodology was based initially upon the quantitative accumulation of complex social data which, through the generation of 'ideal types', suggested the means for qualitative interpretation. Thus in his sociology of religion and studies of the economic ethics of world religions, Weber avoided the monolithic reductionism of Marx when he maintained on a methodological level that to define 'religion' is not possible at the start of a presentation but only at the conclusion of the study in question. Such an approach, which harnesses both theory and substantive definition to empirical interpretation, remains a powerful and salutary challenge to any social scientist concerned with the relation of religion and capitalism which we have tried to respect.

2

Max Weber has thus remained a figure of scarcely diminished importance in the human and social sciences. Often seen as a counterpoise to Marx, Weber provided many of the basic concepts of British and North American sociology: 'rationalization', 'ideal-type', 'unintended consequences of social action', 'charismatic authority', 'the iron cage of bureaucratic life', and 'the Protestant ethic', and so on. Weber disputed the Marxian view of the epiphenomenal status of ideas in bourgeois law, moral values and religion in relation to socio-economic reality without relapsing into the opposing 'idealist' position, characteristic all too frequently of post-Enlightenment Christian and religious thinkers. Weber was both a prophet and an interpreter of the forms of modernity and instrumental rationality associated with the rise and triumph of industrial capitalism. The consequences of the latter for the quality of human life were immeasurable. Weber's much-quoted and despairing prediction in the closing pages of *The Protestant Ethic and the Spirit of Capitalism* is a fitting backdrop to the ambiguous resurgences of both capitalism and religion in our own time:

> No-one knows who will live in this cage in the future, or whether at this end of this tremendous development entirely new prophets will arise, or there will be a great rebirth of old ideas and ideals, or, if neither, mechanized petrification, embellished with a sort of convulsive self-importance. For of the last stage of this cultural development, it might well truly be said: "specialists without spirit, sensualists without heart; this nullity imagines that it has attained a level of civilization never before achieved".
>
> (Weber 1904–5: 182)

Nonetheless, whether the 'cage' is rigid or elastic, gilded or squalid, it should be remembered that Max Weber's interpretative sociology of the religion/capitalism matrix has never enjoyed a monopoly. Whilst in this volume David Gellner and William Swatos provide powerful yet qualified defences of Weber's accounts of Indian religion and Islam, respectively, Paul Morris and Peter Beyer afford insights which show in different but complementary ways that there are viable alternatives to Weber's accounts of the relationship between religious and economic behaviour. Thus Morris challenges Weber's historical interpretation through a close study of Judaism and capitalism, giving particular attention to the context and reception of Werner Sombart's *The Jews and Modern Capitalism*. Beyer opens a way forward through a contextualized study of religion and recently emergent globalization theory.

Morris and Beyer also seek to demonstrate in their respective ways that the intellectual and cultural agency expressed in the ethical and theological reflection of religious traditions in 'economic cultures'[5] possesses a contemporary importance greater than Weber, or the more materialist exponents of the Weberian approach, might normally concede.[6] Whereas Gellner, Swatos, James Grayson and Helmut Loiskandl can be regarded (with greater and lesser degrees of explicit allegiance) as neo-Weberians concerned with the styles of rationality expressed by religious traditions in relation to capitalism and modernity, Beyer and Morris with their shared interest in the cultural agency of religious collectivities do not fall within the former designation.

Part I opens with a revised version of David Gellner's now classic article 'Weber, Capitalism and the Religion of India', in which Weber's book *The Religion of India* (and its subsequent reception) is evaluated in terms which take into account the inadequacies of interpretations grounded in the often imperfectly related disciplines of Indology, Islamic studies and the social sciences of anthropology and sociology. Gellner draws attention to three 'fallacies' that have distorted the debate over Weber's 'Protestantism' thesis. Thus the latter's alleged idealism with regard to the causal power of religious beliefs, reductive represent-ations of the problem of development, and the foisting onto Weber of a simplistic, Humean view of social causality are all tackled as parts of a ground-clearing operation that re-opens a path to *The Religion of India*. Gellner's careful analysis exposes Weber's basic contentions that:

> Protestantism was one element of a situation which, taken as a whole, was sufficient to produce a capitalist spirit, which in turn was . . . necessary for the first unplanned appearance of industrial society.

Although other elements for the production of capitalism sometimes existed, a capitalist spirit as such was absent in South Asia, China, or Islam. Thus:

> Without a protestant ethic or some equivalent no traditional (i.e. agrarian) civilization could develop capitalism "from within itself". Only religious sanctions, Weber assumed, could induce men permanently to defer satis-faction in the way required to produce the capitalist spirit. No this-worldly religious ethic could produce an active rational this-worldly asceticism: only an active type of soteriology could do so.

As Gellner points out, Weber's own studies revealed the existence of an analog-ous ethic in Jainism, and Helmut Loiskandl writing on Japan and Kenneth Grayson on Korea extend consideration of this problematic. Whilst both the latter examples reinforce (but in different ways) the Weberian view of there being elective affinities between certain forms of religious ethic and dynamic economic activity, any such relationships always have to be understood in context and not generated on the basis of any general theory of socio-cultural causation, be it materialist or idealistic in orientation. Gellner's final judgement upon Weber's virtues, that is to say the latter's unrivalled comparative range, historical depth and theoretical apparatus, confronts the reader with an acute problem: the neces-sary imperfection of any contemporary comparative work undertaken in the face of the explosion of knowledge.[7] In the light of this complexity the present volume is more an advance into new areas that must be understood rather as the prior condition of theoretical integration than an attempt at such synthesis, for which the moment is not yet, in this writer's view, fully ripe.

William Swatos turns once again to the Weberian legacy in order to defend it with substantial qualifications and then to employ Weber's conceptual apparatus to clarify the nature of contemporary Islamic states and their associations with capitalism. Like Gellner, Swatos begins, not surprisingly, with an appraisal of the work of Weber on Islam and its reception, besides *The Protestant Ethic and the Spirit of Capitalism*. Unlike many commentators, Swatos (doubtless as a North American scholar having been educated with some awareness of classical rhetoric) grasps the peculiar character of Weber's approach as 'an enthymematic argument about a religious way of acting and a world view'. In other words, Weber was not engaged in dialectical (i.e. logically rigorous) proof as such, but in the educing of what have proved to be highly durable interpretative generalizations, the loci or commonplaces, that guide thought towards more precise, context-specific accounts of the religion/capitalism problematic. As Swatos points out, Weber's interest in comparative analysis was not merely scientific, he regretted the absence of the experience of hard asceticism in German history which had led, so he thought, to her relative economic failure in comparison with Anglo-America.

According to Swatos, for Weber 'Islam was to be the final and most perfect foil of the Protestant ethic thesis'. Conceding Weber's relatively less careful treatment of Islam as compared with his essays on Hinduism and Buddhism, Swatos focuses his discussion around ethics, law and political organization understood as unified by the arbitrariness of patrimonial rule that becomes sultanism in its extreme form. Swatos criticises both Brian Turner's rejection of Weber's interpretation of Islam as a 'religion of warriors' and Susan Croutwater's attack upon Weber's concept of sultanism. He then proceeds to apply the patrimonialism/traditional and sultanism/modern distinctions to the contemporary Islamic states of (e.g.) Kuwait and Iraq. It is, he maintains, somewhat ironic that the capitalist world powers prefer to deal with traditional rather than modern Islamic states because of the relative predictability of the behaviour of the former. Swatos argues from a sociological standpoint for the relative uniformity of Islam in the Mediterranean Basin and the Near and Middle East as a traditional force, despite the Sunni/Shi'ite distinction. Islam on the Pacific rim is understood as a modernizing factor as opposed to patrimonialism. Swatos touches upon Indonesia and Malaysia, thus opening up a contrast between 'traditional' and 'modern' Islam that undergoes further contextual clarification in Anne Eyre's study of Malaysia in part III. Swatos concludes with the identification of a positive parallel between Puritanism and 'merchant' Islam in Southeast Asia which purports to be both modern and legitimate. This is the most explicit contemporary confirmation of the Protestant ethic thesis to be found in this volume.

Helmut Loiskandl and James Grayson provide parallel, yet strongly contrasting accounts of the influence of religous factors on the organization of social and economic interaction. Loiskandl takes up the discussion since Weber and Bellah in order to question the emphasis given by the latter to Confucianism as a rational ethics confronting the pious reality acceptance of both Buddhism, and Shinto as exemplified in 'Tokugawa Religion'. Loiskandl contends, however, that Confucianism is a 'force which not so much created as articulated the values by which Japanese society works'. He then develops an argument which lays particular emphasis upon the evolution in the modern business context of traditional Japanese ethical values orginating in Shinto, as the latter provides the 'strongest religious stimuli influencing economic structure as well as interaction in Japan', rather than Confucian traditions.[8] Yet in contrast with Weber and others' emphasis upon an ethic (which is implicitly equated with 'moral concern'), Loiskandl argues against the contention that 'Japanese religion is only concerned with the internal problems of man' and thus with processes of reality acceptance, rather than its transformation.

A widely current view maintains that because both Buddhism and Shinto propound a 'pious' acceptance, and because neither of these elements of traditional Japanese religion provided supplied ethical principles, it required the Tokugawa government to implant Confucianism in order to make good this ethical deficit. By contrast, Loiskandl outlines and analyses the main aspects of Japanese ethical orientation in terms of different understandings of the individual, respect for social consensus, the life-community, loyalty and the professional ethics of Bushido, and, perhaps most interestingly for those concerned with the impact of capitalism, the nature of 'trans-rationality' and beauty. According to Loiskandl, these elements of Japanese culture are endorsed by both Shinto and Buddhism, thus the Japanese analogues of Weberian 'inner-worldly asceticism' consist in attitudes that are consistent with the Shinto village community and involve the development of the business organization as quasi-sacred communities; indeed, the 'workplace is actually accepted as total community by workers and their families'. The result could be described as a form of collective, rather than individual, inner asceticism. Loiskandl reports that Japanese sociologists now argue that the traditional Shinto pattern of social interaction is the most decisive agent of the Japanese way of modernization. This contrast between East and West (if sustainable) is remarkable: modernization in Japan reinforces and develops community, whereas in the West it destroys communities and atomizes individuals. Such a contrast provides important interpretative background to the accounts of attempts to re-invigorate charismatic, entrepreneurial capitalism in non-Eastern cultures that are reviewed in part II.

James Grayson's account of the 'dynamic complementarity' between Confucianism and Christianity in Korea provides historical insight into a context far less well known than the Japanese example which has been the subject of extended discussion. The history of Korean religious and philosophical culture was permeated with Confucianism, but this influence was primarily upon the cultural and political spheres. When Buddhism came to Korea it complemented Confucianism as it was primarily concerned with the after-life and metaphysical questions, rather than with politics and morals. During the Choson Dynasty (1392-1910) the state became the most consistently Confucian in East Asia, outdoing China itself. Not only this, but the original Confucianism of the Chinese Han Dynasty (206 BC – AD 220) of earlier times was supplanted by Chu Hsi's more invasive form which appropriated cultural and religious space occupied by Buddhism.

In effect, the cultural claims of Confucianism became rigidified, exclusive, reductive and totalitarian. This created a spiritual vacuum which permitted the temporary and dissonant assimilation of Roman Catholic ideas from the mid-seventeenth century onwards, a process which led to a long persecution of the Church from 1800 onwards. The introduction of Protestant Christianity in the 1880s resulted in dramatic growth, owed, according to Grayson, to the existence of 'a religious vacuum which had been created by the aridity of neo-Confucian thought and by the concomitant suppression of Buddhism and all other forms of heterodox thought and superstitious practice'.

The ensuing career of Protestant Christianity in Korea is remarkable. Unlike Japan, where Christianity of all forms has always been culturally problematic, Protestantism in Korea formed an alliance with Korean nationalism, a role which was consolidated during the Japanese occupation. Education (to which Christianity had made an important contribution) played a decisive role in post-war development and Grayson isolates a series of complementarities between Protestant Christianity and the spiritual demands of a growing urban population undergoing rapid social change. Grayson goes so far as to conclude that 'without the spiritual support of Christianity . . . the Korean nation would have lacked the moral and social coherence to survive the massive pressures imposed upon it by the social and economic changes which have occurred over the past three decades'.

The conclusions drawn above reinforce arguments about the necessity of the existence of a sound cultural base for the success of capitalism. Wider implications that relate to having moral and spiritual resources drawn from a religiously-based culture for successful socio-economic development are relevant, it is not unreasonable to suggest, for societies like those of Britain and the United States which have sought to develop a resurgent capitalism. Unfortunately, however, it is precisely at the level of the moral and educational infrastructure, where the circulation of 'cultural capital' takes place, that the religiosities and ethos of 'enterprise culture'[9] and prosperity theology appear to be at their weakest, as we shall see in part II.

Paul Morris and Peter Beyer explore the involution of economic factors and socio-cultural development in historical and contemporary terms, respectively. Paul Morris examines the relation of Judaism and capitalism from the standpoint of Moses Hess, Karl Marx, Bruno Bauer, Werner Sombart, Isaac Deutscher, Irving Kristol and Milton Friedman. The originality of Morris' essay consists not least in his comprehensive and critical articulation of Sombart's alternative theory to Weber's *Protestant Ethic and the Spirit of Capitalism*. Starting out with Marx's anti-semitic attitude towards Judaism, his conception of Christianity as 'completed Judaism', and a model of the capitalist as 'nought but his Jew writ large', Morris reworks in a comprehensive way a post-Marxist, yet Marxian account of the intrinsic bond between capitalism and modern Western culture as refracted through the recent history of anti-semitism and the pre-history of Zionism.

Morris recounts the resultant tensions for Jews committed to forms of socialism which admitted elements of this negative construal of the alliance of Judaism and capitalism. In the face of the near monopoly of discussion of the religious aspects of the genesis of capitalism enjoyed by Weberian and neo-Weberian accounts (a tendency further encouraged by the collapse of Marxism–Leninism and the socialist regimes of Eastern Europe in 1989–90), Morris presents an alternative account culminating (with regard to Sombart) in the claim that it is Jewish law that lies behind Calvinism itself. Weber's response to Sombart and his representation of the Jews as a 'pariah people' need to be understood, Morris points out, in the context of their respective cultural and political agendas. Thus the present-day Jewish 'New Right' is obviously heir to a complex and problematic inheritance.

Morris draws his reflections together with a trenchant plea for the integrity of active Jewish law (*halakah*), on the basis that it is 'an error to allow the dictates of the market system (or socialism) to define the significance of Jewish law'. Indeed, Morris goes further (and this is where the inevitably *theological* character of the question as to the ultimate significance of capitalism emerges)[10] and argues for a widening of the remit of the law: 'The question of being honourable in your dealings must be extended to the sanctioning of a system that re-defines all individual acts'. The question therefore left with the reader is this: after the death of Marxism is the only effective source for structural critiques of the unchallenged (and seemingly unchallengeable) power of global capitalism to be found in the discourses of theology and religion which specialise in the articulation of ultimacy?[11]

In the final contribution to part I, Peter Beyer subjects the hyperbole of recent years, talk of the 'resurgence' of capitalism and religion, or of 'new world order' and even the 'end of history', to testing in the light of globalization theory. Insofar as Beyer continues the task of interpreting the relation of religion to socio-economic structure, he follows in the footsteps of Weber. But Beyer's approach represents a kind of synthetic middle way between the two tendencies, Weberian and neo-Marxist, seen in the essays of the previous contributors, and Paul Morris, respectively.

In effect, the interpretative impulse of neo-Weberianism and the structural analysis of neo-Marxism come together in globalization theory. Beyer addresses two major issues in the light of the latter theory. First, does the collapse of socialism imply the resurgence of capitalism? In other words, to what extent is is it possible to think in terms of qualitative discontinuity and a new beginning in history? Second, what is the role of religion in the globalization process given that religion has an ambiguous status? In the light of these factors Beyer argues that religion is 'at once an important way of communicating and one that, at the global level, is at a structural disadvantage when compared to more powerful modes such as positive law, politics, economy and science'. Indeed, despite its tendency to become privatized, religion has functional characteristics which 'makes it a suitable perspective from which to address the "residual" problems of global society, namely those that the operation of the more powerful globalizing systems (economy, states, and so on) creates but does not solve'.

Beyer pursues his analysis in relation to a qualitative content analysis of public documents issued by Canadian churches, that is the products of a group of potential global religious agents. Beyer advances a defence of the importance of liberal religious reflection in terms of a 'Social Justice Ethic and the Spirit of Globalization' which could serve as a promising means for understanding larger historical change. Such an argument is very preliminary, not least because globalization theory is now in a state of rapid development and the widespread use of the term 'globalization' tends to outrun its testing in empirical and contextual analysis.[12]

Part I serves to provide a theoretical setting for part II, 'The New Handmaid?', which contains five studies (based on field-work in the United States, Sweden, Britain, Africa and Chile) by David Bromley, Simon Coleman, Richard Roberts, Rosalind Hackett and David Martin, respectively. These chapters scrutinize the diverse ways in which religion, religiosity and prosperity theologies co-operate in the empowerment of contemporary capitalism. In part II we examine patterns of synergistic convergence between religion and capitalism that afford an important contrast with the more critical interactions presented in part I.

In his study of the direct sales organization Amway, David Bromley shows how a large North American corporation negotiates the increasing disjunction between the contractually organized public sphere of social life and the covenantally organized private sphere, in circumstances where the former tends to predominate over the latter. In this account the reader first encounters the phenomenon of 'quasi-religion', where the corporation 'promises to reintegrate work, politics, family, community and religion through the formation of *family*-businesses that are linked together into a tightly-knit social network and legitimated symbolically by appeals to nationalism and transcendent purpose'. The origins of such a promised integration are traced back to the North American traditions of the Gospel of Prosperity, harmonial philosophy and positive thinking.

According to Bromley, Amway (as a representative organization) offers the opportunity for competing 'baby-boomers' to break out of the constraints of declining prosperity and diminishing expectations and restore control to their lives. In other words, Amway offers the possibility of restoring the American Dream in an era of reduced circumstances and the threat of loss of class status. The affinities between Amway's 'American Way' and traditional forms of faith commitment are apparent: increasing tension culminating in conversion, risk-taking, and release into a new social world with known and commonly celebrated ground-rules are common to both. Not surprisingly, however, Amway's activities are permeated by ironic tensions in that what it restores is consumer-based capitalism, not the production-driven pioneer capitalism that it idealizes. It is also apparent that the success of Amway, achieved despite a very high turnover of staff, is an indication of the intensity of the social needs it addresses.

Simon Coleman's chapter on North American influenced prosperity theology in Sweden provides an important parallel and comparison with David Bromley's study of Amway. Both the latter and the 'Faith Movement' in Sweden are operating at the leading edge of social change. Coleman examines Swedish experience in the light of the worldwide revival of conservative Protestantism, and the global, but ambiguous resurgence of capitalism. As we have seen in the North American example, the relative decline and crisis of capitalism as an accessible and effective means of enabling self-development and increasing familial wealth forms the background to the activities of Amway as a capitalist restorationist movement.

The so-called 'triumph' of capitalism predicated on the basis of the collapse of Marxist socialism in 1989–90 could, arguably, be understood as an aspect of an ongoing crisis of relative decline in the global economic system. Thus the global relocation of productive activity and the concomitant redistribution of wealth creation exacerbated differentials and created local crises in economies from which production has migrated. Indeed, it is plausible to regard the socially-embedded forms of both North American and Swedish prosperity theology as restorationist and emancipatory in orientation. The former addresses loss of agency through 'natural' economic decline and impoverishment, whereas the latter directs itself against the enforced restrictions and uniformitarianism of the 'all win or none win' ethos and social policies of the Swedish welfare state. Both movements are concerned with what the re-sacralization of capitalism understood, as Coleman puts it, 'as much more than a mode of production, since it implies a cultural totality of political, social and symbolic elements'. It is of course precisely this totalizing tendency which Paul Morris has attacked in part I through his call for an extension of the application of Jewish law.

In Sweden prosperity theology has thus functioned as an anti-institutional catalyst for debate over the future of the democratic institutions of the country as a whole. Aggressive economic and personal risk-taking understood as a sign of effective faith is plausible where a culture of equalitarianism and correlative constraints restricted the range of possible dissonances. Coleman's generalizations are important. Whereas Amway is restorationist in orientation and represents economic activity as imbued with quasi-religious practices dedicated to the celebration of a particular vision of American commercial and cultural identity, the Swedish Word of Life movement relies specifically upon an transcultural, supremely globalizable and autonomous 'Word' that facilitates a split between signifier and signified and the commodification of evangelism in a global information system. Both Amway and the Word of Life movement endorse free market principles and practices, but the mediation of catalytic function in their respective societies is markedly different, and both are distinctively ambivalent with regard to modernity. In terms of globalization, however, a new configuration of supremacy emerges: Sweden, the United States, South Africa and South Korea become the quadrants in a 'kind of globalized, civil religious ethic, incorporating a global division of labour'. Such a tendency contrasts in content and intention with the globalized liberal religiosity which Peter Beyer depicted in the conclusion of his chapter.

In the next contribution to this section, the editor presents a contextualized study of religiosity and quasi-religiosity to be found in the growing and socially ascendent British managerial elite and its trainers and facilitators. Remarkable in this context is the relative absence of Christian participation and the apparent failure of any explicit prosperity gospel of the kind examined in the two earlier chapters in part II to take hold in Britain. Thus whilst it would certainly have been possible to present evidence of the synergy of management training with so-called New Age practices in the United States (and further afield), this chapter looks in some detail at the context in which the 'Thatcher revolution' originated and where it has led to distinctive and, in this writer's judgement, disturbing social consequences.

The British situation is one in which massive social and cultural changes have been promoted, managed by successive Conservative governments in order (ostensibly) to promote popular capitalism. The present study takes a large management conference as a representative microcosm of contemporary British trends. When interpreted in terms of its inclusions and exclusions, this event appears to represent the quasi-religious activities of a managerial elite. The neo-gnostic spiritual practices of this new *classe dirigente* have to be understood in the context of changes in social stratification that at the same time sanction the emergence of a substantial underclass whose existence is not ideologically or ethically assimilated into traditional Christian denominations, religion or indeed the residual political culture. In other words the quasi-religiosity analysed in this paper confirms the socio-psychological (i.e. 'spiritual') functionality of an empowered elite, yet it is simultaneously evidence of a wider societal dysfunctionality which has yet fully to be represented or addressed. The British example also presents the observer with an important example of confrontation between modern and post-modern modes of social organization and their concomitant forms of religiosity. Binary analysis yields a series of oppositions which cohere around the juxtaposition of manager/managed, empowered/disempowered, cultural (and religious) capital/cultural (and religious) deprivation which is not transcended by restricted impact of the ideology of the 'enterprise culture'.

Rosalind Hackett describes the gospel of prosperity in West Africa and accounts for the spread and increasing popularity of aspects of an indigenized Christian revivalism that places a decisive stress upon liberation from poverty. Whilst not entering fully into the argument as to whether such revivalism is in large measure alien to African Christianity because of sources of funding from the United States, Hackett maintains that there is a 'close affinity between the type of religious multi-nationalism, religious enterprise, values and competitive pluralism engendered by the charismatic revival in Africa and global, particularly Western capitalist forces'.

A remarkable feature of West African revivalism has been its impact on higher education institutions and the emergence of educated evangelists, and their continuing promotion of what Hackett discretely terms 'conspicuous salvation'. The correlations of sin/poverty and salvation/prosperity are part of belief practices

11

characteristic of a 'possibilitarian' ideology. Amway, the Swedish Faith Movement and African prosperity revivalism all offer within the ambit of globalizing religion opportunities for self-transformation and even the possibility of status change despite the very considerable differences in cultural setting between North America, Scandinavia and West Africa.

Wealth creation and 'redemption from poverty' are explicitly celebrated and made a central focus of faith commitment. Hackett isolates economic recession and political disillusionment as causal factors in the situation, but there is also a widespread latent belief in the transformative power of religion, a factor that merits further anthropological study. It is apparent that much more than that could be said about the African situation which is distinctive, not least in the persisting influence of indigenous African religion, and its distinctive demands and resources. Whether these religious movements are to be understood as evidence of neo-colonialism and dependency is a sensitive political issue but Hackett detects increasing African agency and creativity. All in all, there is abundant evidence that these forms of religiosity enjoy very considerable cultural resonance and can scarcely be regarded as marginal or socially dysfunctional in the West African context.

In his study of the economic culture of Chilean Pentecostalism, David Martin provides a transitional paper which extends the investigation into the Latin American context where, as in Africa, Christian traditions originating in missionary activity continue to undergo transformation in relation to powerful local socio-cultural factors. The Chilean experience is, however, markedly different from that of Nigeria. Martin regards evangelical Pentecostalism as truly indigenized, and free of the kind of prosperity theology practised in Africa, where North American influence remains overt and powerful. Whilst Chilean Pentecostals operate a 'supernatural technology' lying beneath a 'veneer of rationality', their growth and activity is best explained in the context of social differentiation. Rather than hoping for the extraordinary rewards of prosperity theology, the Chilean Pentecostal exhibits characteristics which maximize wealth through thrift and good living. Martin draws a parallel between these Pentecostals and the early Methodists in Britain: both come from relatively poor backgrounds; both seek to avoid the life-damaging features of economic deprivation; and each experience the limitations to advancement to be found in the inbuilt 'ceilings' of societies with relatively rigid inherited class systems.

The life-world of the Chilean Pentecostal is personal, rather than political and expressed through a pervasive spiritual and moral functionality. It is informed by a series of opposites (spirit and matter, and so on). In collective social terms this life-world represents the emergence of the private corporation in the context of differentiation of spheres, the break up of religious monopoly and the appearance of an open market in religious beliefs. Thus Martin introduces another distinctive way in which relatively successful (albeit socially limited) participation in wealth creation during a period of rapid economic change and development has been facilitated by religious involvement.

The papers placed in the second part of this collection illustrate the diversity of the liaisons that exist between resurgent religion and resurgent capitalism. One of the most prominent features unifying these examples, all taken from within what can be regarded for present purposes as the Christian world, is negative: all reflect transmutations of Protestantism (or in the British example, instrumentalization of 'New Age' religiosity), but none are indicative of contemporary adaptation of Roman Catholicism. Weber's depiction of Roman Catholicism as unlikely to assimilate itself into the 'spirit' of the promotion of wealth creation remains valid, and it is precisely against this apparent antipathy to capitalism in the 'Catholic ethic' (and in liberation theology) that the American Roman Catholic theologian and apologist for capitalism, Michael Novak of the American Enterprise Institute, has directed his efforts.[13]

In part III we examine further aspects of change in economic cultures taking place throughout the world, not least since the revolutions of 1989–90. Whereas part II contained chapters concerned with contemporary instances of active and positive synergy between religion and capitalism, in this final third section a short series of case studies is presented which indicate further modes of relation and accommodation between economic developments and social, cultural and political change. In chapters on Hungary, Greece, Israel, Australia, Indonesia and China we consider various aspects of the impact of capitalist modernization upon a diverse range of societies and economies. Greek society has passed (and indeed is still passing) through a transition from a basically pre-modern to a modern society. The Eastern European example of Hungary represents the common but not uniform experience of rapid transition from a centralized to a market economy, whilst fully recognizing the distinctive contextual factors that are characteristic of each former Warsaw Pact and Comecon country. The other examples illustrate the diversity of societal impact of the general increase of confidence on the part of global capitalism upon many cultures, both traditional and as it were exported during the era of colonial expansion.

Ivan Varga writes on the basis of his distinctive participant involvement in the history he analyses. Having left Hungary in 1956 in the aftermath of the uprising, he taught sociology in Canada for many years. Since the return to democracy he has advised the Hungarian government and he is therefore able to provide an intriguing account of the processes of modernization. This he refers to as the 'pseudo-modernity' and 'pseudo-secularization' (rather than modernity or pre-modernity) that provides the starting point for marketization in Eastern Europe. Varga sets the problem of secularization in East-Central Europe in the context of more than forty years of 'stupor', followed by an apparent sudden increase of religious interest. What Varga sets out to show is that the conceptualization normally applied to the secularization problem needs careful qualification and adaptation in the post-communist setting.

The apparent alternatives of a 'return' to pre-Sovietized society or 'renewal' in terms of the creation of a modern, Western-like society that faced countries like Hungary requires an examination of the socio-economic history of each case:

where, as it were, did the development of each freeze at the moment of the turn to communist socialism? It is within the moment of the onset of relative stasis that Varga also isolates the religious factor, which attracted peculiarly intense repression because, interestingly, its claim to the status of universality and resistance to absorption into class analysis. Varga then juxtaposes a schematic analysis of 'modernization' with the process of 'pseudo-modernization' which took place when centralized Sovietization attempted (but failed) to modernize. He then maps out the consequences of this abortive societal development. Following this introduction, Varga applies theoretical insights drawn from Hans Blumenberg and Jean-François Lyotard to the analysis of the decrease in religiosity and the secularization processes which did take place in order to clarify what amount to the cultural contradictions of Marxist–Leninist society, in the parallel and representative, but in some respects contrasting, experiences of Hungary and Poland. Varga concludes that once the peculiar dialectics of 'pseudo-secularization' are overcome, then East-Central Europe will 'catch up with Europe' and a normalizing assimilation into wider European trends will take place.

Nikos Kokosalakis comments in both historical and contemporary terms upon the distinctive experience of Orthodoxy in Greece. This provides an interesting and informative contrast with Ivan Varga's account of the Hungarian situation. Reflecting a general awareness of the enormity of changes that have led some to speak of a 'new order', Kokosalakis shows how religion continues to play a central role in Greek culture and identity despite recent, sudden and apparently traumatic secularization. Kokosalakis argues that the historically entrenched role and the other-worldly orientation of Orthodoxy allows it to exploit present tensions as an opportunity for growth and persistence. Kokosalakis' chapter serves to test and extend Weber's relatively sparse comments on Orthodoxy within a context in which there has been neither the Reformation nor the Enlightenment as experienced in other parts of Europe. It is only since the Second World War that modernization moved from its bureaucratic imposed form into popular capitalism. With the fall of communism in 1989, the Orthodox Church and Greek politicians of both left and right have emphasized the crucial role of Orthodoxy in preserving Hellenic ethnic identity. According to Kokosalakis' relatively optimistic assessment, if Orthodoxy can successfully combine a public symbolic function, the solemnization of rites of passage for the vast majority of the population and its role as bearer of national identity with the servicing of a privatized piety, then its future in the face of modernity, whilst not secure, is at least open to positive exploitation. Indeed if, as Kokosalakis maintains, 'religion resurges as a cultural response to the secularising ethos of capitalism and its dehumanising impact on the human condition' then Orthodoxy in Greece is arguably well equipped to engage in the civilizing process.

Stephen Sharot analyses an apparent corelation between the greater importance of religion and the demise of socialism in Israeli society. This study of changes in core values and their sustenance in the unique social setting of contemporary Israel is related to stages in the evolution of civil religion. Sharot relates these transformations to demographic change associated with immigration and problems of political and moral legitimation, not least those arising as a consequence of the Six Day War of 1967. Again in political and historical terms, the gradual exposure of internal contradictions in the Labour movement provides evidence of a failure of adaptation on the part of socialists. Sharot once more exposes the inherent complexity of a situation in which a wide range of factors interact and in which no single interpretation is sufficient. In Israel the historic political hegemony of the pioneer Labour movement was displaced by a competitive political pluralism demanded by religious parties, which to a considerable extent reflect the interests of waves of immigration.

In his account of religion and capitalism in Australia, Alan Black guides the reader through the intricacies of Australian politics in which he is prepared to isolate an event which represents the 'resurgence of capitalism'. This event was the highly controversial dismissal of Prime Minister Gough Whitlam on 11 November 1975. It is this political act which marked a crisis in the evolution of the distinctive, even peculiar, economic and social development of Australia. This development, after the initial pioneer and convict period, took the form of 'colonial socialism' and 'settler capitalism' in which there was substantial state intervention accompanying massive immigration. The historic religious affinities of the main political parties, in particular the association between the Labor Party and Roman Catholicism, resulted in a significant parallel between the former's political policy aspirations and Catholic social teaching. State intervention served to promote competition in an economic environment open to monopolistic abuse. The post-war period of prosperity saw substantial immigration from Europe outside Britain and Ireland, a process with consequences in terms of social and cultural identity that have yet fully to be worked out.[14] The period following the dismissal of Prime Minister Whitlam in 1975 has been fraught with ironies in the government of both the (conservative) Liberal–Country Party and the Labor Party. Dr Black's commentary on the religious aspects of these developments are relatively sparse, perhaps because of the nature of Australian culture in which religion is traditionally expressed through political solidarity with ethnic origin (Irish/Catholic, English/Anglican, Scottish/ Presbyterian, etc.) and not through a prominent civil religion, and in which religious rhetoric is largely absent from the public domain. Thus whereas British political conflict between Mrs Thatcher and some of her opponents took on powerful religious and quasi-religious overtones, this was not characteristic of parallel and broadly contemporaneous struggles in Australia. This did not, however, prevent the issue of a joint declaration by the major denominations in Australia on social policy and the economy in 1983 which, like the *Faith in the City* report in England, attracted criticism, not least from the New Right. Black acknowledges the dearth of really detailed information about public attitudes to the ethical issues raised by a continuing general convergence around the market principle.

Anne Eyre shows how the inherited ethnic and religious pluralism of Malaysian society is managed in terms of constitutional arrangements and socio-economic policies that balance Eastern and Western models of development with an Islamization designed to protect the religious, moral and cultural heritage of Malaysia. A remarkable feature of the Malaysian situation is the self-conscious attempt to combine all these factors in a national programme of development promulgated in 1990 which is designed to deliver a fully developed nation by 2020. The national plan, 'Vision 2020', is seemingly a unique experiment in social planning, which whilst it overlies a set of complex social tensions offers an important example of fusion between Western and Japanese patterns of development and a problematic post-colonial ethnic and cultural diversity.

In the last contribution, the sinologist Julian Pas provides us with a lively account of the possible future of religion in China. According to Pas, it is awkward and paradoxical to speak of either 'socialism' or 'capitalism' in China because of the existence of a political system built around a rigid state dictatorship. So-called 'moderate reforms' in the economy have created a peculiarly ambiguous situation under what is still in constitutional terms a continuing 'people's democratic dictatorship'. Pas argues that the present relationship between religion and politics is such that it can arguably be understood as a variation on a permanent theme present throughout Chinese imperial and post-imperial history – the conflict between religion as 'divine mandate' (Tian-ming – dating back to c. 1000 BC) and the eventually unsuccessful attempts of Taoism and Buddhism to sustain autonomy. There were four fundamental ways in which the religious establishment and imperial government interacted: religion as legitimation of imperial authority (a role endorsed by Confucianism); revelation as face-saving expedient; quasi-independent religions (Taoism and Buddhism) used in the motivation of the masses; religious masters called upon as a (sometimes problematic) source of counsel. These existed alongside the performance of seasonal sacrifices made by the emperors themselves. Popular religion (officially concerned with ancestors and cthonic spirits) was tolerated, providing it steered clear of sedition.

This complex and longstanding system was part of an 'absolutist, totalistic world view' which assumed the state control of religion. In the twentieth century the role of religion in China has been intensely problematic and its history fraught with war, revolution and cultural struggle. There is thus disagreement about whether, and to what extent, the Chinese people may be regarded as religious; indeed, the distinction is drawn between 'religion' and 'superstition' in a context in which only the freedom of the former is in principle guaranteed by the constitution. The control and protection of religion is discussed within the framework of 'socialist goals of modernization' and the promotion of foreign and trade policy objectives. The academic study of religion within China is underdeveloped and dominated by outdated Marxist dogmatism. In addition, the religious situation in China is complex and difficult to assess. Present uncertain circumstances would indicate that religion is seen from a political standpoint as having some importance in preserving societal stability. The persistence of religion and the need for its control or for finding substitutes are policy alternatives. Above all, all informed commentary upon religion in relation to economic change in China is handicapped by problems of accessibility and future developments are not easy to predict.

In the three parts of this volume we review aspects of the global interface between religion and contemporary capitalism. In part I, the Weberian paradigm is extended and tested; in part II, examples of a growing symbiosis or synergesis between resurgent capitalism and forms of religiosity and 'quasi-religion' are examined; in part III, a further series of case studies explore ways of managing the modernization process. The material thus assembled does not suggest that any single interpretative model will be capable of assimilating all the evidence. Clearly, each case study operates within a common framework, the modern world system and the complex polarity between it and the sheer diversity and complexity of the local. As Peter Beyer (1993) has shown in a recent study of religion and globalization, the juxtaposition of globalization theory and examples has not yet moved beyond this to the integration of a full theory of the global and the local applicable to the world system. Thus the Weberian paradigm survives in part, but if, as theoreticians like Roland Robertson hope, globalization theory brings about an 'extension and refocusing of sociological work which enables sociology and more generally social theory to transcend the limitation of the conditions of its own maturation in the so-called classical period of the discipline',[15] then a distinct effort will be required to conceptualize the conditions of the diversity explored in this volume and elsewhere. Indeed, far from globalization attaining the status of a central paradigm for sociological interpretation, the 'mixed' character of the evidence gathered in this volume might well indicate that several bodies of theory abut on each other, a situation which reflects with some accuracy the global coincidence of pre-modern, modern and post-modern factors. Whether it will prove feasible to move forward into some form of metatheory comprising this residual diversity is an open question – and a challenge to practioners in the sociological investigation of the interface of religion and resurgent capitalism.

NOTES

1 See such diverse (and doubtless preliminary) assessments as Callinicos, Alex (1991) *The Revenge of History Marxism and the East European Revolutions*, Cambridge: Polity; Collins, Peter (1993) *Ideology After the Fall of Communism*, London/New York: Bowers/Bowerdean; Dahrendorf, Ralf (1990) *Reflections on the Revolution in Europe*, London: Chatto & Windus; Fukuyama, Francis (1992) *The End of History and the Last Man*, London: Hamish Hamilton; Holmes, Leslie (1993) *The End of Communist Power Anti-Corruption Campaigns and Legitimation Crisis*, Cambridge: Polity Press; Fukuyama, Francis *et al.*, 'The Strange death of Soviet Communism: an autopsy', *The National Interest* 31: Spring 1993.

2 See the contributions by Helmut Loiskandl and Richard Roberts in this volume.

3 Michael Novak relishes the designation 'democratic capitalism' as it both confronts a tradition of denigration of capitalism (in which he once shared before his own conversion) and projects what he conceives as the latter's unique capacity to sustain

17

democracy and its special relationship with Judaism and Christianity. Again this is explored further in the works referred to in note 1 above.

4 See the opening pages and attendent references of David Gellner's chapter in this volume.

5 The research of Peter Berger and his associates, including David Martin in his chapter in part II of this volume, is now directed at the exploration of such 'cultures' on the assumption that it is futile to engage in speculation about about socio-political, and indeed religio-cultural, forms of life speculatively conceived in unreal Utopian projections. Thus in the words of Michael Novak, they reject the 'dream' of socialism.

6 This is a major theme in the companion volume to this entitled *Theology, Ethics and Resurgent Capitalism*, and the editors's forthcoming monograph, Roberts, Richard H. (1996) *Religion and the Resurgence of Capitalism*, London: Routledge.

7 Indeed, here the question as to the formation and practice of disciplines arises in the face of unsurmountable complexity. It is helpful to recognize that all disciplinary strategies involve the choice of integrative commonplaces and the exertion of power in a game in which there may be no innocent participants, but in which there should be recognizable rules. See Roberts, Richard H. and Good, J.M.M. (eds) (1993) *The Recovery of Rhetoric: Persuasive Discourse and Disciplinarity in the Human Sciences*, London: Duckworth/Bristol Classical Press and Charlottesville, VA: Press of the University of Virginia.

8 For an account of recent discussion in Japan, see Hayashi, Makoto and Hiroshi Yamanaka (1993) 'The adaptation of Max Weber's theories of religion in Japan', *Japanese Journal of Religious Studies* 20/2–3: 207–28.

9 See Keat, Russell and Abercrombie, Nicholas (eds) (1991) *Enterprise Culture*, London: Routledge; and Roberts, Richard H. (1992) 'Religion and the "enterprise culture": the British experience in the Thatcher era (1979–1990)', *Social Compass* **39** (1): 15–33.

10 Which was approached in other contributions to the project *Religion and the Resurgence of Capitalism*, to appear in forthcoming publications.

11 Thus central to Dietrich Bonhoeffer's critical response to National Socialism in the Ethics was a distinction between the 'penultimate' and the 'ultimate' that no ideology should transgress.

12 The reader's attention is drawn to Peter Beyer's recent book, *Religion and Globalization*, London: Sage (1994).

13 See most recently, *The Catholic Ethic and the Spirit of Capitalism*, New York: The Free Press (1993).

14 The choice in September 1993 of Sydney as venue for the second millennium Olympic Games may well be associated with the rapid evolution of cultural identity and the drive towards full political autonomy and republican status.

15 Robertson, Roland (1992) *Globalization Social Theory and Global Culture*, London: Sage, p. 9.

REFERENCES

Beyer, Peter (1994) *Religion and Globalization*, London: Sage.
Weber, Max (1930) *The Protestant Ethic and the Spirit of Capitalism*, London: George Allen and Unwin.

Part I

REVISING THE CLASSICS

1

MAX WEBER, CAPITALISM AND THE RELIGION OF INDIA

David N. Gellner

INTRODUCTION[1]

The Religion of India (henceforth ROI) has suffered a strange and undeserved fate.[2] Unlike *The Protestant Ethic and the Spirit of Capitalism* (henceforth PESC), it has given rise to rather little discussion of the numerous stimulating theories it puts forward among the specialists most competent to judge them. Part of the reason for this must lie in the fact that South Asian studies,[3] to their detriment, tend to divide up three ways between (i) Sanskritists, (ii) historians of the Muslim and modern periods, and (iii) social scientists, either anthropologists or sociologists. Between these three groups there is only imperfect communication.[4]

Sanskritists frequently dismiss Weber's book out of hand on the ground that nobody who had to rely on secondary sources can have anything to contribute to the study of South Asian religion or society. Occasionally historians have in fact discussed or made use of Weber's work (Bayly 1983; O'Hanlon 1985), but they have tended to damn him with faint praise, or worse. Anthropologists and sociologists, on the other hand, are not in a position, in the nature of their study, to address the more specific historical theses which Weber advances; and they have frequently been ill at ease with Weber's comparative framework (e.g. Appadurai 1986). Thus, Weber's book has remained little read and largely unused by those South Asianists most competent to tackle it. As for sociologists in the West, it is probably the only book on South Asia they ever read. That this is certainly the case with Weber's translators, Gerth and Martindale, is shown by the frequent obscurity and inaccuracies of the translation, the incredible number of misprints in the transliteration of Sanskrit and Pali words (for which they carry over unthinkingly the German transliteration), and by the fact that they translate *yajnopavita* from the German as 'holy girdle' instead of the normal 'sacred thread'.

THREE FALLACIES IN THE INTERPRETATION OF THE WEBER THESIS

In so far as Weber's work has been taken up at all by social scientists dealing with

21

South Asia, the discussion has centred on the connection between Hinduism and capitalism, a debate sparked off by post-Independence economic development or the lack of it. This debate, inasmuch as it deals with Weber, has been almost wholly vitiated by misunderstandings of his central concerns. As Marshall (1982: 168) concludes of the 'Protestant ethic' debate in general, 'Working often with a crude and bastardized version of [Weber's] thesis, most critics have pursued inadmissible data in the wrong times and places'. Weber's writings on South Asia and China, and the projected work on Islamic civilization, were of course the counterpositives to PESC: that is, the latter explained, or began to explain, why capitalism originated only in the West, the other works why it failed to originate elsewhere. Thus in order to understand ROI, and why the above-mentioned interpretations of it are invalid, it is necessary to deal with PESC at the same time.

The debate over Weber's 'Protestantism' thesis, both in the Western and in the South Asian context, has been dominated by three fallacies. These fallacies, though they can be held separately, are related and when held together reinforce each other, as I hope will become clear in the ensuing discussion. In decreasing order of vulgarity, they are:

(i)   Weber was an idealist in the sense that he believed economic behaviour to be straightforwardly determined by religious beliefs, either of individuals or collectively or both.
(ii) There is only one problem of development, or the origin of capitalism, which is the same in essentials in Medieval China, nineteenth century Europe, and twentieth century Peru.
(iii) Weber held a whenever-A-then-B Humean view of social causality; in other words, he thought that if A was the cause of B, it was necessary and sufficient, or at least a necessary, condition of B.

The truth is that Weber was certainly not an idealist in this sense. Though vulgar Marxists and vulgar Weberians may be diametrically opposed, it is quite wrong to suppose that Weber represents historical materialism stood on its head. Protestantism for Weber was an exception to the general rule that ideas do not have an independent power to produce social change.

As far as fallacy (ii) goes, there are three separate problems of development requiring different answers:

(a) Why did one pre-industrial society develop faster than another (say, China than Christian Europe)?
(b) Why did one civilization only (Europe) develop industrial capitalism 'from within itself'?
(c) Why are some societies better at (deliberate, imitative) development in the modern industrial and industrializing world than others (say, Japan and Singapore than China and Indonesia)?

Weber himself was above all concerned with (b) and very little with (c), which was not then the burning issue it was to become.

22

The truth corresponding to fallacy (iii) is harder to state briefly. But it should at least be clear from his methodological writings, if not from the consideration of 'social reality' itself, that for Weber society is causally complex. X may be a necessary precondition for Y only under certain circumstances. In another situation Y may be possible without X. Thus talk of causes, rather than conditions, is misleading, as we may be led to expect a single cause to be 'constantly conjoined', in Hume's phrase, with a given effect. Much misguided criticism of Weber has been based on the assumption that he claimed Protestantism and capitalism to be 'constantly conjoined'.

EXAMPLES OF THE FALLACIES

Fallacy (i) has not normally been committed by those who have read PESC closely. Weber's statement that 'it is not, of course, my aim to substitute for a one-sided materialistic an equally one-sided spiritualistic causal interpretation of culture and of history' (PESC: 183) is too prominently placed for that. This has not prevented it from entering the South Asianists' discussion. Mandelbaum, for example, aligns Weber with William Kapp and Gunnar Myrdal as explaining South Asia's backwardness by citing the attitudes inculcated by Hinduism (Mandelbaum 1970: 638).

Fallacy (ii) is more interesting and it is more important to be clear about it. A concise formulation of it (a confusion of (b) and (c) above) is to be found in the preface by Gerth and Martindale to ROI: 'The central concern of this and other of Weber's studies of countries we today describe as "developing" was with the obstacles to industrialization and modernization. Weber anticipated by several decades a problem that has come to occupy the post-World War II world' (ROI: v). Similarly, Surajit Sinha takes the Weber thesis with reference to South Asia to be that Hinduism is a 'major stumbling block for modernization' (Sinha 1974: 519). In fact, Weber's principal theme was an answer to problem (b): 'no community dominated by powers of this sort [viz. religious anthropolatry on the part of the laity and a strong traditionalistic charismatic clergy] could out of its own substance arrive at the "spirit of capitalism"' (ROI: 325). The sentences which follow this in ROI state two corollaries which are indeed relevant to problem (c): that South Asia could not take over capitalism developed elsewhere as easily as the Japanese; and that, though capitalism had already been introduced to South Asia, only the Pax Britannica, according to some, prevented an outbreak of the old 'feudal robber romanticism of the Middle Ages'. But these are only asides, and not the theme of the book as a whole.

Fallacy (iii) has not directly and openly been espoused, as far as I know, but it lurks in the claim that Weber's project with regard to PESC and the studies of the world religions was an application of Mill's method of agreement and difference. Of course the cases in which Protestantism did not produce capitalism are too well known for such a position to be tenable by present-day Weberians.[5] Consequently, Weberians claim, not that Protestantism invariably produces capitalism, but that it has a potential to do so. However this does not seem to get us very far in the task of explaining why capitalism appeared in one place rather than another, unless it is analysed in turn in a way similar to that attempted below.

Most commonly, fallacy (iii) is committed tacitly along with fallacy (ii). It is assumed that Weber asserted the existence of a necessary and sufficient link between Protestantism and rational capitalistic activity, or at least that the former is a necessary condition of the latter so that even if all Protestants are not capitalists, no Catholic can be one. Put like this it may sound absurd, but much of the debate has been carried on at this sort of level. As H. Luethy (1970: 128) remarked, 'it was as though the essential thread had suddenly been discovered which would lead dialectically from the nailing of Luther's ninety-five theses on the Wittenberg church door to the assembly lines of Detroit and the ramifications of Standard Oil'.

In the Asian context Weber's claim that non-European civilizations could not have developed capitalism endogenously because they lacked the ideological resources to produce a capitalist spirit, i.e. an active rational this-worldly asceticism, is misinterpreted as the 'theory' that Chinese, Hindus, or whoever make bad capitalists. In other words, Weber's answer to problem (b) above is taken as an answer to problem (c), and the causal connection asserted is presumed to be an invariable one. In this way it is possible to attempt to refute his characterization of the Hindu 'spirit' by citing 'the evidence today before us of politically independent Asian states actively planning their social, economic and scientific and technical development' (Singer 1961: 150). This is of course to miss the crucial point that Weber was concerned with the *first* unplanned, endogenous appearance of industrial capitalism, and with South Asia's potential or lack of it for the production of a capitalist *spirit* which was its necessary condition.[6] Capitalist economic *organization* according to Weber is not at all the same thing; the latter may exist, carried on in a traditionalistic spirit, in preindustrial societies without having any potential to transform its environment.

In an approach similar to Singer's, Tambiah seems to assume that because Buddhism and Hinduism can be adapted to modernization, because they can, *ex post*, provide analogues of the Protestant ethic, Weber's theory is disproved (Tambiah 1973: 13–16). But since Weber is addressing problem (b), in order to refute him in this way, one must show that Buddhism and Hinduism had this potential before the impact of modernization. It is quite wrong to attribute to him the thesis that there is an innate hostility between Hinduism or other eastern religions and capitalism. In his book on China he explicitly repudiates such a claim:

It is obviously not a question of deeming the Chinese 'naturally ungifted' for the demands of capitalism. But compared to the Occident, the varied conditions which externally favored the origin of capitalism in China did not suffice to create it. Likewise capitalism did not originate in occidental or oriental Antiquity, or in India, or where Islamism held sway. Yet in each

24

of these areas different and favorable circumstances seemed to facilitate its rise.

(Weber 1951: 248)

What then was Weber's position? It was that the spirit of capitalism was a necessary precondition of the first appearance, or origination of capitalism. It was not of course a sufficient condition, as the case of Jainism, discussed below, shows. Nor was it a necessary condition of capitalism as such: once capitalism stands on 'mechanical foundations' it is capitalism which tends to produce a capitalist spirit, or aspects of it, rather than the other way round. The importance of Protestantism lay in the fact that it produced and legitimated a capitalist spirit; but there was no necessary and/or sufficient link between Protestantism and the capitalist spirit (see PESC: 91). It is therefore quite beside the point to cite against Weber examples of non-Protestant capitalists or of Protestant non-capitalists. Protestantism was one element of a situation which, taken as a whole, was sufficient to produce a capitalist spirit, which in turn was, as stated, necessary for the first unplanned appearance of industrial society.[7]

Weber's studies of South Asia, China, and Islam were designed to show that, although other elements necessary for the production of capitalism sometimes existed (such as the availability of capital and formally free labour, and other factors discussed in his *General Economic History*), a capitalist spirit did not and indeed could not develop. Without a Protestant ethic or some equivalent no traditional (i.e. agrarian) civilization could develop industrial capitalism 'from within itself'. Only religious sanctions, Weber assumed, could induce men permanently to defer satisfaction in the way required to produce the capitalist spirit. No this-worldly religious ethic could produce an active rational this-worldly asceticism: only a particular type of soteriology could do so. In fact the studies revealed, in at least one case, an analogous ethic (Jainism) and the burden of explanation in the South Asian case shifted, as we shall see, to the absence of other conditions.[8]

PROBABLE REASONS FOR THE PREVALENCE OF THE FALLACIES

The three fallacies listed above are by no means always made, but even when they are rejected, the way in which they go together does not seem to have been grasped. Thus Giddens rejects fallacy (ii): 'Weber's concerns were with the first origins of modern capitalism in Europe, not with its subsequent adoption elsewhere' (Giddens 1976: 6). He also seems to reject fallacy (iii) when he says that it is quite valueless to take Weber to task for suggesting that 'Calvinism was "the" cause of the development of modern capitalism' (*ibid.*: 10). But then he goes on to cite 'the supposed lack of "affinity" between Catholicism and regularized entrepreneurial activity' as one of the 'elements of Weber's analysis that are most definitely called into question' (*ibid.*: 12).

Why then is it so easy to make the three mistakes listed above? Two reasons leap to the eye: Weber's order of exposition in PESC, which makes it possible to mistake his initial problem, that other things being equal Protestants in nineteenth century Germany were more likely to be entrepreneurs than Catholics, for his theory; and, second, the different meanings which attach to Weber's use of the word 'capitalism'.[9]

It is indeed misleading that Weber begins PESC with a consideration of the fact that in nineteenth century Germany Protestants showed a greater proclivity for entrepreneurial activity than Catholics, even where one would expect the opposite (i.e. in areas where Catholics are a minority among Protestants). But proper attention to the text makes it quite clear that this is merely the problem, namely the evidence that at an earlier period there was a special connection between Protestantism and the origin of capitalism. That is to say, Weber was not making the quasi-tautological claim that more Protestants are entrepreneurs because they have an innate disposition to be so; rather he claimed that the preponderance of Protestant entrepreneurs in late nineteenth century Germany was a consequence of the fact that 200–300 years previously it was the Protestant ethic which had produced the spirit of capitalism and therefore above all among Protestants that modern bourgeois capitalists emerged.

In Weber and in the debate over PESC 'capitalism' seems to have at least three shades of meaning. In the first place it refers to a type of economic activity to be found in all civilizations: 'The important fact is always that a calculation of capital in terms of money is made . . . at the beginning of the enterprise an initial balance, before every individual decision a calculation to ascertain its probable profitableness, and at the end a final balance to ascertain how much profit has been made' (PESC: 18). The 'capitalistic adventurer' is of this type. Then there is what Weber called modern, rational, or bourgeois capitalism: in addition to the above criterion this is based on formally free labour and double-entry book-keeping; it is separate from the household and 'attuned to a regular market'. Finally there is 'capitalism' as a name for industrial society, or one kind of industrial society, a usage which perhaps owes more to Marx than to Weber, but which Weber certainly encouraged because in looking for the origin of modern capitalism in the second sense, he clearly believed he was also explaining the origin of capitalism in the third sense. Thus in the first two senses 'capitalism' denotes a kind of economic organization, the latter a distinct type of the former; the third sense denotes a type or subtype of society. The capitalist *spirit* on the other hand comprises an historically unusual set of attitudes based on the pursuit of profit for its own sake, which Weber illustrated with the maxims of Benjamin Franklin (PESC: ch. 2).

The connection between the three senses of 'capitalism' for Weber is this: capitalist society (sense 3) results, not from the gradual development of capitalist economic organizations (sense 1), but from the latter's infusion with the spirit of capitalism, which turns it into rational or bourgeois capitalism (sense 2). Weber's central insight was that there was nothing inevitable or 'natural' about this (the appearance of industrial society) as evolutionist perspectives suggest: it was the result of a certain set of unique and unusual conditions.[10] Thus he states in the final sentence of ROI: 'The appearance of [a rationally formed missionary prophecy] in the Occident . . . with the extensive consequences borne with it, was conditioned by highly particular historical circumstances without which, despite differences of natural conditions, development there could easily have taken the course typical of Asia, particularly of India' (ROI: 343).

Confusion has no doubt been increased by failing to notice that the capitalist spirit as defined by Weber is only invariably associated with capitalism in the second of these senses, and then only before it stands on 'mechanical foundations'. Of course, all institutions require certain attitudes on the part of the individuals within them, but what Weber has called the capitalist spirit was not necessarily required by capitalist economic organization. Thus 'the management, for instance, of a bank, a wholesale export business, a large retail establishment, or of a large putting-out enterprise dealing with goods produced in homes, is certainly only possible in the form of a capitalistic enterprise. Nevertheless, they may all be carried on in a traditionalistic spirit' (PESC: 65). This is indeed the way they always, or nearly always, have been carried on, and Weber made it clear that this type of economic behaviour has no power to transform society. Protestantism, by contrast, produced individuals imbued with the capitalist spirit, and as an unforeseen consequence produced a new type of society based on its own attitude to work. In reply to the initial publication of PESC, Sombart had cited the case of Alberti, a Renaissance man, in both senses, who wrote a treatise on household management which displayed a thoroughgoing money-mindedness. Weber replied:

> The essential point of the difference [between Alberti and Franklin] is . . .
> that an ethic based on religion places certain psychological sanctions (not
> of an economic character) on the maintenance of the attitude prescribed by
> it, sanctions which, so long as the religious belief remains alive, are highly
> effective, and which mere worldly wisdom like that of Alberti does not
> have at its disposal. Only in so far as these sanctions work, and, above all,
> in the direction in which they work, which is often very different from the
> doctrine of the theologians, does such an ethic gain an independent influ-
> ence on the conduct of life and thus on the economic order. This is, to speak
> frankly, the point of this whole essay, which I had not expected to find so
> completely overlooked.

> (PESC: 197)

THE CHALLENGE TO THE WEBER THESIS

The real question which Weber's approach has to face has been missed by most of the literature. It is: why was the development that occurred within pre-industrial societies (see problem (a) above) not sufficient to produce modern capitalism? From an evolutionist perspective such as that of Luethy, development within agrarian civilizations ought to be sufficient to produce industrial capitalism. The emphasis that Weber placed on Protestantism 'creating' capitalism is therefore misplaced: 'In the period of the Reformation all the bases of the modern world – capital, wealth, the highest technological and artistic level of development, global power, world trade – all these were almost exclusively present in countries that were and remained Catholic . . . One century later all this was petrification and decay'. The real problem, which according to Luethy is missed by Weber and the Weberians, is to explain 'the sudden breaking of an ascendant curve of development' in the Catholic countries, not its continuance in the Protestant ones (Luethy 1970: 133).

A viewpoint very similar to Luethy's has been advanced by Hugh Trevor-Roper in his stimulating article, 'Religion, the Reformation and social change':

> It was not that Calvinism created a new type of man, who in turn created capitalism; it was rather that the old economic elite of Europe were driven into heresy because the attitude of mind which had been theirs for generations, and had been tolerated for generations, was suddenly, and in some places, declared heretical and intolerable.
>
> (Trevor-Roper 1967: 27)

Consequently Europe was divided into Catholic states with a '"bureaucratic" system of the princes which may encourage state capitalism, but squeezes out free enterprise' and Protestant ones which were the inheritors of 'the mercantile system of the free cities' (*ibid.*: 38). Thus 'it was the Counter-Reformation which extruded [economic enterprise] from society, not Calvinist doctrine which created it, or Catholic doctrine which stifled it, in individuals' (*ibid.*: 42).

Two separate issues are raised by Trevor-Roper's criticism of Weber. First, he takes Weber's thesis to be that there is a necessary and sufficient causal connection between Calvinism and the capitalist spirit, i.e. that all Calvinists must be ascetic capitalists. I need not repeat the reasons for rejecting this. Trevor-Roper's proof that the capitalist spirit predates Protestantism, and his examples of the unascetic behaviour of the most successful Calvinist entrepreneurs (unlikely to be typical for that very reason), do not therefore attack the Weber thesis. The importance of Protestantism lay in the fact that it brought active rational asceticism into the everyday world and provided it with religious sanctions; asceticism was no longer confined, as in Medieval Catholicism or in Asia, to virtuosos. Trevor-Roper ably documents the hostility of Catholic Europe to the capitalist spirit when it threatened the former's political dominance. It was only much later, when the political advantages of Protestant economic attitudes became over-whelmingly clear (and it is important to remember that they were anything but clear beforehand), that Catholic writers began to urge the adoption of Protestant virtues.

Trevor-Roper's second point is the same as Luethy's: it was the Counter-Reformation that prevented the emergence of industrial capitalism in Catholic Europe, not Protestantism that produced it in northern Europe. But if we put the evidence cited by Luethy and Trevor-Roper in a larger comparative framework, as Weber tried to do, we can perhaps see that Weber was justified in concentrating on the creative role of Protestantism rather than the destructive one of Catholicism. In his books on South Asia and China he tried to show that in spite of the 'ascendant curve of development' apparent in both civilizations, neither could have led to a breakthrough to industrial society. The frustration of urban economic growth by ruling but non-productive strata is the norm, not the exception, in agrarian society.[11] Hence the stress that Weber laid on the necessity for the development of capitalism of the existence of rational law and a rational bureaucratic state. It seems to have been evident to Weber that mere technological growth and population increase are not enough to produce capitalism, and he therefore concentrated on the potential these civilizations had for the production of a capitalist spirit. This is why he says that he was 'necessarily dealing with the religious ethics of the classes which were the culture-bearers of their respective countries' (PESC: 30). The implication is that, but for Protestantism, or some equivalent, producing a capitalist spirit, Europe would have gone the way of South Asia or China.

THE CHINESE CASE

The Chinese case is particularly important for the Weberian approach because here many of the conditions for the development of modern capitalism seem to have been satisfied, but there was no capitalist spirit. 'Rational entrepreneurial capitalism, which in the Occident found its specific locus in industry, has been handicapped not only by the lack of a formally guaranteed law, a rational administration and judiciary, and by the ramifications of a system of prebends, but also, basically, by the lack of a particular mentality' (Weber 1951: 104). This crucial lack, which Weber calls his 'central theme', is tackled in part 2 of *The Religion of China*, which attempts to show why a capitalist spirit did not, and indeed could not, given its cultural resources, develop in China.

Clearly Weber's explanation is a negative one: the absence of a capitalist spirit meant that China could not develop modern capitalism, even though in the early Medieval period it was the most advanced society in the world, in terms of agricultural, economic, commercial, and technological development. Weber does not provide a detailed answer to the question why this development should not be self-sustaining, i.e. sufficient to produce modern capitalism, though he gives a few hints in *Economy and Society*:

It would be a mistake to assume that the development of capitalistic enterprises must occur proportionally to the growth of want satisfaction in the monetary economy, and an even larger mistake to believe that this development must take the form it has assumed in the Western world. In fact, the contrary is true. The extension of money economy might well go hand in hand with the increasing monopolization of the larger sources of profit by the *oikos* economy of a prince. Ptolemaic Egypt is an outstanding example . . . It is also possible that with the extension of a money economy could go a process of "feudalization" (*Verpfründung*) of fiscal advantages resulting in a traditionalistic stabilization of the economic system. This happened in China . . .

(Weber 1968: 113)

[A]s always in the area of "techniques" – we find that the advance proceeded most slowly wherever older, structural forms were in their own way technically highly developed and functionally particularly well adapted to the requirements at hand.

(*ibid.*: 987)

A detailed theory of what happens under these conditions has been elaborated by Mark Elvin for the Chinese case, which he calls the high-level equilibrium trap. I shall quote his summary:

In China, demand and the supply of materials were increasingly constrained by a special combination of circumstances that gradually spread across the country until, by about 1820, they held all of the eighteen provinces within the Wall in their grip. These circumstances were: (1) the rapidly falling quality, and hence rapidly falling returns to labor and other inputs, of the small remaining quantity of new land not yet opened to cultivation and capable of being opened under the existing technology; (2) the continuing increase of the population, reducing the surplus per head available above subsistence for the creation of concentrated mass markets for new goods, and also (though less significantly) for investment; (3) the impossibility of improving productivity per hectare in agriculture under a pre-modern technology that was the most refined in the world in terms of manuring, rotations, etc., without the modern inputs such as chemical fertilizers and petrol or diesel pumps that presuppose a scientific and industrial revolution for their production; and (4) the great size of China (close to twice the population of Europe), and its relatively good commercial integration, which made it impossible for pre-modern foreign trade to substitute for internal inadequacies, by providing either the stimulus of a large volume of new demand or the support of large quantities of cheap raw materials. The trap could only be broken by the introduction of new technology exogenous to the Chinese world.

(Elvin 1984: 383–4)

Rational strategy [therefore] for peasant and merchant alike tended in the direction not so much of labour-saving machinery as of economizing on resources and fixed capital . . . When temporary shortages arose, mercantile versatility, based on cheap transport, was a faster and surer remedy than the contrivance of machines.

(Elvin 1973: 314)

30

It is clearly a weakness in Weber that he provided no such analysis. Nevertheless the explanation in terms of the high-level equilibrium trap and Weber's explanation do not necessarily compete (as Elvin assumes they do in the article cited above). Indeed one might even say that they imply each other or some equivalent: because China had no capitalist spirit, it was caught in the high-level equilibrium trap; because Europe produced a capitalist spirit it avoided the high-level equilibrium trap to which its 'ascendant curve of development' would otherwise have led it.[12]

From this point of view Elvin's term 'trap' is a misnomer, which only makes sense from the distinctive perspective of the modern world: the 'high-level equilibrium trap' describes the *normal* relationship between population, resources, and development in pre-industrial agrarian society. It is the development of the West, in spite of the fact that it is widely taken for granted, which is abnormal and in particular need of explanation. It is the development of the West that Weber was particularly concerned to explain.

THE SOUTH ASIAN CASE

The South Asian case is different from the Chinese. For one thing, among the multifarious religious doctrines to be found in South Asia, one, Jainism, showed great potential for the production of a capitalist spirit. Thus the explanation for South Asia's failure to produce industrial capitalism rests on other factors, to do with the general Hindu caste context and the way that it overrode any particular ethic. It is to be presumed on this Weberian perspective that, if South Asian civilization had taken its course uninterrupted by the introduction of industrialism, it would have encountered some equivalent of Elvin's high-level equilibrium trap, though probably at a technically lower level. Thus, in short, South Asian society could develop a minority capitalism as with the Jains, or an emulative capitalism, as in the modern world, but not, Weber claimed, an endogenous capitalism capable of transforming South Asia from an agrarian to an industrial society.

For the sake of clarity in the following discussion of South Asian religions, it is worth making a distinction, due to Schluchter, of three senses which rationality had for Weber: (i) scientific–technological rationalism: control of the world on the basis of empirical laws, or means–end rationality; (ii) metaphysical–ethical rationalism: systematization of an ethos, or the application of logic to a world view; (iii) practical rationalism: a methodical way of life, or rational asceticism (Roth and Schluchter 1979: 14–15). Although South Asia was advanced in mathematics and grammar, it failed to develop (i). (ii) it certainly had: Weber was very impressed by the *karma* doctrine as a solution to theodicy. (iii) developed in the West thanks first to the monasteries, and then to the Reformation. Its failure to develop in South Asia was what Weber wished to explain.

JAINISM

Weber was struck by the similarities between Jainism and Protestantism:

> As with Protestantism, "joy in possessions" (*parigraha*) was the objectional thing, but not possession or gain in itself . . . The Jains believed in absolute honesty in business life . . . [which] excluded the sect, on one side, from typical oriental participation in "political capitalism" (accumulation of wealth by officials, tax farmers, state purveyors) and, on the other, it worked among them and among the Parsees, just as for the Quakers in the Occident, in terms of the dictum (of early capitalism) "honesty is the best policy".
>
> (ROI: 200)

This was so even though Jainism was based on a quite different theology, in which God, in so far as he is admitted to exist, is irrelevant to the concerns of human beings. The Jain community was led by monks, and the laity, to a much greater extent than in Buddhism, were integrated into the ascetic values, and to a certain extent the practices, of their monasticism. However the Jains remained a minority within Hindu society to which they increasingly accommodated themselves. They became in effect a caste or several castes, and could not escape the general consequences of caste society. 'That they remained confined to commercial capitalism and failed to create an industrial organization was again due to their ritualistically determined exclusion from industry and as with the Jews their ritualistic isolation in general. To this must be added the by now familiar barriers that their Hindu surroundings with its traditionalism and the patrimonial character of kingship put in their way' (*ROI: 200; Weber 1917: 424).[13]

CASTE AND STATUS GROUP

Weber explains the different types of religion to be found in South Asia principally with reference to two strata: 'the social world was divided into the strata of the wise and educated and the uncultivated plebeian masses' (ROI: 343). As we approach the present he also posits the category of the 'illiterate middle classes'. He does not discuss what he thinks is the relation between these strata and caste; the very use of the word 'stratum' is perhaps a sign of vagueness. Caste on the other hand Weber takes to be a 'closed status group':

> What is a "status group"? "Classes" are groups of people who, from the standpoint of specific interests, have the same economic position . . . "Status", however, is a quality of social honor or lack of it, and is in the main conditioned as well as expressed through a specific style of life . . . All the obligations and barriers that membership in a status group entails also exist in a caste, in which they are intensified to the utmost degree.
>
> (ROI: 39–40)

Louis Dumont takes Weber to task for this definition of caste: to understand caste as a form of something found in the West (a) is ethnocentric and (b) necessarily makes the religious aspect of caste secondary (Dumont 1980: 26). Weber is aware of the importance of the religious aspect and that it is this which makes a crucial difference between caste among Hindus and caste among Muslims or Buddhists, but he does not see caste as different in kind from the status groups found in other societies, as Dumont does.

Without going further into theories of caste,[14] it is clear that Weber's approach seems to have blinded him to an important fact, viz. that although all Brahmans to be considered as such had, in the traditional situation, to maintain a certain way of life (like the members of a status group), it was by no means the case that all Brahmans could be said to belong to the class of cultured intellectuals. The same applies *mutatis mutandis* to Kshatriyas ('rulers', 'nobles'). 'In India', Weber says, 'the Brahmans represent a status group of literati partly comprising princely chaplains, partly counsellors, theological teachers, and jurists, priests and pastors', though he immediately concedes: 'In both cases [i.e. South Asia and China] only a portion of the status group occupied the characteristic positions' (ROI: 139–40). In fact, although many of the twice-born would comply with Brahmanical customs, and even learn Sanskrit, and thus maintain 'the specific style of life' of a Brahman or Kshatriya, the extent and the manner of this compliance varied enormously; consequently the meaning of this allegiance cannot be explained in terms of their all belonging to a stratum of cultured intellectuals, but only in caste terms – which is presumably Dumont's point. It was therefore possible for Brahmans to participate, and indeed take leading positions, in what Weber saw as uncultured forms of saviour religion or Tantric 'orgiasticism'. Hence the Medieval formula: a Vaidika [i.e. conservative follower of the orthodox Vedas] for *samskaras* (life-cycle rituals), a Shaiva [a devotional adherent of the great god, Shiva] in the market place, and a Kaula [a practitioner of antinomian Tantric rituals] in secret. Thus, in short, the questions of status groups and the types of religion which grew from them, and of the relation of orthodox Brahmanism to Tantric forms of religion, were considerably more complex than Weber realized.

Weber's crucial mistake was to argue back from religious texts to the motivations of those who gave allegiance to them; there is a long tradition of this in Indology to which he merely gave sociological formulation. Nevertheless Weber was acquainted with all the types of religion to be found in South Asia. The fact that they could be combined in this way, in disregard of their 'original' meaning, does not of itself invalidate his conclusions about the 'spirit' of Hinduism and its consequences for economic activity.

Caste did not prevent the division of labour in the workshop, but the existence of caste ritualism, Weber argued, made it inherently unlikely that capitalism could develop. It was 'as if none but different guest peoples, like the Jews, ritually exclusive towards one another and toward third parties, were to follow their trades in one economic area' (ROI: 112). Further, it was the increasing strength of caste, encouraged by Hindu kings, that undermined independent guilds and independent cities. Thus 'individual acceptance for apprenticeship, participation in market deals, or citizenship – all these phenomena of the West either failed to develop in the first place or were crushed under the weight of ethnic, later of caste fetters' (ROI: 131).

Weber emphasizes the 'religious promise' of the caste system:

> No Hindu denies two basic principles: the *samsara* belief in the trans-migration of souls and the related *karman* doctrine of compensation. These alone are the truly "dogmatic" doctrines of all Hinduism, and in their very interrelatedness they represent the unique Hindu theodicy of the existing social, that is to say caste system.
>
> (*ROI: 118; Weber 1916: 728)

These views reveal Weber's textual bias, as does his remark that in consequence of these beliefs the Untouchables had most to gain from ritual correctness, which, he thinks, explains their hostility to innovation (ROI: 123). The work of anthropologists shows that considerations of purity and impurity/sin, which impose themselves or are imposed on the individual, are far more pervasive, 'dogmatic', and built into the social structure than beliefs about *karma* or *samsara*. The evidence is that these beliefs are invoked in an *ad hoc* and retrospective way and do not guide the lives of caste Hindus (e.g. Srinivas 1976: 317).

Weber was on much firmer ground when he deduced this consequence of the caste order: universalist humanism and individualism similar to that of the West is only to be found outside it.

> In this eternal caste world, the very gods in truth constituted a mere caste . . . Anyone who wished to emancipate himself from this world and the inescapable cycle of recurrent births and deaths had to leave it alto-gether – to set out for that unseen realm [*Hinterwelt* in original] to which Hindu "salvation" leads.
>
> (*ROI: 123; Weber 1916: 733)

> Such literature of the Indians as arguably parallels the philosophical ethical systems of the West [i.e. in their universalism] was – or more correctly, became in the course of its development – something altogether different, namely, a metaphysically and cosmologically grounded teaching [*Kunstlehre* in original] of the methods of achieving salvation from this world . . . A religious eschatology of the world was as little possible here as in Confucianism. Only a (practical) eschatology of single individuals could develop . . .
>
> (*ROI: 147; Weber 1917: 358)

Here in essence is the theory later elaborated by Louis Dumont in his famous essay on world renunciation in South Asian religion (Dumont 1960).

BRAHMANICAL RELIGION

Weber's remarks on Brahmanical religion were extremely perceptive. Even if today they would have to be supplemented, his conclusions as to the social implications of the most orthodox part of Hinduism remain valid.

> For the character of official Indian religiosity it was decisive that its bearer, the Brahmanical priestly aristocracy, was a genteel educated stratum, later simply a stratum of genteel literati. This had above all one consequence, ... that orgiastic and emotional-ecstatic elements of the ancient magic rites were not taken over and for long periods either completely atrophied or continued and were tolerated [only] as unofficial folk magic.
>
> (**ROI: 137; Weber 1917: 345)

As we have observed, this may be taken as correct if read as referring to Brahmanical religion, above all to what is known as Smarta Brahmanism; Brahmans themselves by no means always kept to 'genteel' (*vornehm*) religiosity. The similarities and differences with Confucian intellectuals are extremely enlightening:

> In both we find a status group of genteel literati whose magical charisma rests on "knowledge". Such knowledge was magical and ritualistic in character, deposited in a holy literature, written in a holy language, remote from that of everyday speech. In both appears the same pride in education and unshakable trust in this special knowledge as the cardinal virtue determining all good. Ignorance of this knowledge was the cardinal vice and the source of all evil. They developed a similar "rationalism" – concerned with the rejection of all irrational forms of holy seeking.
>
> (ROI: 139)

However, whereas the Confucian literati were paradigmatically office-holders and guardians of a universalistic ethic, the Brahmans were 'by background and nature priests' (ROI: 148) and the guardians of a relativistic ethic.

The view that Brahmans are paradigmatically priests has been contested by Heesterman (1964, 1971). Certainly the evidence is unambiguous that the Brahman who can avoid priestly activity and devote himself to knowledge and teaching, has higher status than the practising priest, especially the temple priest (see, e.g. Parry 1980, Fuller 1984: 62–4). Nevertheless, Brahmans remained guardians of a relativistic caste ethic, whatever their occupation, so long as they gave allegiance to the Vedas (i.e. did not become Buddhists or Jains). Weber quite rightly noted that 'contemplative mysticism as a type of gnosis remains the crown of the classical Brahmanical style of life, the goal of every well-educated Brahman though the number of those who actually pursue it was as small in the medieval past as today' (ROI: 148).

Weber is equally good when he deduces the *aim* of Brahmanical religion from the social position of its adherents:

The status pride of cultured men resisted undignified demands of ecstatic therapeutic practices and the exhibition of neuropathic states . . . [but] could take a quite different stand toward the forms of apathetic ecstasy . . . and all ascetic practices capable of rationalization.

(ROI: 149)[15]

[Thus] the development of such salvation doctrines signified essentially, as is to be expected of intellectuals, a rationalization and sublimation of the magical holy states. This proceeded in three directions: first one strove increasingly for personal holy status, for "bliss" in this sense of the word, instead of for magical secret power useful for professional sorcery. Secondly, this state acquired a definitely formal character, and indeed, as was to be expected, that of a gnosis . . . All religious holy seeking on such a foundation had to take the form of mystical seeking of god, mystical possession of god, or finally, mystical communion with the godhead. All three forms, pre-eminently however, the last named, actually appeared . . . The rational interpretation of the world with respect to its natural, social and ritual orders then was the third aspect of the rationalization process, which the Brahmanical intellectual stratum consummated in reworking the religio-magical material . . .

(ROI: 152–3)

Once again, this is an excellent characterization of Brahmanism, but misses the way in which even its adherents interpreted it in terms of magical powers. Crucial to the way in which anti-magical or anti-deistic doctrines would resurface in magical or deistic interpretations was the fact that texts were learned by heart in Sanskrit, not learned by reading, so that even many of those who could recite them needed explanations.[16] Also, Weber perhaps overestimates the importance of communion with a 'depersonalized' godhead: the other two forms of mysticism he mentions became increasingly important with the rise of the monotheistic sects.

Weber saw very clearly that the development of this mysticism posed certain problems for Brahmanical thought: how to reconcile the ideal of renunciation with caste duty?

For one thing, from such mysticism no ethic for life within the world could be deduced. The Upanishads contain nothing or almost nothing of what we call ethics. For another, salvation through gnostic wisdom alone came into sharpest tension with the traditional content of holy texts. The gnostic doctrines led to the devaluation not only of the world of the gods, but, above all, of ritual . . . [T]he orthodox remedied the situation through "organic" relativism.

(*ROI: 172; Weber 1917: 389)

Thus although this 'denial of the world' was extremely 'radical', it 'did not reject the suffering, or sin, or uncharitableness, or imperfection of the world, but rather

36

it rejected its transitory nature' (*ROI: 167; Weber 1917: 383). So, as Dumont has also been at pains to stress, Brahmanical soteriology is accommodated to Brahmanical social teaching: the ideal of the renouncer is absorbed into Hinduism in such a way as to pose no threat to it, and in such a way that it excluded the possibility of a rational this-worldly asceticism. This was because on the one hand, the ideal was relativized and, on the other, because it was, in its dominant strains, conceptualized as opposed to all activity.

BUDDHISM

As with Brahmanism, Weber is not a reliable guide to the practice of Buddhists. Nevertheless he has some very perceptive remarks to make about Buddhist doctrine which are surely correct in their assessment of the limitations it placed on the action of its adherents. Weber's well-known summary is particularly misleading:

> Ancient Buddhism . . . is a specifically unpolitical and anti-political status religion, more precisely, a religious "technology" of wandering and of intellectually-schooled mendicant monks . . . Its salvation is a solely personal act of the single individual. There is no recourse to a deity or savior. From Buddha himself we know no prayer. There is no religious grace. There is, moreover, no predestination either.
>
> (ROI: 206)

This picture is based on the doctrinal texts of the Pali canon, and if it was ever true of Buddhism it can only have been so for a short period while the Buddha was alive. A similar picture of 'true Buddhism' was arrived at by nineteenth century commentators in Sri Lanka and elsewhere who then went on to condemn what they saw of Sinhalese or other Buddhism as corrupt, degenerate, animistic, superstitious, and so on.[17] By paying no attention to the Vinaya (monastic discipline) texts, Weber underestimated the all-important role of the Sangha (monastic community) in the life of the monk. He also underestimated the degree to which early Buddhism had already accommodated itself to lay religious interests and therefore included elements of prayer, deification of the Buddha, and so on.[18]

The urban origin of Buddhism, its original appeal to the middle classes, its universalism, and sociological egalitarianism, its rejection of magical means to salvation, and its ethical stress on carefulness (Gombrich 1974) might make one think that Buddhism was a South Asian Protestantism. Weber's conclusions on this count are surely valid:

> [A]ll rational action ("goal directed action") is . . . expressly rejected. Thus there is lacking the tendency which in occidental monasticism developed increasingly with time and was so important for its specific character, namely, the impulse toward rational method in the conduct of life in all

spheres, except that of the pure intellectual systemization of concentrated meditation and pure contemplation. The latter, on the other hand, was increasingly developed [within Buddhism] to that level of sophistication usually striven for in India.

(**ROI: 222; Weber 1917: 451)

Not only was Buddhism not rationalistic in Weber's sense, it was also not ascetic, as indeed the Jains charged:

In principle Buddhistic salvation is anti-ascetic if one conceptualizes, as we wish to do here, asceticism as a rational method of living. Certainly Buddhism prescribes a definite way . . . However, this way is neither through rationalistic insight into the principles on which it metaphysically rests, in themselves, indeed, timelessly simple, nor a gradual training for ever higher moral perfection. Liberation is . . . a sudden "leap" into the psychic states of the several stages of enlightenment, for which methodical contemplation is only a preparation. The nature of this leap is such that it puts the seeker in his innermost active dispositions in harmony with his theoretical insights, and grants him thereby the Buddhist *perseverantia gratiae* and *certitudo salutis* . . . As all traditions indicate, this was the Buddha's own self-conscious state of grace.

(**ROI: 220; Weber 1917: 449)

[In short] just as every rational asceticism does not constitute flight from the world so not every flight from the world represents rational asceticism – as convincingly shown by this example.

(ROI: 219)

Buddhism was therefore a 'genteel' or 'elite' (*vornehm*) soteriology:

That it was such a genteel soteriology of intellectuals was precisely the basis of all its differences with ancient Christianity. Opposition to all genteel intellectuality . . . was fundamentally important to the latter.

(**ROI: 371; Weber 1917: 687)

For the laity Buddhism offered the Five Precepts 'as an inferior substitute ethic of the weak (*Unzulänglichkeitsethik der Schwache*) who do not wish to seek complete salvation' (**ROI: 215; Weber 1917: 443). This would seem to mean, not that Weber thinks these are 'paltry stuff' as Gombrich (1971: 245) interprets him, but that the ethic is necessarily inferior to the path of becoming a monk. Thus although

the later Buddhist suttas . . . deal more thoroughly with lay problems . . . [they] seek to treat lay morality as a preliminary step to the higher spiritual ethic . . . This "higher" morality does not lead – this is the decisive point – to increasingly rational asceticism (this- or other-worldly) or to a positive life method. Every idea of the sanctity of work . . . is and remains heretical.

Rather the opposite holds; active virtue in conduct recedes more and more into the background as against . . . the ethic of nonaction . . . in the interest of pure contemplation.

(*ROI: 217; Weber 1917: 445)

This inability to produce a 'positive life method' was legitimated by the Buddhist theological principle of 'skill in means', i.e. 'the Buddhist belief in meeting the audience on their own level' (Gombrich 1971: 247). Thus on the one hand Buddhist monasticism could not produce rational asceticism out of its conceptual inheritance, but nor could Buddhist lay ethics on the other, because they were tied in, as an inferior partner, to those same values.[19]

THE RELIGION OF THE MASSES

The mass of South Asian people, and this included for the most part the Buddhist laity in its religious dealings with this world,

in no way bound itself to a single faith. Rather, the simple Hindu who has not been specifically initiated into a sect treats the [different] cults and deities [of Hinduism] just as the ancient Greek worshipped Apollo and Dionysus according to the occasion, and as the Chinese devotedly attends Buddhist masses, Taoistic magic, and Confucian temple cults.

(**ROI: 327; Weber 1917: 797)

Not the "miracle" but the "magical spell" remained . . . the core substance of mass religiosity. This was true above all for peasants and laborers, but also for the middle classes . . . This was either in the gross form of compulsive magic or in the refined form of persuading a functional god or demon through gifts. With such means the great mass of the illiterate and even the literate Asiatics sought to master everyday life.

(*ROI: 335–6; Weber 1917: 805)

This most highly anti-rational world of universal magic also affected everyday economics. There is no way from it to rational, this-worldly conduct.

(ROI: 336)

From the viewpoint of Weber's interests, these judgements are fair. He was not interested, as an anthropologist would be, in showing how these beliefs formed a system, and therefore possessed their own rationality. It should not be necessary to repeat that Weber was interested in the origins of a particular type of rationality, one which from other points of view might appear quite irrational.

Saviour religion (i.e. the Vaishnava sects) Weber interprets as being originally the preserve of the 'illiterate middle classes' (ROI: 307, 309, 335). In fact it was often the urban lower classes who turned to this form of religion. Its potential for creating a rational asceticism was negated by two facts: its nature which followed from the 'orgiastic and indeed sexual-orgiastic origin of *bhakti* ecstasy' (ROI: 307).[20]

Second, there was the position of the guru: 'adoration of the living savior was the last word of Hindu religious development' (ROI: 324). The influence of the gurus was wholly traditionalistic and anti-rational:

> Instead of a drive toward the rational economic accumulation of property and the utilization of capital, Hinduism created irrational accumulation opportunities for magicians and spiritual counsellors, and prebends for mystagogues and ritualistically or soteriologically oriented intellectual strata.
>
> (*ROI: 328; Weber 1917: 798)[21]

It is worth mentioning here Weber's conclusions on the ethical consequences of the doctrine of the Bhagavad Gita that one should fulfil one's caste duty while remaining unattached to the 'fruit' or results of the action. Milton Singer has claimed that Weber's 'emphasis on its organismic relativistic character and on its "world indifference" led him, I think, to slight a major parallel with the "Protestant ethic" in Hindu thought' (Singer 1961: 147). But Weber was surely correct to say:

> [The professional fulfilment taught by the Bhagavad Gita] was rigidly traditionalistic in character and thereby mystically oriented as an activity in the world but not yet of the world. At any rate, it would occur to no Hindu to see in the course of his economic professional integrity the signs of his state of grace – or what is more important – to evaluate and undertake the rational constitution of the world according to empirical principles as a realization of God's will.
>
> (ROI: 326)

In any case, in spite of the Bhagavad Gita's universal popularity, no sect which has survived into modern South Asia has based its ethical doctrine principally on that text. The inspiration of the Vaishnava sects has come rather from the Bhagavata Purana with its emphasis on the need for emotional abandonment in one's relationship to God. Thus even when Vaishnava sectarianism has represented values of hard work and self-improvement (see, e.g. Pocock 1973: 141), it does not make those values imperative in the way that interested Weber.

Religion, as it developed in South Asia, was incapable of imposing on the masses new sorts of social action, as Protestantism did in the West. The same religion offered different ideals to, and made different demands upon, different social strata. Furthermore,

> with very few exceptions Asiatic soteriology knew only an exemplary promise. Most of these were only accessible to those living monastically but some were valid for the laity . . . The bases of both phenomena were similar. Two above all were closely interrelated. In the first place [there was] the gap which set the person of literary cultivation above the non-literate masses of philistines. Then [there was] the associated fact that in the final analysis all philosophies and soteriologies of Asia shared a common presupposition: that knowledge, be it literary knowledge or mystical gnosis, is

ultimately the only absolute path to the highest spiritual good both here and in the world beyond.

(**ROI: 330; Weber 1917: 800)

[The mystical character of this gnosis] had two important consequences. First was the formation by the soteriology of a redemption aristocracy, for the capacity for mystical gnosis is a charisma and not by a long chalk accessible to all. Then, however, and correlated therewith it acquired an asocial and apolitical character . . .

(*ROI: 331; Weber 1917: 802)

But [Asia's] goals of self-discipline – in some cases purely mystical, in others purely worldly and aesthetic [i.e. especially in China] – could in any case be pursued only by emptying experience of the real forces of life. These goals were remote from the interests of the "masses" and their day-to-day activities, who were therefore left in undisturbed magical bondage.

(**ROI: 342; Weber 1917: 814)

It was this 'emptying' nature of the road to salvation which Weber thinks is the crucial 'spiritual' factor, to be placed alongside caste and the power of the guru, in prolonging the 'enchantment' of the Hindu, i.e. the prevalence of magic as opposed to rationality. It meant that religious means were always, in one way or another, irrational:

Either they were of an orgiastic character and led directly into anti-rational paths which were inimical to a rational way of life, or they were admittedly rational in method but irrational in aim.

(**ROI: 326; Weber 1917: 796)

CONCLUSION

Weber's sociology of Hinduism and Buddhism is a marvel of condensation and, in spite of a superficial appearance to the contrary due to the mass of details, it displays an impressively unitary theme. In order to try and bring out that theme, I have presented and commented on only the most general and prominent points of ROI. To discuss and assess it in all its detail would require another book at least. To ignore Weber's book on South Asia because many of the details are wrong is to ignore also three virtues it conspicuously displays, from which the study of South Asian religion and society could well benefit: (i) comparative range, from China, to Europe, to Ancient Greece, which no single scholar will probably ever again possess; (ii) a genuine historical depth, which is only approached even by the best sociologists and anthropologists; (iii) an impressive theoretical apparatus: (a) he treats society as a whole whose parts are interdependent, unlike even so distinguished a Sanskritist as A.L. Basham, whose otherwise excellent *The Wonder That Was India* has one chapter on politics, one on everyday life, one on religion, and so on, with little indication of the extent to which they are interrelated; (b) Weber tries to understand and explain the functioning and development of Hinduism and Buddhism in terms of a few basic categories, which are the same as those used to explain other societies. In this, as in much else, the foremost disciple of Weber, in the study of South Asia, is clearly Louis Dumont.[22]

NOTES

1 This essay appeared originally in *Sociology* (1982) 16, 1: 526–43, and is republished with revisions by kind permission. Much of the stimulus for writing it came from discussions with Mark Elvin (see below on the Chinese case and Elvin 1984). At about the same time as it was written, Detlef Kantowsky wrote several articles on Max Weber's study of Hinduism and Buddhism (see bibliography) and made similar criticisms of the way Weber has been misunderstood by South Asian specialists. While numerous new references have been added it would have been impossible to survey all the literature which continues to pour forth on Max Weber (Marshall 1980 and 1982, represent the approach closest to that adopted here, and are highly recommended); even publications strictly on Weber and South Asia are too voluminous. The translations from *The Religion of India* have been checked and where I have judged them not even passable they have been adjusted. Where I have changed a word or two this is indicated with an asterisk (*ROI); where I have changed more than this, it is indicated with two asterisks (**ROI). For advice on translation I would like to thank Dr N.J. Allen, Professor T.J. Reed, and Dr Wolfgang Schwentker. However, I alone am responsible for the retranslations; it should be clear that a new translation, based on the forthcoming critical edition of the German text edited by Glintzer and Golzio, by someone competent both in the German language and in South Asian studies, is an urgent scholarly necessity. I would also like to thank David Chalcraft for detailed comments which have persuaded me that the text of PESC is not as univocal as I had supposed (see his 'Bringing the text back in: ways of reading *The Protestant Ethic*', in M. Reed and L. Ray (eds), forthcoming, *Re-Organising Modernity*, Routledge).

2 *The Religion of India* is in fact a translation, and in many places a mistranslation, of part (Weber 1916–17) of Weber's series of long articles entitled 'The Economic Ethics of the World Religions'. It would have been more accurate to call the translation *The Religions of Asia*. Kantowsky (1986: 214–16) describes how such a poor translation came to be published.

3 I use the term 'India' in the title since it appears in the title of ROI and was used by Weber; but the region is today generally referred to as South Asia to differentiate it from the modern political unit called India.

4 For example, Fuller (1977) has traced some of the drawbacks in anthropologists' accounts of caste to the division of labour between them and historians.

5 For an important discussion of the Scottish case, scholarly both in its analysis of Weber and in its presentation of the historical evidence, see Marshall (1980). I shall argue that in fact South Asia (India) was closer to Scotland than to China: i.e. it had an analogue of neo-Calvinism (namely, Jainism), but lacked other ('material') conditions for 'take-off' (cf. Marshall 1980: 272–3). As discussed below, Elvin (1984) argues against Weber that even in the Chinese case the explanation must hinge on ecological and technical factors, not on the absence of functional equivalents of Protestantism.

6 Thus Singer's long analysis of present-day Hindu entrepreneurs in Madras (1972: ch. 8), although interesting enough in itself, fails to attack Weber's main thesis. A similar criticism can be made of Munshi's (1988) otherwise very useful and detailed critique.

Marshall (1980: 11–12, 30; 1982) lists numerous other, even more elementary mis-interpretations springing from lack of attention to Weber's text.

7 Thus – although there is no space to argue this at length here – I claim Weber's theory to have been that Protestantism was what J.L. Mackie (1965) called an INUS con-dition of the capitalist spirit, i.e. it was an insufficient but necessary part of a collection of conditions which together were/are unnecessary but sufficient for the production of the capitalist spirit. According to Mackie this is, in fact, what we generally mean by 'cause'. Marshall (1980; 1982: 58–9) argues that Weber's initial problem was a search for the origins of the capitalist *spirit*, and that this only subsequently came to encompass the separate question of the origin of capitalism itself. The formulation given here is compatible, I believe, but more precise.

8 Turner (1974: 172–3) argues that in the Muslim case also Weber's position was that the main burden of explanation lay with 'material' factors, i.e. with the patrimonial nature of Muslim states.

9 Many commentators and critics, even those of Weber's own time, have ignored the context of his writing, e.g. the fact that PESC was first composed, and later revised, as part of a debate with Sombart. On this background, see Marshall (1980: 1–35; 1982).

10 As Schluchter (1981: 4) puts it, 'Weber's work can be viewed as the gigantic effort to refute the basic assumptions of evolutionism'. He rightly criticizes Tenbruck's (1980) evolutionist interpretation of Weber as one-sided.

11 In this context John Hall (1985) has traced the consequences of Europe's multi-state system as opposed to China's single imperial state. Cf. Collins (1986: 49).

12 In an approach similar to Elvin's, Collins (1986: ch. 3) emphasizes technological innovations, both in Medieval Europe and in China from the eighth to the twelfth century, and the similar economic dynamism of Christian and Buddhist monasteries (a parallel Weber missed).

13 On Jainism one should consult Jaini (1979) and Carrithers and Humphrey (1991), though curiously neither work engages with Weber's ideas. The Jains seem to have had closer connections to industry and to kings than Weber realized.

14 For a longer discussion of Weber on caste, see Stern (1971). For the most recent in a long line of critiques of Dumont on caste, see Quigley (1993). Some South Asianists, tired of the emphasis on caste, for which they hold Weber partly responsible, have in recent times rejected the notion that caste was important in South Asian history. For a representative critique, see Inden (1990: ch. 2), and for a counterblast to an earlier version of the same argument, see Quigley (1988).

15 For reflections in a very Weberian mode on the place of spirit-possession in South Asian religions, see Höfer (1974).

16 See Staal (1979) and Heesterman (1974) for attempts to grapple with the problem of the effects on South Asian Great Traditions of the methods by which they were passed on.

17 The most impassioned critique of these sorts of views is by Southwold (1983). For the Christian model which dominated nineteenth century observers' views of Buddhism, and for a typology of modern anthropologists' views, see Gellner (1991).

18 On these issues, see Gombrich (1971, 1988). On early Buddhist monasticism, see Wijayaratna (1990).

19 For discussion of Weber's remarks on Mahayana Buddhism, which in my view exaggerate the differences between it and early Buddhism, see Gellner (1988: 125–7).

20 Munshi (1988: 24) is surely right that Weber's repeated use of the terms 'orgiastic' and 'sexual-orgiastic' is likely to mislead. Turner (1974: 183) goes so far as to say that 'Weber's mistakes about Islam are closely bound up with his whole attitude towards the relationship between religion and sex'.

21 For a discussion of Weber's use of the term 'prebend', see Turner (1981: ch. 7).

22 See Dumont (1980 [1966], 1977). Others have noticed this debt also. See Burghart (1985: 6), Buss (1985: 13–14, 61–2), Conrad (1986: 172), and Holton and Turner (1989: 86–7); and in a more hostile manner, Appadurai (1986: 745) and Dirks (1987: 9). For interesting personal background to Dumont's study of South Asia, see Collins (1989). Dumont is however open to the charge, as Weber is not, that the single contrast between Europe and South Asia dominates his thought.

REFERENCES

Appadurai, A. (1986) 'Is Homo Hierarchicus?' *American Ethnologist* 13, 4: 745–61.

Bayly, C.A. (1983) *Rulers, Townsmen and Bazaars: North Indian Society in the Age of British Expansion, 1770–1870*, Cambridge: Cambridge University Press.

Basham, A.L. (1967) *The Wonder That was India*, London: Fontana.

Burghart, R. (1985) 'Introduction: theoretical approaches to the anthropology of South Asia', in R. Burghart and A. Cantlie (eds) *Indian Religion*, London: Curzon Press.

Buss, A.E. (1985) *Max Weber and Asia: Contributions to the Sociology of Development*, Munich: Weltforum Verlag.

Carrithers, M. and Humphrey, C. (eds) (1991) *The Assembly of Listeners: Jains in Society*, Cambridge: Cambridge University Press.

Collins, R. (1986) *Weberian Sociological Theory*, Cambridge: Cambridge University Press.

Collins, S. (1989) 'Louis Dumont and the study of religions', *Religious Studies Review* 15, 1: 14–20.

Conrad, D. (1986) 'Max Weber's conception of Hindu dharma as a paradigm', in D. Kantowsky (ed.) (1986).

Dirks, N. (1987) *The Hollow Crown: Ethnohistory of an Indian Kingdom*, Cambridge: Cambridge University Press.

Dumont, L. (1960) 'World renunciation in Indian religion', *Contributions to Indian Sociology* 4: 33–62. Reprinted in L. Dumont (1970) *Religion, Politics and History in India*, Paris/The Hague: Mouton; and in Dumont (1980).

Dumont, L. (1977) *From Mandeville to Marx: The Genesis and Triumph of Economic Ideology*, Chicago: The University of Chicago Press.

Dumont, L. (1980) *Homo Hierarchicus: The Caste System and Its Implications*, complete revised English edition, Chicago: The University of Chicago Press. First published (1966).

Elvin, M. (1973) *The Pattern of the Chinese Past*, London: Eyre Methuen.

Elvin, M. (1984) 'Why China failed to create an endogenous industrial capitalism: a critique of Max Weber's explanation', *Theory and Society* 13, 3: 379–92.

Fuller, C. (1977) 'British India or traditional India? An anthropological problem', *Ethnos* 42, 3–4: 95–121.

Fuller, C. (1984) *Servants of the Goddess: The Priests of a South Indian Temple*, Cambridge: Cambridge University Press.

Gellner, D.N. (1988) 'Priesthood and possession: Newar religion in the light of some Weberian concepts', *Pacific Viewpoint* 29, 2: 119–43.

Gellner, D.N. (1991) 'Introduction: What is the anthropology of Buddhism about?' *Journal of the Anthropological Society of Oxford* 21, 2: 95–112.

Giddens, A. (1976) 'Introduction' in PESC.

Gombrich, R.F. (1971) *Precept and Practice: Traditional Buddhism in the Rural Highlands of Ceylon*, Oxford: Clarendon Press.

Gombrich, R.F. (1974) 'The duty of a Buddhist according to the Pali scriptures', in W.D. O'Flaherty and J.D.M. Derrett (eds) *The Concept of Duty in South Asia*, Delhi: Vikas/SOAS.

Gombrich, R.F. (1988) *Theravada Buddhism: A Social History from Ancient Benares to Modern Colombo*, London: Routledge.

Hall, J. (1985) 'Capstones and organisms: political forms and the triumph of capitalism', *Sociology* 19, 2: 173–92.

Heesterman, J.C. (1964) 'Brahmin, ritual, and renouncer', *Wiener Zeitschrift für die Kunde Süd- und Ostasiens* 8: 1–31. Reprinted in Heesterman (1985) *The Inner Conflict of Tradition: Essays in Indian Ritual, Kingship, and Society*, Chicago: The University of Chicago Press; Delhi: OUP.

Heesterman, J.C. (1971) 'Priesthood and the Brahmin', *Contributions to Indian Sociology* (N.S.) 5: 43–7.

Heesterman, J.C. (1974) 'Veda and Dharma', in W.D. O'Flaherty and J.D.M. Derrett (eds) *The Concept of Duty in South Asia*, Delhi: Vikas/SOAS.

Höfer, A. (1974) 'A note on possession in South Asia', in C. von Fürer-Haimendorf (ed.) *The Anthropology of Nepal*, Warminster: Aris & Phillips.

Holton, R.J. and Turner, B.S. (1989) *Max Weber on Economy and Society*, London: Routledge.

Inden, R. (1990) *Imagining India*, Oxford: Blackwell.

Jaini, P. (1979) *The Jaina Path of Purification*, Berkeley: University of California Press.

Kantowsky, D. (1982a) 'Die Rezeption der Hinduismus/ Buddhismus-Studie Max Webers in Südasien: ein Missverständnis?' *European Journal of Sociology* 23: 317–55.

Kantowsky, D. (1982b) 'Max Weber on India and Indian interpretations of Weber', *Contributions to Indian Sociology* (N.S.) 16, 2: 141–74. Republished in Kantowsky (ed.) (1986).

Kantowsky, D. (1984) 'Max Weber's contributions to Indian sociology', *Contributions to Indian Sociology* (N.S.) 18, 2: 307–14. Republished in Kantowsky (ed.) (1986).

Kantowsky, D. (1985) 'Die Fehlrezeption von Max Webers Studie über "Hinduismus und Buddhismus" in Indien: Ursachen und Folgen', *Zeitschrift für Soziologie* 14, 6. English version in Kantowsky (ed.) (1986).

Kantowsky, D. (ed.) (1986) *Recent Research on Max Weber's Studies of Hinduism*, Munich: Weltforum Verlag.

Luethy, H. (1970) 'Once again: Calvinism and capitalism', in Wrong (ed.) *Max Weber*, New Jersey: Prentice Hall. First published in *Encounter* 22 (January 1964): 26–32. Reprinted in S.N. Eisenstadt (ed.) (1968) *The Protestant Ethic and Modernization: A Comparative View*, New York: Basic Books.

Mackie, J.L. (1965) 'Causes and conditions', *American Philosophical Quarterly* 2: 245–64

Mandelbaum, D.C. (1970) *Society in India*, 2 vols, Berkeley: University of California Press.

Marshall, G. (1980) *Presbyteries and Profits: Calvinism and the Development of Capitalism in Scotland, 1560–1707*, Oxford: Clarendon Press.

Marshall, G. (1982) *In Search of the Spirit of Capitalism*, London: Hutchinson.

Munshi, S. (1988) 'Max Weber on India: an introductory critique', *Contributions to Indian Sociology* (N.S.) 22, 1: 1–34.

O'Hanlon, R. (1985) *Caste, Conflict, and Ideology: Mahatma Jotirao Phule and Low Caste Protest in Nineteenth-century Western India*, Cambridge: Cambridge University Press.

Parry, J. (1980) 'Ghosts, greed and sin: the occupational identity of the Benares funeral priests', *Man* (N.S.) 15, 1: 88–111.

Pocock, D. (1973) *Mind, Body and Wealth: A Study of Belief and Practice in an Indian Village*, Oxford: Basil Blackwell.

Quigley, D. (1988) 'Is caste a pure figment, the invention of orientalists for their own glorification?' *Cambridge Anthropology* 13, 1: 20–36.

Quigley, D. (1993) *The Interpretation of Caste*, Oxford: Clarendon Press.

Roth, G. and Schluchter, W. (1979) *Max Weber's Vision of History: Ethics and Methods*, Berkeley: University of California Press.

Schluchter, W. (1981) *The Rise of Western Rationalism: Max Weber's Developmental History*, trans. G. Roth, Berkeley: University of California Press.

Singer, M. (1961) Review of ROI, *American Anthropologist* 63, 1: 143–51.

Singer, M. (1972) *When a Great Tradition Modernizes: An Anthropological Approach to Indian Civilization*, New York: Praeger.

Sinha, S. (1974) 'The sociology of religion', in *A Survey of Research in Sociology and Social Anthropology*, vol.II, ch.9, Bombay: Popular Prakashan.

Southwold, M. (1983) *Buddhism in Life: The Anthropological Study of Buddhism and the Sinhalese Practice of Buddhism*, Manchester: Manchester University Press.

Srinivas, M.N. (1976) *The Remembered Village*, Delhi: Oxford University Press.

Staal, F. (1979) 'Oriental ideas on the origin of language', *Journal of the American Oriental Society* 99: 1–14.

Stern, H. (1971) 'Religion et Société en Inde selon Max Weber', *Informations sur les Sciences Sociales* 10, 6: 69–112.

Tambiah, S.J. (1973) 'Buddhism and this-worldly activity', *Modern Asian Studies* 7, 1: 1–20.

Tenbruck, F.H. (1980) 'The problem of thematic unity in the works of Max Weber', *British Journal of Sociology* 31: 313–51.

Trevor-Roper, H.R. (1967) *Religion, the Reformation and Social Change and other Essays*, London: Macmillan.

Turner, B.S. (1974) *Weber and Islam: A Critical Study*, London: Routledge & Kegan Paul.

Turner, B.S. (1981) *For Weber: Essays on the Sociology of Fate*, Boston: Routledge & Kegan Paul.

Weber, M. (1916–17) 'Die Wirtschaftsethik der Weltreligionen (Dritter Artikel): Hinduismus und Buddhismus', *Archiv für Sozialwissenschaft und Sozialpolitik* (1916) 41, 3: 613–744, (1917) 42, 2: 345–461, (1917) 43, 3: 687–814. Reprinted in M. Weber (1921) *Gesammelte Aufsätze zur Religionssoziologie*, vol. II, Tübingen: JCB Mohr.

Weber, M. (1927) *General Economic History*, London: Allen & Unwin.

Weber, M. (1949) *The Methodology of the Social Sciences*, trans. E.A. Shils and H.A. Finch, New York: The Free Press.

Weber, M. (1951) *The Religion of China*, trans. H.H. Gerth, New York: Macmillan.

Weber, M. (1958) *The Religion of India: The Sociology of Hinduism and Buddhism*, trans. H.H. Gerth and D. Martindale, New York: The Free Press.

Weber, M. (1968) *Economy and Society: An Outline of an Interpretative Sociology*, 3 vols, G. Roth and C. Wittich (eds), New York: Bedminster Press.

Weber, M. (1976) *The Protestant Ethic and the Spirit of Capitalism*, trans. T. Parsons, 2nd edn, London: Allen & Unwin.

Wijayaratna, M. (1990) *Buddhist Monastic Life, According to the Texts of the Theravada Tradition*, trans. C. Grangier and S. Collins, Cambridge: Cambridge University Press.

2

ISLAM AND CAPITALISM

A Weberian perspective on resurgence

William H. Swatos Jr

Like his projected work on revolution, Max Weber never completed a free-standing essay on Islam within his world religions corpus. Treatments of his understanding of Islam must be garnered from fragments scattered throughout his work, particularly *Economy and Society*. At the same time, however, as Karl Jaspers points out, all of Weber's works 'are really *fragments*. A work would end with the note. An additional article follows' (italics in original (1920), 1989: p.40). To present a discussion in the contemporary context based on 'Weber on Islam', is simply to acknowledge at the outset that all of Weber's theses have a tentativeness about them. Only those who misunderstand science as a revelation of eternal truth rather than as a process for gaining knowledge should be disturbed by this observation. The ultimate test of a conceptual apparatus is its use value, and in this chapter I want to make use of Weber's analyses in a comparative way to highlight both the positive and negative associations between Islamic states and capitalism currently.

I will focus on two broad Islamic sectors of the globe. One of these is the 'traditional lands of Islam', running from the West African coast of the Maghreb through the Levant to Persia. The other is Islamic Southeast Asia, principally Malaysia and Indonesia. These two cases provide contrasting pictures of the relation of Islam to capitalism, and I will argue that they reflect broader cultural orientations that both underscore and limit the accuracy of Weber's assertions. In making this comparison, I am leaving out two other big Islamic sectors: Subsaharan Africa and the Slavic peoples. I am also excluding Turkey and those areas of the Indian subcontinent and Mongol world that remain Islamic. Each of these cases can be addressed within a Weberian framework (as Murvar (1989) has, for example, for some of the Balkan states), but each also has cultural dynamics that are much less clearly relevant to capitalism at present than the two areas I do propose to examine.

ASSESSMENTS OF WEBER ON ISLAM

The literature on Weber on Islam is relatively limited and may be placed into one of four categories:

Exegetical works are those that primarily attempt to tell the reader what Weber said about Islam. They in effect write the chapter on Islam Weber failed to write, either in general or with respect to application to a specific Islamic population. Examples of this style are provided by articles of Raj Gandhi (1976) and Robert Bocock (1971). Because Weber's remarks on Islam are scattered, these pieces provide a proportionally greater service than do exegetical works on some other topics where Weber's texts are themselves straightforward.

Weber relevant texts appear to be written, to borrow Dieter Henrich's (1987) phrase, 'with Max Weber in mind'. These are primarily anthropological works that take inspiration from Weber but move away from him fairly quickly to develop a substantive quality of their own. Premier exemplars of this strategy are Ernest Gellner (1963) and Clifford Geertz (1968). Also I would include here the myriad essays that attempted to explore what Robert Bellah (1970) termed 'the Protestant ethic analogy in Asia' or elsewhere, to the extent that they apply to Islam.

Critiques of Weber constitute a third category. Many of these build upon an even wider body of criticism of Weber's Protestant ethic thesis, to which I will turn shortly. The most extreme position is probably that of Maxime Rodinson (1973), who attempts a Marxist–Freudian alternative. A similar, though ultimately more Weber-amenable, approach is offered by Sami Zubaida (1972). Less ostensibly hostile criticisms are offered by Bryan Turner in a series of essays and in the only substantive monograph on the topic (1974a, 1974b, 1978), but these are quarrelsome and tendentious works that as a whole paint Weber in an unfavourable light. Susan Croutwater's essay on sultanism (1985) reflects Turner's influence, if not his attitude. Perhaps the most helpful treatments as a group are contained in a collection of essays edited by Wolfgang Schluchter (1987), which is available only in German. Taken as a whole, however, the Weber critiques have a tendency to cancel each other out. For example, Croutwater and Zubaida make much of the interconnections between militarism and Islam, while Turner tries to break the connection – though more by assertion than documentation.

Neo-Weberian studies constitute a final category. Neo-Weberian studies give primacy to Weber's conceptual arsenal while simply setting aside the content of his own historical studies. In research on Islamic societies, this orientation has an outstanding example in Said Arjomand's work on Shi'ite Iran up to 1890, *The Shadow of God and the Hidden Imam* (1984). It has also been used to great effect by Robert Antonio in his study of the fall of Rome (1979), and I have employed this strategy in work on the slave South in North America (Swatos 1987). In a broader compass of considerable relevance to the contemporary interaction of Islam and capitalism, Vatro Murvar has produced a magisterial essay on modern patrimonialism (1985: 40–85), though unfortunately his application of it to Islam (*ibid.* 203–15) is historical rather than contemporary.

In this chapter, I intend to draw primarily from the first and fourth categories in this taxonomy. In order to do so credibly, however, something needs to be said at the outset principally about matters relevant to the Weber critiques. These occur at two levels, one having to do with the way Weber uses Islam in his world religions studies, the other historical and theological arguments about data and their meaning.

THE PROTESTANT ETHIC CONUNDRUM

It is virtually inevitable that discussions of Islam and capitalism return to Weber's Protestant ethic thesis, since it is indeed the point from which Weber began his consideration of the world religions. At the same time, as a number of scholars have pointed out at one time or another, the debates surrounding these essays constitute something of a hermeneutical vortex.[1] I sincerely wish I could avoid all discussion of it here; yet it is so prominent in the literature as to make ignoring it imprudent. I shall try to be as brief as possible. I have made longer statements elsewhere (e.g. Swatos 1987; Kivisto and Swatos, 1988; Swatos and Kivisto 1991a, 1991b), which may be consulted further and from which these remarks are abstracted.

The Protestant Ethic and the Spirit of Capitalism in its present, generally used English translation (1930) is a 1920 revision by Weber of two essays he first published in 1904–5. To these are prefixed the introduction to his entire world religions corpus, which was the context for his revision. Along with his 1909–10 reaction (translated 1978a) to criticisms of the original essays by Felix Rachfahl, this introduction is extremely important for understanding what it was Weber thought he was (and was not) doing in his work. There is also a third Protestant ethic essay, related to his observations on the Protestant ethic in America, that appeared in 1906, and is translated separately in both its revised 1920 version (1946) and the original (1985).

In spite of occasional claims to the contrary, the work is accurately titled. It is an enthymematic argument about a religious way of *acting* and an economic world view. Religious beliefs, as Gianfranco Poggi has aptly noted (1983: 56), are 'upstream' of Weber's thesis. The original context for Weber's writing was his assumption of the co-editorship of the *Archiv für Sozialwissenschaft und Sozialpolitik*, on the one hand, and his frustration on the other of finding a political solution to what he perceived to be a German national identity crisis. The 'Protestant' in *The Protestant Ethic* properly contrasts to 'Lutheran', not Catholic (see Liebersohn 1988); though by the time of the 1920 revision this was altered, and a universal–historical dimension seeking to discern *impediments to the capitalist ethos* in the action systems of the world religions was added. The essay remains basically historical in character, however, and offers an intentionally one-sided argument (1930: 27), that is 'unambiguous and breathtakingly simple' (Marshall 1982: 70), that the breakthrough to modern rational capitalism as a life-world was facilitated by Protestant morality (the 'work ethic'). It does not argue that Protestantism as a specific set of Christian dogmas was either necessary or sufficient to 'cause' modern rational capitalism to appear, but that it did in fact create a system of meaningful action that functioned historically as the 'last intensification' in a causal chain that in fact led to modern capitalism, 'the most fateful force in our modern life' (1930: 17).[2]

This historical point is all Weber needed to carry on not only a 'dialogue with the ghost of Karl Marx', as Albert Salomon phrased it (1945: 596), but also with other theorists in the social sciences as well as his German political and religious allies and adversaries.[3] What Weber lamented in Germany and in himself (see Jaspers 1989: 169) was 'the fact that our nation has never experienced the school of hard asceticism in *any* form'. On this cultural critique he lay tremendous weight as an explanation for the failure of Germany to attain the international political-economic stature of Anglo-America. This historical logic can be seen, for example, in his somewhat exasperated comment in his response to Rachfahl that 'the great centers of the Middle Ages such as Florence, . . . were, God knows, capitalistically developed to quite another degree than . . . the American colonies', yet Anglo-America became the cultural centre of the *spirit* of capitalism (Weber 1978a: 1119).

THE ISLAMIC FOIL

It is my view that in the world religions studies, Islam was to be the final and most perfect foil for illustrating the validity of the Protestant ethic thesis. Unfortunately, Weber's comments on Islam lack the sometimes painful care that characterizes, for instance, his essays on Hinduism and Buddhism. Basically, however, he is dealing with three interdependent elements – ethics, law and political organization – the unifying tendency among which is *arbitrariness* rather than rationality. With regard to political organization, this means patrimonial administration that at its extreme Weber terms *sultanism*. It also means the absence of independent cities; the Islamic city is only a unit for political administration by the caliph or sultan. With regard to law, the critical feature is *qadi* justice, the 'irrational' personalistic judgements of wise men. Weber particularly liked to contrast qadi justice to Western rational forms. The Islamic ethic derives from *jihad*, Holy War, and is linked therein to the 'upstream' theological concept of *predetermination*, rather than predestination. One might in a shorthand way say that the Islamic ethic is 'overdetermined' by this-worldliness.

There is general agreement among scholars who have looked at Weber on Islam that his discussion of patrimonialism within Islam as its major impediment toward capitalism is accurate. Less unanimity exists regarding both the 'Islamic ethic' hypothesis and qadi justice. It would take us too far afield to pursue these topics in detail, and in any case, it is in the nature of interpretive sociology that conclusions rest on what Lipset has called 'method of the dialogue' (1968) – that is, the validity of conclusions rests more on persuasion than falsification. Suffice it to say, that I am unpersuaded, in particular, by Bryan Turner's assertion that Weber was 'hopelessly incorrect in purely factual terms' when he claims that 'Islam as a religion of warriors produced an ethic which was incompatible with the "spirit of capitalism"' (1974b: 2). I think Turner is wrong for two reasons: first, methodologically, there is no such thing as a 'pure' fact using the kinds of historical data to which circumstances force us here – and, indeed, there may not be such a 'fact' ever. Second, I find Turner's own data subject to an interpretation much more consistent with the booty–sex–luxury ethic of a warrior religion (*Kriegerreligion*) than he apparently does.[4]

Although Turner's work is replete with references to the army and military life which by their sheer quantity might overwhelm his interpretation, two specific examples are particularly telling against his critique. First, in discussing the Islamic city – which is a salient point to the larger patrimonialism issue, since one of Weber's central arguments is that the Islamic city was a purely political-administrative entity, whereas in Europe the city was a stepping stone toward economic independence – Turner explains the peculiar character of the Islamic city by noting that 'Islamic cities which had emerged from army camps and garrison cities (*amsar*) continued to reflect the organization of tribal bedouins . . . [T]he continuity of clan and tribal organization within the city context imported rural feuding arrangements into urban life' (1974b: 100). This statement clearly shows the military basis upon which the cities were founded, and thus the historical priority of the warrior ethic to the development of patrimonialism. The second example comes from a quarrelsome chapter in which Turner faults Weber for using the term 'saint' for the Islamic 'sheikh'. Turner wants to show the 'this-worldliness' of Islamic sheikh deeds as distinct from the other-worldliness of Christian saint deeds (i.e. miracles). 'Sexual intercourse with a saintly person [sheikh] is considered beneficial. Chenier speaks of a saint [sheikh] in Tetuan who seized a young woman and had commerce with her in the midst of the street', a blessing which was well-received by all, including her husband (1974b: 68). 'Sheikh' or 'saint' aside, my point is that the example centres on (male) sexual conquest, very much a part of what Weber terms the Islamic ethic. This is like minimizing the fact that Muhammed granted himself more wives than Quranic law allowed by the observation that 'only one was a virgin'.

I am similarly unpersuaded by Susan Croutwater's argument that Weber's concept of sultanism 'as a recurrent type of Islamic government diverges so significantly from the historical record that it is virtually useless as a heuristic device' (1985: 183). In my view, she misrepresents Weber by attaching 'arbitrary will and grace' to sultanism as distinct from patrimonialism. What Weber says, rather, is that *both* patrimonialism and sultanism are distinct from 'the traditional limitations of patriarchal and gerontocratic structures' by the extent to which *both* sultanism and patrimonialism 'broaden the range of [the ruler's] arbitrary power and put himself in a position to grant grace and favors'. Patrimonialism and sultanism as types are differentiated from each other by the relative degree of discretion pertaining to the ruler:

> Where domination is primarily traditional, even though it is exercised by virtue of the ruler's personal autonomy, it will be called *patrimonial authority*; where it indeed operates primarily on the basis of discretion, it will be called *sultanism*. The transformation is definitely continuous . . . Sometimes it appears that sultanism is completely unrestrained by tradition, but this is never in fact the case.
>
> [italics in original] Weber 1978b: 232

Indeed, it is difficult in reading Croutwater to see how she would distinguish her reading of sultanism from charismatic authority, since her primary critique of Weber is that sultan figures ultimately appealed to traditional religious sources of legitimation. In terms of Weber's typological scheme, the proper term for a leader who displays only arbitrary will and grace is 'charisma', not sultanism. It may in fact also be the case that much of what Murvar (1985) terms 'modern patrimonialism' could be more accurately conceptualized as 'modern sultanism'.

CONTEMPORARY APPLICATIONS

The foregoing discussion is not intended simply as an academic exercise. It could be asked in one sense, for example, 'Who cares?' if Weber is right or wrong about Islam. What difference does it make to our study today? In my view, it is important because the Weberian conceptual arsenal contains powerful tools for understanding contemporary developments in at least some parts of the Muslim world. These tools, furthermore, are not ahistorical, though their applicability will have to be rethought for different times and places. In this process, however, we can illuminate a number of issues of significance and arrive at valuable understandings of the world around us and what we might anticipate in the future. We want to try to understand the cultural contexts out of which meanings or significances arise and how these shape and are shaped by other aspects of the total human environment.

THE ARAB WORLD

Let us take the patrimonialism–sultanism distinction as an example. When the Iraq–Kuwait conflict ended, many Westerners seemed surprised and dismayed by the undemocratic quality of the Kuwaiti regime. In fact, however, what the Emir of Kuwait and the rulers of most of the monarchic regimes of the Middle East represent is patrimonialism. What Saddam Hussein represents is sultanism. Sultanism is more dangerous to the global system precisely because it leaves more discretionary authority in the hands of a single individual. The irony of sultanism in modernity is that because of the relatively higher degree of non-traditionalism that superficially appears to characterize his regime – Iraq is a republic after all – he may appear to be more like a modern world leader. But, as Weber (1978b: 232) notes, 'The non-traditional element is not, however, rationalized in impersonal terms, but consists only in an extreme development of the ruler's discretion. It is this which distinguishes it from every form of rational authority'. We should not mistake the fact that Saddam Hussein – or the President of Syria – wears business suits and Western fashions for the nature of their regimes as sultanates.

Because the Emir of Kuwait, for example, is a patrimonial leader in the traditionalist sense of that type, it is possible for Western regimes to 'calculate' to a much higher degree how he will behave and thus to predict his moves. In this sense patrimonialism is more congenial to the background conditions of capitalism than is sultanism, which is far more 'irrational'. Though the tradition upon which patrimonialism is based is not itself based on rationality, the applications of that tradition are based on a relative rationality that in some cases may be reconciled to capitalist presuppositions. If we understand this relative calculability inherent in traditionalist patrimonialism, we can see why the United States, for example, supported what might at first blush appear to be a similar invasion to that of Kuwait by Iraq in that by Morocco of the Spanish Sahara. In the latter case, the alternative was a Marxist regime, which would have (at the time at least) been less amenable to integration by the dominant powers of the capitalist globe than was Moroccan patrimonialism. This is not, however, to suggest that patrimonialism is ultimately consistent with capitalism, but rather that capitalism, once established, finds it easier to deal with a relatively fixed (and therefore calculable) tradition than it is to deal with the discretionary powers of a single individual and his cadre of personal retainers.

A fascinating Weberian study by James Duke and Barry Johnson (1989) of religion and political democracy takes up a variant of the Protestant ethic thesis to demonstrate that Protestantism has acted causally with respect to the development of political democracy. More to the point presently, however, is that using four different indicators of democracy Islamic nations appear at the bottom of five major religious groups on two of the four indicators and next to the bottom (higher only than tribal religions) on the other two. This is intensified by the fact that whereas in the poorest nations (per capita GNP less than $399) democracy is weak across the board, states with tribal religions drop out of the picture at the uppermost end of the GNP spectrum, but Islamic nations do not. In addition, the undemocratic nature of Islamic regimes is unrelated to whether or not a previous colonial regime was of a more or less democratically orientated religion (e.g. French Catholicism or English Protestantism).

It should not be assumed from this, however, that the *economic* character of the Protestant ethic argument is incorrect. Rather, patrimonialism inhibits the background conditions necessary for the emergence of an institutional infrastructure to support capitalism. Nor should this be taken to mean that Islam is not a relevant variable, because it is 'religious', whereas we have now identified a 'political' impediment. Precisely because in Islam there is no separation of

53

religion and politics, the political impediment of patrimonialism is *pari passu* a religious dynamic. In other words, the faith of Islam in the Arab world sanctifies the political system of patrimonialism (historically, the caliphate, latterly the sultanate). This occurs because the warrior (or military) ethic mediates between 'upstream' doctrine and day-to-day practice. In this way, Islamic patrimonialism occupies a unique position in the global system, and we should not be surprised, for example, if the Arab world is ultimately less amenable to penetration by capitalism than Eastern Europe. Nor should we see this tendency counter-indicated by extra-territorial capitalistic involvements by Muslims or even Islamic states. Precisely because of the us–them tributary character of Arab Islam through history, it is quite possible for Arabs to make money abroad without adopting capitalism as a way of life. Profits earned abroad are tribute from an alien – and corrupt – people.

Weber makes the point, further, that in all religions there is a tendency for there to be two underlying orientations operating concurrently. With respect to Christianity in the West, we would term them churchly and sectarian. One draws to a centre, the other pulls away. These both exist in any tradition at any time. In monopolistic situations, the churchly orientation clearly has the upper hand, while pluralism encourages sectarianism. In mainstream Islam, these may be denoted as the Sunna and Sufi (or more generally, the brotherhoods). Today this latter form of expression often is styled 'Islamic fundamentalism', though the phrase from a history of religions standpoint is undesirable (see Swatos 1989; Nasr 1987). This dynamic has run throughout the bulk of Islamic history, though the specific terms have differed across time. Ironically for the West, movements toward pluralism have allowed brotherhood Islam actually to grow in its degree of influence. Those societies – such as Turkey and Pakistan – that have most intentionally aped Western democratic models have created the conditions for the growth of Sufi parties, who in their extremism simply reinforce the anticapitalist factors that are already latent in patrimonialism. Again, by failing to see that Islam is a politics as well as a religion, Westerners have failed to anticipate adequately the cultural conditions of capitalism. While we have indeed in the West spoken of 'political culture', we have nevertheless considered 'politics' primarily a *structural* variable. A Weberian perspective would sensitize us to the 'one-sidedness' of such a view just as it does to an economistic construction of capitalism.

The 'over-determining' character of the Islamic warrior ethic can be seen in the transformation of the Baath party, particularly in Iraq but also in Syria, from a secular party founded by a Christian into a party of Arab sultanism dominated by what Thomas Friedman has termed 'Hama rules' – the total destruction of opposition elements within the society (1989: 76–105). That cultural precon-ditions are a necessary part of this process – that in this case Arab nationalism and Islam interpenetrate to form a single unit – can be seen by contrast in the failure of the attempted 'Islamic' coup in Trinidad and Tobago in the summer of 1990. The absence of cultural preconditions made it abundantly clear both within and without the country that the religious rhetoric of the revolt was spurious, and it was not taken seriously. Although we cannot say sociologically that the motivations of the leader of the coup were not sincerely religious, the structural and cultural elements that would legitimate his claims were lacking. This case serves as a helpful example of the importance of both structural and cultural conditions in the determination of the success or failure of legitimate domination, regardless of its type.

It may be objected that Shi'ite Islam is of an essentially different character, and this is inadequately accounted for in my discussion. As a matter of fact, however, Shi'ism in its present form is simply a variant of Sunni Islam – though, admittedly, it grew from anti-centre roots and does have a richer revolutionary tradition. In short, the Ayatollah Khomeini was no less a patrimonial figure than any Arab sultan.[5] He and his followers were somewhat more successful in manipulating the charismatic qualities of his office than the Emir of Kuwait, but as types they are hardly different. In each case personal rulership based on tradition is the operative mode of political existence. In each case, too, the appeal for legitimacy is to the *religious* tradition of Islam. Failure to recognize the depth to which these cultural components structure political organization leads Westerners to think that the assumptions of modern rationalism can provide a basis for 'reasonable' *compromise*, when in fact they do not. Instead, the warrior ethic sees *stand-off* as a transcendent scenario in which different 'strong men' contend for power.

Citizenship represents another background condition for capitalism in Weber's model that is particularly amenable to neo-Weberian analysis in the context of *boundaries*. Again the Iraq–Kuwait case is paradigmatic, but it can also be extended easily to Israel–Palestine and the several states that border this region as well as to the status of Lebanon. The drawing of boundaries is a largely artificial act in modernity that is perhaps more than any other political deed the apotheosis of rationality over personal considerations. Lines drawn on paper based on mathematical representations of physical space determine who is a citizen of what nation-state. In the Iraq–Kuwait conflict, the Iraqi claim was simple: The line-drawing that created the state of Kuwait was an external imposition of colonial power upon the nation of Iraq. At the same time, the Iraqis conveniently forgot that Iraq itself was created by a series of line-drawings that were equally artificial.

By the creation of 'legal' boundaries in the process of nation-state definition and the treatment of this entity as coequal to national identity, contemporary international systems define nationhood as coincident with statehood and generally accept state sovereignty as evidence of nationality. This relatively artificial definition – often the creation of colonialism – ignores a host of cultural factors (including religious factors, but not limited to religious factors) involved in nationhood at the level of participants in the action system, and by so doing creates a context for religious resurgence as providing the only feasible alternate discourse to legal rationalization. The Iraqi case, for example, had a ready-made support system in the Arab nationalism of the Islamic warrior ethic. (By contrast, this juxtaposition of the irrational and the rational is what creates the 'offence' of the modern state of Israel: the state of Israel caused the undermining of the secular ideology of the nation-state in the Muslim world because, in a Western betrayal of its own commitments to the secular state, a religious ideology was used to justify the creation of that state.)

Saddam Hussein embraced fully the rhetoric of Islam upon his invasion of Kuwait. Indeed, as *Washington Post* columnist Nora Boustany (1990: A22) pointed out early after the Iraqi move into Kuwait, 'In his call of *jihad* . . . and in religious symbols he used in his speeches, Saddam is using the same appeal to religious extremism that he once claimed he was opposing when it was used by Iran' in its war with Iraq. This may well be perceived by Westerners as simple demagoguery. The point at issue, however, is that this *religious language* has the power it does not merely in the eyes of a naive followership, but also in the mind of a cunning leader. Saddam is willing to use the language of religion, even though it 'contradicts the relentless secular ideology of his Baathist Party', precisely because he perceives its power to move the masses. At the same time, however, the post-war rebellions of both Shi'ites in the southern part of Iraq and Kurds in the north show how limited the idea of citizenship is within Iraq and how dependent preservation of the regime is upon sultanism.

THE ALTERNATIVE ISLAM OF THE PACIFIC RIM

In spite of the fact that Indonesia is the largest Muslim nation in the world, relatively little attention is paid to Islam on the Pacific rim. For example, when John Esposito decided to expand his brief text on Islam by adding case studies (1991), none was drawn from the Pacific. Likewise, Bryan Turner might have found stronger empirical arguments against the 'Islamic ethic' thesis if he had looked at Indonesia and Malaysia than by the more troublesome routes of issues of varying interpretations of historical data and meanings of words. As there is considerable consensus that the Pacific will form the new 'pond' around which successful world capitalists will settle, there is good reason to look at Islam in this part of the world to see its relationship to the spirit of capitalism today.

An admittedly Western bias inheres in talking about 'Protestant ethic' analogies in Asia. 'Protestant' is, after all, a Western category. On the other hand, what we observe in the most successful countries of the 'new Pacific' is in fact a process of Westernization, what one might even term a 'Westernization beyond the West'. By this I mean, for example, that 'Japanese' management was the brain child of Americans who took such things as role objectivity and statistical analysis to their logical conclusions and applied them beyond the limits that the West was willing to accept in the 1950s or 1960s. Of course, Japanese theorists were able to understand these ideas and have now extended them beyond the original theses of Joseph Moses Juran and William Edwards Deeming, but there is nothing inherently Eastern in what is being proposed – though it may well be that an Eastern world view makes these proposals easier to adopt than Western romantic individualism, which is tied to post-modern consumerism, not modern rational capitalism (see Campbell 1987).

Among the early studies of the emergence of Weberian perspectives on Islam in Southeast Asia is that of Said Alatas (1963), who notes that the traits of the capitalist spirit among Muslims in Southeast Asia first developed in response to colonial domination and out of the 'tradesman' ethos of early Islam. In a similar essay some twenty years later, John Clammer (1985) also suggests the import-ance of looking beyond superficial Protestant ethic analogies to historical, ethnic, and political-economic elements within the different societies. These help us to specify the complexities of the issues. At the same time, we can note that the Asian societies have recognized different perspectives on Islam as well. For example, Joseph Tamney (1987: 60) provides the following report from the 1980 Southeast Asia and Pacific Regional Islamic Missionary Conference held in Malaysia as evidence of how Muslim leaders there 'are trying to dissociate Islam and Arab culture':

> Speaker after speaker carefully drew the line between what the Koran said and what merely happened to be practised in the deserts and oases in which Islam first spread. As the conference progressed it was being made clear that what was merely Arab was not by any means necessarily Muslim.

The Islam that spread into Southeast Asia appeared much more as a 'trader' religion and thus has a more modern character – that is, it is a sign of social 'progress' – than it did as a reform movement within a pre-existent Arab tradition in the Middle East (see Esposito 1991: 14–21).

This more 'rational' approach to Islam can be seen most clearly in Indonesia, where the government was formed on principles derived from Islam but inten-tionally chose not to be an 'Islamic republic'. The core of Indonesian 'civil religion' is the *Panchasila*, or Five Principles.[6] These are 'belief in God, humani-tarianism, national unity, democracy based on consensus, and social justice. Pancasila is an ideology designed specifically for a modern state' (Tamney 1987: 57). While the Panchasila may be more theistic than Americans would allow, many Western capitalist nations would not find this an unacceptable national creed. As Fred von der Mehden points out (1986: 50), furthermore, '[m]any scholars have equated rational with secular without the care employed by Weber'; that is, it is not necessary for us to demand total secularization of a regime before we can conceive it as having adopted the conditions of rationality. A further evidence of rationalizing tendencies within the rubrics of official support for the Panchasila may be seen in the efforts of the Indonesian state to stress *kepercayaan*, or belief, over against *agama*, or religion – i.e. a privatization of spirituality.

In Indonesia, Islam acts as a bridge between the past and the future of the nation, where both folk religion and Christianity still hark back to a time of weakness. Tamney describes the role that Islam plays in Indonesia as an agent of

modernity and how it differs from what Westerners might ascribe to Christianity
– even Protestant Christianity – in our own developmental history:

> Islam is perceived in the Indonesian context as modern. In the West,
> modernization was accompanied by the ideological struggle between Chri-
> stianity and Science. In this confrontation, the latter was identified with
> "modern", and the challenges to Science emanating from Christianity tended
> to give this religion the burden of being perceived as "backward". In the
> Third World the universal religions are not caught in the same ideological
> set. Rather, Muslim peoples perceive a world with alternative explanations
> identified as Folk Culture (usually a magical-mystical orientation) and
> Islam. Given this alternative, many find Islam more appealing.
>
> (Tamney 1987: 61)

To see Islam as essentially *modern*, then, is to see it in a guise quite different from
the tradition-based character of patrimonialism. Here we see the connection
between the patrimonialist (or sultanist) use of Islam in the Middle East and
Islam's function in Southeast Asia. Islam is also much more consciously chosen
in Southeast Asia from a pluralist palette, whereas in the Arab world it is an
extension of preexisting patterns.

In Malaysia the case is slightly more complicated because of the identification
of Islam with the Malay peoples in opposition to the Chinese. Islam is the religion
of the historically oppressed, now dominant, indigenous population, and as a
result there is more official indulgence toward Islam than in Indonesia. Nevertheless, the continued rapid integration of Malaysia into the world capitalist
economy is likely to result in the increasing economic success of the Malay
population, and one might predict that as this occurs there will be less Muslim
protectionism than is now the case. One can measure the comparatively rational
character of the Malay system versus that of Arab states, however, by the relative
ease with which it was possible for Singapore to withdraw from the Malay
confederation and establish its independence. Contrast Malaysia–Singapore with
Iraq–Kuwait, and two different worlds appear. These worlds are also underwritten, of course, by very different economies, but to a great extent, that is just
the point.

CONCLUSION: 'ETHICS' REVISITED

Gianfranco Poggi (1983: 37) makes the important observation that the Protestant
ethic thesis involves not only a way of acting but a *'body of personnel'*, who stand
to gain by adopting a new way of acting because it is consistent with their life
situation. These conditions incorporate the Weberian concepts of 'elective affinities' and 'carriers'. In the case of Weber's original statement 'certain groups,
already involved in the practice of business', found Puritan preaching congenial
to their life-world and became advocates for the new faith (Poggi 1983: 56, italics
in original). We might say that these people adopted 'merchant Christianity' and

by doing so gave generation to processes already in an unmistakably progravid state.[7] Essential to the legitimation of their cause, however, was the claim that what they were proclaiming was actually original, authentic, or 'true' Christianity, since of course as merchants they needed the support of the rulership in order for their way of life to prevail. In other words, it was essential to the Puritan cause that they not be condemned as heretics. (Condemned persons are rarely financial successes.)

When we take this model over into Islam, what we find in Southeast Asia is 'merchant Islam', shorn of Arab national aspirations. It is motivated by a similar dynamic to be at once both modern and legitimate – or, so to speak, new and old. Alatas (1963: 32), for example, writes that, 'Before the second world war in Malaya and Indonesia, we could come across several Arab traders and small industrialists manifesting the traits of the capitalist spirit. They were also known for their religious enthusiasm and with many of them also the innerworldly asceticism'. On the one hand, then, there is a desire to jettison the Arabness of Islam, but on the other, in so doing, to claim authenticity in the process. We should not be surprised that there are revivalist movements – muffled in Indonesia, more militant in Malaysian *dakwah* – but these more likely represent the consequences of social dislocation by groups outside of the rising classes than they do reassertions of patrimonial systems.

It is important to underscore, however, that these movements toward capitalist hegemony are strengthened by religious affirmations that underwrite their claim and that are inherent in Islam, just as Puritan affirmations are inherent in Christianity. The proper comparison, then, might be of Arab Islam, with its disdain for commerce (which was ultimately turned over to Jews and Christians) and Eastern Orthodoxy, which 'God knows' has no ethic that would lead to capitalism. Freed from the warrior ethic ('real men don't make change') the Southeast Asian Muslim could 'recapture' the merchant ethic of the Prophet and ultimately transform it into an ethos consistent with the values of capitalism. This is not a refutation of Weber's understanding of the Islamic ethic, which refers to an early period in the expansion of Middle Eastern patrimonialism, but rather a confirmation of the *processes* inherent in the Protestant ethic thesis as a case study of the *complex interactionism* that characterizes Max Weber's understanding of the cultural integration of economic development.[8]

NOTES

1 I am indebted to Donald Wiebe for this particularly apt expression, though he generated it in another context.
2 The phrase 'last intensification' is from Randall Collins (1986: 93). Unfortunately Collins qualifies it with the modifier 'only', which is over-reacting. If we might think of a complex firecracker, for example, the flame that sets the whole thing off could be called the 'last intensification', but it is hardly '*only* the last intensification'. Specifically, if John Doe ignites such a firecracker with his cigarette lighter, he will be held *accountable* or *responsible* for the consequences. This legal notion of responsibilty is

precisely what Weber had in mind in his concept of 'adequate causality', which is at the heart of the ideal-typical method that underlies his analysis of Protestantism and capitalism (see Turner 1985).

3 The word *ghost* is significant in Salomon's characterization. Weber was engaged in refuting 'vulgar' Marxism, not any specific text of Marx himself, in fact quite to the contrary, he affirms in the introduction to the world religions studies that every attempt to explain modern Western capitalism 'must, recognizing the fundamental importance of the economic factor, above all take account of the economic conditions. But at the same time the opposite correlation must not be left out of consideration' (1930: 26). Weber was clearly more sympathetic to Marx's analysis than some champions of idealism have alleged him to be, but to claim, as Bryan Turner (1974b: 16) does, that Salomon's assertion is not correct, is belied by Marianne Weber's observation only a few years after Max's death that his work was precisely intended to correct the one-sidedness of economistic analyses ((1926) 1988: 335 *et passim*). Precisely because it was a dialogue with the 'ghost' of Marx, it was also possible, for example, for Weber to be in dialogue with the ghost of Adam Smith, as Marshall suggests (1982: 33).

4 Cf. Turner (1974b: 98) also: 'Whatever Islam may have been, it was not a warrior religion'. Weber (1978b: 623–24) writes: 'In the first Meccan period of Islam, the eschatological religion of Muhammad developed in pietistic urban conventicles which displayed a tendency to withdraw from the world. But in the subsequent developments in Medina and in the evolution of the early Islamic communities, the religion was transformed from its pristine form into a national Arabic warrior religion, and even later into a religion with a very strong status emphasis'. John Esposito, in a text that can only be characterized as Islamic apologetics (1991: 17), writes: 'Muhammad's use of warfare in general was alien neither to Arab custom nor to that of the Hebrew prophets. Both believed that God had sanctioned battle with the enemies of the Lord'. If Islam were not a warrior religion, why would Esposito bring it up and justify it in this way?

5 As both Weber and the Anabaptists in their respective historical periods knew well, there was little difference in the system of domination that characterized state church Lutheranism from Roman Catholicism so far as religious freedom is concerned.

6 Also *Pantja Sila* or *Pancasila*.

7 This I take to be the positive contribution of the findings in David Zaret's book *The Heavenly Contract* (1985) which unfortunately is so confused about what Weber actually said that the significance of its material is easily lost.

8 I am not a little impressed by the fact that in a core text for the total implementation of 'quality' approaches to industrial organization (i.e. 'Japanese' management), the process is referred to as 'cultural change' and its adoption as 'getting religion' – see Huge (1990). This resonates robustly with the underlying dynamics that Weber was articulating in *The Protestant Ethic and the Spirit of Capitalism*.

REFERENCES

Alatas, S.H. (1963) 'The Weber thesis and South East Asia', *Archives de Sociologie des Religions* 15: 21–34.

Antonio, R.J. (1979) 'The contradiction of domination and production in bureaucracy: the contribution of organizational efficiency to the decline of the Roman empire', *American Sociological Review* 44: 895–912.

Arjomand, S.A. (1984) *The Shadow of God and the Hidden Imam: Religion, Political Order, and Societal Change in Shi'ite Iran from the Beginning to 1890*, Chicago: University of Chicago Press.

Bellah, R.N. (1970) 'Reflections on the Protestant ethic analogy in Asia', in R.N. Bellah, *Beyond Belief: Essays on Religion in a Post-Traditional World*, New York: Harper & Row.

Bocock, R.J. (1971) 'The Ismailis in Tanzania: a Weberian analysis', *British Journal of Sociology* 22: 365–80.

Boustany, N. (1990) 'Doctrine, dreams drive Saddam Hussein', *Washington Post*, 12 August: A1, A22.

Campbell, C. (1987) *The Romantic Ethic and the Spirit of Modern Consumerism*, Oxford: Blackwell.

Clammer, J. (1985) 'Weber and Islam in Southeast Asia', in A. Buss (ed.) *Max Weber in Asian Studies*, Leiden: Brill, pp. 102–14.

Collins, R. (1986) *Max Weber: A Skeleton Key*, Beverley Hills, CA: Sage.

Croutwater, S.K. (1985) 'Weber and sultanism in light of historical data', in V. Murvar (ed.) *Theory of Liberty, Legitimacy, and Power: New Directions in the Intellectual and Scientific Legacy of Max Weber*, London: Routledge & Kegan Paul, pp. 168–84.

Duke, J.T. and Johnson, B.L. (1989) 'Protestantism and the spirit of democracy', in W.H. Swatos, Jr (ed.) *Religious Politics in Global and Comparative Perspective*, New York: Greenwood Press, pp. 131–46.

Esposito, J.L. (1991) *Islam: The Straight Path*, expanded edn, New York: Oxford University Press.

Friedman, T.L. (1989) *From Beirut to Jerusalem*, Garden City, NY: Doubleday/Anchor.

Gandhi, R.S. (1976) 'The economic ethic of Islam', *Sociologus* 26: 66–74.

Geertz, C. (1968) *Islam Observed: Religious Developments in Morocco and Indonesia*, Chicago: University of Chicago Press.

Gellner, E. (1963) 'Sanctity, puritanism, secularization, and nationalism in North Africa', *Archives de Sociologie des Religions* 8: 71–86.

Henrich, D. (1987) 'Karl Jaspers: thinking with Max Weber in mind', in W. Mommsen and J. Osterhammel (eds) *Max Weber and His Contemporaries*, London: Allen & Unwin, pp. 528–44.

Huge, E.C. (ed.) (1990) *Total Quality: An Executive's Guide for the 1990s*, Homewood, Ill: Dow Jones-Irwin.

Jaspers, K. (1989) *On Max Weber*, New York: Paragon House.

Kivisto, P. and Swatos, W.H., Jr (1988) *Max Weber: A Bio-Bibliography*, New York: Greenwood Press.

Liebersohn, H. (1988) *Fate and Utopia in German Sociology, 1870–1923*, Cambridge, Mass.: MIT Press.

Lipset, S.M. (1968) 'History and sociology', in S.M. Lipset and R. Hofstadter (eds) *Sociology and History*, New York: Basic Books, pp. 20–58.

Marshall, G. (1982) *In Search of the Spirit of Capitalism: An Essay on Max Weber's Protestant Ethic Thesis*, New York: Columbia University Press.

Murvar, V. (ed.) (1985) *Theory of Liberty, Legitimacy, and Power: New Directions in the Intellectual and Scientific Legacy of Max Weber*, London: Routledge & Kegan Paul.

Murvar, V. (1989) *Nation and Religion in Central Europe and the Western Balkans – The Muslims in Bosnia, Hercegovina and Sandzak: A Sociological Analysis*, Brookfield, WI: FSSSN Colloquia and Symposia.

Nasr, S.H. (1987) *Traditional Islam in the Modern World*, London: KPI.

Poggi, G. (1983) *Calvinism and the Capitalistic Spirit: Max Weber's Protestant Ethic*, Amherst, MA: University of Massachusetts Press.

Rodinson, M. (1973) *Islam and Capitalism*, New York: Random House.

Salomon, A. (1945) 'German sociology', in G. Gurvitch and W.E. Moore (eds) *Twentieth Century Sociology*, New York: Philosophical Library, pp. 586–614.

Schluchter, W. (ed.) (1987) *Max Webers Sicht des Islams: Interpretation und Kritik*, Frankfurt: Suhrkamp.

Swatos, W.H., Jr (1987) *Mediating Capitalism and Slavery: A Neo-Weberian Interpretation of Religion and Honor in the Old South*, USF Monographs in Religion and Public Policy No.3, Tampa, FL: Department of Religious Studies, University of South Florida.

Swatos, W.H., Jr (1989) 'Ultimate values in politics: problems and prospects for world society', in W.H. Swatos, Jr (ed.) *Religious Politics in Global and Comparative Perspective*, New York: Greenwood Press, pp. 55–73.

Swatos, W.H., Jr and Kivisto, P. (1991a) 'Beyond *Wertfreiheit*: Max Weber and moral order', *Sociological Focus* 24: 117–28.

Swatos, W.H., Jr and Kivisto, P. (1991b) 'Max Weber as "Christian sociologist"', *Journal for the Scientific Study of Religion* 30: 347–62.

Tamney, J.B. (1987) 'Islam's popularity: the case of Indonesia', *Southeast Asian Journal of Social Science* 15: 53–65.

Turner, B.S. (1974a) 'Islam, capitalism and the Weber theses', *British Journal of Sociology* 25: 230–43.

Turner, B.S. (1974b) *Weber and Islam: A Critical Study*, London: Routledge & Kegan Paul.

Turner, B.S. (1978) 'Orientalism, Islam and capitalism', *Social Compass* 25: 371–94.

Turner, S.P. (1985) 'Explaining capitalism: Weber on and against Marx', in R.J. Antonio and R.M. Glassman (eds) *A Weber-Marx Dialogue*, Lawrence, KS: University Press of Kansas, pp. 167–88.

Von der Mehden, F.R. (1986) *Religion and Modernization in Southeast Asia*, Syracuse, NY: Syracuse University Press.

Weber, Marianne (1988) *Max Weber: A Biography*, New Brunswick, NJ: Transaction.

Weber, Max (1930) *The Protestant Ethic and the Spirit of Capitalism*, New York: Scribners.

Weber, Max (1946) 'The Protestant sects and the spirit of capitalism', in C.W. Mills and H.H. Gerth (eds) *From Max Weber: Essays in Sociology*, New York: Oxford University Press, pp. 302–22.

Weber, Max (1978a) 'Anticritical last word on *The Spirit of Capitalism*', *American Journal of Sociology* 83: 1105–31.

Weber, Max (1978b) *Economy and Society*, Berkeley, CA: University of California Press.

Weber, Max (1985) '"Churches" and "sects" in North America: an ecclesiastical sociopolitical sketch', *Sociological Theory* 3: 1–13.

Zaret, D. (1985) *The Heavenly Contract: Ideology and Organization in Pre-Revolutionary Puritanism*, Chicago: University of Chicago Press.

Zubaida, S. (1972) 'Economic and political activism in Islam', *Economy and Society* 1: 308–38.

3

RELIGION, ETHICS AND ECONOMIC INTERACTION IN JAPAN

Some arguments in a continuing discussion

Helmut Loiskandl

Since Weber and Bellah, the discussion of the possible influence of religious stimuli on the organization of social and economic interaction in Japan has not subsided. Weber's expectation that the inner-worldly asceticism he finds in early Calvinism might have had a counterpart in Confucianism is readily continued by foreign and Japanese scholars alike. As inner-worldly asceticism, in the tradition of Kantian ethics, is understood as being an individualistic and rational force directed towards change or at least control, it is not surprising that Bellah, for instance, accepts the arguments that, as Buddism teaches people how to accept the given environmental situation, and as Shinto has the same central attitude of pious acceptance of reality, there was a need for rational ethics which was satisfied by the central position of Confucianism in what he called 'Tokugawa Religion'. But it could be argued that Bellah overstated the importance of this special impact. Confucianism did not have too much influence on the business world of the Tokugawa period, and even less on the world of the Japanese economy today. And Confucianism in Japan is more and more seen as a force which not so much created as articulated the values by which Japanese society works (Ellwood and Pilgrim 1985: 130).

Thus the argument proposed on the following pages is that the values central to modern Japanese business organization can be best understood as a continuation or development of traditional Japanese ethical values, which are the ethical values of an irrigation society, and that the strongest religious stimuli influencing economic structure as well as economic interaction in Japan originate in the Shinto tradition. That ranges from structures of social interaction reflecting designs of village Shinto cult organizations to the incorporation of material elements of Shinto religiosity into the business environment. One could argue that in an Durkheimian way elements of religion are used to heighten the integration of society, up to the point where the secular institution imported from the West is made sacred by immersion into religious tradition.

HELMUT LOISKANDL

JAPANESE ETHICS AND VALUES

Ethics in sociological understanding has to do with the value basis of human interaction. Normally this value basis is somehow interrelated with religion. Surprising, however, in the case of Japan this is often denied (see Hideo 1967). It is argued that religion in Japan shows a different picture from religion in the West. While Christianity entails an essentially moral concern, Japanese religion is only concerned with the internal problems of man. Worries and anxieties are not overcome by fighting outside causes but by changing the mind structure. Consequently, social interaction simply is not a primary concern. This is certainly true for Buddhism's insight that human suffering is a consequence of desire. The environment stimulates conflicting desire which must remain unfulfilled by its very nature. Worries and anxieties are an outgrowth of this disorder.

Unlike Indian Buddhism, in which the solution to the problem lies in the extermination of such basic desire by ultimately negating life, Buddhism in Japan developed a more positive attitude. Mahayana Buddhism in Japan affirms life but tries to correct the desire-structure in man. Desire *per se* is now interpreted as ambivalent or even as good, since it is the reason for all life-activities. The problem is a wrong desire-structure. The issue for Japanese Buddhists, then, is not to erase desire, but to remould it. Different schools in Buddhism have developed different disciplines to reach this goal. Their final hoped-for effect, enlightenment, indicates the appearance of the right mind structure. With this, outside stimuli will no longer provoke conflicting desires. There will be no need to change anything in the environment in order to remake a life of misery into a life of happiness.

Thus, one could argue that Buddhism 'teaches people how to accept the given environmental situation' (Hideo 1967: 115), and therefore is not concerned with ethics. Implicitly it is assumed here that pure acceptance is not ethical and ethics necessarily contain an element of intended change.[1] By using this argumentation the religious tradition of Shinto falls into the same category as religions unconcerned with ethics. After all, acceptance is a central attitude of Shinto, too. Here, even more than in Buddhism, a 'pious' acceptance of reality is expected. The purpose for a believing visitor to a Shinto Shrine is only to 'feel the deity in his heart' (Hideo 1967: 113). Names of gods specifically venerated in a shrine matter not, nor does a theological rationale for this.

The point made in most discussions therefore is that traditional Japanese religion did not supply ethical principles to Japanese society and it took the Tokugawa government to eventually implant Confucianism as a much needed ethical code into a society without a system of established ethical principles.

This chapter therefore will first challenge the assumption that Japanese religion left Japan a society without any kind of ethical system (Hideo 1967: 116).[2] This will be done by enumerating generally accepted characteristics of Japanese ethical orientation and then analysing the established traits against the background of traditional religion.[3]

FACETS OF JAPANESE ETHICAL ORIENTATION

Individual and group: acceptance

Any observation of Japanese life is sure to note the different social value of the individual in Western and Japanese society. In the West, the Greek and biblical traditions made individual decision a paradigm of the ethical process. This experience of individual decision making becomes synonymous with ethics in that tradition. Not so in Japanese culture. As Chie Nakane puts it:

> The Japanese are devoid of any such religious practice as controls individual thinking and behavior on the strength of a supernatural being. What plays an important role for the Japanese is not religion or philosophy but a very human morality. And this morality always governs people with the contemporary trends as a yardstick. A feeling that "I must do this because they are also doing it" or "because they will laugh at me unless I do so" rules the life of individual persons with greater force than anything else and thus affects decision-making. Certainly, there are those who keep an attitude of "going-my-way" but they are exceptionally rare in Japanese society.
>
> (Nakane 1970: 150).

In short, a moral decision is a decision respecting the social consensus which is not for the individual to check or change. Change might come in a ground swell like the turn of the tide, but it is never left to the discretion of an individual.

This general attitude (different from the West) shapes an understanding of ethics in contemporary Japanese society. The American system of democracy, for example, feels no ethical qualms about imposing the majority's will on a minority and might even ridicule those who do not like it as 'sore losers'. The Japanese ethical expectation is that any societal decision should be made on the basis of a consensus including minorities and groups lower in the hierarchy. It has been a long-standing tradition in Japanese villages to proceed in such a way in any decision-making process, and procedures in modern business companies are rather similar.

Neither the individual conscience nor generalized rules pertaining to abstracta like 'mankind', 'humanity' or similar concepts decide the morality of an action as does the yardstick of acceptance within the life-community. This life-community is comprised of the people one lives with. Originally family-orientated, later centuries saw the life-community expanded. However, it is interesting to note that 'ie', the Japanese word used to describe the original family, today is also used to describe modern companies with tens of thousands of employees. Employees are also regarded as members of a household with the employer at its head (cf. Nakane 1970: 150).

The famous 'Nixon-Shokku' of the 1970s, the shock of being faced with totally new directions in American foreign policies without being consulted beforehand, was for the Japanese public not only a political insult but shamefully

65

unethical behaviour. Not to try to establish consensus with a long-standing partner was an abuse of power at its worst. 'Lonely decisions' may be a trademark of Western hero-hagiography, but they do not have the ring of ethical authenticity in Japan. Lonely decisions imply rational analysis and separation from the life-community; in contradistinction, the Japanese interpretation of what makes decisions ethical includes loyalty and transrationality.

Loyalty

Since the introduction of Confucianism in the Tokugawa period the concept of loyalty has become more deeply entrenched within the Japanese value system. But it has been part of the Japanese orientation before and the Confucian structures have been reformulated against the background of Japanese exigencies (cf. Nakane 1970: 28).[4]

Loyalty, as proposed in the Bushido-ethic of the Samurai, has been explained by doing one's duty without any regard for the consequences. Duty, however, is no Kantian generalized rule, but again something dependent on social consensus and individual inner experience. In a certain way, the duty postulated in group identification through group symbols such as lords or the emperor, is an identification negating the ultimate importance of the individual. The *Hagakure*, a book written around 1716, states, 'Bushido is a single straight way to death, practising over and over again every day and night how to die a samurai's death on every possible occasion and for every possible cause' (Tesshi 1967: 230). Furukawa Tesshi interprets this statement as intend to transcend the limits of individual human existence.

> A human being essentially contains in his constitution such an utmost limit, which constantly presses upon him and makes him return to the daily possibilities of his real existence. And, in proportion to the intensity and sincerity with which a man tackles this utmost limit of his existence, its possibilities are just that much more enriched and diversified in content.
> (Tesshi 1967: 231).

As Nitobe Inazo has shown, Bushido has developed from being the professional ethics of the Samurai caste into a general Japanese morality (Inazo 1905). The extremes of loyalty are still with us, from Kamikaze to the total identification of Japanese employees with their company as this claim goes. But again, loyalty works both ways. When in 1976 a major company in Nagoya went out of business, the last action of the management was to arrange for every one of the approximately 10,000 employees to obtain a new job. While Western societies hail enlightened self-interest as an ethical stance, the expectations of Japanese tradition hold that individual potential is only activated to its limit by identification with others. Historically this identification was on a relatively limited basis. It is only in the new religions of Japan now that loyalty extends to all humanity, but the Bushido-paradigm is still recognizable (cf. Köpping 1974). The

old expectation that in Bushido the individual should become pure and simple –
an expectation raised again in the new religions – is just an expression of the
conviction that individualism is taking away from the purity of the right framework of desires.[5] If Japanese tradition knew an original sin it probably would be
that of individualism.

An additional typical feature of the loyalty-complex is the expectation that
purity and simplicity cannot be reconciled to rationality. Rationality took over in
the West after religion was no longer accepted as the guarantor of ethical systems.
The assumption that rational thinking could lay bare the necessary structure of the
physical world as well as of human interaction was not shared by Japanese ethics.

Trans-rationality

Japanese ethics distrusts rational processes. While in Western traditions, deliber-
ation and rational analysis help render a decision ethical, the Japanese claim is to
the contrary. The right way of doing, as explained in the *Hagakure*, is to act
without delay or hesitation. Thoughts make for second thoughts. To be pure and
simple, it states, one should act without heeding the possible consequences and
without paying attention to eventual perils or final disasters.

To the Western tradition, the understanding of a situation is confined to the
perimeters of a subject–object–predicate analysis. This process, while not totally
alien to Japanese tradition, is regarded inferior to that of immediate experience.
This attitude might be related to the structure of the Japanese language and as a
matter of fact is often explained that way.

The immediate action of unreflected and unanalysed experience then is the
basis for ethical imputation. To appreciate this, one must grasp the Western
differentiation between nature and culture. Nature in Western tradition is regarded as fallen nature. The wide diffusion of this ideology can be laid at the
doorstep of the Biblical tradition. Even in evolutionary interpretations of man
there sometimes looms the fear of man, the brute beast, hiding behind his cultural
veneer. If the ideal structure of man and society is understood as cultural, what
better symbol could the religious phase of Western civilization have but 'the
Book', the Bible? It seems fitting that the rationalism of a post-religious phase
simply exchanges 'the Book' for books.

The Japanese tradition chooses an alternative. Basic laws and structures cannot
be learned out of books but stem from insight into reality and understanding of
nature. This attitude is not only a teaching of Zen but a generally accepted
primary belief of Japanese life.

The radical empiricism of immediate experience makes unrestrained life the
source of ethical behaviour while Western ethical concern reflects the Socratic
dictum about the 'unexamined life' not worth living. Refuting this statement, the
Japanese propose a sacredness of life and nature which transcends the surgical
scalpel of reflective analysis. In emphasizing experience, they minimize the
import of intellectual examination. Reality does not consist of neatly labelled

categories but of paradoxes, contradictions, absurdities – scientific clarity and logical neatness is only second-hand life.

No wonder that Western ethicians view 'Japan's ethics as little beyond the ethics of pure utility and expediency and the acceptance of sociological principles and mores in which the basic western virtues lose status' (Moore 1967: 298). The realism of Japanese ethics easily might be misunderstood as opportunism or hedonism because it refuses to accept universals familiar to Western tradition.

Appreciation of beauty

It is easy to realize that an ethics based on immediate experience and total acceptance of life and nature will necessarily place less emphasis on analysis and reason. On the other hand, the Western tradition identifies rational and ethical, at least to the extent that the rational is understood to be the sole access to truth. So the old adage 'the good and the true are convertible' still holds. The East does not believe in the identity of goodness and truth. Indeed, the Japanese tradition substitutes the identity of beauty and moral goodness. The search for beauty in Japan might well be equivalent to the search for truth and rationality in the West. That does not mean, however, that the search and appreciation of beauty encompasses Japan. As Western history and culture is pockmarked by deceit and irrationality, so too Japan exhibits it share of vulgarity, crudeness and disharmony.

However, this basic orientation explains for example why suicide is viewed differently in the West and in Japan. Ceremonial suicide, *seppuku* (known to Westerners as harakiri), has been observed officially until the end of the feudal times in the middle of the last century. Unofficially it still is occasional. (One of the more recent instances was the death of the famous author Mishima Yukio.) To Western observers the attitude of Japanese towards *seppuku* often seemed close to blind adoration. But in Japanese society committing suicide never has been regarded as sinful or shameful. To choose death and to die in a beautiful manner makes this decision a highly ethical one. To the Japanese mind, life and nature are characterized by harmony. Thus, a harmonious death, induced or non-induced, is a good death. To create beauty and harmony in the human world is the mark of morally superior people.

THE RELIGIOUS ROOTS OF MORAL ATTITUDES

The main ethical concerns then show an orientation slightly different from Western interpretations of ethics. It is reasonable to assume that this difference is either caused by or at least concomitant to specific theological or religious traditions.[6] The main difference might be summarized:

(a) While in Western tradition individual decision-making is recognized as an integral part of morality, the Japanese approach gives more weight to the group.

68

(b) Consequently, the Japanese prototype of ethical orientation is less of a lonely moral hero but a person characterized by strong loyalties.

(c) While in Western tradition ethical behaviour includes the use of rational analysis in the process of decision-making, Japanese culture prefers actions not mutilated or weakened by the paleness of analysis and thought. Not mediation but immediacy makes life moral.

(d) The immediacy of experience is supposed to communicate the sacredness and beauty of nature. While the Western tradition holds the concept of a fallen nature and the ethical consequence of necessary change, Japanese understanding stresses the sacredness and harmony of nature. Beauty is therefore regarded as expressing a religious and an ethical dimension as well. The quality of goodness is seen as exchangeable with beauty and not with truth as in the West.

Religion and group consciousness

If we now want to examine the religious background of these differences, we can begin with a look at the individual. Individualism is a rather late stage in the development of human culture and it took yet longer to make this ideology the basis of an ethical system. Even in the older books of the Bible, God is still the god of the forefathers and morality follows the law of the group – an attitude typical for simple societies. The interesting thing in Japan is that their society was able to transmit value-orientations of early times into the technological age.

Primitive Shinto, the religion of early Japan, was centred around two concepts. The *ujigami* concept is intertwined with the Japanese family structure. Each family had its own shrine as a symbol of group identity, a shrine dedicated to the ancestral spirit. Strictly speaking it was not the veneration of individual ancestors. Individuals were not expected to keep their identity after death but were believed to join into a vague community of ancestral spirits. The main function of this cult was obviously to integrate into a moral unit all members of the family. The concept of *hitogami*, a divine force which was transmitted by shamans and medicine men, allowed the extension of group identification beyond the family. This system was characterized by the primacy of political values (cf. Bellah 1957: esp. 70–3).

A religious belief system not stressing individual transcendence but emphasizing the moral and even metaphysical unity of family and group is obviously easily reconcilable with an ethical system giving maximum weight to the group as the normative basis for judging right or wrong, good or evil. And it is surprising to see that not only is this ethical system alive and well in contemporary Japan, but the old religious beliefs are still very influential, even among the core of converts to Christianity (cf. Dörner 1977: 151).

Religion and loyalty

It has been shown quite convincingly that the interplay of loyalty based on the two concepts of *on* (obligation, indebtedness) and *ko* (filial piety, gratitude) is very closely related to the concept of ancestor and ancestor worship (Inazo 1905: 166–7). To remember the ancestors is to remember the toil, perseverance and tolerance it took to develop and to continue the family group and eventually the enlarged group with its roots in the past. The people living now are indebted to their predecessors, they have incurred *on* to them. Their reaction is expected to express gratitude, to perform *ko*. In contemporary Japanese society *on* is not geared to the ancestors only, but includes the wide area of group interaction. As Ruth Benedict explains,

> The word for "obligation" which covers a person's indebtedness from greatest to least is on. In Japanese usage it is translated into English by a whole series of words from "obligations" and "loyalty" to "kindness" and "love", but these words distort its meaning. If it really meant love or even obligation the Japanese would certainly be able to speak of on to their children, but that is an impossible usage of the word. Nor does it mean loyalty, which is expressed by other Japanese words, which are in no way synonymous with on. On is in all its uses a load, an indebtedness, a burden, which one carries as best as one may. A man receives on from a superior and the act of accepting an on from any man not definitely one's superior or at least one's equal gives one an uncomfortable sense of inferiority.
>
> (Benedict 1954: 99–100)

So it is safe to say that the indebtedness to one another which is so typical for the Japanese society and probably one of the main reasons for the restraint with which individualism is even judged today, goes back to the religious notion of ancestor (and implicitly group) worship in ancient Shinto. No doubt this original orientation was strengthened by the coming of other religions. The Buddhist virtue of *jihi* (mercy) and the Confucian virtue of *jin* (human-heartedness), however, also view the individual as a dependent entity. So the individual in Japanese tradition always has been seen as someone 'absorbed in the interest of the collectivity to which he belongs, and the interest of the collectivity is recognized as having primary importance, while the interest of the individual has merely a secondary importance' (Takeyoshi 1967: 268).

Trans-rationality and religion

Every religion encompasses a certain amount of trans-rationality. The knowledge attained and transmitted by religion claims to be of a different nature than the insights gained by the analytical methods of science. Religion seeks the immediacy of enlightenment.

The trans-rational structure of early religions which lack a strict boundary between the world of divine powers and the world of man, between the sacred and the profane, is clearly visible in primitive Shinto as well. A world which is full of divine powers, of *kami*, does not need the scrutiny of rational inquiry. In fact,

Shinto has long maintained that there should not be a rational interpretation of it. An analytical approach seems to be a vilification of the sacred to the believer. And nature simply is the sacred in Shinto. The right action of man therefore follows from being in harmony with nature and group; a harmony which is not the consequence of rational analysis but of pious acceptance.

This attitude of original Shinto was strongly endorsed by Buddhist philosophy and praxis. In Buddhist teaching two ways of understanding are contrasted, *prajna* (intuition) and *vijnana* (discursive understanding). *Prajna* goes beyond *vijnana*. Discursive understanding divides. This division creates parts, and parts conceived without reference to what unifies them are just disconnected parts and therefore without real existence according to Buddhist understanding Only *prajna* allows for seeing things from an unitive point of view. *Prajna* wants to see its object quickly apprehended, giving us no intervening moment for reflection, analysis or interpretation (Teitaro 1967: 67). Because knowledge gained through *prajna* is superiorly regarded, so is action resulting from this lightning of insight. In Buddhist teaching the act of intuition creates identification between subject and object. The object of all *prajna* knowledge is ultimately reality or the Absolute or god. Hence, to act out this immediacy is to do the will of the Absolute; a will which is strictly beyond the powers of discursive understanding.

Beauty and religion

The mysterious harmony of this will can only be experienced, not communicated by words. Beauty in nature shares the same fate, so beauty becomes the paradigm of religious and ethical perfection.

It is no coincidence that tradition in Japan allowed the people to experience the beauty of nature at a time when Europeans abhorred everything beyond the context of humanly construed structures. In Europe it was only the Renaissance which allowed a Petrarch, for instance, to rediscover the beauty of mountains. This rediscovery took centuries to reach the masses. The anthropocentrism of the Greek and Roman tradition combined with the Christian message of a fallen nature relegated the concept of beauty to an ideally human world. Beauty in Japanese tradition, however, does not go for the human measure but for the dimensions of nature (which includes human nature) and the harmony of the universe. Nature is a synonym for the Divine and *kami* are everywhere. In Shinto, mountains and trees and bodies of water are epiphanies of the sacred. This Shinto attitude reshaped even Buddhism. It is a singular Chinese–Japanese contribution which took the negative world view of Buddhism and turned it into a philosophy like Zen. Here the original Buddhist abhorrence of beauty (because beauty might strengthen the desire for life) was changed into a situation in which Zen monks become protagonists in the development of poetry, painting and a number of other things revealing the original beauty of life.

It would be a misunderstanding of the nature of ethics then to deny ethical tradition in early Japan. The original ethics of Japan, however, is different from the mainstream of Western ethics and the difference is related to differences in religious and philosophical outlooks. The West is characterized by individualistic anthropocentrism and distrust against a fallen nature, while Japanese tradition stresses man's place in nature and proclaims trust in the harmony of a world of which we are a part. Western ethics is an ethics of conversion and change, mediation and individualism: Japanese ethics is an ethics of acceptance and loyalty, of immediacy, and the experience and expectation of being part of a harmonious whole.

SHINTO AND ECONOMIC INTERACTION

A question of special interest is the degree to which this basic ethical orientation can be shown to be influential in the formation of specific structures of economic interaction in contemporary Japan. This causal relation is a difficult area of argumentation, even more so than in the case of Europe, as Yawata[7] has pointed out:

> An approach based mainly upon doctrines and ethical codes of Japanese religions could not really be effective, because Japanese religiosity does not consist essentially in doctrine and the profession of it. Rather it lies totally in the concrete commitment to concrete religious activities of a community. The most important traits of religious life are neither verbalized nor codified.
>
> (Yawata 1981: 293)

Consequently the argument presented here will rest on the proposition that a closer look at Japanese economic interaction shows attitudes comparable to the 'inner-worldly asceticism' Max Weber invoked, that these attitudes go hand in hand with the continuation of interaction structures developed in village Shinto, and that increasingly business organizations embrace at least the paraphernalia of the traditional 'sacred community' as tools of an effective management practice.

As can be expected, these propositions are developed against a background of controversy. A well-known study by Robert M. Marsh and Hiroshi Mannari for instance claims that the more Japanese the variables of the social organization of a company are, the less their performance (Marsh and Mannari 1976). On a TV symposium on TV Asahi Tokyo (1 January 1981) the president of the Sony Corporation, Akio Morita, claimed that differences influencing the styles of management between Japanese and American enterprises are the real cause of the difference in competitiveness between the two countries, a claim which seems to be supported by various research. Dore (1973) points out that as newcomers are mostly employed on the basis of reliability as members of the organization, being 'reallocated' in the organization to fit in neatly, a specific 'enterprise consciousness' is created; while this does less to develop individualism. Individualism is also counteracted by a Japanese company's recognition that employees are not just individual sellers of labour, but family men. Thus 'a man's family are peripheral members of the company family' (Dore 1973: 219). While that entails benefits, Japanese business and civil service organizations alike require co-operation and co-operation of families for the sake of better work performance of employees. 'In the case of conflicts between work and family life, it is common-place in the Japanese society that family life has to give precedence to the requirements of work' (Yawata 1981: 286). A behaviour characterized by some degree of inner-worldly asceticism is thus not only expected from employees proper. The workplace is actually accepted as total community by workers and their families. In an NHK survey (1978), 70 percent of those interviewed had a strong emotional attachment to it, while only 25 percent looked at it with a functional orientation. As space for intensive and extensive social interaction, neighbourhoods and relatives are clearly losing out to the total community of the workplace. It is surprising that the central aim of a capitalistically operated enterprise, namely the maximization of profits, is rarely even mentioned by the enterprises in question. They prefer to identify themselves as communities looking for mutual prosperity through mutual work. Yawata (1981: 288), following Nakagawa and other Japanese sociologists, argues that in a trial-and-error struggle for survival, the Western capitalist business style was eventually changed into the typical Japanese style of management by a conversion of the Western secular type of organization into the framework of traditional sacred community.

The traditional Japanese irrigation village was a community based on co-operation, consensus and equal rights. This co-operative work was sanctioned by religion (Takatori and Hashimoto 1979). Folk Shinto provided each act in every-day life in a village, both private and communal, with a sacred meaning. Every space in village and house was thought to be related to transcendent powers, and the time flow was marked by a yearly calendar of work, issued by the local Shinto shrine. Shinto thus functioned as an institution to regulate the sequential flow of life. In festivities the community projected its system of social interactions into the sacred area and thus ensured sacred sanctions for secular social systems. Shinto switched and intermediated between sacred and secular spheres of life throughout the year.

Generally it can be ascertained that structures of interaction based on folk Shinto are still influential in Japan today. For example: between ninety and one hundred million Japanese visit Shinto shrines at New Year; Shinto rites of passage are generally observed for children of 3, 5 and 7 years; and more than 90 percent of Japanese households are organized in neighbourhood organizations (Chonai-kai) usually organized around a shrine. In new city areas new Chinju shrines are established as centres of neighbourhood organizations on a regular basis.

When it comes to modern business organization in Japan, the structures used show striking similarities to the organizational structures of the traditional village community. There is a strong tendency not to demonstrate rank differences in factory structures; one and the same cafeteria serves top managers, white collar and blue collar workers, and there are no executive toilets. Company uniforms do not provide for rank insignia. The modes of decision making are based on consensus – the *ringi* system of traditional villages lives on. A great amount of high quality corporate information is shared throughout the company, and entering a company is not being given a contract, but being accepted as a new member into a community with high-visibility ritual. The most striking symbol of the claim of modern Japanese business to be a sacred community is the appearance of the company Shinto shrine. While it used to be hidden away from foreigners on the top floor of corporation headquarters, like at Toyota Motors, Nissan Motors, Idemitsu Kosan (Oil company), Mainichi Shinbun (news conglomerate) or Nippon Paint, the new business centre fronting Yurakucho Station in Tokyo has a Shinto shrine guarding the entrance to the building. This solution is sometimes explained as being based on aesthetic reasons, but as beauty is clearly integrated into traditional ethics, this explanation means something different to the Westerner and to the Japanese.

Following Otaka (1984), these traditional and essentially Shintoistic patterns of social interaction and integration in modern Japanese business are not to be understood as mere legacy of a culture gone. Rather, Japanese companies have rediscovered these features as managerial instruments to improve corporate achievement. While since the beginning of industrialization, and especially after the Second World War, Western business theories were put into practice in Japan, concomitantly Japan rediscovered these traditional patterns of organization and social integration as efficient instruments to overcome difficulties of implementation.

Thus Japanese sociologists argue that the traditional Shinto pattern of social interaction is now the most decisive agent of the Japanese way of modernization. It gave the Japanese population its work ethic and provided discipline, the principle of co-operation and the communal sharing of risks. While European modernization eliminated to some extent the existing communities and used individuals as the basic elements of the new social order, Japanese modernization used Shinto community orientation, which is also central for Japanese achievement orientation. Economic interaction is consequently sufficiently calculable and represents a case of alternative modernization.

NOTES

1 It is interesting to note that a Japanese scholar is following a typical Western line of argumentation. Change-orientation as a necessary ingredient of an ethical system can only be postulated on the basis of a theology of original sin and a fallen world – a typical Western paradigm of thinking from the Bible to Karl Marx.

2 Obviously Kishimoto Hideo's statement is based on an ideological definition of 'ethical system'. Interaction has to follow established rules and norms and their foundation is nothing else but basic, shared values.

3 Max Weber's proof that the ethics of capitalism can be traced down to religious sources will be used as a paradigm.

4 The example given, however, also might indicate the redefinition of originally Confucian universals even in Chinese society.

5 It is interesting to see that there is a certain hesitation among some of the new religions in Japan against democracy because they feel it might easily be falsely interpreted as egoism and individualism.

6 The old discussion whether religion is either just a reflection of societal reality or one of the main factors responsible for specific structures of society has been going on since a sociology of religion came into existence. It is not necessary, however, to repeat the arguments here. For the original formulation, see Emile Durkheim *Elementary Forms of Religious Life*, New York: The Free Press, 1965 (first published 1895), and Max Weber, *Protestant Ethics and the Spirit of Capitalism* (trans. Talcot Parsons), New York: Scribners, 1958 (first published 1904–05).

7 This chapter owes much to Yasusada Yawata, Professor of Sociology at Sophia University, Tokyo. In long discussions the importance of Shinto became clearer to both of us, resulting in a paper presented at the IIS Conference in Rome 1989, 'Tokugawa Religion or Shinto – A Discussion of Religious Influences on Economic Interaction in Japan' (unpublished). Quotes are taken from Yawata (1981).

REFERENCES

Bellah, R.N. (1957) *Tokugawa Religion*, New York: Glencoe Free Press.
Benedict, R. (1954) *The Chrysanthemum and the Sword: Patterns of Japanese Culture*, Tokyo: Charles E. Tuttle.
Dore, R. (1973) *British Factory–Japanese Factory: The Origin of National Diversity in Industrial Relations*, Tokyo: Tuttle.
Dörner, D.L. (1977) 'Comparative analysis of life after death in Folk Shinto and Christianity', *Japanese Journal of Religious Studies* 4: 2–3.
Ellwood, R. and R. Pilgrim, (1985) *Japanese Religion*, New York: Prentice Hall.
Hideo, K. (1967) 'Some Japanese cultural traits and religion', in C.A. Moore (1967) *The Japanese Mind*, Honolulu: University of Hawaii Press.
Inazo, Nitobe (1905) *Bushido: The Soul of Japan*, New York.
Köpping, K.-P. (1974) *Religiöse Bewegungen in Modern Japan*, Köln.
Mannari, H. and Marsh, R. M., (1976) *Modernization and Japanese Factory*, Tokyo: Tokyo University Press.
Moore, C.A. (1967) *The Japanese Mind*, Honolulu: University of Hawaii Press.
Nakane, Chie (1970) *Japanese Society*, Berkeley: University of California Press.
Otaka, K. (1984) *Nipponteki Keiei* (Japanese Management), Tokyo: Chūo-koran-sha.
Takatori, M. and Hashimoto, M. (1979) *Shukyo Izen* (Ethnology of Japanese Religiosity), Tokyo: Nikon Hoso Shuppan Kyokai.
Takeyoshi, Kawashima (1967) 'The individual in law and social order', in C.A. Moore (1967) *The Japanese Mind*, Honolulu: University of Hawaii Press.
Teitaro, Suzuki Daisetz (1967) 'Reason and intuition in Buddhist philosophy', in C.A. Moore (1967) *The Japanese Mind*, Honolulu: University of Hawaii Press.
Tesshi, Furukawa (1967) 'The individual in Japanese ethics', in C.A. Moore (1967) *The Japanese Mind*, Honolulu: University of Hawaii Press.
Yawata, Yasusada (1981) 'Religiosity, communality and modern business organizations in Japan', *Listening* 16, 3: 282–95.
Yawata, Yasusada (1989) 'Tokugawa religion or Shinto: a discussion of religious influences on economic interaction in Japan', paper presented at IIS Conference, Rome, 1989 (unpubl.).

4

DYNAMIC COMPLEMENTARITY

Korean Confucianism and Christianity

James H. Grayson

INTRODUCTION

The relationship between Confucianism and Protestant Christianity in Korea is one of dynamic complementarity. Whereas the advent of Roman Catholicism in Korea in the eighteenth century brought about a situation of immediate hostility and the persecution of Christianity by the Confucian establishment, the advent of Protestantism in the late nineteenth century resulted in a dynamic relationship which, although in some cases was and is still hostile, is essentially complementary. It is the contention of this paper that the effects of 1500 years of Confucian influence on Korean civilization created circumstances conducive to rapid modernization in the twentieth century. On the other hand, deficiencies in the Confucian world view were supplemented by the emergence of Protestant Christianity in the twentieth century. This provided the spiritual and moral basis for rapid modernization which Confucianism by itself could no longer do. Further, the means by which mission work was initially undertaken created situations and attitudes which resonated with certain core values of Confucianism. Thus, although Confucianism and Christianity have certain areas of hostility and tension in their relationship, the general situation is one of complementarity rather than of confrontation. Modernization and industrialization in the Republic of Korea grew from a spiritual and cultural ground in which Confucianism and Protestantism have reacted together in conditions of mutuality.

CONFUCIANISM AS THE FOUNDATION OF TRADITIONAL KOREAN VALUES

Confucianism has formed an important component of the religious and philosophical culture of Korea since at least the fifth century. During that century and the following two centuries, the three kingdoms of ancient Korea – Koguryŏ, Paekche and Silla – underwent a process of Sinification or modernization involving the absorption of significant aspects of Chinese civilization. However, Confucian influence on Korean civilization was uneven, and had three distinct

76

aspects, a cultural aspect, a political aspect, and a social aspect. Up until the creation of the Chosŏn Dynasty (1392–1910) at the end of the fourteenth century, the influence which Confucianism had on Korea was largely confined to the cultural and political spheres.

In the author's definition, the cultural influence of Confucianism refers to its influence on concepts of education, the advent of writing, the recording of history and its commentary (historiography), certain aesthetic values, and the adoption of the Confucian ritual system. The political influence of Confucianism in my view refers to the influence which Confucianism exercised on the system of government – the structure of government and the political and moral values which underlie the processes of government. Social influence, however, refers to the mores and social values held in the general society, and to the social changes which these mores and values exerted on the structure of society itself.

The Confucianism adopted by the early Korean states derived from the Confucianism of the Han Dynasty (206 BC–AD 220) of China during which period Confucianism was seen principally as a philosophy of government rather than as either a system of religious belief, or a system of moral values capable of reshaping the structure of society. Two of the earliest cultural influences which Confucianism had on the ancient kingdoms of Korea were (1) the adoption of a system of writing, and (2) the creation of a system of formal education. In the kingdom of Koguryŏ, a national college called *T'aehak* with a formal curriculum of study was created in 372. The establishment of this college was followed shortly by the creation of several private Confucian academies called *kyŏngdang*. The purpose of the national college and the private academies was to educate the sons of the aristocracy, to instill in them a knowledge of Confucian virtues, and to prepare them to govern the state.

The influence of these schools on the elite sector of society can be seen in the creation of a literary tradition using Chinese characters, the keeping of state records, and the writing of national histories which analysed the successes and failures of the reigns of the various kings according to Confucian values. At the Koguryŏ court from the fourth century onwards official records of each reign called *yugi* were kept. In 375, the *Sŏgi*, the first analytical history of the kingdom of Paekche, was written. In Silla, an historical record similar to the *Sŏgi* of Paekche was written in 545 and a national Confucian academy, the *Kukhak* was established in 682. Thus, by the seventh century, all three kingdoms of ancient Korea had an established tradition of Confucianism which exercised a strong cultural influence on the society (Grayson 1989: 60–4).

From the seventh century onward, with continued changes in the structure of the state and especially in the aftermath of the peninsular wars of the 660s when the kingdom of Silla became the master of the Korean peninsula, Confucianism exercised considerable influence in the political sphere. Generations of Confucian scholars who had absorbed the values of systematic, bureaucratic Confucian government came to exercise a profound influence on the political structure and functions of the kingdom of Unified Silla (670–936).

Until the seventh century, Silla had been a tribal kingdom in which the functions of government had been dominated by the leaders of the great clans. Various positions in the government were reserved for members of the aristocracy based upon their position within a highly stratified, aristocratic social system. Members of the lower ranks of the aristocracy could not hope to aspire to the highest level of government, whatever their capabilities or merits were. Amongst the Confucian bureaucrats and scholars a movement began to remove the influence of the Bone Rank System – as the system of aristocratic hierarchy was known. Although this could hardly be called a democratic movement, it was an attempt to spread the power of government more widely amongst the elite sector of society, and to give power and authority only to those who had the requisite skills and capabilities.[1]

Throughout the Unified Silla period and the succeeding dynastic era, the Koryŏ period (936–1392), the relationship between Confucianism and Buddhism was one of complementarity rather than competition or opposition. Throughout this period of 800 years, Buddhism dominated the religious scene with its concerns for the after-life and metaphysical questions about the ultimate nature of the world whilst Confucianism dominated the political and moral scene. Especially during the Koryŏ period, government meant Confucian government – government according to Confucian values.

Not only did the Koryŏ government create a national Confucian academy to train bureaucrats, but it also set up two national archival libraries. These libraries would provide the sources for histories which would analyse the moral success or failure of a particular king's reign. More importantly for the development of Confucianism in Korea, the government instituted in the tenth century a civil service examination which required explicit and detailed knowledge of the Confucian classical literature. Anyone who wished to take part in government would have to study a prescribed Confucian curriculum and to pass the Confucian civil service exam. In addition to the government-sponsored academies a number of private academies were created in the capital and throughout the country. Thus from the tenth century onward a firm link was created between politics, education and Confucianism (Grayson 1989: 115–18).

The comfortable relationship of complementarity which had existed between Buddhism and Confucianism altered dramatically with the rise of the Chosŏn Dynasty (1392–1910). The rulers of this avowedly Confucian state created a nation and society which was the most thoroughly Confucian society in East Asia – even more thoroughly Confucian than China itself. From the late fourteenth century on, Confucianism exercised considerable social influence as well as political and cultural influence upon the Korean people. One of the reasons for the rejection of the complementary relationship with Buddhism was the corrupt relationship which was perceived to have existed between the Buddhist church and the Mongol-dominated court which had ruled Korea during the thirteenth and fourteenth centuries (Grayson 1989: 128–35; Lee 1984: 199–200).[2]

The form of Confucianism which came to dominate Chosŏn society was the

78

Neo-Confucian philosophy of Chu Hsi (1130–1200), the great philosopher of the Southern Sung Dynasty (1127–1279). Chu Hsi's thought was significantly different from the Confucianism of the Han period in that it had a metaphysical basis, certain elements of which were derived from philosophical Taoism. This metaphysical system put Confucianism into direct conflict with Buddhism. With the rejection of Buddhism for political and nationalistic reasons, Confucianism came to dominate the religious, philosophical, and moral scene of Korea to an extraordinary degree (Grayson 1989: 146–51).[3]

Traditionally, Confucianism was based upon the concept of the five human relationships, which when well ordered would create a well-governed, harmonious society. The five relationships were the relations between ruler and subject, father and son, elder and younger siblings, husband and wife, and friend and friend. Each of these five relationships was hierarchically arranged and characterized by a unique virtue. For example, the relationship of ruler and subject was characterized by the quality of *jên* (Korean *in*, benevolence) on the part of the ruler, and by the quality of *chung* (Korean *ch'ung*, loyalty) on the part of the subject.[4]

Confucianism as a philosophy of ethics and politics was transformed greatly when it absorbed certain metaphysical concepts from philosophical Taoism. In the Chu Hsi form of Neo-Confucianism, the moral relationships existing between people, which originally had only social value, came to be connected to questions about the ultimate nature of the universe. Thus, violations of the virtues of the one of five relationships which initially would only have had social significance now became violations of the ultimate character of the universe – error in the most profound sense.[5]

One of the most striking characteristics of Korean Confucianism from the fifteenth century onward was the passionate concern amongst the Confucian literati for the reformation of society into some ideal image. One group amongst the scholarly elite, known literally as the *Sarim-p'a*, were particularly uncompromising in their attempt to reform radically Korean society. It was now no longer true that Confucianism had only political and cultural influence. It was now thought that it was essential that the social influence of Confucianism should transform all aspects of the society – not simply the system of government. Kim Chong-jik (1431–1492) and Cho Kwang-jo (1482–1519) were the most outstanding of the literati who tried to impose Confucian values on the ruling class and the ruled (Grayson 1989: 139–41, 144–6; Lee 1984: 204–9).

One method for bringing Confucian practice down to the lowest level of society was the *hyangyak* (village code), an agreement between the members of a particular village to abide by the principles of Confucian propriety and ethics. These codes tended to have four objectives: the mutual encouragement of moral practice, the supervision of improper conduct, the establishment of decorum in social relationships, and mutual assistance during times of difficulty or hardship. Adherence to Confucian practice on the social level also meant the acceptance of the Confucian ritual system, the system of formal reverence for the ancestors of the clan. Full acceptance of Confucianism on the social level increasingly meant the exclusion of women from participation in the ritual system itself and from benefits such as the inheritance of property (Grayson 1989: 140; Lee 1984: 205, 207–8).

With the establishment of Chu Hsi's thought as the orthodox philosophy of the Chosŏn state, all other forms of thought became unorthodox. From the beginning of the dynasty, rigid regulations were set in place which severely limited the numbers of temples which were permitted to be open, and the numbers of monks who would be permitted to pursue monastic life. But Buddhism was not alone in being considered to be a system of heterodox thought and belief. Even other forms of Confucianism, such as the thought of Wang Yang-ming (1473–1529), were considered to be heterodox and the study of their teachings strongly discouraged (Grayson 1989: 151–5; Lee 1984: 199–200).[6] Thus, in their reforming zeal, the idealistic literati came to limit severely the area of political, moral and religious discourse. This limitation of the area of discourse in turn created a spiritual vacuum which was waiting to be filled.

CHRISTIANITY: CHANGES AND ADAPTATIONS IN THE SYSTEM OF TRADITIONAL VALUES

The advent of Roman Catholicism

The length of the period of Neo-Confucian supremacy in Korea and the extent to which it was able to dominate all areas of life meant that there was no society in East Asia which was as Confucian as was Chosŏn Korea. The negative effect of this supremacy was the stultifying effect it had on philosophical enquiry, religious practice, and moral behaviour. The positive effect of this supremacy was that it firmly fixed within Korean culture the importance of moral values (propriety and right conduct), the importance of education and learning, and especially such concepts as benevolence of superiors towards social inferiors and the loyalty of inferiors towards social superiors. Confucianism also reinforced the idea of the rightness of hierarchy as essential to a harmonious society, and the differentiation of the roles of men and women, and the assignment to women of a lower position in society beyond the home.

As a consequence of the devastation wrought by the Japanese invasions of the 1590s and by the invasions of the Manchus in the first third of the seventeenth century, there developed within Korean Neo-Confucianism a unique tradition of philosophy which concerned itself to an unusual degree with the agricultural, commercial and general economic affairs of the nation. This strand of Confucianism, latterly called *Sirhak* or Practical Learning. has no parallel in either China or Japan. The scholars within this broad tradition could trace their intellectual origins back to the so-called Matter First School (*Chugi-p'a*) of the sixteenth century. Like their intellectual ancestors, these practical scholars were passionately concerned with the reformation of their society. Whereas their forebears had been solely concerned with the moral renovation of the nation, these practical scholars were deeply concerned about the means to achieve the people's economic prosperity. Beginning with primary agricultural concerns, the scholars of Practical Learning developed interests in national and international commercial affairs, and even had some detailed ideas about the means to achieve a socially egalitarian state – because of its implications for economic prosperity (Grayson 1989: 161–8; Lee 1984: 232–8).

Within the body of the *Sirhak* scholars, some began to question not only the economic, political and social implications of Chu Hsi's Neo-Confucian thought, but the religious implications as well. In Neo-Confucian thought the Great Ultimate (Chinese *T'ai-chi*, Korean *T'aegŭk*) was an abstract concept without personality. The universe was a moral but ultimately mechanical world. Because of the aridity of abstract concepts such as this, many of the literati had privately dallied with Buddhism, but only a few had done so publicly because that religion was seen to be a superstitious creed unsuitable for a true scholar (Grayson 1989: 161–8).

From the middle of the seventeenth century on, the Confucian literati of Korea were aware of Roman Catholic doctrine through direct and indirect contacts which they had with the Jesuit missionaries in China. By the middle of the following century, several of the *Sirhak* scholars had seriously studied the teachings of the Jesuits contained in various pamphlets and had become practising Catholic Christians. In a recent paper given at the 1991 annual conference of the Association for Korean Studies in Europe, Donald Baker put forward the idea of a monotheistic revolution which had swept Korea during the eighteenth century. In part this revolution in theological thought and religious belief was stimulated by the intellectual trends which were being pursued by the *Sirhak* thinkers at that time (Baker 1991).

Because practising Catholics were not permitted to participate in the *chesa* ritual, the ancestral memorial rites, there was tension between the Confucian establishment and the early Catholics from the beginning. Based upon decisions which had been taken by the Vatican with regard to similar rites in China, participation in such memorial rites was seen to be participation in idolatrous rituals – the worship of the spirits of the dead. Upon the death of the liberal-minded King Chŏngjo (r. 1766–1800) who had held at bay the worst excesses of religious persecution, the active and regular persecution of the Catholic Church began. The persecution of the Church persisted for three-quarters of a century, resulting in thousands of martyrs, and ended only with the establishment of formal diplomatic relations with European and North American powers. The ferocity with which the Catholics were persecuted was for philosophical and nationalistic reasons. The Confucian establishment feared that by refusing to participate in the ancestral rites, the centrepiece of visible Confucian morality, Roman Catholics would be endangering the whole moral fabric of Korean society. There was also expressed concern about entanglements with foreign powers which was implied in Catholic belief (Grayson 1989: 161–8; Lee 1984: 239–40).

In spite of the severe persecutions which the Roman Catholic Church underwent, it survived and in so doing laid the ground for the growth of the Christian Church in Korea, and for a significant alteration in the religious and moral values of the people.

The development of Protestant Christianity

The Protestant form of Christianity entered Korea in the 1880s through the agency of Korean New Testaments brought in from Manchuria by Koreans who were resident there, and by Western missionaries. The growth of the Protestant church was dramatic. In 1910, within the span of a single generation after the arrival of the first foreign missionaries, 1 percent of the Korean population professed belief in Christian teachings and adhered to one of the Protestant denominations. This remarkable growth can be attributed to a peculiar set of circumstances characteristic of late nineteenth century Korean society. Simply stated, there was a religious vacuum which had been created by the aridity of Neo-Confucian thought and by the concomitant suppression of Buddhism and all other forms of heterodox thought and superstitious practice. Five hundred years of Neo-Confucian dominance had created a situation of spiritual hunger.

In addition to these spiritual and intellectual developments, the Confucian polity, the Chosŏn state, intelligent young Koreans at the end of the nineteenth century were looking for new scientific, economic, political and religious ideas. The late nineteenth century was an unusual era of intellectual and spiritual ferment which provided an opportunity for Protestant Christian missions that had not existed in the eighteenth century for Catholic missions. In the nineteenth century the state and the society were at the nadir of their development (Clark 1986: 6–14; Grayson 1989: 194–207).

The rapid growth of the Protestant denominations is attributable not only to the ripeness of the moment for Christian missions, but also to the methods used by the missionaries. In part due to the initial refusal of the Korean government at the end of the nineteenth century to permit direct evangelism, and in part due to the social conscience of the pietistic, first generation of missionaries, early Protestant missionary endeavours involved medical and educational work rather than evangelism. This emphasis on social works and education appealed to Koreans not only because of its practical value, but also because it resonated with certain aspects of the Confucian tradition. Christian schools would be esteemed because of the importance which Confucianism had always placed on learning and education. Furthermore, the strict moral teachings of the conservative and pietistic first generation of missionaries would have resonated with the austere code of morality taught by Neo-Confucianism (Clark 1986: 6–14; Grayson 1989: 194–207). Acceptance of a firm moral code linked to belief in a personal Supreme Being would mesh with spiritual trends which derived from the *Sirhak* tradition of Confucianism.

Catholicism itself would also have acted as a forerunner to Protestantism, helping to lay the foundation for future Christian growth. The essential teachings of Christianity would already have been known to many people because of Catholic missionary efforts and Christian martyrdom. Although in the eighteenth century Confucianism and Catholic Christianity had clashed over the issue of the ancestral rites, in the late nineteenth century and early twentieth century Neo-Confucianism became an ally for Protestant Christianity. This was due to the fact that by the very end of the nineteenth century performance of the ancestral rites had become a matter of personal choice rather than a legal requirement. In a very real sense, Protestant Christianity was built on the foundation laid by the moral concerns of Neo-Confucianism, by the intellectual and spiritual trends which had been taking place within the *Sirhak* camp, and by the advent of Roman Catholicism.

THE EFFECTS OF THE JAPANESE COLONIAL PERIOD (1910–1945)

One of the unique features of the development of Protestant Christianity in Korea was the degree to which that form of Christianity became intertwined with Korean nationalism. Protestant Christianity had an appeal to the Korean people as a whole, but it was particularly attractive to the progressive members of the young intelligentsia. Their interest in Christianity was aroused both by moral and spiritual reasons and by concerns for the safety and socio-economic development of their nation. For instance, Korean Christians followed the example of the early Protestant missionaries and founded Christian schools for the purposes of religious propagation and social development. It is no wonder that following the annexation of Korea by Japan in 1910 Christians should be in the forefront of the nationalist movement to restore the independence of Korea (Clark 1986: 6–14; Grayson 1989: 194–207).

In 1912, the Japanese Governor-General of Korea falsely accused ninety-eight Christians of being participants in a plot to assassinate the Governor-General, Terauchi Masatake (1852–1919). This paranoic plot against the Christian leadership is some indication that even at this early stage of Japanese colonialism there was some concern about the link beween Korean nationalism and Christianity. Another indication of this connection between Christianity and patriotism would be the fact that half of the signatories to the Declaration of Independence from Japan which was read out publicly on 1 March 1919 were Christians. Through such actions an unbreakable link was made between Christian faith and patriotism, which is a unique component of Korean Protestantism (Clark 1986: 6–14; Grayson 1985: 115–20, 1989: 194–207).

During the 1930s a militaristic form of Japanese patriotism, which could be called Shinto nationalism, came to typify the attitudes and actions of both the military and the government of Japan. There was a strongly held belief in not only the divinity of the Japanese emperor, but also of the Japanese people themselves. The Japanese were perceived to have a divine mission in East Asia. Consequently, as an expression of patriotism, regular participation by the members of the Japanese Empire was required at the rituals of State Shinto, the state cult which was based upon the traditional religion of Japan. Although it was difficult for Japanese Christians to avoid participation in these rites as patriotic acts, it deeply offended the patriotic and religious consciences of Korean Christians. Many Christians were imprisoned and a few martyred for refusal to take part in what were seen to be idolatrous acts. It is possible to see in the Shinto Rites Controversy a clash of nationalisms in the form of religious conflict. In this case, Protestant Christianity represented Korean nationalism (Grayson 1985: 115–20).[7]

It is clear to the author that the extraordinarily rapid development of the Republic of Korea (south Korea) following the liberation of Korea from Japanese colonial domination is due in part to the fact that there existed a significant industrial and commercial infrastructure in the peninsula. Roads, railways, port facilities, and other industrial facilities had all been built by the Japanese to serve their greater purposes on the East Asian mainland. None the less, the Koreans upon liberation were immediately capable of utilizing these facilities and extending them. The reason for this ability lies in the fact that the general Korean populace is amongst the most highly literate and highly educated in the world. This fact is a reflection of the importance which Koreans – strongly influenced by 1500 years of Confucian civilization – place on education.

Although the Japanese built an extensive school and university system, the upper level of this system reserved the vast majority of places for Japanese colonials. Even prior to the advent of Japanese colonial administration, the most extensive system of education in Korea was the Christian system, built and maintained by Korean Christians and foreign missionaries (Lee 1984: 367–8). During the Japanese colonial period most Koreans who received higher education in Korea did so in Christian institutions. Thus the Christian Church benefited from a Confucian predilection for learning and education, and in turn it contributed both to the social development of Korea and to the sustaining of Korean nationalism.

RELIGION AND ECONOMICS IN THE REPUBLIC OF KOREA

The Korean War (1950–3), like all fratricidal civil wars, took a ferocious toll in lives and in the damage inflicted upon the economic structure of Korean society. Beginning with the military revolution of General Pak Chŏng-hui (Park Chung Hee, 1917–79) in 1961, successive South Korean governments have created a series of five-year plans which gave detailed plans for the phased development of the nation. The success of these five-year plans depended to a significant degree upon the educational level of the general populace, their patriotic dedication to the task of national development, and the general discipline of their work habits. The enduring influence of Confucianism on contemporary Korean society may be seen in the emphasis which Koreans place upon learning and education, and upon such concepts as loyalty (ch'ung). Koreans' desire to acquire knowledge also meant that a high degree of discipline was required from an early age in order to absorb the vast body of facts demanded by the rigid educational system. Habits of personal discipline learned at an early age, of course, are useful at a later stage in life when discipline in work habits is necessary. Also, concepts such as loyalty to the ruler or to one's clan leader, a virtue which is strongly emphasized in the Confucian classical literature, may also be applied to the larger concept of the nation, especially if the nation is perceived to be an enlarged family or clan.[8]

In the opinion of the author, Confucian attitudes towards education should be seen to be the key to understanding why the Republic of Korea rapidly emerged, phoenix-like, from the ashes of a devastating civil war, to become within a generation the tenth largest commercial nation in the world. There is another Confucian attitude which has greatly influenced the speed of Korean economic development – the concern for a correct moral interpretation of history. We have seen that from a very early period, Koreans have kept detailed historical records of events, the reigns of individual rulers, and entire dynastic periods. As a result of this propensity to record history, Koreans have developed to an extraordinary degree a sense of the meaning of civilization and of their own place on the world stage of culture. It is unquestionably true that one of the great impetuses for national development was the strongly felt desire on the part of the Koreans to recapture their rightful place on the world stage and to erase the shame of Japanese colonial domination.

Christianity played a part in recent Korean socio-economic development in its contributions to education, and in its perceived support for Korean nationalism. Many of the major institutions of higher education are of a Christian if not a missionary origin. For example, three of the five most prestigious universities in Korea are of Christian origin. Christianity has also contributed to the moral and spiritual stability of the nation in that it continued to fill the spiritual gap left by the collapse of Neo-Confucianism as a coherent spiritual and political system, and by the decayed state of Buddhism.

During the 1960s through to the end of the 1980s South Korea changed radically from being a rural agrarian society to an urban industrial state. The movement of the bulk of the populace from the rural areas to the cities, and the change from agricultural to industrial work, meant social and psychological dislocation and disorientation on a scale which few societies – if any society – have experienced in such a short span of time. Although there are churches in virtually every village in South Korea, Korean Christianity is primarily an urban phenomenon. The Christian churches grew at an extraordinary rate during the 1960s because of the lack of any serious spiritual competitor and because massive social changes had created yet another significant area of spiritual need.[9]

If the residual cultural and social influences of Confucianism aided Korea in her economic development, it is also true that Christianity, particularly Protestantism, helped maintain the moral and spiritual qualities of the nation. Without the spiritual support of Christianity, it is the author's opinion that the Korean nation would have lacked the moral and social coherence to survive the massive pressures imposed upon it by the radical social and economic changes which have occurred over the past three decades.

CONCLUSION

It would seem to the author that the success of a process of modernization or industrialization undertaken by any nation will be largely dependent upon the preexistent culture and particularly upon the culture's values, and its philosophical and religious presuppositions. The author believes that successful change to an urban–industrial society is dependent upon preexistent ideas about the ultimate value of education and the importance of diligent work habits. Further, during the period of massive social and economic change, with all of the concomitant dislocations involved, it is necessary that there be a religious or philosophical system which will enable the people to endure the tensions and strains entailed in the transition to a new mode of social existence. In the case of Korea, Confucianism did provide the requisite social and cultural factors which would enable the nation to pursue modernization at an extraordinary rate. Likewise, Protestant Christianity provided the necessary religious and philosophical explanations for the massive socio-economic changes going on around the people. In a strange way, Confucianism and Christianity entered into a state of dynamic complementarity which provided the right foundation for the social and economic changes which had to be made in order for the transition to an urban–industrial society to have occurred.

NOTES

1 One of the major social changes which took place from the late seventh century was the degree to which the members of the petit aristocracy were able to assume positions of power and authority in the government. This was actively encouraged by the kings because these developments strengthened the position of the throne *vis-à-vis* the grand aristocracy. For a discussion of this period and the role of Confucianism in these developments see Grayson (1989: 70–2) and Lee (1984: 73–8).

2 The transition from a largely tolerant Buddhist state to a state dominated by a rigid form of Neo-Confucianism was one of the most significant social and ideological changes which has occurred in Korean history, ranking with the dissemination of Buddhism in the fourth century and the rapid development of Christianity in the twentieth century.

3 A thorough discussion of various aspects of the development of Neo-Confucianism in Korea may be found in de Bary and Haboush (1985).

4 The *locus classicus* for the statement of the concept of the Five Relationships is in the Confucian classical work the *Chung-yung* (The Doctrine of the Mean), ch. 20. For an English translation of this passage and a commentary see Chan (1963: 105–7). The hierarchical implications of this passage are clearly indicated by the Han Dynasty Confucian scholar Tung Chung-shu (179–104 BC) in his work the *Chun-ch'iu fan-lun* (Luxuriant Gems of the Spring and Autumn Annals). See Chan (1963: 277–8) for a relevant passage from this work and a commentary. The passage in *The Doctrine of*

the Mean should be compared with a passage from the third chapter of the *Mencius*. See Chan (1963: 69–71).

5 A survey of the development of the various strands of Neo-Confucian thought may be found in Creel (1953: 206–16). A fuller discussion of the thought of Chu Hsi may be found in Chan (1963: 588–653). Another discussion of the emergence of Neo-Confucianism may be found in Fung (1953: 407–33). Fung's analysis of Chu Hsi's thought may be found on pp. 533–71.

6 As a result of the Manchu conquest of China, Koreans in the seventeenth and eighteenth centuries came to see themselves as the preservers of the authentic traditions of East Asia, i.e. the Confucian philosophical traditions, the Confucian system of government, and the moral attitudes and appropriate behaviour of a Confucian society. For a discussion of the effects of this view on eighteenth century statecraft, and an explanation of why Korean Confucians became so conservative in their social and political outlook, see Haboush (1988).

7 For a thorough discussion of the Shinto Shrine Controversy see Lee, Kun Sam (1966). A brief description of the Japanese colonial period may be found in MacDonald (1988: 37–44). A fuller treatment is in Lee (1966: 306–72). See also Hoare and Pares (1988: 50–64). This latter book also has a good discussion of the Korean system of values and the Korean educational system.

8 An overview of the history of the five-year plans used by the Republic of Korea may be found in MacDonald (1988: 179–210). Pages 210–18 provide good comparative information on North Korea. See also Hoare and Pares (1988: 91–114).

9 A survey of recent historical events may be found in Clark (1986: 15–37) and Grayson (1989: 202–7, 210–12). More detailed information may be found in the *Britannica Yearbook* and the *Annual Register* for the appropriate year.

REFERENCES

Baker, D. (1991) 'Tasan's world: Korea on the eve of a monotheistic revolution', conference paper, 1991 Annual Conference, Association for Korean Studies in Europe, Dourdan, France, 26 March 1991.

de Bary, Wm. Theodore and Haboush, JaHyun Kim (eds) (1985) *The Rise of Neo-Confucianism in Korea*, Washington: Columbia University Press.

Chan, Wing-tsit (1963) *A Source Book in Chinese Philosophy*, Princeton, NJ: Princeton University Press.

Clark, D.N. (1986) *Christianity in Modern Korea*, Lanham, MD: University Press of America.

Creel, H.G. (1953) *Chinese Thought from Confucius to Mao Tse-tung*, Chicago: University of Chicago Press.

Fung, Yu-lan (1953) *A History of Chinese Philosophy*, Princeton, NJ: Princeton University Press.

Grayson, J.H. (1985) *Early Buddhism and Christianity in Korea: A Study in the Emplantation of Religion*, Leiden: E.J. Brill.

Grayson, J.H. (1989) *Korea: A Religious History*, Oxford: Oxford University Press.

Haboush, JaHyun Kim (1988) *A Heritage of Kings: One Man's Monarchy in the Confucian World*, Washington: Columbia University Press.

Hoare, J. and Pares, S. (1988) *Korea: An Introduction*, London: Kegan Paul International.

Lee, Ki-baek (1984) *A New History of Korea*, trans. Edward W. Wagner, Seoul: Ilchogak.

Lee, Kun Sam (1966) *The Christian Confrontation with Shinto Nationalism*, Philadelphia: Presbyterian and Reformed Publishing.

MacDonald, D.S. (1988) *The Koreans: Contemporary Politics and Society*, Boulder, CO: Westview Press.

5

JUDAISM AND CAPITALISM

Paul Morris

The supposed characteristics of the ubiquitous medieval Jewish moneylender – *der ewige Jude*, the fictional merchant Shylock, the Jew of Malta, long associated not only with usury but with demonic powers and the subversion of Christian society – were recast and universalized in the nineteenth century and identified with a new notion, that of the capitalist. Capitalism, or the capitalist era, to use Marx's designation, was a phase – the penultimate – in a developmental series of historical stages marked by their distinctive economic arrangements. One of the aims of this chapter is to explore and explicate the vital historical, albeit asymmetrical, links between Judaism and Capitalism, both terms of comparatively recent coinage.

Capitalism (capital and capitalist are earlier) appears to have first been used by the early French radical socialists and anarchists in the sense of a particular historical stage – that following the French and Industrial Revolutions.[1] Proudhon in 1861, for example, defined it as an 'economic and social regime in which capital, the source of income, does not generally belong to those who make it work through their labour'.[2] Although Marx himself did not use the term, it readily became the label for his third evolutionary stage – slavery, feudalism, *capitalism*.[3] *From its inception, the very idea of capitalism itself entailed a view of Judaism and its supposed role in these progressions*. Pulzer's claim, that 'anti-capitalism was, after all, one of the oldest and most natural forms of anti-Semitism',[4] fails to note this new context and phase of anti-semitism. To engage with the discourses of capitalism, inconceivable without reference to the portrayals of Judaism, is to be implicated in this anti-semitism.

It was only at the turn of this century in works such as Sombart's *Modern Capitalism* (1902), that the nature and history of capitalism became the subject of wide public debate. In his *The Jews and Modern Capitalism* (1911), Sombart[5] offered an alternative theory to Weber's *The Protestant Ethic and the Spirit of Capitalism*[6] and revived Marx's contentions that Judaism is the origin of capitalism and that the modern age is Judaized. Further, Sombart, a sometime supporter of Zionism, provides a link to the earlier debates between Marx and Hess over

Judaism and socialism. Jewish socialism has been the principal arena in which the relationship of Judaism and capitalism has been debated by Jews themselves.

Jewish emancipation, first raised in the debates concerning the Jews after the French Revolution,[7] became the subject of pressing public controversy where these rights subsequently extended to Jews in the areas that came under French control, were rescinded after the defeat of Napoleon in 1815. The relationship of Judaism to capitalism became a major concern in the context of this withdrawal of rights. The Jewish question became a prominent issue in the theorizing of the possibilities for post-feudal society in the new states of Western Europe – a test-case for the competing models of the state. The rise of political anti-semitism as a central feature of European politics after 1870 led to the conservative Right and the 'whole socialist movement' becoming 'seriously preoccupied with the Jewish problem' at the end of the nineteenth century.[8]

This chapter will focus on this constellation of positions: beginning with Marx, via Hess and Jewish socialism, to Sombart and Weber, and will end with a review of the arguments of the recent triumphalist, post-socialist, Jewish New Right.

A number of issues need to be noted by way of background. Jewish sources, both rabbinic[9] and secular academic, contain few references to capitalism.[10] The former largely due to the general lack of engagement with secular debates and the latter – except for the traditions of Jewish socialism and scholarly studies of anti-semitism – due to different agendas. There are no parallels to the Protestant and Catholic materials. Second, the poor and poverty have generally not been celebrated in the traditions of Judaism, and commercial and religious life has always been viewed as quite compatible. Third, much of the substance of this chapter is concerned with essentialist notions of Judaism, now overtaken by more recent, less reductionist methodologies and scholarly norms. Further, from the French thinkers, through Marx, via Sombart to Nazi and Soviet characterizations of the Jew and the identification of Judaism with capitalism, we find a literature so willful in its historical distortions and based on such little evidence that we are forced to read it not as describing Judaism at all but as serving some ideological function. It is surprising that this intellectually arid literature was ever taken seriously by scholars or political activists and can only be explained by the pandering to already existing, deeply embedded anti-semitism. Last, while socialists have identified Judaism with capitalism, those on the political Right have located the essence and origins of socialism (and capitalism!) in Judaism. This alone should warn us against such essentializing.

'MONEY IS THE JEALOUS GOD OF ISRAEL' (KARL MARX 1844)

Marx's writings on Judaism and capitalism form part of his legacy to the radical tradition, creating the single most significant factor in the historic anti-semitism of the Left. He integrated French socialism and German Idealism, both of which structurally utilized anti-semitism. The medieval Christian distaste for the sin of usury and commerce was taken up by the French radicals who identified Jews with the growth of industrialization and international trade. For Charles Fourier, trade, which he associated with Jews, was the 'source of all evil' (1808: 61). He advocated that they become enforced farm workers so as to be included in the life of his 'phalanstèries', where there would be no need of commerce. Proudhon, notorious for his private anti-semitism, saw the world being poisoned by the greed and materialism of the Jews, who had 'rendered the bourgeois, high and low, *similar* to them all over Europe'.[11] His solution was to 'send this race back Asia or exterminate it'. Alphonse Toussenel, Fourier's student, discerned a worldwide Jewish financial conspiracy against humanity.[12] These reconstructions of the Jewish merchant/moneylender as the enemy of humanity and its liberation were strategic ingredients of socialist theories and were indiscriminately adopted by Marx.

From Kant to Hegel, the German Idealist tradition, was consistently negative concerning Jews and Judaism. The former argued that Jews were incapable of developing a true ethics and described them as 'a nation of swindlers' and 'a people solely composed of merchants'. And the latter saw Jews as an historical anachronism. They were marked by a Jewish 'egoism' which alienated them from nature, humanity and even themselves. Judaism was a mere foil for Christian philosophy.

Marx addressed the Jewish question directly only in two relatively short and early essays.[13] These were crucial for the development of his historical materialism.[14] In *The Holy Family* (1845), Marx returned to the issue and it continued to feature in his later essays and correspondence.[15] He was consistently opposed to Jews and Judaism, both theoretically (there was no place for Jews *qua* Jews or Judaism in his system) and personally. But Marx's abusive anti-semitism is less significant than his model of the capitalist, which is nought but his Jew writ large. Further, capitalism and Judaism serve parallel functions respectively in Marx's early and later works.

Marx was responding to Bruno Bauer, who opposed Jewish emancipation.[16] How could Christians grant freedom to the Jews when they themselves still needed to be liberated? Judaism had already been superceded by Christianity and Christianity itself was a barrier to human emancipation. He considered that Christianity was 'completed Judaism' and Judaism was 'underachieved Christianity'.[17] Bauer's Hegelianism led him to construct a crude historical dialectic – from 'lustful Judaism', outside history (thesis) via Christian community in history (antithesis), to the final atheistic state of liberated humanity (synthesis). Jews could only be given civic freedom and begin to take part as human beings in his redemptive humanist programme at the cost of their Jewishness.

Bauer saw need as the basis of all social interaction in civil society – 'everyone utilizes everyone else to satisfy his own needs, and he in turn is utilized by others for the same purpose'. Christian society used to constrain this egoism by controlling trade, but Jews, unbound by these restrictions wormed themselves into the 'gaps and crevices of society' exploiting the 'insecurity' generated by historical progress. He concluded that Judaism (here, the customary reiteration of the nefarious links between Jews, money-lending and the market) has had no independent existence since the advent of Christianity, and 'cannot be helped'.

While for Bauer the question was the intrinsic spirit of the Jew, for Marx, it was the essential nature of emancipation. The feudal order was fatally fractured after 1789. The former estates, castes and guilds were now reduced to 'man', bound by selfish need and individualism. Marx agreed with Bauer about the egoism of bourgeois society on its way to becoming the secular, socialist state. But he rejected Hegel's – and Bauer's – assertion that general and individual interests will merge in the synthesis of the state and civil society. Marx saw clearly that the modern state merely served to foster the selfishness of the bourgeoisie, who used their civil rights not for the benefit of all but for their own ends. Neither Bauer or Hegel recognized that the deeply rooted concerns of the bourgeoisie ran counter to the public good. He distinguished human rights, which cannot be granted by any state, from political rights, which do not change the underlying asymmetries of economic power. He used the case of America to establish that the political freedoms of bourgeois society are quite compatible with conditions that thwart human emancipation, such as religion and trade. Religious freedom is not emancipation *from* religion, nor freedom *to* trade liberation *from* trade.

Marx chose bourgeois Jewry as a concrete instance of a cohesive community that appeared to have benefited collectively from the gaining of political rights. He was familiar with the Jewish situation, using them as an example in order to analyse the 'essence' of emancipation and to attack the social element they represented. Accepting Bauer's judgement of the Jews and of their centrality in civil society, Marx added a new and lethal dimension. He deconstructs Bauer's (and Hegel's) theological probing for the essence of the 'Sabbath Jew' in his religion, with an material account of the 'everyday Jew' based on his analysis of the social and historical role of the Jews in the development of rational, atomised, bourgeois society. He demanded:

> What is the secular basis of Judaism? Practical need, self-interest. What is the worldly cult of the Jew? Bargaining. What is his worldly god? Money. Very well. Emancipation from bargaining and money, and this from practical real Judaism would be the emancipation of our era.

Coalescing Christianity ('theoretical Judaism') with what he called Judaism ('the worldly application of Christianity'), he argued that historically the former never overcame the latter, 'except in appearance'. Bourgeois Christianity had now dissolved itself back into Judaism – 'the material egoism of the Jew has overcome the Christian world'. With great insight, he insisted, that Judaism survived not in spite of history but 'because of history'. Judaism could reach its mastery only in Christian, bourgeois society. For Marx, Christianity and Judaism – as forms of religion – are but shameful excuses for egoism and Judaism is simply the religious ideology of the bourgeoisie.[18]

Marx went far beyond his precursors in associating all aspects of emerging capitalism with Judaism. His argument is not just that the spirit of capitalism arises out of Judaism. Or that Jews representing the money economy prospered in the transition from the feudal Christian natural economy to the essentially market relationships of capitalism. But that our era itself is dominated by Judaism. Marx is referring to not just the market arrangements of the economic sector, but to very spirit of contemporary culture, society and civilization. This era (the Jewish/capitalist) is of universal significance – the theoretical Jew (that is the Christian) has become the practical Jew (that is the capitalist!).

Marx could see no reason why Jews should not be granted political rights in a society that followed 'Jewish practices'. But he undermined the importance of the whole issue, by claiming that as they possessed monetary power, Jews were already emancipated 'in a Jewish way'. Further, although progressive, he considered civil rights to be transitional. Jews protecting their petty interests and private property would only serve to increase general alienation and highlight the contradictions between political and financial power. While the public debate over the assimilation of Jews raged, Marx turned the question on its head by contending that Europe itself had became assimilated into Judaism!

Judaism is by its nature 'anti-social' and its parasitical Jewish agents have enslaved humanity. Marx argued that the existence of Judaism is dependant on capitalism and that 'as soon as society succeeds in dissolving the empirical essence of Judaism the Jew will become impossible'. When there is no further need for 'the bargaining and the conditions which give rise to it', Judaism will simply dissolve. Thus liberating both Jews and others for 'the social emancipation of the Jew is the emancipation of society from Judaism'.

The view that the development of bourgeois 'Judaism' and its impersonal relationships are a necessary stage in the progression of humanity is implicit in 'Zur Judenfrage' and only later explicit in *The Holy Family*. Although Marx legitimately criticized Hegel and Bauer for their essentialism concerning the Jew, he is guilty of the same charge with his essence of the Jew as 'trader'. Marx's 'empirical' usage of the term Judaism (*Judentum*), which can refer to commerce, is also clearly figurative. Apologists claim that Marx's reference is not in any sense literal but applies only to some vague Jewish spirit. But as he is most precise in his use of terminology and his illustrations are taken directly from Jewish life, it is clear that Judaism was specifically selected to be extended, condemned, and its allusions consciously intended. In Marx's mature thought[19] it is evident that his construction of the capitalist ('the old-fashioned but perennially renewed form' of the usurer) is almost an exact parallel to his earlier account of the Jew. Also, capitalism served a equivalent function to that of anti-semitism in Bauer and the other Young Hegelians.

Marx's complete identification of Judaism and capitalism was revived in the last third of the nineteenth century, becoming part of a variety of anti-semitic ideologies. His account generated an extensive literature by socialists and their opponents and by Jewish socialists attempting to answer Marx and the anti-Semites.[20]

MOSES HESS – 'COMMUNIST RABBI' (MARX)

Marx was right in that most Western European and American Jews sought to join the ranks of the emergent bourgeoisie, or construct their own parallel bourgeois life-worlds. Many did, however, join socialist movements, submerging their identity or conceding that national issues were secondary to those of class. Others followed Marx's one-time collaborator, Moses Hess, 'the first religious socialist of Jewry', as Buber called him, in attempting to develop a rapprochement between Judaism and socialism. Hess[21] was largely self-educated and an idiosyncratic thinker. He converted Engels to communism[22] and was an important factor in Marx's move from Hegel's bureaucratic state to social collectivism.[23] Inspired by the Parisian radicals, the German romantic tradition and the philosophy of Hegel, he forged the first synthesis of Feuerbach and French socialism. Hess was an 'ethical socialist' and never subscribed to the inevitability of history or violent class struggle. He was, however, a life-long activist driven by the belief that a society ensuring equality and liberty could be strived for now and achieved in the future.[24]

Hess's *The Holy History of Mankind* (1837), was the first socialist text in German addressing Germans.[25] It is an eccentric Hegelian history of human societies. Hess traced the movement from the original identity of matter and spirit, via their separation, to their coming re-integration. He discovered the primordial unity in the ancient Hebrews, as reflected in their union of religion and state. And he saw them as communists who divided 'up possessions equally and sought to maintain their equal possessions'. This unity was lost in the medieval period giving rise to the iniquities of private property and their maintenance by inheritance.

Hess saw 1789 as the beginnings of the new era ('the Sabbath of history') in Europe ('the new Jerusalem'). History was moving towards the full realization of the original biblical truth and there would once again be a coalition of religion and state. This would be the basis for a universal humanistic socialism based on the rejection of competition and private property. He stressed that as the gap between 'the aristocracy of wealth' and 'pauperism' increased, so too would the revolutionary potential of the 'proletariat'.

In his second and more influential book,[26] *The European Triarchy* (1841), Hess argued that whilst theory had reached its zenith in Hegel, it needed to be harnessed to the developments taking place in France and England in order to be transformed into practical political and social action. His concern was with the revolutionary future but he contended that Hegel's thought was restricted to the 'present, as determined by the past'. Only the triarchy – Germany, France and England – could save mankind from the capitalists (and the Russians) by abolishing private property and adopting socialism. Hess developed a 'philosophy of action' that would make communism a reality, based on his analysis of the relationship of economic to social factors.

Although hindsight leads us to discern elements that would later be crucial for his Jewish socialism, it is apparent that in these two studies the Hebrews play foundational role. They established the prototype of collective social union and the notion of the universality of mankind, the very models of communism itself. Hess was equally convinced that the Jews had *already* completed their historical task by bequeathing these truths via Christianity to humanity. The Jewish mission now was to assimilate into the nations and participate as individuals in the 'redemption'. Hess was shaken by the revival of the medieval ritual murder charge in 1840 (the Damascus affair) but had great faith in the protective powers of the triarchy.

Having formulated his 'spiritual religion' of humanity based on a non-violent transition to universal communist salvation, Hess rejected further abstract, 'theological' theorizing. He devoted his considerable energies to political action and the philosophical grounding of his communism. These efforts are found in his essays in *Einundzwanzig Bogen aus der Schweiz* (1843). He distanced himself from the French socialists by insisting that atheism was necessary for any true liberation. As all forms of the state are theologically informed, there is a necessary link between politics and religion. In *'Sozialismus und Kommunismus'*, for example, he argued that the idea of equality is still 'tied to heavenly politics' and only beyond that is the 'spiritual' freedom from all religion. And, in *'Philosophie der Tat'*,[27] he charged that the abstractions of both religion and politics rob the individual of his 'real life'. Private property and the state itself can only increase man's self-alienation. He rejected all compromises, intellectual freedom – from religion and politics – is a necessary precondition of any true revolutionary action.

He published an attack on Bauer's deliberations on the Jewish question in 1843, and in the same year submitted his essay, *'Über das Geldwesen'* to Marx for inclusion in his new journal. This was a pioneering application of Feuerbach's notions of alienation to economics. Hess forged a parallel between the idea of God and money. Both estrange us from the reality of 'social value', the former theoretically, the latter practically. And both have come to enslave us. He defined life as 'the exchange of productive activity' and argued that all our social exchanges have been commercialized. Money is now 'the worth of men expressed in figures, the hallmark of our slavery'. Man's natural tendencies towards co-operation are blocked by his egoism. He considered this egoism to be an intrinsically modern phenomenon which he identified with Christianity – 'Christianity is the theory, the logic of egoism'.

The Christian separation of the body from the spirit and the attendant message that only the body was ever truly enslaved, made 'Christian slaves out of heathen slaves'. And whilst the French revolution meant that men could no longer be bought and sold this was at the cost of the communal systems of the medieval estates. Now contemporary conditions are even worse, with a populace of egoistic, isolated, individuals separated by property and money living in a society based on a total competitive 'war against all'. Modern slavery is meaner than the past for the modern wage-slave 'sells himself' whereas those in the past were simply sold. Hess, however, saw some value in money in that it acted as a mediator between men, establishing social relations, thus overcoming alienation at some level. But any transitional use that it might have had is now over. His plaintive cry was simply that 'human beings are not goods'.

Hess linked money with sacrifice, the consumption of flesh and blood. He described money 'as social blood' and cautions that 'we', workers and capitalists, 'are the victims who suck our own blood, consume our own flesh'. He traced yet another three stage progression from the ancient Israelite blood cult (*substitute* blood), via Christ (*symbolic* blood), to the oppression of man by 'the modern Jewish–Christian shopkeeper' world (*actual* blood). Thus, as does Marx, he closely identified the development of the money economy and its evils with Judaism – Christianity. And like Marx, behind Christianity lies Judaism, which Hess argued, 'brought out the predator in mankind'. Unless we accept communism and allow the natural realization of the new society based on love, capitalist accumulation and the subsequent devaluation of the value of labour will destroy us all.

In 1862, Hess published the inaugural text of Zionist theory, *Rome and Jerusalem*.[28] It begins with his pendulum swing away from socialist internationalism, described in almost revelatory terms. Although this first synthesis of socialism with Judaism does not challenge Marx directly, much of it can be read as a corrective to the work of his erstwhile colleague and his own earlier thought. The Rome of the title referred to that of the new independent Italy and not to Catholicism. Hess called for a 'new Jerusalem' to mark the parallel Jewish liberation from the medieval period, insisting that the Jewish question required analysis in the context of the contemporary movements of national emancipation and was not just as an issue of the civic rights of a minority group.

With great prescience he recognized that the religious emancipation of groups in the context of the new European nation-states was no liberation at all, for the issue simply became the possibility of the assimilation of that group within the new political entity. Emancipation, entailing the loss of all the distinctive marks of language, history, culture and religion, was impossible and only led to humiliation. The gap between the universalistic rhetoric of the French Revolution and the reality of nations was the cause of this 'empty cosmopolitanism'. Nations, like families, were natural groups and would not simply disappear. To deny this reality was to engage in futile theorizing.

In order to fulfil its historical role in creating a true socialist internationalism, every nation required national liberation in its own land. Hess considered that the masses would be emancipated by science and industry, and nationalism would be the major force bringing the coming socialist era. Jews too must recognize their fundamental national identity and acquire land (Israel) for their socialism to develop naturally. They have a special role to play in that Judaism is the basis of all notions of socialism and equality – 'Judaism is, above all, a nationality whose history, outlasting millennia, goes hand in hand with that of humanity'.[29] Jews have always stressed the unity of all creation and their history knows nothing of feudalism and developed no fixed social divisions, castes or classes. While the old form of Jewish religion had 'preserved its nationality' in the diaspora,[30] Hess saw a new form of Judaism, albeit in 'its secular aspect', based on natural national solidarity renewing the liberated Jewish people in their own land.

Marx rejected any idea of a Jewish nation except 'as the nationality of the merchant, the money-man'. Hess countered Marx's, and his own earlier claims of Jewish egoism by insisting that Judaism 'sanctifies' both 'individual life *and* social life' and this was always preparation for the 'final end of social evolution and the messianic state'.[31] Judaism with its unity of matter and spirit is not materialistic. The individual is never separated from the family, nor the family from the nation, nor the nation from humanity, nor humanity from God. The salvation of the isolated individual had never been a feature of Judaism. He concluded that 'no people is further removed from this egoism than the Jews'.[32]

Hess distinguished traditional Jewish teachings from the 'modern Judaism' of Western Europe with its separation of matter and spirit.[33] Unlike Christian individualism, which ultimately leads to capitalism, Judaism is about social justice. He reconstructed Jewish history as a movement towards socialism. Mosaic law is based on 'socialist principles' and the Sabbath and sabbatical and jubilee years are socialist institutions. Hess referred to the communal life of contemporary Eastern European Jewry, especially Hasidism, to demonstrate the living reality of Mosaic socialism. The old religious context would provide the basis for a true future socialism.

Ever practical, Hess understood that the whole project for the establishment of a Jewish socialist state would need to be underwritten by France. Also that bourgeois Western Jews were too entrenched in Europe and that it would be the Jewish proletariat of Eastern European and North Africa that would go. He wanted the land of Israel to be to be secured by the entire Jewish people as a bulwark against future exploitation. The Jewish socialist state would be established without the need for a revolution. Owning the land and all means of production, it would fund and organise economic activity in workers' co-operatives, based on Mosaic–socialist tenets.

Hess, thus, understood the Jewish question to be equally a socialist and a nationalist issue. Communism and Zionism were perfectly compatible, both having developed out of the same critique of bourgeois society. Further, the liberation of the Jews was a test case for the possibility of universal human emancipation. For all peoples, religious and national realities were not contingent facades to be overcome but the very vehicles for the development of socialism. He supported Arab nationalism for the same reasons. To be a member of a nation is to be part of humanity and the future reality of socialism is dependent on it being adopted by free states. Hess rightly criticized Marx for underestimating the significance of religious and national factors and developed the first theory of nationalist socialism. While Marx equated capitalism and Judaism, Hess discovered the roots of socialism in the same tradition.

'JEWISH HERETICS' (DEUTSCHER)

There was a curious overlapping of personnel and ideas between Right and Left towards the end of the last century, particularly in Germany and Austria.[34] Marx's identification[35] of capitalism and Judaism bequeathed to the socialist tradition[35] was readily appropriated by the conservative Right and the one-platform anti-semitic parties.[36] Many among these latter camps also linked Judaism with revolutionary socialism. Either way, these connections were viewed as evidence of the Jewish conspiracy to undermine the established Christian or national order. That numerous Jews, or those of Jewish descent, became socialists is undeniable. But as this normally entailed the rejection of Jewish identity, what are we to make of this link? Isaac Deutscher, in his essay, 'The Non-Jewish Jew',[37] interpreted *this repudiation of Judaism as itself a Jewish act rooted in the realities of modern Jewish life*. He traced a tradition of 'Jewish heretics' – from Spinoza via Heine, Marx, Lassalle, Rosa Luxemberg to Trotsky and Freud – 'great revolutionaries', who moved beyond 'parochial' Judaism to 'its logical conclusion', hailing 'the message of universal human emancipation'.

Jews in Western Europe joined socialist movements[38] in increasing numbers. For many any explicit relationship between their Jewish tradition and this heretical secular messianism was lost. Others saw more compelling connections between their idealistism, anti-capitalism and Judaism.[39] Many Jewish socialists later came to associate Judaism with socialist ethics, reflecting the dominance of Kantian ethics at the end of the last century. The Jewish neo-Kantian philosopher, Hermann Cohen, was a socialist of the liberal humanist ilk. His merging of the ethics of the Hebrew prophets, Kant and socialism, became an important inspiration for Jewish socialists in linking their political beliefs with their Judaism.[40]

In Western Europe, the formal Jewish community, as reflected in its official press, was as a rule nationalistic and while not in any way pro-capitalist was anti-socialist. Socialism tended to be viewed as atheistic, opposing traditional Jewish values and a challenge to the communal economic life.

In Eastern Europe, however, where there were large Jewish communities with their own distinctive culture, language and literature, Marx's ideal of disappearance by assimilation was a less viable option. Socialist theorists were forced to rethink the Jewish question in the light of the realities of Jewish life in Russia.[41] A secular, anti-traditionalist, Yiddish culture intimately bound up with the labour movement developed. As the new economies developed their conditions worsened and their already precarious borderline existence became ever more threatened. Their situation and their politics were marked by desperation and urgency. Numerous intellectuals came to subscribe to the Marxist remedy, later followed with the direst consequences by the Bolsheviks, Mensheviks and by Trotsky.

In addition to the Jewish Marxists who made a major contribution to the Russian revolutionary movement, two distinct forms of Jewish socialism developed – those advocating Jewish autonomy, and socialist Zionism. Jewish socialists raised the national dimension of the revolutionary struggle, all too easily missed in the premature reduction of complex realities to issues of class. They followed Hess in trying to synthesize socialist internationalism and Jewish nationalism. Both forms built on the existing proto-trade unions and self-help communal structures and the work of the Haskalah (Jewish enlightenment movement). Jewish socialists were convinced that any Jewish future would arise out of the productive labour and co-operation of the more than five million that made up the increasingly marginalized Jewish masses of the Pale of Settlement. They also shared the convictions that their difficulties were due to the anomalous conditions of the diaspora,[42] with its coalition of rabbis and merchants, anti-semitism, and oppression by Jewish and other capitalists. And, that only socialism and some form of autonomy would liberate them from all forms of oppression. Unlike Marx and even more so than Hess, Jewish socialism was based on intimate knowledge of the community and its traditions. Both were mass movements that arose directly from the people, and Carlebach writes of 'the profound and spiritual element in the Jewish "class struggle"'.[43]

The principal group calling for Jewish autonomy after 1903 was the Bund (General Jewish Workers' Union in Lithuania, Poland and Russia), founded in 1897[44] to 'propagate socialism among the Jewish masses'. The Bund drew on Otto Bauer's national model of socialism[45] and attempted to create an autonomous Jewish nations in Russia and Poland. They rejected any Jewish international identity and sought to struggle alongside non-Jewish socialists to defeat the tsar. Affiliated to the Russian Social Party, the Bund was a significant factor in the 1905 revolution. They sided with the Mensheviks in 1917, were banned in 1921, finally being disbanded by Stalin in 1939.[46] The massive emigration from the Russian Empire after 1881 brought Jewish socialism to every centre of Jewish settlement and was a significant factor in the development of trade unionism and the involvement of Jews in left-wing politics in the West and America.

The socialist Zionists[47] sought to establish a socialist Jewish nation-state in Palestine (or sometimes elsewhere). After the terrors of 1881 the choice for Jews increasingly became 'revolution or exodus'.[48] Socialist Zionism included within its numbers Marxists[49] and non-Marxists.[50] It rapidly became the predominant Zionist group and the view that there was some inherent link between Judaism and socialism became part of its ideology. Even the religious Mizrahi party developed a 'socialist' youth movement. The State of Israel was founded on 'socialist' principles and many of its institutions are socialist in orientation. For example, the Histadrut ('Unions of unions'), and the religious and non-religious, kibbutz and moshav movements which were based on the Soviet[51] early communes and Fourier's models.

The traditions of Jewish socialism that began with Hess demonstrate that large numbers of Jews became anti-capitalists and found stronger (Hess) or weaker (Deutscher) connections between the Jewish tradition and their socialism. Abram Léon, the Trotskyist thinker, is probably right that the defining mark of capitalism was its new mode of production and in this sense Jews were not historically capitalists at all but rather served as a 'commercial class'.[52] And there is more than a grain of truth in Otto Heller's claim that 'modern capitalism sealed the fate of Jewry' by denying them their traditional socio-economic roles.[53] Crudely formulated, the rise of capitalism in the West ensured that millions of Jews assimilated into the nations, while in the East it was a major factor in the revival of Jewish nationalism.

NON-EGOISTIC JUDAISM OR ORTHODOX RELIGIOUS SOCIALISM

The 1920s and 1930s saw the growth of Zionist socialist youth movements in Germany. These idealistic groups developed a discourse of the religious and spiritual aspects of their activities but rarely embraced traditional Jewish practice.[54] A number of the prominent founders of the kibbutz movement came from their ranks. A parallel movement developed amongst young Orthodox Jews and in the mid-1930s their members established the Religious Kibbutz Federation in Israel. They find the rationale for their socialism in the Hebrew Bible and in the tradition of authoritative rabbinic teachings. The social teaching of Maimonides, the twelfth century Jewish theologian, provides a model for their structured communal and personal lives. The construction of the moral community is a religious commandment. This must be done in order to allow the individual to become virtuous. Here, we see a compatibility between socialism and traditional Judaism based on egalitarianism, self-discipline, and reflective rational organization. The economically and socially flourishing religious kibbutz system is poor support for Marx's 'Jewish egoism'.[55]

WERNER SOMBART AND MAX WEBER: JEWS, PROTESTANTS AND CAPITALISM AND THE 'GHOST OF MARX'

Willhelm Roscher, the founder of the 'historical school' of political economy, undertook the first systematic scholarly exploration of religious identity and economic behaviour. Roscher's argument was that the Jews' unique capacity for business led them to be summoned into medieval Christian Europe to foster commercial and material development. Later when rival Christian functionaries became established, Jews were expelled as competitors. These Christian ventures provided the basis for the modernization of the European economy.[56] Roscher presented his thesis in support of their full emancipation. It was, however, soon appropriated by those, such as Heinrich von Treitschke, who were opposed to

Jewish rights. Regardless of the context in which it was used, for decades it was held to be the authoritative study of the issue. One of von Treitschke's students was Werner Sombart.

Sombart was part of the circle, which included Max Weber, that debated Marxist notions of political economy at the end of the last century.[57] He was a life-long German nationalist and his earliest work was concerned with the threat to the traditional pre-industrial order posed by capitalism. Later he rejected this conservatism and adopted socialism, incorporating a number of Marxist elements, including the value of the new industrial technologies in improving the lot of the proletariat. *Sozialismus und soziale Bewegung* (1896), his 'national' socialist manifesto, argued that workers' associations would be instrumental in the revival of Germanic solidarity. It had considerable impact and was rapidly reprinted a number of times and translated into more than a dozen languages.[58]

In *Der Modern Kapitalismus* (1902), Sombart offered a spirited attack on capitalism and its bourgeois trader class, presented in the context of the historical development of capitalism.[59] Condemned by socialists as a defence of the status quo and also by the Right, these volumes nevertheless found a wide audience. A careful reading of Marx is evident and Sombart's definition of capitalism comes very close to that of Marxists. Many of the themes – the internationalization of trade; the introduction of 'rational' production and marketing methods; the growth of the money markets; and the reduction of all life to the financial calculation of the bourgeoisie – reappear later as Jewish innovations.

During the next decade Sombart published a succession of programmatic studies concerned with national reconstruction. A number of related developments in his thinking can be traced. First, he lost his faith in the German proletariat as the vehicle for national renewal. Second, he came to consider that capitalism offered the best possibility for creating the new Germany.[60] Finally, he attempted to refine Marx's thesis on Judaism and its relationship to capitalism.[61] While he agreed that Judaism was the necessary underpinning for the rise of capitalism, he was not convinced that materialism and egoism were the significant factors. Sombart considered will, motivation, abstraction and restraint to be the salient features of the Jewish tradition.

In 1910 Sombart gave a lecture series on the relationship of Judaism to capitalism. These were published as *The Jews and Modern Capitalism*[62] the following year, and came to provide the framework for much of the subsequent discussion of this issue. It was heralded by anti-Semites as 'public, scientific' confirmation of their views.[63] Sombart's sought to re-work Marx in the light of Weber. He aimed to prove that the Jews had played the essential role in the development of modern economic life and thus offer a corrective to Max Weber's work on Protestantism. There was little disagreement with Weber on the characteristics of capitalism, but Sombart argued that these were found both earlier and to a greater extent in Judaism.

Sombart attempted to ground Marx's equation methodologically. He approached his subject both historically and conceptually. He began by explaining the shift of the financial centres of Europe from the Mediterranean to northern Europe by the parallel migration of Jewish communities.[64] Historically, the capitalist transformation of Europe necessitated the establishment of a number of institutions (the modern nation-state with its armies; new methods of production; international trade; the New World and modern colonialism; and urbanization) and systems (competition, credit and accounting methods, and the stock exchange). With tremendous zeal, chapter by chapter, he 'demonstrated' that each and every one of these factors originated and/or was developed by Jews. He is greatly aided in this endeavour by his preposterously inclusive definition of a Jew. It is racial as he includes as Jews those whose ancestors were baptised centuries before, but he also counts a variety of people who have Jewish sounding names and those who 'appear as Christians' but are, for his purposes, Jews.[65]

He claimed that all industrial manufacturing was pioneered by Jews. And, America ('the Jewish spirit distilled') not only owed its independence to Jewish efforts but the whole New World was colonized 'for them alone' with 'Columbus and the rest . . . but managing directors for Israel'.[66] Further, he contended that to think about the development of the modern state without reference to the Jews 'would be like Faust without Mephistopheles'.[67] These Jewish successes were accounted for by a number of related factors. First, their wealth! Second, their geographical dispersion had given them an international network of Jewish contacts and experience of different languages and cultures. Third, as continual strangers and 'semi-citizens', by necessity Jews had mastered the skills of adaption and became 'tradition-free world citizens'. Finally, their exclusion from public life allowed them to concentrate on trade and accumulating wealth.[68]

The movement of Jews moved into a static Europe bound by the Aristotelian and Thomist theory of just price determined by station was decisive in the history of capitalism. Sombart maintained that Jews excluded from existing practices developed the characteristic institutions and systems of contemporary economic life. Jews, he insisted, had always subscribed to 'modern' commercial practices and their successes led to the breaking up of the medieval world and the 'conversion' of Europe to Jewish trading norms. All that distinguishes the medieval from the modern economic world can be laid at the feet of the Jews.

Sombart considered that underlying these various 'outer' Jewish conditions was the 'spirit of Judaism'. This, if not eternal, Sombart was convinced, had remained constant 'from Ezra's day to ours'. He argued that this spirit was to be found in the religion of the Jews. And there, in its most essential characteristic feature, the halakhah (rabbinic law), based on the 'contract' between God and the Jews. Jewish prayer is a 'bargaining' and Jewish morality is mere accounting. The law not only gave instruction in abstract credit arrangements and taught the centrality of gain for its own sake, but generated the 'extreme intellectuality of the Jew'.[69] Sombart insisted that all the Jew's 'peculiarities are rooted in this'.[70] He saw these peculiarities as impersonal analysis, calculation (particularly of

101

risk), reflection and great mental flexibility.[71] In addition, the law led Jews to manifest energy, ascetic self-discipline, and a teleological sense, which allowed for deferred gratification and the accumulation of wealth.

Sombart held that it is Jewish law that lies behind Calvinism ('Puritanism is in reality Judaism')[72] and its features display a more direct and closer affinity to the spirit of capitalism. The law shaped the religious Jewish individual, producing the ideal type of the entrepreneur. He argued that capitalism and Judaism have 'the same leading ideas': [73] rationalism is their principal trait;[74] both are 'alien constructions' imposed on 'the natural, created world';[75] and both develop systems based on legal contract.[76]

Having proved to his satisfaction that Jews are totally answerable for modern capitalism, Sombart contrasted the cold, hard, calculating mentality of the desert nomad,[77] with his quick but, at base, shallow intellect and eternal restless character – the reasons behind the Jewish dispersion – with the Germanic peasant farmer. The former, essentially an artificial, contrived being, has come to dominate the latter, a being rooted in the natural order.[78] Sombart is finally most ambiguous about capitalism. On the one hand, he cannot deny some of its benefits, but on the other, he despises it.

Almost every detail of Sombart's analysis of Jewish history has been refuted by expert scholars and his work denounced for its poor argumentation and evidence. And yet, it continues to be read and discussed. It has recently been re-published yet again, leading to another round of reviews and debate. It seems to appeal equally to Jews who wish to celebrate capitalism and to those who desire to condemn both Judaism and capitalism. We shall return to one such contemporary debate below.

The Jews and Modern Capitalism secured Sombart's reputation as the national academic authority on Jews and Judaism and it was in that capacity that in 1911 he delivered a series of lectures throughout Germany, entitled 'The Future of the Jews'. These lectures, attended by Jews and non-Jews, were published the following year.[79] Sombart precipitated a dispute within the Jewish community between Zionists and German Jewish liberals. He contended anti-semitism was caused by Jews and that it was impossible for Eastern European Jews to be assimilated into German life. He supported Zionism as the solution to the Jewish problem. Further, he advocated a 'heads down' policy for Jews who chose to remain in Germany. Germans and Jews were racially distinct,[80] he argued, and Germans must arrest the Judaizing of German public life.[81] The Zionists supported Sombart. There was an outcry from both Jewish liberals and the religious orthodox and Sombart was denounced as an despicable anti-semite. As the controversy intensified it led to public debate at the national level on Eastern Jews, Jewish nationality and Zionism, and the place of Jews in Germany.[82]

Sombart continued to be obsessed with the issue of Jews and capitalism and came to somewhat resolve his ambivalence about capitalism by distinguishing the two distinct elements that combine to form 'capitalism'. The first was the Jewish-bourgeois spirit, and the second, the 'heroic' Germanic entrepreneurial spirit which fosters national solidarity.[83] He went to great lengths to 'prove' that Germans had nothing to do with the former, and were entirely responsible for the latter.[84] And, Sombart contended that only the latter could restore Germany to its pre-capitalist glory. In his Nazi tract, *Deutscher Socialismus*,[85] he advocated that Jews be excluded from the economic and spiritual life of Germany because of the Jewish spirit gave rise to decadent capitalism.

Max Weber knew Sombart well. From 1902 they worked together as editors of *Archiv für Sozialwissenschaft und Sozialipolitik*. Both spent their working lives trying to understand the evolution of modern capitalism and shared a concern with the unity of the German nation. The debates between them persisted over decades.[86] Weber's work on religion and economics is of quite a different order to that of Marx or Sombart. He rejected their massive generalizations such as religion, Judaism or Christianity. Instead he gave elaborate confessional distinctions, set in their specific national and historical contexts. In *The Protestant Ethic and the Spirit of Capitalism*, after a discussion of national Protestant groups, he noted that minority Protestant communities also tended to develop capitalist economies. He mentioned the French Huguenots, the English nonconformists and the Quakers, and added 'last but not least, the Jew for 2000 years'.[87] Weber accepted Roscher's views but added a caveat. Jewish, speculative, 'pariah-capitalism' was very different from sober, modern Protestant industrial capitalism. And, it was the latter that was significant for subsequent developments. In this study, Weber referred to Sombart's work and acknowledged his neglect of Judaism.[88]

Weber returned to his analysis of Judaism in *Ancient Judaism* and *Economy and Society*.[89] That the former, written towards the end of his life (1917–18), was intended as the first of a trilogy on the social and economic history of the Jews, indicates that he had not completed his thinking through of the Jewish question. In the latter, he addressed Sombart's thesis. Weber understood ancient Judaism to have broken the hold of magic on the world and thus created the possibility of the modern world and capitalism.[90] And, he agreed with Sombart that their legalistic and rational ethic was transmitted by rabbinic Judaism and Christianity. Further, they were in accord in that both Calvinism and Judaism produced a personality type particularly fitted for modern capitalism.[91] In fact, they both would have assented to Marx's claim that the Jewish spirit had become dominant in the modern world.

Weber advanced two reasons why modern capitalism could not have evolved from the Jews. First, self-discipline was developed to a greater degree and more systematically in Protestantism. This led to a specific model for the organization of labour which was an essential feature of capitalism for Weber but not for Sombart. Second, since their biblical exile Jews had been a pariah people. Having separated themselves from the wider environment (particularly non-Jews), they did not see the world as the realm of salvific activity.[92]

Ancient Judaism began with a discussion of this pariah status:

103

The problem of Jewry, unique in the socio-historical study of religion, can best be understood in comparison with the Indian caste system. Because, what were, viewed sociologically, the Jews? A pariah people . . . All essential features of its behaviour to its environment especially its voluntary ghetto existence that predates by far its forcible internment and the kind of dualistic interior and exterior ethic can be derived therefrom.[93]

Jews, unlike all the other groups studied in Weber's massive project of exploring the socio-economics of the world religions, were separated from their environment and the focus, here, is primarily on the group itself rather than on its ethical code. Weber claimed that the Jewish dual ethic caused the ghetto and not the other way round. He set his agenda as answering the question – How did the Jews became 'a pariah people with this highly specific character?'[94]

Weber read the prophets, in the light of contemporary Protestant scholarship, as in perpetual tension with the priests. The priests 'policed' the people but were not only influenced by the prophets but incorporated their teachings in authoritative codes of ritual practices.

It was the prophetic insistence on linking the national community with the ancient covenant that transformed Israel from a politically defined community into a religious segregated one. This was the foundation of the pariah people, which – via the embedding of separatist ritual by the priests and their rabbinic descendants – found its way to the ghetto.

Even if we subscribe to Weber's narrative, in what sense was this becoming a pariah 'voluntary'? First, Weber's own contention was that it was the result of the indirect imposition of the ideology of the prophetic elite on the masses. Second, he argued, that the choice facing those in exile in Babylon was to create new socio-political structures or *disappear by assimilation*.[95]

All of the characteristics of a pariah people, outlined by Weber, are problematic and his commitment to the Indian parallel bears little systematic scrutiny.[96] The dual ethic, according to Weber based on Deuteronomy 23.20, is part of the cause of the historic separation of the Jews from others. Leaving aside the fact that all human groups develop different ethics for their members and others,[97] is this feature not especially evident among Protestants? Weber also understood Jewish law as static and did not grasp its considerable and complex post-biblical historical evolution. His entire view of Judaism is bound to the notion that its is ahistorical and unchanging, at least since antiquity. Weber wrote that Jewry has been:

tarrying in its self-chosen position as pariah people as long and insofar as the spirit of the Jewish law . . . the spirit of the pharisees and of the rabbis of late antiquity continued uninterrupted and still does so today.[98]

Weber considered Jews to be an essentially alien[99] and anachronistic people, persisting in time, separated from non-Jews and their historical situation.[100] He described them as being deceitful in business and to combine 'pious humility with cunning shrewdness'.[101] Their ahistorical nature entailed that they were equally at home in any economic system[102] and, more importantly, *by definition* excluded the possibility of them having had any historical impact on the modern world.

Sombart and Weber both discussed Jews in the contexts of their own ideological agendas. The former came to castigate Jewry for its supposed part in creating the terrors of modernity. The latter came to write Jews out of the picture altogether. The contributions to the debate over the relationship of Judaism and capitalism, while proving to be influential, were marred by their inability to finally lay the 'ghost of Marx' to rest.

THE NEW JEWISH RIGHT

The contemporary world is drastically different from that of Weber and Sombart with the present situation of Jewry shaped by the Holocaust, the establishment of the State of Israel and the post-war period of relative affluence and stability in the United States and Western Europe. Demographically the changes have been immense with the vast majority of Jews now living in the United States and Israel. The recent collapse of state socialism in Eastern and Central Europe and huge migrations of Jews to Israel are already transforming the Jewish state. In the United States, although Jewish poverty still exists, the Jewish community as a whole has become comparatively prosperous and well educated.

In *The Political Behaviour of American Jews* (1956), Fuchs detailed the disproportionately high levels of Jewish involvement in trade unionism, left-wing politics and support for the Democratic Party. He argued that the extensive anti-capitalism of Jews was a direct result the values derived from Judaism.[103] This pattern, which lasted until the 1970s, now appears to be declining. In the United States and in Western Europe, Jews, as so many others, have moved politically to the Right. In the 1970s, new conservative movements, associated with right-wing think-tanks and journals developed, particularly in the United States and in Britain. This so-called New Right, contesting the dominant post-war 'Keynesian agreement' on the basis of supply-side economic and libertarian doctrines, was made up of neo-conservatives and, to use Irving Horowitz's term, palaeo-conservatives (long-time conservatives newly in the public eye). Capitalism, that nefarious invention of the socialists, was until then still largely a pejorative term. The New Right launched an intellectual and moral defence of capitalism that re-defined the earlier justifications in support of democracy, and led to the nature of capitalism becoming a widely debated public issue. For many neo-conservatives, the twin enemies of capitalism are socialism (all forms of central intervention and planning) and secularism (as opposed to the 'Judeo-Christian tradition). Its doctrines later became, at least partly, enshrined by the Reagan and Thatcher governments.

Posing a challenge to the Fuch's view, a number of the leading American neo-conservative intellectuals are Jewish. In their writings and addresses they have raised the question of the relationship of capitalism and Judaism. Kristol, a member of the American Enterprise Institute and the author of *Two Cheers for Capitalism!*, for example, in an article entitled, 'The Spiritual Roots of Capitalism and Socialism',[104] writes:

> The difference between capitalism as a system and the existence of mere commercial activity . . . is that capitalism says that . . . free commercial transactions should not merely take place, but should be permitted to shape the civilization as a whole.[105]

Kristol, a Trotskyist in his youth, argues that socialism is a form of 'gnosticism' while capitalism has its non-Utopian roots in the Jewish and Christian 'Orthodox' traditions. These traditions provide the moral 'limits' of capitalism. Further, while Christian ambiguity about commerce led to its misplaced opposition to capitalism, Judaism with its acceptance of the 'real world' and positive inclusion of business life is especially compatible with the capitalist system.

Milton Friedman, Nobel laureate in economics, is one of the doyens of monetarist theory. He is an influential and vocal advocate of capitalism and the author of *Capitalism and Freedom* and *Free to Choose*. A perceptive if misguided commentator, Friedman considers that 'socialism and Judaism are a natural contradiction'. He insists, 'the idealism and Jewish character as they developed in two thousand years bear a marked capitalist character' and that 'without this capitalist trait I don't believe that the miracle of the State of Israel would have happened'. And, he argues that 'there is conflict between socialism and the interest of the state in Israel'.[106] In a later article,[107] he addresses what he takes to be 'the great paradox' at the heart of the issue of Jews and their relationship to capitalism – why have Jews who have benefited so much from capitalism been among its most vociferous critics?

Friedman draws on the works of historians like Rivkin, who emphasise that 'developing capitalism is the prime factor in the liberation and emancipation of the Jews'.[108] He defends the proposition that forms the first part of his question by reflecting that only where there has been free entry to markets, for him a crucial feature of capitalism, have Jews thrived in the modern world. Further, Jewish survival itself for two millenia was, and still is, dependant of some aspect of the market allowing them free entry. The greater the level of free competition, the greater the flourishing of the Jews. He dismisses the Israeli counter case on the grounds that in Israel, socialism is healthily subverted by older and more deeply rooted 'capitalistic traits'.

He refers to Sombart's 'important and controversial book', *The Jews and Modern Capitalism*, extolling it as having grasped something essential about Jews and capitalism. He find himself totally in accord with the thesis that Jewish religion and culture evidence 'a capitalist outlook'. Friedman cites the German sociologist's claim that 'the Jewish religion has the same leading ideas as capitalism' and 'the whole religious system is in reality nothing but a contract between Jehovah and his chosen people'.[109] Friedman seems quite unaware that Sombart's desire was to blame Jews for their links with the development of capitalism. And, although he does not go as far as Sombart in seeing Jews as largely responsible for the capitalist system, Friedman remarks that this is 'high praise' and a badge that one should wear with pride. Noting that the book was unfavourably received as the work of an anti-Semite, he argues that 'the violence of the reactions of Jewish intellectuals to the book is itself a manifestation of the Jewish anti-capitalist mentality'.

Friedman rejects the Fuch's explanation that it is Judaism that predisposes Jews to the Left. He presents two alternative accounts. The first, he bases on the fact that in the nineteenth century the pro-market parties were linked to Christianity. Second, he says that Jews threw out the baby with the bath water by subscribing to the view that *all* Jewish business activity was the result of oppression, and points to 'the subconscious attempts by Jews to demonstrate to themselves and the world the fallacy of the anti-semitic stereotype'.[110] It is important to note that a number of American Jewish sociologists, with their application of Weber's Calvinist characteristics to American Jews, have also came very close to Sombart's views of them.[111]

The claims of the Jewish New Right regarding Judaism have been vigorously opposed by other American Jews. Typical of this response is Shorris's *Jews Without Mercy*.[112] He castigates Jewish neo-conservatives (including Irving Kristol, Norman Podhoretz and those associated with the journal, *Commentary*) as traitors to the Jewish tradition. He reaffirms, 'Socialism found fertile ground among the Jews because it was, in essence, nothing more than a restatement of Jewish ethics'.[113] In the 1980s the organization New Jewish Agenda was set up to revive the Jewish commitment to social action. And, the journal *Tikkun* was founded in 1986, in a conscious attempt to counter *Commentary* and the association of Jews with the Right. Claiming Marx and Freud as exemplars, its founding statement defining its title reads:

> The universalist dream of a transformation and healing of the world, the belief that peace and justice are not meant for heaven but are this-worldly necessities that must be fought for, is the particularistic and religious tradition of the Jews.[114]

Within the context of this intensified Cold War polemic with its black and white opposition between American capitalism and Soviet oppression, many Jews rightly advocate the former. The post-1989 situation has served only to intensify these Jewish defences of capitalism. The New Jewish Right and its anti-capitalist opponents continue to play out the question – Hess, or Marx and Sombart?

HALAKAH AND CAPITALISM

The economic theory and practices of Jewish communities has only recently been the subject of systemic historical study and as yet there is no established consensus. Although pioneering, the work of Salo Baron is both too obviously apologetic and committed ideologically to a evolutionary reading of Jewish history – the enlightenment must have been positive.[115] Jonathan Israel, for example, has shown that even if a small number of Jews did play a significant role in the creation of a number of essentially modern institutions, the seventeenth and eighteenth centuries represented an economic 'decline' of Jewry as a whole.[116] It is also evident that Sombart *et al.* overstate their case and that even where Jewish merchants were dominant, as in Amsterdam and other centres, this was rather short-lived.

It is equally clear that the medieval Christian limitations imposed on Jews *were* a major factor in determining Jewish economic activity and that Jewish existence in some areas did become dependent on the fact that Christian toleration of the 'witness people' entailed a toleration of banking and commercial activities.[117] The question of usury, addressed in a number of studies,[118] indicates that extensive changes were required in rabbinic law to permit the new economic activities and that these decisions were linked to communal survival.

The claim that rabbinic literature contains a mass of materials pertaining to commercial life is undeniable. This claim is often made both to distinguish Judaism from Christianity and to support free enterprise or capitalism. The Aristotelian and Thomistic notions of just price within a static economy are contrasted with Jewish conceptions. Neusner has argued that in the Mishnah, the earliest definitive code of rabbinic law, we find just such a static idealized vision of a distributive economy centred on the Temple, although he notes that mishnaic legislation is designed to both legitimate and control a market economy. But he is adamant that economic activity is only a part of the total life of the people of Israel and is set firmly within the larger comprehensive framework of the just society. Laws pertaining to economic practices are merely the vehicle through which righteousness is to be established.[119]

In this penultimate section I want to briefly explore a strange literature that has appeared in recent years. This is almost exclusively by traditionally observant Jews who are both to some extent economically and rabbinically informed. There is some merit in the argument that Fuch's (and Friedman's) anti-capitalist Jews are in the main drawn (with some notable exceptions) from those estranged from the rabbinic traditions of learning. Before the seventeenth century, rabbinic authorities had a series of sanctions extending up to 'excommunication' that ensured compliance with the law. Since then, it is *de facto* only Jews who hold themselves to be so bound that are so. In the Jewish state the situation is somewhat more complex as the rabbinic legal system is part of the state judicial apparatus, but even there rabbinic authority is severely curtailed. In Israel and the diaspora, the decisions of Jewish courts can serve as legal precedents for future cases. Rabbis writing legal texts do so either as authoritative guidance for their own group to the complexities of the law or as general exhortation, clarification, and advice. This new literature falls into the latter category and is intended to be a guide for contemporary Jewish business practice for Orthodox Jews. Typically, it runs through a series of topics, ranging from monopolies to noise pollution. It is both parallel to the recent materials on business ethics and part of a much larger literature which seeks to re-examine the sources of Jewish law in order to explicate its relevance for contemporary life.

One strand of this literature attempts to show that the modern economic theory has rabbinic parallels and that rabbinic sources could make a significant potential contribution to contemporary debates. Many of these writers conclude that the rabbis advocated a proto-capitalism. For example, Ohrenstein argues that there are rabbinic parallels to Adam Smith's 'invisible hand', opportunity cost, the business cycle, price inflation and the quantity theory of money and that the rabbis 'encouraged a competitive price system as a regulatory mechanism of the market'.[120] He considers that the rabbis with their conviction that 'apparently discordant passions strangely harmonize to the end that 'private vices' are turned into 'public benefits', were precursors of eighteenth century *laissez-faire* economic liberalism.[121] And, that their recognition that supply *and* demand plays a role in the determination of price anticipated nineteenth century theoretical developments.[122]

Other writers are a little more cautious. Meir Tamari writes that 'Judaism is not an economic system and has no clearly defined economic theory'.[123] He follows Leo Jung in insisting that Judaism is not capitalist or socialist but it should morally underlie some sort of perfect synthesis of the two.[124] He argues that the recent revival in traditional religion marks a rejection of the alternatives of socialism and capitalism, in favour of the recognition that religion must a create a moral context for economic activities. He advocates a whole gamut of rabbinic controls, as if these would secure the morality of capitalism. But, Tamari still presents a picture of Jewish law that is especially suited for capitalism, with the proviso that these limiting regulations are fully imposed.[125]

Almost all of these recent materials on Jewish law, while recognizing the need for regulation, offer what amounts to a rabbinic defence of the capitalist free-market, or at very least a particular model of the market – a model that undergirds capitalism.[126] The deficiencies of this approach lie in the fact that they tend to assemble materials set in very specific contexts and generalize from these to a market model. And, at the same time as they insists on the *practical* focus of the Jewish sources, they actually construct an *idealized* framework. In effect, they merely serve to support the New Right, many of whom already advocate some necessary moral basis for capitalism.

HAVE YOU BEEN HONOURABLE IN YOUR DEALINGS? (TALMUD, SHABBAT 31b)

The rabbis taught that on arrival in the world-to-come, the first question asked is, have you been honourable in your dealings? The enquiry relates to the acts of an individual. These acts were understood to relate directly to others and not to the operation of a system. Jews are obligated to construct a moral social system that allows justice to flourish. Such a system, it could be argued, might be socialism, capitalism, a model of welfare capitalism or some new socio-economic system.

The sources can be equally marshalled to support any of these. The question that must be asked is why so many rabbinic and other authorities interpret the tradition as bolstering some partially regulated form of market capitalism. It should not come as a shock that the rabbinic tradition within the context of the Jewish community should generally have been conservative, but it might well surprise us that it should turn out to be largely conservative in the context of the broader society. The cultural context of the rabbi in contemporary cosmopolitan society appears to necessitate a universal relevance.

The most basic error committed by our rabbinic authorities is that they, like the New Right, view the capitalist economy in terms of its eighteenth century model. This model refers to a time when businesses were largely still individually owned, property fairly widely distributed and commodities tended to refer to goods necessary, or at least useful, for life. Contemporary capitalism requires addressing a series of different concerns in order to account for the corporatization and bureaucratization of business. Private property – its rabbinic defence so blithely linked to a defence of capitalism – becomes increasingly insignificant. And, the shift from a work ethic to a consumption ethic can hardly be grasped by a reference to Genesis, chapter 2. Our staunch rabbinic defenders of capitalism, with their advocation of the market and a return to traditional values, fail absolutely to comprehend the radical modern transformation of individual consciousness. The challenge posed by the anti-traditionalism of the autonomous individual of classical political economy has yet to be fully appreciated, never mind its impending demise in fragmentation. As Anthony Giddens has recently argued, all the exhortation in the world about the amorality of elements of capitalism will not change anything if the nature of contemporary consumerist addiction is not addressed (e.g. pornography).

It is the ignorance of these and other integral structural features of current capitalism that make the rabbinic plea for the freedom of the market so naive. The rabbinic tradition does allow, within fixed parameters, a market system to operate, but it is only a shallow engagement with anti-socialist rhetoric that prematurely equates this defence of the market system with capitalism. It is an error to allow the dictates of the market system (or socialism) to define the significance of Jewish law. Capitalism in its current guise can only further destroy the traditional Jewish values. And, a full appreciation of the nature of capitalism would render Judaism and capitalism incompatible. Judaism has little to do with either socialism or capitalism. Rabbinic attention would be better served involving itself with the critique of contemporary culture – there are wonderful precedents – in order to give substance to the claim that Judaism is beyond the immediacies of any particular political system. Even a cursory review of traditional texts leads one to the conclusion that the construction of the moral society – a community based on love of fellow where economic issues are by definition secondary – requires something more radical than a few moral regulations for addressing the iniquities of our present system. The question of being honourable in your dealings must be extended to the sanctioning of a system that re-defines all individual acts. Twersky insightfully argues that the impersonality of welfarism or 'high powered mechanized philanthropy' is just as dangerous as both 'obliterate' the personal element. He interprets the halakhah as demanding nothing less than an 'all encompassing humanitas'.[127] And, it is this humanitas that Judaism teaches and seeks to embed in our daily lives.

NOTES

1 On the origins of the terms capital, capitalist and capitalism, see Braudel (1982: 232–42). There was increased usage after 1917, but no article in *Encyclopedia Britannica* until 1926 or 1936 in the *Dictionnaire de l'Académie français*.

2 Pierre-Joseph Proudhon cited in Braudel (1982: 237).

3 'Kapitalismus' was used by Engels.

4 Pulzer (1988: 42). This new context is clearly demonstrated in Pulzer's own work.

5 Sombart (1922 [1902], 1911, 1982).

6 Weber (1930).

7 Morris (1990: 179–201).

8 Deutscher (1981: 65).

9 See below.

10 There is no entry on capitalism or much that refers to the issue in either Cohen and Mendes-Flohr (1987) or Roth (1972). In Sacks (1991), an authoritative group of Orthodox leaders do not even count capitalism as one of the conditions of modernity that challenge or have to be confronted!

11 Cited in Johnson (1985: 43).

12 Toussenel (1845). Toussenel claimed that as his usage conformed to its 'popular sense', Jew and usurer are synonymous. He defined Jews, as 'Jews, bankers, dealers in spices' (1845: 4). Using Jew to designate 'deviant' Christians who are guilty of 'Judaizing', begins in the Fathers and was a common medieval practice (e.g., Bernard de Clairvaux referred to Christian usurers as 'baptised Jews', *Epistle* 343). Nineteenth century writers followed this (not yet written history of) extended usage. On the French socialists, see Silberner (1963).

13 Marx, 'Zur Judenfrage' (1844), in Marx (1971: 85–114).

14 E.g. McLellan (1972: 135–208, 266–82; 1969: 154–5) argues that these essays are vitally important as Marx's first re-working of Feuerbach's alienation thesis with reference to economics.

15 Marx and Engels (1956: 117–21, 127–33, 143–59) accused Bauer of not recognizing that the 'Jew is a necessary link' and that the bourgeois stage *must* be passed through and overcome. They supported Jewish emancipation as a phase in the 'emancipation of humanity', but still aimed to liberate mankind from bourgeois society, which was 'Jewish to the core'. Later essays continued to offer extremely negative views of Jews (e.g. on the relationship of their praxis to tyranny). The same is true of Marx's correspondence with Engels. Here, the anti-semitism was so evident that the 1913 edition (Bernstein and Bebel) was heavily censored. For example, the crude anti-semitic attacks on Lassalle, characterized by Stanley Hyman as 'obsessively anti-Semitic' (Hyman 1968: 286).

16 Bauer 'Die Judenfrage' (1843). See also, Rosen (1978). Bauer asserted that 'to Hegel, the Jewish religion could be adjudged only as a historical dead-end street committed to the endless repetition of "dead formulas"' (1843: 106). His later works include a racial theory of the incorrigible Jew (1843), which became an important source for the German political/racial anti-semitism. Marx's language and method reflect his recent reading of Feuerbach's *The Essence of Christianity* (on Judaism, see Feuerbach 1841,

trans. 1857: 113–20). For Feuerbach, theology is a reflection of humanity – the Jewish God is a mirror of the Jews – and he saw the Jewish spirit as a 'Jewish egoism', which 'makes him theoretically narrow, because indifferent to all which does not relate to the well-being of the self' (1857: 114). See also, Schuffenhauer (1965).

17 Feuerbach's formulation is 'Judaism is worldly Christianity; Christianity spiritual Judaism – the Christian religion is Judaism purified' (1841, trans. 1857: 120).

18 The attacks on Marx's gratuitous identification of Jews with capitalism by contemporary Jews (e.g. Heine 1968: 357) inaugurated an extensive literature debating Marx's anti-semitism. Marx never moved far from his notion that 'Judaism was repulsive' (Marx and Engels 1957: 418) and the evidence supports Silberner's contention that 'Marx can be and must be regarded as an out-spoken anti-Semite' (Silberner 1949: 3–52). Isaiah Berlin writes of the 'violent anti-Semitic tone of this essay' and considers that this attitude 'became more and more characteristic of Marx in his later years', affecting 'the attitudes of multitudes of communists, particularly Jewish communists, towards the Jews, and is one of the most neurotic and revolting aspects of his masterful but vulgar personality' (1981: 225; on Marx, 252–86). See Carlebach (1978); Wistrich (1976); Misrahi (1972); Hirsch (1980); Künzli (1966); Stepelevich (1974). Cuddihy (1987: 121–50) argues that Marx's attack on the 'courtesy' of civil society is conscious and that the true 'anti-philo-Semitism' of his essay is easily mis-read as 'unadulterated antisemitism' (150)!

19 *Das Kapital*, 23, 2.

20 Marx's essay was reprinted in the leading socialist organs, e.g. in *Neue Sozial-Demokrat* (1872) and *Der Sozialdemokrat* (1881).

21 See Silberner (1958, 1966); Berlin (1959 in Berlin 1981: 213–51) and Buber (1943).

22 See Marx and Engels (1975: 406). Hess also led Bakunin to the 'cause'.

23 The extent of Hess's influence on Marx is disputed, see, Wistrich, (1976: 358), Carlebach (1978: 110–24), Silberner (1966: 184–92). Marx's 'Zur Judenfrage' and Hess's 'Über des Geldwesen' (in Cornu and Mönke 1961: 329–48), both written in 1843, share fundamental concerns. Whilst Marx had probably seen Hess's essay before writing his own, there is little evidence of direct influence. Carlebach argues convincingly, however, that Marx drew heavily on this essay in his *Economic and Philosophical Manuscripts* (1844, in McLellan 1971: 130–83). Hess was one of the founders of the *Rheinische Zeitung* in 1841 and met Marx in the same year. They were part of the same group (that included Max Stirner, Bauer and Proudhon) of Paris 'exiles'. Marx later condemned Hess as 'Utopian', although Marx and Engels used part of his draft of the *Communist Manifesto* and he wrote several chapters of *The German Ideology*. In 1848 the deteriorating relations between Marx and Hess finally came to an end. Marx, Engels and Arnold Ruge referred to him as 'Rabbi Moses'.

24 Hess ('the first German socialist'; Berlin 1981: 218) organized the General Federation of German Workers – the model for all later European democratic movements – with Ferdinand Lassalle (the German (Jewish) nationalist who saw Judaism as 'most complete alienation of the spirit' and identified Jews with the basest aspects of capitalism), and is often referred to as 'father of German communism'. Hess joined Marx's International Workingmen's Association in 1867, represented Berlin workers at the First International and was a Marxist delegate in the 1860s.

25 *Die heilige Geschichte der Menschheit von einem Jünger Spinozas* (1837), reprinted in Cornu and Mönke (1961: 1–74).

26 *Die europäische Triarchie* (1841), reprinted in Cornu & Mönke (1961).

27 'Philosophie der Tat' (1843); 'Philosophy of the Act', in Fried and Saunders (1964: 249–75).

28 Hess (1862) *Rom und Jerusalem* , English trans. by M.J. Bloom (1958).

29 *Ibid.*: 21.

30 *Ibid.*: 8.

31 *Ibid.*: 18–19.
32 *Ibid.*: 22.
33 *Ibid.*: 30.
34 Popular anti-semitic pamphlets, such as *Die Juden und der deutsche Staat* (1861), drew heavily on the motifs of Jewish egoism, the Jewish God as money or profit and Judaism as trade. Socialist and conservatives influenced each other. For example, the important, socialist anti-semite, Eugen Dühring, like so many, later became a racial theorist. And conservatives, like Rudolf Meyer, who linked Jews with capitalism in the wake of the 1873 stock exchange crash, had an impact on socialist thinking. The widely accepted socialist interpretation of anti-semitism as a progressive precursor to revolution (e.g. Bebel (1906), Mehring (1957)), acted during the 1870s and 1880s as an implicit 'common cause' between Right and Left. Marxist anti-Judaism found its way into *völkische* rhetoric, often accompanied by the caveat that the masses should not oppose capitalism *per se* but Jewish capitalism.
35 Anti-semitism always a factor in socialist ideology, became acute with Eugen Dühring's popular *Kursus der Nationalökonomie und des Sozialismus* (1873). A limit was set on the widespread anti-semitism in socialist circles, marked by Engel's *Anti-Dühring* (1878); the reactions to the anti-socialism and populist political anti-semitism of Stoecker's new Christlich-soziale Arbeiterpartei (he claimed that Jews were responsible for the capitalist trends that were leading Germany away from Christianity), and the expulsion of anti-semites (as anarchists) from the party in 1880. But even after this, the socialist leader and editor of *Der Sozialdemokrat*, Eduard Berstein, wrote that many socialists saw Jews 'as the chief representatives of capitalism', and his paper declared that 'bargaining had become the fundamental principle of the German Reich', which had become 'completely Judaized' (1881). The Social Democratic Federation of 1884 reported that 'Jewish moneylenders now control every foreign office in Europe' (cited in *Jewish Quarterly* 31, 4, 1984: 89). The Jewish label was frequently launched at bourgeois 'Judaized Christians'. Many of those who attacked Judaism were themselves Jews or former Jews, for example, Bruno Schoenlank, whose series in *Neue Zeit* (1887) condemned Jews as capitalists. Franz Mehring, party official and the first 'authorized' biographer of Marx, did much to popularize Marx's 1844 essay and the equation of Judaism and capitalism. In the 1890s anti-semitism was renounced as the 'socialism of fools'. Engels (*Arbeiter Zeitung* May 9, 1890) explained it as the last ditched and transitional, reactionary attempt of those who would disappear with the demise of capitalism to try and hold back the clock. Bebel argued that the links between Jews and capitalism were historically determined by centuries of Christian ghettoization. And although he understood that Jews were the most accessible face of capitalism and that in a bourgeois society if there were no Jews then the capitalists would be Christians, he could still write 'our whole society is based on bargaining and moneymaking and is, therefore, a Judaized society' (1893, reprinted 1906: 38).
36 In the 1870s, the clarion call of anti-semites was for Germany to 'be emancipated from the Jews' (Wistrich 1976: 90) and conservatives increasingly drew on socialist materials to oppose capitalism. Later, Jews as capitalists were condemned by anti-modernist, romantic conservative parties in France, Hungary and elsewhere. The involvement of the churches in these parties linked the old to the new anti-semitism. E.g. *Civilita Cattolica* (5 February 1898), the official organ of the Jesuit order in Rome, argued that only when Jews were excluded from the nation in France, Germany, Austria and Italy would 'the old harmony be re-established and the peoples again find their lost happiness' (cited in Halasz 1955: 123).
37 Deutscher (1981: 25–41). Among the many parallel notions to Deutscher's (Jews that have severed their links with actual Jewish communities as they moved 'beyond' Judaism) are Hannah Arendt's followers of the 'hidden prophetic tradition' (*Die*

verborgene Tradition, 1976); George Steiner's 'meta-rabbis' (Villiers 1976: 75), Steiner argues for a link between traditional Jewish hermeneutics and abstract theorizing and historical analysis; and Daniel Bell's 'prophets of alienation'.

38 See Wistrich (1976). It is hard to think of socialism at all without reference to its Jewish contributors (Ferdinand Lassalle, Rosa Luxemburg, Trotsky, Eduard Bernstein, Leon Blum, Otto Bauer, Rudolf Hilferding, etc.). Brossat and Klingberg (1983) trace the history of Pale revolutionaries (Marxist, Bundist, Zionist) and their contribution to the socialist struggle. E.g. one in eight of the International Brigades during the Spanish Civil war was Jewish.

39 A link noted by non-Jewish socialists too. For example, Karl Kautsky noted that Jewish historical conditions had created a literate body of idealists committed to opposing social injustice.

40 These include Eduard Bernstein, Hugo Hasse, Johann Jacoby and Ludwig Frank.

41 Kautsky rejected Engel's explanation of anti-semitism (see note 35) after the Kishinev pogroms of 1903 and considered that the causes of anti-semitism were the enforced, and self-chosen, separation of Russian Jews, coupled with the systematic diversion of the proletariat's revolutionary energies. He advocated speedy and total assimilation. Later he argued that the Jews were a 'caste' and not a nation.

42 This was the call for 'normalization', that is, the correction of the over-concentration in marginal economic activities.

43 Carlebach (1978: 203).

44 There were many groups such as the Hebrew Socialists.

45 Otto Bauer, the Austrian Marxist, argued that emancipation had irrevocably broken international Jewish solidarity and they were no longer a nation, but, like Hess, he did see the progress of socialism through the vehicle of discrete nations.

46 There are still Bundist groups in Israel and America. On the Bund, see Tobias (1972) and Mendelssohn (1970). Also, see Frankel (1981).

47 The three separate socialist Zionist parties co-operated in Russia (the Marxist Poalei Zion; the Zionist Socialist Workers' Party; and the Jewish Socialist Workers' Party). The Left held power in Israel from 1948 until 1977.

48 Frankel (1981: 4).

49 E.g. Ber Borochov ('Our ultimate aim is socialism. our immediate aim is Zionism. The class struggle is the means to achieve both aims'), a founder of Poale Zion, developed a dialectical materialist account of nationalism. Within any given economic system there are, what we might call, the historically conditioned cultural specificities of production. These specificities gives rise to classes in tension with groups that cut across this category – peoples and/or national groups. Under conditions of stable production classes are stronger than national groups and vice versa. These tensions can and are exploited by the ruling classes. The cultural specificities of diaspora Jewry entailed that Jews lived in an aberrant inverted economic pyramid with 'no peasantry' and many too many small traders. This, coupled with anti-semitism fostered by interested parties, led to them being almost totally excluded from the emerging capitalist system. Borochov argued that for the usual economic triangle, with a majority Jewish proletariat at its base, to develop at all a territorial base – the single most significant factor in production – was required (in Israel). Only then would the conditions necessary for a class struggle ensue, leading to socialism. See Borochov (1971).

50 An interesting but rather forced example of a post-revolutionary attempt to synthesize the Talmudic Judaism and Marxist theory (slavery, the class struggle, the rise of the entrepreneur and the middle class) is found in the work (1938–50) of Soldukho (1973).

51 E.g. Nahman Syrkin's *The Jewish Problem and the Socialist State* (1898; abridged English version in Syrkin, M. (1961: 255–93)), also A. D. Gordon and Berl Katznelson. Hess's *Rome and Jerusalem* became a source for the socialist Zionist parties and also for Jewish socialist intellectuals such as Gustav Landauer, Martin

Buber and Franz Oppenheimer.

52 See Léon (1970).
53 Heller (1931: 77).
54 Cf. Unna (1934).
55 See Fishman (1989).
56 Roscher (1944). M. Arkin (1975) offers the same basic thesis.
57 Sombart's father was one of the founders of the *Verein für Sozialpolitik*, whose members became known as the *Kathedersozialisten*. He, along with Max and Alfred Weber and Friedrich Naumann were members of a younger and more socialist wing.
58 Sombart, *Sozialismus und soziale Bewegung im 19. Jahrhundert* (1901, trans. 1909). A Hebrew translation (1911) was published, translated by David Ben-Gurion, the Labour Zionist leader, who was later Israel's first Prime Minister. On Sombart, see Mitzman (1973: 135–264); Mendes-Flohr (1976).
59 Sombart (1902: vol. I, 196–7). The seventh and last edition (Leipzig, 1928) ran to six volumes.
60 In *Dennoch: Aus Theorie und Geschichte der gewerkschaftlichen Arbeiterbewegung* (1900), Sombart voices his first doubts about the transformational potential of the proletariat, and these doubts become certainties in *Das Proletariat* (1906). The possibilities and appropriateness of capitalistic development for Germany is discussed in *Volksgemeinschaft. Die deutsche Volkswirtschaft im 19. Jahrhundert* (1903), where the influence of Tönnies' communitarian ideal is evident.
61 Sombart (1903: 128–30). Arthur Mitzman (in Mommsen and Osterhammel 1987: 99–105) accounts for Sombart's work from 1900 to 1910 in psychological terms, his opposition to his father and his marital breakdown.
62 Sombart (1911, 1982).
63 Due to Sombart's book anti-semitic prejudices linking Jews with money and capitalism 'attained academic respectability' (Mosse 1981: 141). E.g. Theodor Fritsch's *Handbuch der Judenfrage* (1933: 290–2).
64 Sombart (1911: 36), references are to the 1951 translation.
65 *Ibid.*: 30–1. Weber also defined Jews racially. In his book *The Sociology of Religion* (259–61) he classified Jews as: Jewish Freethinkers; pious Orthodox Jews; Reformed Jews; Baptised Jews and Assimilated Jews.
66 Sombart (1911: 50–61).
67 *Ibid.*: 67.
68 *Ibid.*: 169–87.
69 *Ibid.*: 199, 243.
70 *Ibid.*: 248.
71 *Ibid.*: 251.
72 *Ibid.*: 187, 236.
73 *Ibid.*: 68.
74 *Ibid.*: 199–200.
75 *Ibid.*: 199–200.
76 *Ibid.*: 202.
77 *Ibid.*: 299.
78 'Homo Judaeus and Homo Capitalisticus' are exemplars of 'species homines rationalistici artifiales', *ibid.*: 239.
79 *Die Zukunft der Juden* (1912). Also, see, Sombart's views in Lansberger (1912: 1–6).
80 *Ibid.*: 52.
81 *Ibid.*: 58.
82 On this debate, see Reinharz (1975: 281).
83 In *Der Bourgeois* (1913a); *Kreig und Kapitalismus* (1913b); and *Luxus und Kapitalismus* (1913c), Nietzschean influences became a major feature of Sombart's ideal of the capitalist entrepreneur.

84 Sombart (1924': 154–6; 1934, trans. 1937: 178).
85 Sombart *Deutscher Sozialismus* (1934, trans. 1937: 74, 178).
86 On the debate between Weber and Sombart over Calvinism versus Judaism as the basis for capitalism, see the new introductory essay by S. Klauzner in the recent edition of *The Jews and Modern Capitalism* (Sombart 1982: lxxiv -lxxxv).
87 Weber (1930: 39). On Weber's views on Judaism, see ch. 10 of Liebeschütz (1967).
88 *Ibid.*: 187.
89 Weber, *Ancient Judaism* (1952); *Economy and Society* (1968).
90 Cf. this break with magic and superstition 'created the basis for our modern science and technology and for capitalism' (Weber 1961: 265).
91 Weber (1961: 611–4).
92 *Ibid.*: 615–23.
93 Weber (1952: 1). See also (1952: 336–45; 1930: 271; 1968: 250).
94 Weber (1952: 5).
95 *Ibid.*: 424.
96 Weber (1968: 614–5). See Abraham (1991).
97 E. Gellner (1983: 103–5) has argued that a dual morality is imposed by majority groups on minority groups.
98 Weber (1952: 424).
99 Weber spoke of having received from his Jewish colleagues (Simmel Eulenburg, Jellinek, etc.) 'the fine fragrance that blows to us from the mellow and ripe sensibility of the Orient'.
100 *Ibid.*: 417.
101 *Ibid.*: 50.
102 *Ibid.*: 345.
103 Fuchs (1956: 197).
104 Kristol, 'The Spiritual Roots of Capitalism and Socialism', in Novak (1979: 1–14). See Kristol (1983), especially 'Christianity, Judaism and Socialism', pp. 315–26.
105 Kristol (1983: 14).
106 *Yediyot Ahronot*, 8 July 1977.
107 Friedman 'Capitalism and the Jews', in Black *et al.* (1985: 401–419).
108 Rivkin (1971: 160).
109 Friedman, in Black *et al.* (1985: 408).
110 *Ibid.*: 416.
111 E.g. Glazer, in Blau *et al.* (1965: 42).
112 Shorris (1982).
113 Cited in Bershtel and Graubard (1983: 20).
114 (1986) *Tikkun* 1, 1: 3.
115 Baron (1975).
116 Israel (1975).
117 Poliakov (1965: 129).
118 E.g. Gottfried (1985); Gordon (1975: 111–120; 1982; 1987). Also Gamoran (1976).
119 Neusner (1990). See also Silver's insightful *Prophets and Markets, The Political Economy of Ancient Israel* (1982) and Sperber (1974).
120 Ohrenstein (1968).
121 Ohrenstein (1970a).
122 Ohrenstein (1970b; 1981) and Ben-David (1974).
123 Tamari (1986: 393–421); see also Tamari (1987, 1991a, 1991b). See also Levine (1980, 1987); Zipperstein (1983); Herring (1984); Herzog (1968); Wiesfeld (1974); Ejges (1930); Agus (1965); Shemen (1963); Shapiro (1970); Rakover (1980); Solomon (1991: 37–104).
124 'Judaism pledges its adherents neither to socialism nor to capitalism. Socialism borrowed from Judaism its emphasis on responsibility for a fellowman's welfare,

and the creation of a society in which every human will receive essential protection and security. Capitalism borrowed from the Hebrew Bible the emphasis on a man's rights to the rewards of his honest labour, limited only by the common good. If any 'ism' attaches to Judaism, it would be 'Tsedekism', the rule of tsedek, which means righteousness, fair play and human compassion' (Jung 1976: 332–43, quotation: 340). See also Jung (1964, 1945) and Jung and Levine (1987).

125 For a statement of shallow trust, see Tamari (1991), 'I think that the Israeli economy has very deep roots in Jewish thought . . . I feel that the non-Jewish traditions are the cause of our problems and that if we were to stick to the halakhah we would be alright'.

126 A case in point is the new British Chief Rabbi, Jonathan Sacks, who rightly maintains that religions are primarily concerned with 'moral ecology' – 'the environment within which a political system must work, rather than the system itself' – and are not reducible to party programmes or support for 'the free market or the welfare state' (1991: 12–13). But he can still advocate the present position that is significantly closer to free-market capitalism than anything else (1990: 183–202). The same could be levelled at his predecessor, I. Jakobovits, a very public supporter of Mrs Thatcher, whose *From Doom to Hope* (1986) advocated a market solution to poverty, particularly amongst Afro-Caribbeans, in Britain.

127 Twersky (1982: 140).

REFERENCES

Abraham, G. (1991) *Max Weber and the Jewish Question*, Chicago.

Agus, I.A. (1965) *Urban Civilization in Pre-Crusade Europe*, 2 vols, New York.

Arendt, Hannah (1976) *Die verborgene Tradition*, Frankfurt.

Arkin, M. (1975) *Aspects of Jewish Economic History*, Philadelphia.

Baron, S. (1975) *Economic History of the Jews*, N. Gross (ed.), Jerusalem.

Bauer, B. (1843) *Die Judenfrage*, Brunswick; and 'Die Fahigkeit der heutigen Juden und Christen frei zu werden', in Herwegh, G. (ed.) (1843), *Einundzwanzig Bogen aus der Schweiz*, Zurich (56–71), trans. Lederer, H. (1958), *Bruno Bauer: The Jewish Problem*, Cincinnati.

Bebel, A. (1906) *Socialdemokratie und Antisemitismus*, Berlin.

Ben-David, A. (1974) *Talmudische Okonomie*, Hildesheim.

Berlin, I. (1959) 'The lives and opinions of Moses Hess' in Berlin (1981) *Against the Current*, Oxford, pp. 213–51.

Berlin, I. (1981) *Against the Current*, Oxford.

Bernstein, E. and Bebel, A. (eds) (1913), *Der Briefwechel zwischen Friedrich Engels und Karl Marx*, Stuttgart.

Bershtel, S. and Graubard, A. (1983) 'The mystique of the progressive Jew', *Working Papers Magazine* 10, 2.

Black, W., Brennan, G. and Elzinga, K. (eds) (1985) *Morality and the Market*, Vancouver.

Blau, J.L., Glazer, N. and Handlin, O. (1965) *The Characteristics of American Jews*, New York.

Borochov, B. (1971) *Essays on Nationalism, Class Struggle and the Jewish People*, London.

Braudel, F. (1982) *The Wheels of Commerce*, vol. 2 'Civilization and Capitalism', London.

Brossat, A. and Klingberg, S. (1983) *Le Yiddishland Révolutionnaire*, Paris.

Buber, M. (1943) 'Moses Hess', *Jewish Social Studies* 7: 137–48.

Carlebach, J. (1978) *Karl Marx and the Radical Critique of Judaism*, London.

Cohen, A.A. and Mendes-Flohr, P. (eds) (1987) *Contemporary Jewish Thought*, New York.

Cornu, A. and Mönke, W. (eds) (1961) *Philosophische und sozialistische Aufsätze*, Berlin.

Cuddihy, J.M. (1987) *The Ordeal of Civility*, Boston.

Deutscher, I. (1981) *The Non-Jewish Jew and Other Essays*, London.

Ejges, S. (1930) *Das Geld in Talmud* (Yiddish), Wilno.

Feuerbach, L. (1841) *Das Wesen Christentums*, trans. G. Eliot (1857) *The Essence of Christianity*, London.

Fishman, A. (1989) 'The religious kibbutz: a note on the theories of Marx, Sombart, Weber on Judaism and economic success', *Sociological Analysis* 50, 3: 281–290.

Fourier, C. (1808, 1966) Théorie des quartres mouvements et des destinées générales, in *Oeuvres Complètes de Charles Fourier*, vol. 1, Paris.

Frankel, J. (1981) *Prophecy and Politics: Socialism, Nationalism and the Russian Jews*, Cambridge.

Fried, A. and Saunders, R. (eds) (1964) *Socialist Thought*, New York.

Fritsch, T. (1933) *Handbuch der Judenfrage*, Leipzig.

Fuchs, L. (1956) *The Political Behavior of American Jews*, Glencoe, IL.

Gamoran, H. (1976) 'Talmudic usury: laws and business loans', *Journal for the Study of Judaism* 7: 129–42.

Gellner, E. (1983) *Nations and Nationalism*, Ithaca, NY.

Gordon, A.D. (1950) *Ha Adam ve Ha Tevah*, Jerusalem.

Gordon, B. (1975) *Economic Analysis Before Adam Smith*, New York.

Gordon, B. (1982) 'Lending at interest: 800 BC – AD 100', *History of Political Economy* 14: 406–26.

Gordon, B. (1987) 'Biblical and early Judeo-Christian thought: Genesis to Augustine', in S. T. Lowry. (ed.) *Pre-Classical Economic Thought*, Boston.

Gottfried, P. (1985) 'The western case against usury', *Thought* 60: 89–98.

Halasz, N. (1955) *Captain Dreyfus*, New York.

Heine, H. (1968) *Heines Werke* V, Berlin.

Heller, O. (1931) *Der Untergang des Judentums*, Vienna.

Herring, B. (1984) *Jewish Ethics and Halakhah for our Time*, New York.

Herzog, I. (1968) *Judaism: Law and Ethics*, Jerusalem.

Hess, M. (1862) *Rom und Jerusalem*, Leipzig. English trans. M. J. Bloom (1958) *Rome and Jerusalem*, New York.

Hirsch, H. (1980) *Marx und Moses: Karl Marx zur 'Judenfrage' und zu Juden*, Frankfurt.

Hyman, S. (1968) *The Tangled Bank*, New York.

Israel, J. (1975) *European Jewry in the Age of Mercantilism 1550–1750*, Oxford.

Jakobovits, I. (1986) *From Doom to Hope*, London.

Johnson, P. (1985) *Time and Tide*, Summer.

Jung, L. (1945) 'Judaism and the new world order', *American Journal of Economics and Sociology* 3: 385–93 & 4: 515–28.

Jung, L. (1964) *The Rabbis and the Ethics of Business*, New York.

Jung, L. (1976) 'The ethics of business', in M. Fox (ed.) (1978) *Contemporary Jewish Ethics*, New York, pp. 332–43.

Jung, L. and Levine, A. (1987) *Business Ethics in Jewish Law*, New York.

Katznelson, B. (1945–50) *Kitve B. Katznelson*, 12 vols, Tel Aviv.

Kristol, I. (1983) *Reflections of a Neo-Conservative*, New York.

Künzli, A. (1966) *Karl Marx: Eine Psychographie*, Vienna.

Lansberger, A. (ed.) (1912) *Judentaufen*, Munich.

Léon, A. (1970) *The Jewish Question: A Marxist Interpretation*, New York.

Levine, A. (1980) *Free Enterprise and Jewish Law*, New York.

Levine, A. (1987) *Economics and Jewish Law*, New York.

Liebschütz, H. (1967) *Das Judentum im deutschen Geschichtsbild von Hegel bis Max Weber*, Tübingen.

Marx, K. (1971) *Karl Marx: Early Texts*, trans. David McLellan, Oxford.

118

Marx, K. and Engels, F. (1956) *The Holy Family*, Moscow.
Marx, K. and Engels, F. (1957) *Werke* I, Berlin.
Marx, K. and Engels, F. (1975) *Collected Works* vol. 3, London.
McLellan, D. (1969) *Young Hegelians and Karl Marx*, New York.
McLellan, D. (1972) *Marx Before Marxism*, Harmondsworth.
Mehring, F. (1957) *Karl Marx*, New York.
Mendelssohn, E. (1970) *Class Struggle in the Pale*, London.
Mendes-Flohr, P. (1976) 'Werner Sombart's *The Jews and Modern Capitalism*', *Leo Baeck Institute Yearbook* 21: 87–107.
Misrahi, R. (1972) *Marx et la Question Juive*, Paris.
Mitzman, A. (1973) *Sociology and Estrangement: Three Sociologists of Imperial Germany*, New York.
Mommsen, W. and Osterhammel, J. (eds) (1987) *Max Weber and His Contemporaries*, London.
Morris, P. (1990) 'Judaism and pluralism: the price of religious freedom' in I. Hamnett (ed.) *Religious Pluralism and Unbelief*, London, pp. 179–201.
Mosse, G. (1981) *The Crisis of German Ideology*, New York.
Neusner, J. (1990) *The Economics of the Mishnah*, Chicago.
Novak, M. (ed.) (1979) *Capitalism and Socialism: A Theological Inquiry*, Washington.
Ohrenstein, R. A. (1968) 'Economic thought in Talmudic literature in light of modern economics', *American Journal of Economics and Sociology* 27: 185–96.
Ohrenstein, R. A. (1970a) 'Economic self-interest and social progress in Talmudic literature', *American Journal of Economics and Sociology* 29: 59–70.
Ohrenstein, R. A. (1970b) 'Economic aspects of organised religion in perspective', *Nassau Review*: 27–43.
Ohrenstein, R. A. (1981) 'Some studies of value in Talmudic literature in the light of modern economics', *Nassau Review*: 48–70.
Poliakov, L. (1965) *Les Banquiers juifs et le Saint-Siège*, Paris.
Pulzer, P. (1988) *The Rise of Political Anti-Semitism in Germany and Austria*, London.
Rakover, N. (1980) 'Unjust enrichment', *Jewish Law Annual* 3: 9–32.
Reinharz, J. (1975) *Fatherland or Promised Land: The Dilemma of the German Jew 1893–1924*, Ann Arbor.
Rivkin, E. (1971) *The Shaping of Jewish History: A Radical New Interpretation*, New York.
Roscher, W. (1944 [1875]) 'The Jews' function in the evolution of medieval life', *Historia Judaica* 6: 3–12. First published (1875).
Rosen, Z. (1978) *Bruno Bauer and Karl Marx: The Influence of Bruno Bauer on Karl Marx*, The Hague.
Roth, C. (ed.) (1972) *Encyclopaedia Judaica*, Jerusalem.
Sacks, J. (1990) 'Wealth and poverty: a Jewish analysis', in *Tradition in an Untraditional Age*, London, pp. 183–202.
Sacks, J. (ed.) (1991a) *Orthodoxy Confronts Modernity*, New York.
Sacks, J. (1991b) *The Persistence of Religion*, London.
Schuffenhauer, W. (1965) *Feuerbach und der junge Marx*, Berlin.
Shapiro, A. (1970) 'Rabbinical responses and the regulation of competition', *American Journal of Economics and Sociology* 29.
Shemen, Ben (1963) *The Jewish Attitude Towards Labor* (Yiddish), 2 vols, Toronto.
Shorris, E. (1982) *Jews Without Mercy*, New York.
Silberner, E. (1949) 'Was Marx an anti-semite?', *Historia Judaica* 11, 1: 3–52.
Silberner, E. (1958) *The Works of Moses Hess*, Leiden.
Silberner, E. (1963) *Sozialisten zur Judenfrage*, Berlin.
Silberner, E. (1966) *Moses Hess: Geschichte seines Lebens*, Leiden.
Silver, M. (1982) *Prophets and Markets: The Political Economy of Ancient Israel*, New York.

Soldukho, Y. A. (1973) *Yu. A. Soldukho: Soviet Views of Talmudic Judaism*, Jacob Neusner (ed.), Leiden.

Solomon, N. (1991) *Judaism and World Religion*, London.

Sombart, W. (1900) *Dennoch: Aus Theorie und Geschichte der gewerkschaftlichen Arbeiterbewegung*, Jena.

Sombart, W. (1901) *Sozialismus und soziale Bewegung im 19. Jahrhundert*, Jena. English trans. M. Epstein (1909) *Socialism and the Social Movement*, London. First published (1896).

Sombart, W. (1903) *Volksgemeinschaft: Die deutsche Volkswirtschaft im 19. Jahrhundert*, Berlin.

Sombart, W. (1906) *Das Proletariat*, Frankfurt.

Sombart, W. (1911) *Die Juden und das Wirtschaftsleben*, trans. M. Epstein (1951) *The Jews and Modern Capitalism*, Glencoe, IL.

Sombart, W. (1912) *Die Zukunft der Juden*, Leipzig.

Sombart, W. (1913a) *Der Bourgeois*, Munich. English trans. M. Epstein (1915) *The Quintessence of Capitalism*, London (1951 Glencoe, Illinois: Free Press).

Sombart, W. (1913b) *Kreig und Kapitalismus*, Munich.

Sombart, W. (1913c) *Luxus und Kapitalismus*, Munich.

Sombart, W. (1922) *Der moderne Kapitalismus* 2 vols, Leipzig & Munich. First published (1902).

Sombart, W. (1924) *Der proletarische Sozialismus*, Jena.

Sombart, W. (1934) *Deutscher Sozialismus*, Berlin. English trans. Geiser, Karl F. (1937) *A New Social Philosophy*, Princeton.

Sombart, W. (1982) *The Jews and Modern Capitalism*, S. Klauzner (ed.), New Brunswick.

Sperber, D. (1974) *Roman-Palestine 200-400: Money and Prices*, Ramat-Gan.

Stepelevich, L. (1974) 'Marx and the Jews', *Judaism* 23, 2: 150–60.

Syrkin, M. (1961) *Nachman Syrkin: Socialist Zionist*, New York.

Syrkin, N. (1898) *Die Jundenfrage und der sozialistische Judenstaat*, Berne.

Tamari, M. (1986) 'Judaism and the market mechanism', in W. Block and I. Hexham (eds) *Religion, Economics and Social Thought*, Vancouver, pp. 393–421.

Tamari, M. (1987) *With All Your Possessions: Jewish Ethics and Economic Life*, New York.

Tamari, M. (1991a) *In the Marketplace: Jewish Business Ethics*, Southfield, Michigan.

Tamari, M. (1991b) 'Religion as an antidote to socialism and capitalism', paper delivered to conference on *Religion and the Resurgence of Capitalism*, University of Lancaster, July 1991.

Tamari, M. (1991c) article in *L'Eylah* 32: 2–6.

Tobias, H. (1972) *The Jewish Bund in Russia*, Stanford.

Toussenel, A. (1845) *Les Juifs rois de l'époque*, Paris.

Twersky, I. (1982) 'Some aspects of the Jewish attitude to the welfare state', in *Studies in Jewish Law and Philosophy*, New York.

Unna, M. (1934) 'Die Jüdische form des religiösen Sozialismus', *Zion* 6, 1, Berlin.

Villiers, D. (ed.) (1976) *New Year in Jerusalem*, London.

Weber, M. (1930) *The Protestant Ethic and the Spirit of Capitalism*, London. First published (1904–5).

Weber, M. (1952) *Ancient Judaism*, Glencoe, IL. First published (1917–19).

Weber, M. (1956) *The Sociology of Religion*, London.

Weber, M. (1961) *General Economic History*, New York.

Weber, M. (1966) *Sociology of Religion*, London.

Weber, M. (1968) *Economy and Society*, New York. First published (1922).

Weisfeld, I. (1974) *Labor Legislation in the Bible and Talmud*, New York.

Wistrich, R. (1976) *Revolutionary Jews from Marx to Trotsky*, London.

Zipperstein, E. (1983) *Business Ethics in Jewish Law*, New York.

6

RELIGION AND THE TRANSITION TO A 'NEW WORLD ORDER'?

Some preliminary evidence from Canada

Peter Beyer

INTRODUCTION: RESURGENT CAPITALISM IN A NEW WORLD ORDER?

The world scene of the past few years has been anything but dull. As a symbolic starting point, let us take the weekend of 3–4 June 1989. Those two days saw the death of the Ayatollah Khomeini, a rail–gas pipeline disaster in the central Soviet Union that took hundreds of lives, and the massacre of students in Tienanmen Square. Intriguingly enough, the second of these events, the one that probably the fewest people remember, was in a symbolic sense the most indicative of what was to come that fall: the virtually total collapse of Soviet-style socialism. Real and symbolic walls came tumbling down; not even Albania was to escape the effects. In many parts of the world, but especially in First World countries, the mood was optimistic, even euphoric. The Cold War was over. While the cracks in the planned command economies of the East turned into open fissures, the capitalist heartlands were experiencing a period of economic growth that had lasted throughout much of the 1980s. In this atmosphere, various observers began using terms like 'resurgence of capitalism', 'new world order', and even 'end of history'.[1]

As we know, the optimism did not last. Periodic boom gave way to periodic recession. Saddam Hussein decided to use the military capital he had amassed during his eight year battle with the 'fundamentalist' revolution to his east in order to invade Kuwait. The result was the first post-Cold War war, a one-sided, devastating, and inconclusive affair that gave George Bush's own proclamation of a new world order a hollow and ironic ring. In general, the break-up of the Soviet Union left in its wake not Pax Americana but uncertainty and regional horrors like the Bosnian civil war.

Faced with this daunting sequence, we should perhaps all throw up our hands and admit that something is happening, but we don't know what it is. There is, however, at least one undeniable common thread running through these events, and that is their global reach and global involvement. Around the world, we are more than incidental observers of the phenomena. The Gulf war was one of the clearest examples of near global involvement; as have been subsequent United Nations 'peacekeeping' operations in places like Somalia and Cambodia. For these and all the other events, especially Tienanmen and the demonstration effect of the Eastern European developments, the fact of global observation itself affected what happened next, albeit not in an easily predictable way. Because such global communicative entanglement is so noticeable, those who speak of a new world order featuring resurgent capitalism may be pointing to a key aspect of the current world-historical juncture. They may also, at the very least, be oversimplifying or getting too much caught up in the drama of the moment.

The operative questions, of course, centre around the ideas of resurgence and newness. Does the collapse of socialism mean an actual resurgence of capitalism? Does the fact that there are, as it were, manifest contradictions in state-centred socialism mean that the manifest contradictions of market capitalism are no longer problematic? Then again, does the end of the Cold War era mean a new world order or simply the altered continuation of the old one? In this chapter, I set myself two tasks. To begin, I apply recent globalization/world-system theory to the questions just posed. This theory is directly relevant because it posits a globally extended social system as its primary unit of analysis; and thus addresses precisely the sort of global communicative entanglement that current events demonstrate. Using certain variants of this theory, I defend the hypothesis that we are today perhaps in the midst of a particular phase in the globalization of our social world and that contemporary upheavals are symptomatic of being in this phase; but that, by and large, the continuities between, say, the early 1980s and the early 1990s, are so strong as to make talk of resurgence or new order – let alone the end of history – an indulgence in hyperbole, although perhaps not an entirely misleading one.

My second task is to test this hypothesis in a very preliminary way by focusing on the role of religion in the globalization process. For reasons that I explain below, religion is in an ambiguous position in global society. It represents at once an important way of communicating and one that, at the global level, is at a structural disadvantage when compared to more powerful modes such as positive law, politics, economy, and science. As such, it tends to become the privatized concern of its adherents. And yet, the functional characteristics of religion also make it a suitable perspective from which to address the 'residual' problems of global society, namely those that the operation of the more powerful globalizing systems (economy, states, etc.) creates but does not solve. Put in slightly different terms, globalization privatizes the priestly functions of religion, but encourages its prophetic applications.

This implication of religion in the globalization process, I suggest, makes it one area of human endeavour where we can attempt to gauge whether we are in fact experiencing the dawning of a new world order of resurgent capitalism. In particular, we can ask if the prophetic criticism that religious leaders and activists level at the global system is shifting in some dramatic fashion. If so, then that would constitute at least a preliminary indicator from a group of global actors who have, through their pronouncements, organizations and actions, responded clearly to previous phase changes in the process of globalization. If they shift, this may point to a global shift. The above hypothesis would lead us to expect no consistent trend in this direction.

Religious people, of course, do not share a uniform outlook. The applications of religious resources in the modern global context are in fact quite diverse. One of the more significant axes of variation, however, is going to be the attitude that religious actors take toward the global system as such. Do they see it in liberal fashion as a largely positive development, albeit perhaps with critical problems? Or do they take a more conservative position, viewing the globalization of the social world as a negation of what they hold sacred and of the good human life in general? In this chapter, I focus primarily on the former, and specifically on the attitudes of the Canadian liberal Christian elite. That narrowing is to some degree arbitrary. Theoretically, other religious segments should also be sensitive to global phase shifts; and empirically have been. From the turn of the last century, we might pick movements as diverse as the Christian Fundamentalists in America and the Hindu Arya Samaj in India; and from the post-Second World War period, the Buddhist Soka Gakkai in Japan and Latin American liberation theology. Canadian liberal Christianity has had its corresponding movements, most notably for my purposes here, the social justice radicalization of the late 1960s to early 1970s. It therefore promises to make a good case study since past developments within the same organizations can serve as the basis of comparison for possible changes in direction today.

In searching for local expressions of a wider global process, this chapter examines the attitudes among the Canadian liberal religious elite to fundamental issues such as what is required to achieve social justice and move toward world peace. Have these changed in a more 'pro-capitalist' direction in the sense of a revaluation of capitalist values, and the relative devaluation of socialist goals? Or have they changed dramatically at all?

To carry out this task, I have done a qualitative content analysis of public documents issued by the churches in question, but above all by the inter-church bodies in which they participate. The dates of these documents range from the mid-1970s to 1993, with heavy concentration on more recent years. The documents chosen address a wide range of issues, both national and global. Special attention was paid to those issues that touch directly on globalization and the capitalist economy, in particular Third World development and debt, the arms race, human rights around the world but especially in Eastern bloc countries, and global trade. The results of this analysis offer confirmation of the hypothesis, albeit inconclusively. Liberal Canadian religious attitudes in the very late 1980s and early 1990s show a great deal of continuity with the immediate past, but criticism of the capitalist system may be getting more nuanced, reflecting perhaps a gradual acceptance of that system as part of the global picture.

123

GLOBALIZATION AND RELIGION: THE CURRENT PHASE

Globalization

The globalization discussion among social scientists is relatively new. With hindsight, we can trace its beginnings for practical purposes to the late 1960s and early 1970s. It is during this time that we begin to see theoretically elaborated views of the contemporary world that take as their primary unit of analysis a social system geographically coterminous with the globe (see, e.g. Nettl and Robertson 1968; Luhmann 1971; Wallerstein 1974). This feature distinguishes such positions from others with a worldwide orientation, for instance, the field of international relations.

The participants in the globalization debate are by now quite numerous; but certainly the names of Immanuel Wallerstein and Roland Robertson stand out in the sense that their somewhat differing views of the structures and processes involved have been nodal points around which many other contributions have centred.

For Wallerstein, what he calls the world-system is primarily economic: it is the capitalist world-economy. The system has various other features, such as states and global-cultural themes, but these are dependent manifestations. Following Marxist and dependency theory perspectives, the most basic structure of the global system is its division into dominant core and dependent peripheral or semi-peripheral regions (Wallerstein 1979, 1990). Wallerstein expects the problems of capitalism to result in its eventual demise, yielding a single world socialist state.

Robertson, by contrast, focuses precisely on those aspects that are dependent variables for Wallerstein: national societies and global-cultural themes. He is centrally concerned with the way individuals and collectivities construct global/ universal and particular identities in the context of systemic globalization (Robertson 1992; Robertson and Lechner 1985). Robertson thereby allows cultural life-world factors an independent and constitutive role in the globalization process, while not denying the systemic aspect that Wallerstein stresses.

These connections are perhaps suggestive, but they do not by themselves show precisely how empirical religious attitudes can be reflective of more macrosocietal transformations. Rather than follow either the Wallersteinian or Robertsonian versions too closely, I take a synthetic approach, one that incorporates key elements from Niklas Luhmann's theories.

Pursuing this path, globalization has come about as a result of the rise in early modern Europe of functionally oriented societal systems that came to displace communal and status-oriented systems as the dominant systems of the society. The most powerful of these systems were a capitalist economic system, a political system of formally equal states with corresponding positive legal systems, and a scientific-technological system. Largely because of their instrumental, cognitive orientation, these systems eventually spread around the globe in spite of the diversity of established cultures.

As Robertson's emphasis on identities and culture makes clear, however, the instrumental systems are not the whole story. Just because they are functionally specialized, these systems leave much of social life out of consideration, if not unaffected. Various terms refer to this realm: it is the life-world, the private sphere, the domain of expressive action, the realm of individual and cultural identity. Moreover, the continuing operation and elaboration of the dominant globalizing systems is not unproblematic. The very efficacy of these systems enhances not only wealth, power, knowledge, and other means by which humans can control their surroundings; it also generates new problems such as constant and rapid social change with an attendant unpredictability, exacerbated disparities in life-chances among humans, unavoidable juxtaposition and power-struggles among often very different world views, the build-up of ever more potent means of destruction, and natural environmental alteration/degradation. On the other hand, the same globalizing developments have generated certain core values which intensify the unacceptability of these problems, most especially the inter-related values of progress, equality, freedom, pluralistic inclusion, and – more recently – sustainability. For those who adhere to these values, including most liberal religious people, the operation of the globalizing systems carries at least a measure of unfulfilled expectation. To many, it amounts to an inherent contra-diction in the world system.

Although these problems occur as a direct result of the dominance of the instrumental systems, they are not problems of these systems as such. Inequality in life-chances is not a problem of the capitalist economic system; profitability and capital growth are. Ecological destruction is not as such a scientific problem; its understanding is. Hence, from the point of view of the dominant systems, these are *residual* problems. In calling them residual, I do not imply that they are marginal: they are just as constitutive of the global social field as the dominant systemic preoccupations (cf. Robertson 1992).

Religion in global society

For the key arguments of this chapter, residual problems are important because religion has a strong affinity for them. That is, addressing residual problems is perhaps the most significant way in which religion makes its presence felt in global society. To see how this is the case, we must first situate religion in the globalizing context.

Although it has also generated a functionally oriented system, religion is not like the world capitalist economy or the global system of sovereign states. Like other functional domains, religion is potentially applicable to everything. But because of its holistic approach and supra-empirical reference, functional differenti-ation aimed at the creation of a specialized system of purely religious communication runs the risk of making religion generally relevant in all situations, but instru-

125

mentally relevant in comparatively few. In pre-modern societies, this functional peculiarity was often an advantage; today it is far less so. Put more concretely, before the ascendancy of such instrumentally specialized social systems as for economic production, political decision-making, scientific explanation, or academic education, religious modalities provided essential support for a large portion of communication in these domains. Since then, however, we have witnessed significant pressure to displace, marginalize, or privatize religiously based approaches to these tasks as different regions have become enmeshed in the global system.

If we accept this description, then the core problem of religion in global modernity is that it does not lend itself well to the sort of instrumental specialization typical of functional subsystems like economy, polity, or science. That difference does not mean the irrelevance of religion, however.

From its holistic point of departure, religion addresses all those matters about which the other functional systems communicate, plus all that they leave out. As I noted above, these systems are effective and globalizing, but there is much that they exclude. In its general applicability, therefore, religion can and, I suggest, often does serve as a kind of system 'specializing' in what, from the perspective of the dominant functional systems, are residual matters. Religion's view, under modern and globalizing conditions, is therefore typically 'anti-systemic' in the sense that religious adherents, professionals, and leaders tend to see their communication as essential because it addresses the problems that the dominant systems either leave out or create without solving. This does not necessarily make residual problems religious, but it does establish a structural and functional affinity between the two.

Religion and phases of globalization

Periodizations are almost always problematic. This is especially so if the historical development under scrutiny is centuries long and, furthermore, still incomplete. Precisely because of these features, however, some attempt at phasal analysis is probably inevitable, if only to lend requisite flexibility and complexity to theoretical interpretations.

In the case of globalization theories, both Roland Robertson and the Wallersteinians have attempted to approach the historical development in terms of successive phases. The latter have generally used economic cycles such as Kondratieff (45–60 years) and so-called long waves (150–300 years) (see Bergesen and Schoenberg 1980; Wallerstein 1984). In his more recent work, Robertson has presented his own, significantly less economically oriented version of the phases of globalization (Robertson 1992). In spite of their differences, the two theorists agree on the broad timing of the phases.

Both Wallerstein and Robertson agree that the current phase began in the mid to late 1960s. For Wallerstein it has been a period of cyclical economic decline, of political uncertainty in the relations among states, and of upheaval in the realm of anti-systemic movements (see Wallerstein 1976, 1988). Although his view is less mono-systemic, Robertson largely agrees. What he calls 'the uncertainty phase' has several interrelated features. These include a heightened awareness of globalization along with enhanced concern with humanity as a species-community, the inclusion of the Third World, a great increase in global institutions and movements, the end of the Cold War and therefore a more fluid international system (Robertson 1992: 58f.). Before the current one, Wallerstein and Robertson see previous phases occupying the late nineteenth/early twentieth century, the inter-war period, and the post-Second World War decades up to the 1960s. Neither specifically predicts a next phase featuring resurgent capitalism, although the Wallersteinian position would postulate another prolonged period of global economic expansion beginning sometime around the turn of the next century. Important for the current context, both theorists characterize the present phase as in key ways uncertain.

Synthesizing these two points of view is perhaps not that difficult. For Robertson, the current phase of globalization is witnessing the end of what he calls dispute over the 'terms of the dominant globalization process' (1992: 59). In Wallersteinian terms, it is today not only less and less possible for a country or region to pursue an independent path outside and in opposition to the world capitalist system; it is also much more difficult even to conceive this as possible. A heightened sense of interdependence results, whether in core or peripheral areas. The major globalizing subsystems have entered a stage of consolidation in which their dominance as global-structural realities is no longer or at least far less in question. Of course, this says nothing about the future of the world system, its sustainability or fragility, its quality as good or evil. It does mean that the communicative net of global society is now sufficiently dense to create the kind of increase in global consciousness to which Robertson refers. The uncertainty that both theorists stress may well be a sign of this actual globality. For better or worse, there may now only be 'one game in town'. Speculating, we might say that, in the current phase we are coming to realize that fact; in the next phase we will take it as given.

In turning to the role religion plays in the more recent phases of globalization, I restrict myself to liberal religion. Religious leaders, organizations, and movements of this stripe will embrace the increased density as exhibiting the wholeness and singleness of the human community. They will orient themselves explicitly and positively to the global system; but will also focus very specifically on its residual problems. The orientation will, in general, be pro-systemic and anti-systemic at the same time. If we are entering a new phase marked by a significant strengthening of capitalism, then the attitude to the fact of globality will not change; but the assessment of residual problems should change in one of two directions: either in a pro-capitalist direction that sees capitalism as 'the only game in town', or in an almost conservative one that despairs in the light of the intractability of residual problems after the bankruptcy of what seemed for long to be a socialist alternative.

127

Canadian liberal religious attitudes

As a religious segment, the Canadian liberal mainline is representative of this type of Christianity throughout the Western world. Developments in its history, while different in detail, have been similar to those of the corresponding churches in Western Europe, the United States, Latin America, and Australasia. In this regard, they are the successors to those religious organizations involved in the worldwide missionary spread of Christianity that was an aspect of European imperial expansion. From the Christian perspective, they were key players in the globalization of the religious system and therefore have always been intimately involved in the globalization process as a whole.

Following either Wallerstein's or Robertson's phasal model, the Christian mainline in Canada as elsewhere unequivocally reflected the more recent phase shifts as the globalization process has intensified. Among the Protestants, the late nineteenth and early twentieth century saw the effective liberalization of theology, the spawning of inclusive ecumenism, and the development of the residual-problem-oriented Social Gospel movement. The more conservative Roman Catholic church launched its pillarizing social Catholicism direction, a noticeable shift from a previous, more reactionary period. The post-Second World War era witnessed the formation of the globally inclusive World Council of Churches and, somewhat later, the Second Vatican Council. Both these developments involved the recognition of Christianity's global extent and a de-emphasis of its European/North American based cultural identity; or, conversely, they signalled the recognition in principle of equal status for Third World Christians (cf. Lee 1992; Wuthnow 1987: 215–64).

Of critical importance for my purposes here, however, were the changes of the late 1960s and early 1970s. Corresponding to the downward turn of the latest Kondratieff long wave and to the beginning of Robertson's 'uncertainty' phase as exemplified for instance in the counter-cultural new social movements, both Roman Catholic and mainline Protestant Christianity produced a new, radically this-worldly, religious direction focused above all on 'social justice' problems. Perhaps the most well-known manifestation of this shift was Latin American liberation theology and its attendant movements; but that beginning became much more widespread within a very few years (cf. e.g. Brown 1978; Ferm 1986). Among the more significant results in Canada were the sudden proliferation of increasingly radical social statements on the part of various church leaders (see Baum and Cameron 1984; Williams 1984) and the spawning of ecumenical social action organizations, including those known as inter-church coalitions. Both these changes contrast markedly with the more subdued character of previous leadership pronouncements and with the relative absence of social justice oriented ecumenical organizations, especially ones including the Roman Catholic church.

These rather clear manifestations of previous liberal religious phases can serve as a basis of comparison for looking at what has been happening lately within the same Christian segment. I continue to restrict myself to the representative Canadian case.

To begin, one must note the absence of new organizational developments. The various ecumenical and/or social justice organizations such as the Canadian Catholic Organization for Development and Peace, the Canadian Council of Churches, or the various inter-church coalitions are still in place and internally unchanged. Economic hard times have in many cases reduced their budgets; and, following the example of the World Council of Churches, ecological issues have been raised to a level of importance somewhat comparable with social justice issues (cf. Beyer 1994: ch. 9). Unlike in the United States (see Kearns 1990), this high profile for environmental issues since the late 1980s has not resulted in significant new Canadian mainline Christian organizations dedicated to those concerns. Given the strong organizational developments associated with previous phases, this absence may well be significant for the question under discussion.

More clearly telling, however, are developments – or the lack thereof – in the social justice pronouncements of these churches and their ecumenical bodies. Here a brief look at the typical statements of the 1970s to early 1990s is necessary to appreciate what has and has not changed.

Between the early 1970s and the early 1980s, the official statements issued by liberal church leaders and elite activists often displayed an increasingly radical or anti-systemic tone. Condemnations of capitalism, the global economic order, transnational corporations, international financial institutions, and government policies supporting these appeared in documents recommending an 'option for the poor', a symbolic position that favoured socialist alternatives and some degree of withdrawal from the capitalist world-system. Perhaps the most widely commented and clearest example of this trend was a 1982 statement issued by the Canadian Catholic bishops entitled, 'Ethical Reflections on the Economic Crisis' (CCCB 1982; cf. Williams 1984; Sheridan 1987). But one of the ecumenical inter-church coalitions, originally named GATT-Fly and later changed to Ecumenical Coalition for Economic Justice (ECEJ), has been particularly consistent in this regard, directing its efforts at grass-roots, anti-systemic mobilization (see GATT-Fly 1985; ECEJ 1990). Beginning in the early 1980s, however, a more moderate, more pro-systemic position began to assert itself among the same elite group of church actors. Its difference *vis-à-vis* the more anti-systemic direction is that, while adopting many of the same positions, its advocates hoped to influence the actions of governments, corporations, and international bodies such as the Conference on Security and Cooperation in Europe and the World Bank. Their documents therefore exhibit the more moderate tone and technical analyses that would enhance their chances of being taken seriously in the corridors of wealth and power (see e.g. CCC 1985; TCCR 1989). The anti-capitalism here becomes much more implicit.

In recent years, the more moderate position seems to be on the ascendant among the church leadership and the activist elite. This contrasts with the situation of the early 1980s. While that is certainly a change, it probably reflects the developing expertise of the church activists in matters such as arms proliferation and international finance rather than a more basic change in the direction of criticism and activism. Compared with the much greater changes of the late 1960s or the post-Second World War periods, it pales in comparison. Moreover, the continued presence and legitimacy of the more radical perspective alongside the moderate one indicates not so much change as precisely uncertainty.

CONCLUSIONS

The continuity of positions and organization among the Canadian liberal Christian elite from the late 1980s to the early 1990s supports the notion that we are not as yet experiencing a new phase of globalization, a new world order of resurgent capitalism, for instance. That is of course only a very preliminary and, some might say, even weak indicator. Yet these representatives of one segment in a globalized religious system have responded rather clearly to previous changes of this nature. It is not illogical to expect them to do it again. Two more general conclusions follow, one concerning global society and the other religion's place in it.

If the evidence I have presented here is indeed indicative, then it points to a global society which has become so highly interconnected and complex that even such a momentous 'local' event as the collapse of the Soviet empire may be no more than an outstanding symptom of larger, more gradual developments that directly involve us all. By itself, it does not amount to a resurgence of capitalism. In Wallersteinian terms, it simply shows how powerful this economic system has been for quite some time.

With respect to religion, the conclusion is somewhat more complicated. Although the actual influence liberal religious elites and organizations have on world events may be doubted, the evidence does suggest that here is a segment that has been consistently in tune with global developments. We may, perhaps, even go so far as to say that what has been happening in Canadian liberal Christianity is largely incomprehensible except in the context of global processes. As such, while a local, small, and seemingly insignificant case, Canadian religion as an example of global liberal religion bears a similar relation to contemporary globalization as seventeenth and eighteenth century Protestantism bore to modernization, most particularly the incipient development of what has since become the global capitalist system. This is not to say that we should now talk about the 'Social Justice Ethic and the Spirit of Globalization' to parallel Weber's 'Protestant Ethic and the Spirit of Capitalism'. If anything, this evidence points away from a necessary or causal relation between the latter two. Nonetheless, in spite of privatization, marginalization, and even perhaps a trend toward deinstitutionaliz-ation, liberal religion does still represent a promising domain for understanding larger historical change. While the sectarians and the 'fundamentalists' may as yet be attracting most of the scholarly and media attention, liberal developments may be the more significant for discerning and comprehending the next phase of globalization: with rapidly growing diasporas in many religious traditions, it is not out of the question that we may finally see a consolidation of liberal trends in religions beside Judaism and Christianity.

NOTE

1 The last phrase was, of course, revived by Francis Fukuyama in his 1989 article, 'The end of history' (see Fukuyama 1989, 1992).

REFERENCES

Baum, G. and Cameron, D. (1984) *Ethics and Economics: Canada's Catholic Bishops on the Economic Crisis*, Toronto: Lorimer.

Bergesen, A. and Schoenberg, R. (1980) 'Long waves of colonial expansion and contraction, 1415–1969', in A. Bergesen (ed.) *Studies of the World-System*, New York: Academic, pp. 231–77.

Beyer, P. (1994) *Religion and Globalization*, London: Sage.

Brown, R.M. (1978) *Theology in a New Key: Responding to Liberation Themes*, Philadelphia: Westminster.

CCCB [Canadian Conference of Catholic Bishops] (1982) 'Ethical reflections on the economic crisis', in E.F. Sheridan (S.J.) (ed.) (1987) *Do Justice! The Social Teaching of the Canadian Catholic Bishops (1945–1986)*, Sherbrooke & Toronto: Editions Pauline & The Jesuit Centre for Social Faith and Justice, pp. 399–410.

CCC [Canadian Council of Churches] (1985) *Canada's International Relations: An Alternative View. An Enhanced World Role for Canada*, Toronto: CCC.

ECEJ [Ecumenical Coalition for Economic Justice] (1990) *Recolonization or Liberation: The Bonds of Structural Adjustment and Struggles for Emancipation*, Toronto: ECEJ.

Ferm, D.W. (1986) *Third World Liberation Theologies: A Reader*, Maryknoll, NY: Orbis.

Fukuyama, F. (1989) 'The End of History', *The National Interest*, 16, Summer: 3–18.

Fukuyama, F. (1992) *The End of History and the Last Man* , New York: Free Press.

GATT-Fly (1985) *Debt Bondage or Self-Reliance: Popular Perspectives on the Global Debt Crisis*, Toronto: GATT-Fly.

Kearns, L. (1990) 'Redeeming the earth: eco-theological ethics for saving the earth', Paper presented to the Association for the Sociology of Religion, Washington, DC.

Lee, R.W. (1992) 'Christianity and the other religions: interreligious relations in a shrinking world', *Sociological Analysis*, 53: 125–139.

Luhmann, N. (1971) 'Die Weltgesellschaft', *Archiv für Recht sund Sozialphilosophie*, 57: 1–35.

Nettl, J.P. and Robertson, R. (1968) *International Systems and the Modernization of Societies: The Formation of National Goals and Attitudes*, London: Faber.

Robertson, R. (1992) *Globalization: Social Theory and Global Culture*, London: Sage.

Robertson, R. and Lechner, F. (1985) 'Modernization, globalization, and the problem of culture in world-systems theory', *Theory, Culture & Society*, 2, 3: 103–18.

E.F. Sheridan (S.J.) (ed.) (1987) *Do Justice! The Social Teaching of the Canadian Catholic Bishops (1945–1986)*, Sherbrooke & Toronto: Editions Pauline & The Jesuit Centre for Social Faith and Justice.

TCCR (1989) 'The international debt crisis: a discussion paper prepared for the Canadian churches', prepared in co-operation with representatives of GATT-Fly and the Inter-Church, Inter-Coalition Debt Network, July.

Wallerstein, I. (1974) 'The rise and future demise of the world capitalist system: concepts of comparative analysis', *Comparative Studies in Society and History*, 16: 387–415.

Wallerstein, I. (1976) 'Semi-peripheral countries and the contemporary world crisis', *Theory & Society*, 3: 461–83.

Wallerstein, I. (1979) *The Capitalist World-Economy*, Cambridge: Cambridge University Press.

Wallerstein, I. (1984) 'Long waves as capitalist process', *Review of the Fernand Braudel Center*, 7: 559–75.

Wallerstein, I. (1988) 'Typology of crises in the world-system', *Review of the Fernand Braudel Center*, 11: 581–98.

Wallerstein, I. (1990) 'Culture as the ideological battleground of the modern world-system', *Theory, Culture and Society*, 7, 2–3: 31–55.

Williams, J.R. (ed.) (1984) *Canadian Churches and Social Justice*, Toronto: Anglican Book Centre & Lorimer.

Wuthnow, R. (1987) *Meaning and Moral Order: Explorations in Cultural Analysis*, Berkeley: University of California.

Part II

THE NEW HANDMAID? RELIGION AND THE EMPOWERMENT OF CAPITALISM

7

QUASI-RELIGIOUS CORPORATIONS

A new integration of religion and capitalism?

David G. Bromley

The historical connection between religion and capitalism has been a major intellectual issue in social science from the time of Marx and Weber. Whatever the final resolution of that storied debate, the relationship between religion and capitalism has continued to evolve through Western history and has assumed a variety of forms in different locations within the social structure. Among the most significant trends in the recent history of Western societies has been an increasing disjunction between the contractually organized public sphere of social life (structured principally by the economy and state) and the covenantally organized private sphere (structured principally by the family, community and religion), with an increasing hegemony of the former over the latter.[1] This chapter examines one organized response to the disjunction between the two spheres, the flourishing of what I here term quasi-religious corporations.[2]

Quasi-religious corporations promise to reintegrate work, politics, family, community and religion through the formation of *family*-businesses that are linked together into a tightly-knit social network and legitimated symbolically by appeals to nationalism and transcendent purpose.[3] These hybrid entities mix corporate and social movement organizational forms at the distributor network level, manifesting characteristics that sociologists of religion traditionally refer to as sectarian. There are a substantial number of quasi-religious corporations in the United States, and increasingly in Europe as well.[4] In addition to Amway, the more prominent quasi-religious corporates include Mary Kay Cosmetics (beauty aids), Herbalife (vitamins, food supplement products), A.L Williams Insurance (term life insurance), Tupperware (food containers), Shaklee (nutritional products) and Nu Skin (cosmetics and nutritional products). Amway, the largest and most fully developed of these quasi-religious corporates, is utilized as an illustrative example of this phenomenon.

SOCIOCULTURAL ROOTS OF THE QUASI-RELIGIOUS CORPORATE FORM[5]

Throughout American history material success has been a preeminent cultural

135

goal that has structured both institutional arrangements and the lives of individual Americans (Merton 1968: 185–214). One important source of cultural under-pinning for pursuit of economic success emanates from what social historians term the Gospel of Prosperity. The Gospel asserts that America has a special covenant with God – that in return for obeying his mandates and creating a Christian nation that will eventually carry His message and the American way of life to the entire world, God will raise up America as His most favoured people. The Gospel of Prosperity, which has taken a number of forms through American history, assumed its modern form in the post-Civil War period when individual prosperity came to be viewed as the reward for personal virtue and integrity.

An important development linking spirituality with material success of indi-viduals was harmonial philosophy, which has as one of its major tenets that 'spiritual composure, physical health, and even economic well being are under-stood to flow from a person's rapport with the natural order of the cosmos' (Ahlstrom 1972: 1019). Failure to realize personal prosperity is therefore mental and self-imposed. By this logic, individuals can literally think their way to wealth by being attuned to the Infinite and appropriately using their God-given faculties. Waldo Trine, a popular writer around the turn of the last century, wrote that ' . . . in just the degree that you realize your oneness with this Infinite Spirit of Life, and thus actualize your latent possibilities and powers, you will exchange dis-ease for ease, inharmony for harmony, suffering and pain for abounding health and strength' (Trine 1897: 56). Material abundance too would flow naturally. Writes Trine (1897: 176), 'He who lives in the realization of his oneness with this Infinite Power becomes a magnet to attract to himself a continued supply of whatsoever things he desires'. A second central tenet of harmonial philosophy is the concept of *true success*, which means using wealth in the service of greater humanity rather than simply amassing a personal fortune. Service to others is thus the purest expression of success as well as a certain path to ensuring one's own attainment of wealth.

The cultural themes of economic success, positive thought, service to others and transcendent purpose have been evident in economic organizations over the last century of American history. Perhaps the most lionized corporate leader in American history, Henry Ford, made such appeals in the form of a vision of automobile manufacturing that transcended the innovative production processes he developed. To Ford his invention was 'concrete evidence of the working out of a theory of business which I hope [is] more than a theory of business – a theory towards making the world a better place to live' (Collier and Horowitz 1987: 70). More specifically, Ford believed that companies like his would offer 'a cure for poverty and misery far superior to the humanitarian projects of reformers', and he went so far as to assert that the abolition of poverty in fact 'is the only legitimate purpose of business' (Greenleaf 1968: 16).

Edward Fuller, the founder of Fuller Brush Company, which is the historical forerunner of the contemporary quasi-religious corporates discussed here, projected a similar lofty vision of door-to-door sales of brushes and cleaning materials. In his autobiography he states that 'the ultimate goal [of business] is not to make money, but to secure the future of many persons, the nation under which they prosper, and the world at large' (Fuller and Spence 1960: 237). He thought of himself as 'a reformer, eager to attack the dirt and domestic labor of the city, destroying the one and alleviating the other' (Fuller and Spence 1960: 87). This crusade against domestic drudgery rendered the selling of useful products synonymous with service to others. When one served others by making certain that the product offered 'as much altruistic benefit as it yields the seller in money,' then personal success would soon follow (Fuller and Spence, 1960: 87). Fuller insisted that his own success was due not to exceptional talent but to being in tune with the Infinite. As he put it, 'The only conclusion I can reach from my own personal experience is that there is a tremendous power somewhere that can lift any person, however mediocre, to great opportunity, affluence and happiness' (Fuller and Spence, 1960: 3).

There are a number of similarities between early direct sales organizations, like Fuller Brush, and their contemporary counterparts, such as Amway. Direct sales organizations most commonly sell personal use products with high profit margins in face-to-face transactions that take place in the buyer's home. The economic viability of direct sales rests on avoiding direct competition with other products in retail stores, eliminating middlemen and minimizing costs associated with advertising, sales staff salaries and benefit packages. The best known quasi-religious corporates incorporate the appeals to positive thought, service to others, economic success and transcendent purpose that traditionally have been employed by direct sales organizations. In contrast to earlier direct sales organizations, however, the ideologies and organizational structures of quasi-religious corporates are designed to create considerably higher levels of participant mobilization. They seek to enlist entire families in an enterprise that is touted as having vital significance in restoring meaning and control to the lives of members as well as the potential for transforming American society. For the quasi-religious corporates, personal commitment and belief in the cause are more important than specific skills or prior experience. Likewise, there is no financial barrier to participation as the cost of becoming a representative is nominal compared to that of obtaining a franchise with any major national business chain. Once recruited, distributors form tightly-knit networks of true believers who are on a mission and who seek to enlist others to their cause. Quasi-religious corporates usually have charismatic leaders, minimal bureaucracy, few rules and little hierarchy of authority. Their allure is the promise to restore a naturally ordained order of prosperity and unity of life.

THE SOCIAL SIGNIFICANCE OF QUASI-RELIGIOUS CORPORATIONS

Direct sales organizations have a long history in the United States, but recent decades have witnessed a notable expansion in the number of such organizations, their sales volume and the number of industry workers. Most of the prominent firms in the industry have been founded since 1950. Amway, Mary Kay, Shaklee, Tupperware and Home Interiors and Gifts all were established in the 1950s and 1960s; Herbalife and Nu Skin were founded in the 1980s. Available data (Biggart 1989: 51–2) suggest that sales volume and the size of the sales force expanded steadily from the mid-1960s through the mid-1980s. Overall industry sales were approximately $3 bn in 1964 and soared to just over $8.5 bn by 1984. The number of distributors grew from 1,500,000 in 1964 to nearly 6,000,000 by 1984. As a result, quasi-religious corporates now constitute a major force in the American economy. Direct sales organizations produce nearly $10 bn worth of goods and services and are a major source of employment. National survey data indicate that 16 percent of American adults have at some time worked in direct sales, and 8 percent currently work in the industry (Biggart 1989: 2, 50). The labour force in the direct sales industry is 80 percent female (Biggart 1989: 50); many of those women work on a part-time basis as a means of boosting family income without forfeiting their domestic role.

The reason for the popularity of quasi-religious corporates like Amway is not difficult to discern. Career success is an important basis of Americans' sense of achievement and self-validation, and the economic resources generated through occupation pursuits are used to pursue the rich and fulfilling private lives that Americans regard as the ultimate source of personal meaning. Although economic success remains a preeminent goal in American society, for many Americans it has become increasingly elusive.

The relationship between families and the economy during recent years has been dramatically altered by a number of factors. One of the most significant is the increase in the number of women in the labour force. The Bureau of Labor Statistics reports that the percentage of women who work increased from 39 percent in 1970 to 49 percent in 1978 and to 57 percent in 1989. Projections for the 1990s indicate that two out of every three new workers in the labour force will be female, but women entering the labour market frequently work at low-paying jobs. The result is that even though the number of working wives has doubled, average family income has risen only 6 percent since 1973 (Gibbs 1989: 58–67). Work-related activity also has been appropriating a larger share of each day. Survey data indicate that the average American's leisure time decreased by 37 percent between 1973 and 1989; during that same period the average working week increased from 41 to 47 hours (Hewlett 1990: 54).

Money and time are not the only issues, however critical these are, as the very nature of contemporary work life is changing. The scale of corporate enterprise continues to burgeon as a result of the formation of immense corporate holding companies. For example, in 1945 the 200 largest corporations controlled 45 percent of American industry's total assets; by 1984 that figure had soared to 61 percent (Simon and Eitzen 1990: 88–9). The pace of corporate mergers and consolidations continues to accelerate. The value of corporate mergers, which was $44 bn in 1980, rose to $190 bn by 1986 (Simon and Eitzen 1990: 88–9). Businesses such as restaurants, convenience stores, auto service centres and real estate firms that once were locally owned and operated now increasingly are organized as local franchises of national corporations. The result is that a very large number of Americans work for vast, bureaucratically organized corporations in which work life has become increasingly competitive and regimented. Salary increases, promotions in rank and recognition for work well done are the measures of success in these hierarchically organized bureaucracies, and there are few opportunities for dramatic career breakthroughs. As a result, the mid-career baby boom generation fears

> . . . becoming trapped in junior positions for the rest of their lives. Their fellow baby-boomers, an extremely large and able cohort of men and women, [are] competing with them for a limited number of positions at the top . . . . Anxiously scanning the business and financial worlds in search of opportunities for rapid advancement beyond their fellows, the ambitious [are] attracted by the promises of various self-help schemes.
>
> (Starker 1989: 141)

Traditional job security has declined even for white collar workers as corporate policies and decisions reflect the economic priorities of their holding companies. This erosion of job security enhances the attractiveness of alternatives to traditional employment. It may not be surprising, therefore, that both men and women responding to a recent national survey question probing the nature of their 'dream job' selected as their first choice 'to own or manage their own company' (Gibbs 1989: 64).

Americans have been forced to come to grips with the reality that the American dream is becoming expensive, even if both spouses work. Family income has actually declined in recent decades. The median annual incomes of workers increased from $15,000 to $24,000 between 1955 and 1973, but income then declined by 19 percent to just under $20,000 by 1987. Between 1972 and 1988 real wages for middle and low income workers actually dropped by 12 percent (Gwynne 1990: 80). In the meantime, the cost of owning a home and providing for a college education for children, the twin pillars of the American dream, has skyrocketed. The price of housing has increased 56 percent and college tuitions have increased 88 percent *in real dollars* over the past twenty-five years. Home ownership among young families is actually declining because the carrying cost of home ownership has almost doubled, from 21 to 40 percent of income. US government data released in 1986 reveal 'the first sustained drop in home ownership since the government began keeping records in 1940' (Stacey 1990: 256). Families are absorbing the escalating cost of the American dream by incurring more debt and financing expenditures over ever longer periods of time. The result is that household debt soared from 77 percent of annual income in 1980 to 94 percent of annual income in 1990 (Hewlett 1990: 54). Many Americans looking ahead now discover that their futures quite literally are mortgaged. Families face an even graver threat since there has been a decline in the proportion of families in the middle income range, from 46 percent in 1970 to 39 percent in 1985. (Stacey 1990: 257). For a growing number of American families even their class position is at risk.

American families thus find themselves confronted with countervailing behavioural imperatives that episodically generate considerable tension. Family and economy remain integral to one another but in some critical respects are mutually incompatible. Families rely on the economy as the source of employment that yields both income and the goods and services necessary to sustain domestic life. Families also compose the labour pool for the economy and, in a consumption-based economy, the primary outlet for products and services. This integrality notwithstanding, economy and family make simultaneous, competing demands on individuals' time, energy and commitment. The escalating cost of realizing the traditional American dream of economic success requires greater involvement in the economy; the equally valued modern goal of attaining self-fulfilment and self-actualization requires greater involvement in private life. This dilemma gains force from the behaviour and characterological imperatives of the two spheres. The contractually organized public sphere requires autonomous, rational-calculative, impersonal, self-interested conduct compatible with bureaucratic organization. By contrast, the covenantally organized private sphere calls for mutually supportive, cathectically responsive and spontaneous, personalized, committed conduct appropriate to family, religion and informal interpersonal networks. The impact of the countervailing imperatives of economy and family lends a rhetorical hollowness to the cultural maxim of 'having it all' and constitutes the ultimate source of the pervasive search for some means to reintegrate these divergent elements of life.

AMWAY: AN ORGANIZATIONAL SKETCH

Rich DeVos and Jay Van Andel, the founders of Amway, were high school friends who went into business together after graduation as distributors for Nutrilite, a food supplements company. They were extremely successful, building a sales organization with over 2,000 distributors. When they feared that Nutrilite faced imminent financial collapse in the late 1950s, DeVos and Van Andel formed a new company, 'The American Way Association', later renamed Amway. The product line initially was based on marketing two of the first biodegradable detergent products sold in the United States as well as a variety of other household cleaning products. Again, DeVos and Van Andel were extraordinarily successful. Retail sales grew from a $500,000 in 1959 to $500,000,000 twenty years later, and sales surpassed the billion dollar mark in the early 1980s. Based on this rapid growth, Amway became one of the 300 largest industrial corporations in the United States, second only to Avon Products in the direct sales industry. Amway expanded its operations into international markets and diversified its product line to include not only beauty aids, toiletries, hosiery and jewellery, but also durable goods such as furniture, electronics products, automobiles and even satellite dishes.

The Amway system is disarmingly simple (Juth-Gavasso 1985: 98–111; Lester 1974: 12–18). The corporation operates as a supplier of products and support services to distributors; individual distributors purchase products from Amway but own and operate their own distributorships independently.[6] No credentials and only a minimal financial investment are necessary to establish a distributorship. One becomes a distributor through sponsorship by an already established distributor, and new distributors initially must purchase Amway products from their sponsors. After maintaining a stipulated business volume for a prescribed period of time, however, new distributors may 'go direct'. Becoming a 'Direct Distributor' makes one eligible to purchase products at wholesale cost directly from Amway. Once they have reached direct distributor status, individuals are able to increase their incomes through some combination of selling more Amway products themselves at retail prices, earning graduated bonuses based on sales volume, acting as wholesalers to new distributors who they sponsor, and receiving a percentage of the profits of the distributors they sponsor. Beyond Direct Distributor, there is a system of ranks designated by precious stones – Ruby, Pearl, Emerald, Diamond, Double Diamond, Triple Diamond, Crown, and Crown Ambassador. Attainment of these ranks brings greater prestige and income as well as a variety of bonuses, such as cruises on the Amway yacht or expense-paid trips to exclusive resorts. The top distributorship levels offer the potential for additional, and more controversial, sources of income. Successful and visible Amway distributors can receive lucrative fees for speaking at Amway seminars and rallies, and some sell a variety of motivational books and tapes to lower ranking distributors. Achieving a level of success commensurate with the high expectations of most new distributors hinges primarily on recruiting an extensive network of 'downlines' rather than on retail sales of Amway products.

At the national corporate level, Amway and its leadership also support a range of conservative causes that champion traditional capitalism (Morgan 1981). In 1977 the corporation purchased the Mutual Broadcasting System, to air more 'balanced' coverage of political events through its network of radio stations, and it funds the Institute for Free Enterprise, to offer teachers instructional materials for communicating basic economic concepts to schoolchildren. Amway distributors were a major influence in establishing Citizens Choice, a conservative equivalent to the more liberal advocacy group, Common Cause. DeVos and Van Andel have given substantial financial support to conservative foundations such as the Heritage Foundation and the American Economic Foundation. Both have also made substantial donations to conservative religious groups such as the Christian Freedom Foundation, Gospel Films, Radio Bible Hour, Back to God Hour and Robert Schuler's Hour of Power. DeVos and Van Andel are closely connected to the Republican Party, as evidenced by Ronald Reagan's speaking appearances before Amway audiences and DeVos' appointment as the Finance Chairman of the Republican National Committee.

141

DAVID G. BROMLEY

AMWAY AS A QUASI-RELIGIOUS CORPORATION

Among the characteristically sectarian features of Amway as a quasi-religious corporate are (1) a transformative ideology and supporting rituals, (2) an organizational style featuring charismatic leadership, conversion experiences as the basis for volitional membership, tightly-knit community and distancing from conventional society, minimal bureaucracy and egalitarian relationships among participants; and (3) persistent tension with the institutions of larger society.[7]

Amway ideology and ritual

Amway ideology draws heavily on the harmonial philosophy tradition. As Lester observes, Amway distributes written and oral materials that

> constantly refer to a source of power in the universe to which every man may have access through certain technical procedures. Every human being is a potential vessel for this power, and can learn to tap its source. The body is described as a set of channels through which this power can run, though it may be dammed up by negative blocks. The key to tapping into this source of power is utter and absolute belief that one can do so. Any doubt, any negative feelings, and power is impossible to come by. Thus the secret to success is to continually intensify one's desire to succeed and one's belief that one will succeed.
>
> (Lester 1974: 30)

The basic message of Amway ideology is that Americans have lost touch with their roots, with the qualities that made America great – individual freedom to achieve, strong families and unswerving devotion to God and country. Once upon a time, the ideology preaches, an individual's financial success in life was limited only by ability, imagination, initiative and persistence. Somewhere along the way America lost the essential elements of its greatness.

> America – the Land of Opportunity. The place where an individual has always had an honest shot at the Big Time. However poor the start in life, there is an opportunity to break out to a richer life. That is the American Way, the tradition of hungry, hard-working men and women breaking out of the life of the have-nots, to take their places among the haves. That tradition has in recent years felt the squeeze of new grim realities. The golden promise of the New World has receded a bit, and some argue that it is gone altogether – that for a person to begin with nothing and work his way into the ranks of the wealthy is virtually a thing of the past, a casualty of our times. People just don't have an honest chance to do that anymore, they say.
>
> (Conn 1982: 35)

As the dream and the opportunities on which it was based receded, American workers became resigned to the fact that 'the job is just a job, a way to put bread

142

on the table, a forty-hour chore between weekends' (Conn 1982: 174). Even though the labour force is predominantly white collar, those comfortable incomes offer no guarantee of real personal freedom. A successful surgeon-turned-Amway-distributor captured the sense of frustration he experienced at feeling trapped despite achieving considerable financial success: 'The better I did, the worse off I was. My practice owned me. The more successful it became, the less I enjoyed it' (Conn 1982: 30).

According to Amway ideology, there still is a way to achieve the American dream of freedom and opportunity, one limited only by one's belief and commitment. As Amway apologist Charles Conn (1982: 35) puts it, 'In Amway, the tradition of breaking out is still alive and well'. Amway is *the* answer because it is the

> most efficient system of economic organization known to man . . . guaranteeing the right of free choice [where] the consumer is king . . . . [It] encourages and protects human freedom because political liberty and economic freedom are impossible without each other. And, finally, free enterprise offers the individual the greatest opportunity for self-expression and self-improvement because it guarantees each individual the right to pursue his own objectives and dreams.
>
> (Green and D'Aiuto, 1977: 312)

The fate of individuals becoming trapped in stultifying, regimented jobs is not the only consequence of the receding American dream. Perhaps even more damaging to society is the fragmentation of families. Both husbands and wives increasingly pursue individual careers; as a result, they spend much of their lives apart and have little to share with one another even when they are together. Children also suffer as they have little opportunity to experience, or even observe, what it is their parents do outside of the family. The consequence is a weakening of the fabric of the family as closeness between spouses diminishes and children lack strong role models. Both individual achievement and strong, loving families take on larger meaning when placed in the context of democratic freedoms and divine purpose – God and country – that make them possible. Unfortunately, religion and patriotism also have become marginal to the daily work and family lives of many Americans.

Amway promises to remedy these vexing problems of modern society. The vision is of a real, attainable opportunity for individuals to regain control over their own lives and at the same time to bring work, family, community, country and religion back into their proper relationship. Rich DeVos captured the Amway sense of buoyant optimism in a speech to distributors:

> This is an exciting world. It is cram-packed with opportunity. Great moments await around every corner . . . . I believe in life with a large "yes" and a small "no". I believe that life is good, that people are good, that God is Good. And I believe in affirming every day that I live, proudly and enthusiastically, that life in America under God is a positive experience.
>
> (Birmingham 1982: 60)

In De Vos' view the very essence of the American way of life is the free-enterprise system, and he asserts that it is 'a gift of God to us, and we should understand it, embrace it and believe in it' (Morgan 1981: A2). There are even some Amway enthusiasts who envision potential for contributing to world peace and understanding. One asserted that 'If there were Amway in every country, people wouldn't bomb each other, they're not going to kill each other. They'd be killing their own distributors – no way' (Biggart 1989: 120).

In the tradition of Social Darwinism (Hofstadter 1955), there is a harsh side to the individualistic, free-enterprise ideology. Failure is regarded as the product of a lack of personal belief in and commitment to success. There is little sympathy among Amway adherents for failure. For example, Rich De Vos rejects the idea that there are 'a lot of people in this country whose needs are not being met' and insists that residents of areas like Chicago's South Side slums live there because that is 'the way they choose to live' (Morgan 1981: A2). The path to success involves a variety of proscriptions as well as prescriptions for living that reflect traditional American values. The leader of one of the major distributorship lines lectured a gathering of distributors:

> There's no dirty jokes or vulgarity, ever, offstage or onstage, ... There's no alcohol ever . . . and that goes for other mind benders, dope and things like that . . . . We believe, basically, that communism is satanic. We don't believe in Darwinism . . . socialism . . . heathenism and all those other 'isms'.
>
> (Allen 1988: A-6)

The Amway vision that there is a realistic probability for dramatically transforming one's life circumstances requires a leap of faith for most potential participants. A number of parables are told in Amway circles in order to fortify participants' resolve against their own doubts as well as scepticism from outsiders.[8] For example, one of the tales told and retold within Amway ranks is the story of the reluctant spouse, which forewarns recruits and recruiters alike to anticipate resistance to accepting the Amway dream. An enthusiastic husband who sees the potential of Amway encounters a 'negative wife' who responds to her husband's initiative by insisting, 'Chuck, I will never sell *anything* to *anybody* at *anytime*' (Conn 1982: 69). In the reluctant spouse narrative, once the wife comes to realize that Amway builds strong marriages and cohesive families the couple joins in a mutual commitment to Amway as a business and a way of life. This story is also important to Amway because it emphasizes the importance of a family partnership and Amway's contribution to a strong family. Even after joining Amway, new distributors remain vulnerable to criticism and rejection from sceptical acquaintances, co-workers and relatives. It is therefore not surprising that another favourite Amway tale used to buoy the resolve of novitiates is one of the resolute distributor who perseveres in the face of doubt and opposition and ultimately proves the cynics wrong. For example, one distributor tells of quieting scoffing co-workers by mailing them photocopies of ever larger bonus cheques. Another recounts how he made a statement simply by moving out of his old home into an exclusive neighbourhood. He recalls

> You know, neighbors laugh .... But I can't hear them over here, they're so far away. They're over there in that section where the houses cost about a third of what they cost where I live.
>
> (Lester 1974: 26)

Amway ideology is preached in frequent gatherings at which participants reinforce one another's commitment to their way of life. The most striking of these ceremonies are the periodic seminars and rallies that bring together separate distributor networks. These events feature testimonials by successful distributors who offer encouragement and advice while conspicuously displaying their wealth in order to bolster neophytes' motivation and commitment.[9]

> A master of ceremonies opens the event with miscellaneous facts or stories about successful distributors and the growth of Amway. Then the featured speaker(s) are introduced and enter the stage area amid cheers, applause, and the theme music from Rocky. The Guests speak for about an hour delivering what may be termed their variation of "How we got involved in Amway and became successful". In addition, the speakers usually have with them color slides depicting some of their material possessions (homes, boats, cars) and pictures of the places they have travelled (Hawaii, Hong Kong) in conjunction with their Amway business.
>
> (Juth-Gavasso 1985: 177–8)

The rallies resemble religious tent revivals as 'Speeches and award presentations are continually punctuated by shouts of "Ain't it great?" and "I believe". Directs call out "How sweet it is!"' (Lester 1974: 26).[10]

These ritualistic observances represent dramatic enactments of bedrock American values. They attest that Amway has succeeded in restoring fairness (i.e. equality of opportunity) to the Contest of Life. The successful engage in communion with the soon-to-be successful, and the corporation creates a level playing field by acting as a neutral referee, offering the same encouragement, resources and recognition to every distributor, great or small. The testimonials of ordinary individuals who have become fabulously wealthy confirm that Amway has eliminated the modern corporate requirement for large amounts of capital or educational credentials to enter the contest. Personal effort, commitment and belief are the important ingredients of success, qualities that any individual can bring to the contest. The unity of the gathering demonstrates that the quest for success does not mandate cut-throat competition because the divinely ordained opportunity for success is limitless. Contestants therefore freely celebrate each other's successes and form mutually supportive social networks as they each pursue their own destiny. Sales and recruitment activities become honourable pursuits since selling useful and beneficial products to others or selling others on joining the company is a form of serving and caring for others. These rituals also represent an attempt to downplay and manage the enormous inequality that in fact exists within Amway ranks. During the course of these ceremonial occasions, successful distributors mingle with, offer encouragement to, and share the 'secrets' of the success with aspiring neophytes. Unity is fostered by insisting on a distinction not between successes and failures (outsiders are the failures) but between those who have already achieved success and those who are on the verge of success.

Amway thus offers a world of security and certainty. Success is defined in material terms, creating a clear distinction between 'winners' and 'losers'. Everyone has been endowed by their Creator with the natural potential to achieve success. The key to success is understanding this divinely intended right to prosper, remaining absolutely convinced that one will succeed despite present circumstances and constantly rekindling the motivation to succeed. Maintaining the proper frame of mind will create the diligence of effort required to succeed. Failure results from having a negative mental attitude, and individuals who are failing are due little sympathy since they could choose to do otherwise.[11] The most generous and constructive way to help others who are struggling in life is to share the Amway vision with them so that they will have an equal opportunity to succeed. Material success leads naturally to self-fulfilment, as individuals gain a sense of confidence and mastery, and to freedom, as families garner the resources to live as they wish.

Conversion

As envisioned by its most ardent proponents, Amway is not just a business, it is a way of life. Even if ultimately Amway merely provides a supplementary source of family income, many Amway distributors initially anticipate much more. The risk of giving up a relatively predictable corporate career, a stable income and perquisites such as health insurance, life insurance and retirement plans in pursuit of the Amway dream is daunting, however, and requires a leap of faith. Upon listening to a presentation of the Amway marketing plan or attending an Amway sponsored function, some individuals experience precisely both that kind of transformation in their world view and a concomitant sense of excitement, anticipation and commitment. In short, they undergo a conversion experience. One husband described the feelings that he and his wife experienced during a weekend Amway rally in terms which closely parallel the symbolism of a religious conversion:

> I don't think my wife and I said a word most all weekend long, and I know we didn't sleep any. Well, we got excited. We made a commitment to ourselves and I made a commitment to her and we made a commitment to ourselves to this business that we're going to make it grow. My people say, "When do you know when you're committed? How do you know when it's time?" Well, it's just like, you know, when you're in love – you know! Nobody has to tell you.
>
> (Lester 1974: 41)

In other cases the decision to become involved in Amway is expressed in more explicitly religious language that captures the sense of integration of life that new participants feel.

> . . . on Sunday morning, I came to know the Lord more than I ever had in my life. And we really enjoyed that. It's the greatest thing that's ever happened. That really got us started in the business. And I think if everybody'd take the Lord in their business, ask him to help you, and do the business right and listen to your sponsor, that things'll really start going for you.
>
> (Lester 1974: 41)

Yet another individual who for years had suffered from an ulcer and a speech impediment reported a physical healing as well as renewed personal confidence and optimism about the future as a result of his affiliation with Amway.

> My energy level was up and I found my speech becoming fluent. It was the excitement of the business and getting my mind off myself. People at work were flabbergasted that I was volunteering to stand up in front of people and talk. Most of us reach a plateau where there is no future. What Amway does is to remove that lid.
>
> (Morgan 1981: A2)

The Amway distributors seeking to convert new prospects often conceive of themselves as helping others to attain what they have always wanted out of life. The process of evangelizing, of course, also reinforces the proselytizer's own commitment. Describing the Amway plan to potential new distributors involves a visual depiction of how the plan leads to financial success, referred to as 'drawing circles'. One distributor described his own feelings about this process in the following way:

> Drawing circles is my therapy. When I get in front of that board, I pour my heart out. I always feel good and clean when a get through, because I know I've given it my best shot. Life can get you down if you let it, but I won't let it.
>
> (Conn 1982: 102)

One way that sponsors attempt to increase new distributors' confidence in the commitment they have made is through pledging a reciprocal commitment to the neophyte's success.

> If you will give this thing your best, I'll give you my best. I'll work harder than you will. I'll stay up later than you will. I'll drive more miles; I'll talk more hours; I'll invest more time; I'll do more in every area than you will, to help *you* be successful in this business . . . . And if you don't believe it, try me!
>
> (Conn 1982: 63–4)

Once individuals (or hopefully husband–wife teams) have converted, sponsors reinforce the initial conversion euphoria with intense involvement in Amway activities.

What is the demographic pool from which most Amway converts are drawn? The corporation advertises itself as the ultimate equal opportunity employer by showcasing the diverse gender, occupational, social class, and ethnic and racial backgrounds of its distributors. Research on Amway distributors indicates that distributors are not a representative sample of the overall American population, however, even if a broad spectrum of Americans have participated in Amway. On average, distributors are likely to be in their young adult years, have finished high school but not college, earn low incomes, and hold politically and religiously conservative attitudes (Juth-Gavasso 1985: 84; Johnston 1987: 112–18). In contrast to prominent quasi-religious corporates such as Mary Kay and Tupperware, Amway ranks are not as dominated by women and there is strong emphasis on male leadership in business activity. It is not surprising that younger families with modest incomes and limited educational credentials are most likely to find Amway appealing, for they have fewer resources at their disposal to pursue the traditional American dream. These same families also are most likely to resonate with the spiritual and patriotic overtones of the Amway message.

Organization

Central organizational attributes of quasi-corporates like Amway include charismatic leadership, strong group solidarity and egalitarianism. The awe approaching reverence with which Rich DeVos and Jay Van Andel, the founders of Amway, are viewed is compelling evidence of their charismatic authority. From the perspective of Amway distributors, it was these two men who possessed the special vision not only to discern the dilemma confronting contemporary American families, but also to conceive of a remedy that would give families control over their own futures. When Rich DeVos speaks at Amway gatherings, he is quite literally treated like a conquering hero. When he 'arrives to greet an audience, the thunderous applause, whistles and foot stomping must be seen to be believed' (Birmingham 1982: 58). Outsiders and novitiates frequently are astonished by such veneration. One new distributor confided that 'When I got into the business and people would talk about . . . Rich DeVos I would go, "Oh, my God, they talk about him like he's God or something"' (Biggart 1989: 142). Lower levels of leaders possess less of this prophetically based charisma but may command a parental level of moral authority and influence over their downlines.

> In Amway, where the sponsors perform the task of resocialization, the relationship between the sponsor and distributor is, ideally, intense and time consuming, and especially so at the outset. The extent to which distributors are encouraged to view their sponsors as performing an essentially parental role is striking.
>
> (Lester 1974: 42)

As one distributor put it, 'Just like a mother, you gotta have a sponsor' (Lester 1974: 42). Like model parents, sponsors spend a great deal of time with their novice distributors in order to ensure that they will 'duplicate correctly', which means having total trust in their 'uplines', doing exactly as they are told and attending every function organized by their uplines (Johnston 1987: 31).

The high level of group solidarity in Amway is a product of both scepticism from outsiders and intense involvement in Amway-related activities. The constant round of selling, business meetings, demonstrating the Amway plan, reading and listening to motivational materials, fortifying the resolve of new distributors, socializing with other distributors who share the faith, and attending seminars and rallies can leave little time for former friends and activities. Periodic seminars and rallies unify ordinarily autonomous distributor networks. For many distributors, becoming part of these distributor networks creates a sense of community. One distributor who had been through a difficult divorce declared, 'I found a family I never had. There was a tremendous amount of love and acceptance, support in growing' (Biggart 1989: 86). This sense of acceptance and trust is fostered by encouraging distributors to enjoy and participate in one another's victories rather than regarding fellow distributors as competitors. Co-operation is based on the belief that the opportunity for success is limitless and therefore can best be achieved through mutual support. The socially alienating component of competition is thereby muted as individuals need only struggle against their own lack of faith.

Since the Amway ideal is a family-run business composed of a husband–wife team, the corporation goes to great lengths to strengthen joint spousal commitment to the business. The vision of family that Amway seeks to instill and reinforce poses no threat to traditional family organization. Both husband and wife are treated as equal partners in the business, but husbands are the leaders and wives are encouraged to support their husbands. As the leader of one of the major distributorship networks admonished his audience:

Ladies, I'm not putting you down – I think you're better than your guys are.
But I'm just stating a simple fact: that men should make business decisions.

His wife then responded

Number 1: Support your husband . . . and the beaches of the world will be yours. I was a secretary for 16 years, and now I have my own.

(Allen 1988: A6)

The emphasis upon Amway as a business prevents feminization of the male role by too close an association with the household, and the supporting role women play in business activity blunts any implication that women are abdicating their primary roles as wives and mothers. Providing acceptable roles for both spouses permits Amway to mobilize the family unit rather than individuals, which fosters a high level of organizational commitment.

The intense commitment exhibited by many Amway members may also be a product of different forms of organizational involvement. Research on mainline religious denominations 'suggests that persons with high status are more likely than lower-class persons to be committed at an instrumental level – through investment of time and money in the formal structure. Lower-status persons are more likely than higher-status persons to be committed at the affective level – through close friendship networks' (Roberts 1990: 222). Some research on Amway suggests a comparable phenomenon (Johnston 1987: 130–63). A survey of just over 100 Amway distributors indicated that moral involvement (based on non-material incentives such as helping others, promoting religious values, friendly people) is more strongly related to organizational commitment than calculative involvement (based on material incentives resulting from such instrumental activities as showing the Amway plan, motivating downlines and intensive involvement in Amway organizational endeavors). Further, the study found a weak relationship between moral involvement and distributor success but a strong relationship between calculative involvement and success. Moral and calculative involvement were only moderately related to one another.

These findings suggest that the Amway dream and the community of believers may be important factors in sustaining organizational commitment for at least some individuals, irrespective of financial success. Amway leaders clearly recognize that these differences exist. In a public address Rich DeVos stated that

> The great performers in Amway are a unique breed of people. Those are the real goers, the tigers of the world. But there are all sorts of people in Amway. There are the Maudes and the Nellies out there, and the Johns, too, who just sell a hundred bucks worth a month. How do we keep them? They don't have any great results . . . they get a $3-a-month bonus check. We keep them around, because they have a sense of involvement. Because we recognize their self-worth. We keep telling them we love them for whatever they do.
>
> (Morgan 1981: A2)

Ultimate victory according to Amway ideology, of course, is attaining a level of economic success that yields the personal freedom to live life as one pleases without any economic constraints. However, there are other levels of personal victory – in believing that one can and will succeed and in becoming one of the elect associated with the organization that makes success attainable to everyone. From this perspective, all Amway adherents can count themselves winners. Clearly, despite Amway's legal status as a corporation, many adherents continue involvement out of affiliative rather than sheerly economic motives. Intense commitment is often short-lived, however, and the turnover rate among distributors is high. Estimates for the direct sales industry as a whole are that turnover is about 100 percent annually, and there is little reason to believe that Amway departs significantly from those estimates.

Conflict

Tension between Amway and the larger societal environment in which it operates emanates from the very organizational structure through which Amway generates its strength and effectiveness. Amway combines sectarian/social movement and corporate/economic organizational forms that create hybrid combinations of religion and business and of family and business. The resulting organizational style and practices run counter to cultural conventions and, in some instances, legal conventions. One source of conflict is the mixing of salvationist hopes with explicit promises of financial returns on investment; another is the totalistic lifestyle that is engendered by tightly integrating work, family, religion and community.

As a champion of economic salvationism, Amway markets hope as aggressively as soap. While Amway ideology and rituals only encourage adherents to hope, dream and visualize unbounded material success, some distributors seeking new recruits for their Amway networks are less circumspect in their descriptions of the monetary success new distributors will enjoy. Government officials in a number of states have investigated or prosecuted Amway and other quasi-religious corporates for blending salvationist hopes, ultimately based on belief in a divine covenant that is the centrepiece of the Gospel of Prosperity, with financial agreements to establish Amway distributorships, based on specific income projections that assume highly improbable economic scenarios. There is convincing evidence that actual income rarely matches the Amway dream. Financial records demonstrate that only a tiny proportion of Amway distributors ever become independently wealthy and relatively few produce an income sufficient to support a middle class lifestyle. Indeed, the data from one investigative report reveal that only 1,000 of over 200,000 distributors ever achieved the rank of Direct Distributor or higher (Green and D'Aiuto 1977: 314). Further, an analysis of the state tax returns of Amway distributors in Wisconsin revealed

> the average annual adjusted gross income of these distributors to be $267. Only the 139 Direct Distributorships in operation during the two year period 1979–1980 (less than 1 percent of all the Wisconsin distributors) had an average annual adjusted gross income of $12,000 or more. The average annual net income, after business deductions, for all Wisconsin distributorships was determined to be a NET LOSS of $918. The average Direct Distributorship, comprised of two individuals, was found to have an annual adjusted gross income of $14,349.
>
> (Juth-Gavasso 1985: 155–6)

The same report also calculates that if each Amway distributor were to sell the volume of goods projected in promotional literature, 'this would require the annual purchase of $400 by each of the 1,652,261 citizens in Wisconsin' (Juth 1985: 13). And Butterfield (1985: 135) estimates that 'For one person to change [social] class using the Amway vehicle, at least 2083 new active people must be brought in, trained, motivated, programmed and supplied'.

Conflict derives as well from the tightly-knit organizational style that collapses the boundaries between family, religion, community and economy. In contrast to the predominant mode of coping with family–economy tension, a cordoning off and insulation of private life from public domain intrusions that increases institutional differentiation, Amway conjoins the two spheres in a sect-like organization that decreases institutional differentiation. The result is an often totalistic organizational style that is deemed inappropriate to the affective neutrality normative for economic relationships and to the non-regulated, highly personalized relationships of private life. Outsiders thus are disturbed both by the spectacle of what are billed as business seminars dissolving into revivalistic unity rituals and by highly regimented families that apparently have become mere corporate pawns. As one perplexed observer put it: 'Again and again, I have seen hard-nosed, rational, cautious, unemotional individuals of every station and background swept up by "the dream", the components of which are the expectation of vast wealth, positive thinking, constant reinforcement through programmed small-group activities and mass rallies, and a product that somehow benefits mankind in ways far beyond the powers of normal, lower-priced commercial items' (Streiker 1984: 227).

Based on the encapsulating quality of Amway as a way of life, some critics have gone so far as to label Amway a 'cult' that practises mind control and have drawn explicit comparisons to Sun Myung Moon's Unification Church.

> The similarity between Amway and the Moonies is so profound that one wonders if the two are in cahoots . . . Both groups have a Leader who offers himself as an object of edification and devoted hero-worship. The Leader and his teachings are the guide for the major decisions of a member's life. Both claim to be the salvation of America, a purpose to live for, a faith to live by. Both indoctrinate their followers with books, tapes, and special mass meetings. Both provide a substitute for the extended family, and regulate the influences over members and construct their identity and their consciousness. Both practice thought control.
>
> (Butterfield 1985: 148–9)

These concerns about manipulativeness are not without foundation, of course. For example, some Amway true believers are so convinced that anyone who truly understands the Amway message will accept it, that they have employed deceptive techniques in their recruitment practices in order to reach disinterested outsiders. In her participant observation of a major Amway distributor network, Lester heard one distributor counsel his charges:

> Okay, the first thing you want to learn to do is how to approach a person. Now, number one, if they're a brand new person that is a friend of yours and you're new in the business, the first thing you do is learn how to invite them – right? You call 'em on the phone, you get 'em curious, *and you don't tell 'em anything.*
>
> (Lester 1974: 20)

The potential for exploitation of true believers also exists. Some distributor networks, sometimes referred to as 'Black Hat' lines, push sales of motivational materials to downlines to such a degree that proceeds from such materials actually exceed profits from the sale of Amway products (Johnston 1987: 17–18). For example, in a 1984 legal complaint filed against Amway it was revealed that one distributor grossed $59,000 from Amway products and $500,000 from non-Amway motivational products (Juth-Gavasso 1985: 185).[12]

Still, although Amway has been accused of being simply a pyramid scheme and a 'cult', detractors have not been successful in creating a public definition of Amway comparable to the image of controversial groups such as the Unification Church (Bromley and Breschel 1992). How does Amway avoid such stigmatizing categorization? As a business enterprise, Amway is closely connected both to traditional cultural values and to dominant institutions. Its distributor ranks are filled with hard-working, middle class families seeking to improve their economic lot, a culturally laudable goal. The corporation is fervently patriotic, even if it views contemporary America as having lost its way. Amway is also big business. It is well entrenched within the powerful direct sales industry and connected with a plethora of other industries which supply direct sales corporations with products, services and financing. And Amway boasts a number of influential political figures and celebrities who lend their names and legitimacy to the corporation. For example, in a second speaking engagement at an Amway convention Ronald Reagan was lavish in his praise of Amway:

> Ladies and Gentlemen, I want to tell you, you have made me an honest man in my own family. Because I was here not too many years ago, as you know, not in this exact place, but speaking to this meeting. And I went home and told Nancy, who wasn't with me at the time, about it, and I don't think I could quite make her believe it. Now she knows . . . . Well, it's a great pleasure to be back here and a great pleasure to be talking to you again. Because I think I told you the first time, you really are capitalism in America!
>
> (Kerns 1982: 108)

Amway also has been represented by Bob Hope in its commercials and counts Pat Boone and Gerald Ford among its supporters. These types of legitimation serve to insulate Amway from attacks that more marginally positioned groups experience although in popular culture Amway recruiters appear to be regarded with the same aversion as Hare Krishna fundraisers and Jehovah's Witnesses proselytizers (e.g. Willimon 1982).

CONCLUSIONS

The objective of this paper has been to interpret sociologically the organization of what I have termed quasi-religious corporations. I have argued that direct sales organizations trace their socio-cultural roots to the traditions of entrepreneurial capitalism and harmonial philosophy. The contemporary quasi-religious corporations can be distinguished from traditional direct sales organizations, however, in that their ideologies and organizations possess the attributes of sectarian social movements at the distributor network level. The appeal of quasi-religious corporates emanates from a disjunction between the contractually ordered public sphere (state and economy) and the covenantally ordered private sphere (family and religion). Tensions between the two spheres of American social life have flared episodically through much of American history, although their intensity and form of expression have varied. The current crop of quasi-religious corporates, which have posted substantial gains in distributor network size and sales volume since the mid-1960s, constitute one contemporary response to this persistent tension. Quasi-religious corporates present themselves as providing vehicles for re-integrating important spheres of life that have become dis-integrated. The solution is embodied in their reciprocally related sectarian social movement organizations and transformative ideologies.

Amway and other quasi-religious corporates begin with the premise that there are ordering principles in the universe that naturally yield abundance and fulfilment for humanity. By the logic of harmonial philosophy, the important elements of life should be congruent with one another, and individuality and group life should be mutually sustaining. The root problem of modern existence is that this natural order has been disrupted, which individuals experience as dis-integration and contradictory behavioural imperatives. The ideology thus interprets contemporary dis-ease as a fall from a natural state of 'grace'. The concurrent announcement of the discovery of Amway as a means of restoring wholeness to life creates the possibility of a 'new beginning'. In this fashion the ideology constructs an interpretive system for adherents that defines accountability and structures motivation. While adherents could not be held accountable for events in primordial time, they become responsible in the present by virtue of knowing there is an accessible solution to life's problems that is contingent only on their own individual faith and effort. By heightening expectations for imminent salvation, the ideology creates an energy-structuring symbolic system for directing and intensifying activity and for accepting a period of sacrifice that is a prelude to ultimate salvation.

The organizational solution proposed by Amway is the creation of *family*-businesses that will restore wholeness and integration to life. The relationship between family and economy is transposed as the corporate world is distanced, operating simply as a supplier of goods and services at the behest of the *family*-business. Quasi-religious corporate sponsored *family*-businesses are thus to bridge the gulf between family and economy and reintegrate the two spheres. The new form of organization falls outside the realm of family and economy, and it mediates between the two by simultaneously being neither and both. The networks of *family*-businesses are organized as sectarian social movements.

At base, sectarianism is an organizational form that is characterized by a high level of member commitment to the group, attenuated external relationships and significant tension with the surrounding social environment. Since the prevailing adaptation for managing public–private life dysjunction has been an insulation of the two spheres from one another, acceptance of Amway ideology requires a paradigmatic shift in participants' world views. Likewise, participation in Amway requires a major realignment of participants' social activity and commitment patterns. Sectarian organization fosters both the cultural and social transformations necessary for participation in Amway.

Conversion is effected by drawing simultaneously on the dissatisfactions and tensions in converts' present lives and on their culturally ingrained hopes and aspirations. At rallies, seminars or one-to-one recruitment sessions, dissatisfactions are amplified while an alternative vision of life is juxtaposed that serves to increase the perceptual distance between present realities and future possibilities. Displays of wealth, 'drawing circles' (which personalizes the ideology and models the convert's ascension to financial success), testimonials from successful distributors, pledges of commitment to the convert's financial success, and preliminary participation in the Amway 'community' all bridge the transition from outsider to insider. Converts are then offered an organizationally sponsored line of action that promises to transform their lives. Conversion of both spouses is designed to insure internal family solidarity and family-unit commitment to the organization.

Tightly-knit organization and intensive internal relationships are imperative if converts are to maintain commitment to the cause since both public and private life are restructured and distanced from conventional social life. Current career lines assume secondary priority as time and energy are committed to Amway in an effort to achieve autonomy and eliminate the need for a conventional career. The family unit is reorganized, with spouses and (sometimes) children becoming business partners who have a shared commitment to Amway. High levels of social support are necessary whether Amway-sponsored transformations of social life are immediate or gradual. In the less frequent case in which families abandon conventional careers and make a total commitment to Amway, the inherently high-risk and vulnerability mandate constant social reinforcement. In the more typical case, families attempt to engineer a gradual but steady transition to an independent *family*-business. The problems confronting these new distributors are that they must continue to participate in two social worlds between which there is real tension, to satisfy two competing sets of occupational demands and to sustain a high level of commitment over an extended period when real success is modest at best. The charismatic authority of uplines and participation in Amway unity rituals are critical to faith maintenance during this process.

Over the last two decades both demographic factors and diverse individual adaptations within the organization have contributed to the intense organizational commitment so conspicuous at Amway gatherings. The organization has experienced high rates of conversion, defection and growth (the balance of conversion over defection). The result is a steady infusion of enthusiastic recent converts and self-deselection of the disenchanted, which yields a continuing preponderance of adherents most likely to exhibit high levels of commitment. Beyond these important demographic underpinnings, adherents have adapted in very different ways to the limited economic success that is the reality in all of the quasi-religious corporates. Amway is dominated by a relatively small number of highly successful distributors who have a major financial interest in the proliferation of downline distributor networks. These individuals lead and orchestrate Amway's emotionally charged unity rituals. Recent converts attempting to make the transition to income self-sufficiency through their distributorships are encouraged by their uplines and are disposed by their own aspirations to exhibit high levels of commitment. Finally, those adherents for whom Amway serves more congregational and status enhancing functions are among the most devout participants in organizational rituals. The result is that what seems to outsiders to be passionate and unswerving loyalty in fact is considerably more complex than it appears.[13]

The Amway prescription for socio-cultural revitalization is not without its ironies. Quasi-religious corporates closely resemble some orthodox and fundamentalist groups in that they reconfigure the very traditions they claim to restore/revitalize (Hunter 1991; Lechner 1990). Amway depicts itself as restoring the lost American traditions of individual freedom and initiative; it is the network of *family*-businesses that are to constitute the primary restorative mechanism. However, as one of the few hundred largest corporations in the United States, Amway is tightly integrated into the contractually organized public world dominated by corporate bureaucratic forms. The workers upon whom Amway depends for product development, manufacturing, storing and transporting the products Amway distributes are wage-earning *employees*, not liberated members of the Amway community (i.e. distributors). Amway also is closely connected to the complex of corporate attorneys and accountants, banks and insurance companies, advertising and promotional firms, communication and transportation companies that are at the heart of the contractual order.

The nature of the economy Amway is an active participant in creating also bears faint resemblance to the *laissez-faire* capitalism it claims to resurrect. For example, the economy that Amway idealizes was rooted in production while the contemporary American economy is driven by consumption. Amway celebrations feature conspicuous consumption of consumer goods, and self-fulfilment is defined through choice of leisure-time activity. In a similar fashion, the form of community Amway invokes is distinctly modern. Adherents do not form *gemeinschaft* associations on the traditional axes of ecology, ethnicity or kinship but rather form *gesellschaft* limited scope networks based on mutual economic interests. In essence, then, Amway refashions in contemporary terms the tradition it purports to restore and maintains a symbiotic relationship with the modern world that it purports to reject. In classic sectarian style, Amway is both rooted in and opposed to its societal environment. This contradiction engenders persistent tension with the larger society.

Whatever the ultimate historical destiny of Amway and other quasi-religious corporates, they cannot be dismissed as sociologically epiphenomenal. There surely is compelling evidence that few families generate liveable incomes under their auspices, membership turnover rates are extraordinarily high and deviant practices abound. However, these very attributes render quasi-religious corporates significant sociologically. Although there are few dramatic success stories in quasi-religious corporates, they continue to flourish. Further, individual commitment to the organization is intense, albeit temporary in most cases. The number of individuals who experiment with quasi-religious corporates and the passionate nature of their involvement are convincing measures of the tensions that they seek to redress. Their culturally anomalous practices and ambivalence toward the social order of which they are part can be understood as an attempt to reintegrate a world that which has become fragmented. In this regard quasi-religious corporates offer revealing insight into the dynamics of modern society.

NOTES

1 Contractual social relations are those in which individuals coordinate their behaviour through pledging themselves to specific reciprocal activity and covenantal social relations are those in which individuals coordinate their behaviour through pledging themselves to one another's well being. Contracts are articulated through a logic of calculative involvement and individual interest, and covenants are articulated through a logic of moral involvement and unity (Bromley and Busching 1988: 16).

2 For a discussion of quasi-religious therapeutic groups paralleling this analysis, see Bromley and Shupe (in prep.).

3 The term *family*-business as envisioned by quasi-religious corporates has a more specific meaning than a firm owned and operated by members of the same family unit or lineage. It refers to the a merger of family and business with the latter placed in the service of the former.

4 Information on other quasi-religious corporates may be found in the following sources. For Tupperware: Rex Taylor (1978); Dorothy Peven (1968). For Mary Kay: Adele Kingan (1982); Roul Tunley (1978). For Shaklee: Rodney Smith (1984); (Editorial) 'Panacea, placebo, nostrum, amen: Shaklee Corp got rich on its founder's tent-show formulas', *Forbes* (15 October): 83–90. For Herbalife: Ellen Paris (1985). For Nu Skin: Marjorie Williams (1991).

5 Some of the material in this section is derived from Bromley and Shupe (1990).

6 Because Amway is composed of independently owned and operated distributorships, organizational practices are quite diverse. Most of the research conducted on Amway has involved studies of specific distributor networks, and like other corporations, Amway has not always been receptive to research that does not serve its own interests. As a result, research-based descriptions of specific organizational practices may or may not be representative of all distributorship lines.

7 For a discussion of the attributes of sectarian organization, see Benton Johnson (1963); Richard Niebuhr (1957); Rodney Stark and William Sims Bainbridge (1979); Ernst Troeltsch (1961).

8 This point is illustrated nicely by a husband–wife team who began a Nu Skin distributorship (Williams 1988: C1–C3). They report that 'The dream-stealers went to work on them . . . . People started to tell us it was a pyramid . . . . This was the crisis of faith. Suddenly . . . we just in ourselves weren't sure this was as great as it was'.

9 Several staff members at a local hotel in which an Amway rally was held reported to

157

the author that Amway distributors were notoriously tight-fisted tippers and that housekeeping services found numerous instances of individuals preparing meals in their rooms. It appears that low-level distributors were husbanding resources for display at formal occasions.

10 These celebrative rituals are the central mechanism for unifying the decentralized organization and building and maintaining group solidarity. The following account depicts a similar ritual in Mary Kay.

> A whirlwind of excitement fills the convention center. Thousands of women are taking their seats, eagerly anticipating the evening ahead. An orchestra is playing themes from popular musicals. Water fountains surge 30 feet high, reflecting lights that change color in time with the music. Backstage, more women are lining up, dressed in the most elaborate evening gowns. Suddenly, a figure in white, trimmed with fur and diamonds, emerges onto the runway. The audience quickly rises. The applause is thunderous. "Are you ready?" she asks, as the cheers for her, Mary Kay, become deafening. "Here it comes, the most exciting night of your life . . . when dreams come true!" (Kingan 1982: 12)

11 The ideological reinforcement that inhibits discontinuation of effort is critical to sustained effort in the fact of lack of immediate success. For example, confronted by earnings that did not match their expectations, the Nu Skin couple quoted previously concluded that

> If they were falling behind, it must be their fault . . . . They decided that their prospects had probably sensed their lack of faith. Ever since then, they've worked on getting their belief levels up . . . . [They decided to] just keep going, no matter what, and believe in yourself, you can do it! (Williams 1991: C3)

12 According to Juth-Gavasso (1985: 149–95; Juth 1985), other examples of deviant practices include misrepresentation of distributor incomes, misrepresentation of distributor earnings potential, use of unrealistic hypothetical examples, deceptive product presentations and inventory loading.

13 Amway creates the kind of pure capitalist motivational system that Robert Merton (1958) describes, and this tripartite division of Amway distributors could be interpreted as paralleling his conformist, innovator and ritualist forms of adaptation. The 'Black Hats' are innovators (accept cultural goals but reject institutional means). This group is very powerful within Amway ranks, and the corporation seems to face great difficulty in curtailing its excesses (Johnston 1987: 19; Juth-Gavasso 1985: 189–91). Conformists (accept both cultural goals and institutional means) spend considerable time in sales rather that recruiting and recruit only a moderate sized downline distributor network, with the result that they earn modest supplemental incomes. Ritualists (reject the cultural goals but accept the institutional means), who in essence are 'free' riders, are extremely active in organizational activities but are not financially successful.

REFERENCES

Ahlstrom, S. *A Religious History of the American People*, 2 vols, New Haven: Yale University Press.

Allen, M. (1988) 'Amway is more than business to true believers who came here'. *Richmond Times Dispatch* (21 March): 1, A–6.

Biggart, N.W. (1989) *Charismatic Capitalism: Direct Selling Organizations in America*, Chicago: University of Chicago Press.

Birmingham, F. (1982) 'Rich DeVos: faith and family', *The Saturday Evening Post* (July/August): 58–60.

Bromley, D. and Breschel, E. (1992) 'General population and institutional elite support for social control of new religious movements: evidence from national survey data.' *Behavioral Sciences and the Law* 10: 39–52.

Bromley, D. and Busching, B. (1988) 'Understanding the structure of contractual and covenantal social relations: implications for the sociology of religion', *Sociological Analysis* 49S: 15–32.

Bromley, D. and Shupe, A. (1990) 'Rebottling the elixir: the gospel of prosperity in America's religioeconomic corporations', in T. Robbins and R. Anthony (eds) *In Gods We Trust: New Patterns of Religious Pluralism in America*. New Brunswick: Transaction Publishers, pp. 233–54.

Bromley, D. and Shupe, A. *Strange Gods and Cult Scares*, in prep.

Butterfield, S. (1985) *Amway: The Cult of Free Enterprise*, Boston: South End Press.

Collier, P. and Horowitz, D. (1987) *The Fords: An American Epic*, New York: Summit Books.

Conn, C. (1982) *An Uncommon Freedom*, New York: Berkeley Books.

(Editorial) 'Panacea, placebo, nostrum, amen: Shaklee Corp got rich on its founder's tent-show formulas', *Forbes* 120 (October, 1977): 83–90.

Fuller, A. and Spence, H. (1960) *A Foot in the Door*, New York: McGraw-Hill Book Co.

Gibbs, N. (1989) 'How America has run out of time', *Time* (24 April): 58–67.

Green, J. and D'Aiuto, J. (1977) 'A case study of economic distribution via social networks', *Human Organization* 36 (Fall): 309–15.

Greenleaf, W. (1968) 'Preface', in K. Sward, *The Legend of Henry Ford*, New York: Atheneum.

Gwynne, S.C. (1990) 'Rounding up those personal loans', *Time* (19 November): 80.

Hewlett, S.A. (1990) 'Running hard just to keep up', *Time* (Fall): 54.

Hofstadter, R. (1955) *Social Darwinism in American Thought*, Boston: Beacon Press.

Hunter, J. (1991) 'Fundamentalism and social science', in D.G. Bromley (ed.) *Religion and the Social Order: New Developments in Theory and Research*. Greenwich, CT: Association for the Sociology of Religion & JAI Press, pp. 149–64.

Johnson, B. (1963) 'On Church and Sect', *American Sociological Review* 28 (August): 539–49.

Johnston, G.P. (1987) 'The Relationship Among Organizational Involvement, Commitment, and Success: A Case Study of Amway Corporation', unpublished Ph.D. Dissertation, Virginia Polytechnic Institute and State University.

Juth, C. (1985) 'Structural factors creating and maintaining illegal and deviant behavior in direct selling organizations: a case study of Amway corporation', paper presented at the annual meeting of the American Sociological Association. Washington, DC.

Juth-Gavasso, C. (1985) 'Organizational Deviance in the Direct Selling Industry: A Case Study of the Amway Corporation', unpublished Ph.D. Dissertation, Western Michigan University.

Kerns, P. (1982) *Fake It til You Make It! Inside Amway*. Carlton, OR: Victory Press.

Kingan, A. (1982) 'Entrepreneur's corner', *The Executive Female* (November/December): 12–14.

Lechner, F. (1990) 'Fundamentalism revisited', in T. Robbins and R. Anthony (eds) *In Gods We Trust: New Patterns of Religious Pluralism in America*, New Brunswick, NJ: Transaction Publishers, pp. 77–98.

Lester, L.O. (1974) '$ucce$$: A Phenomenological Analysis of the Belief System of the Amway Corporation', unpublished Master's Thesis, University of North Carolina at Chapel Hill.

Merton, R. (1968) *Social Theory and Social Structure*, New York: Macmillan Publishing Co.

159

Morgan, D. (1981) 'Selling free enterprise: Amway combats liberal ideology in politics', *Washington Post* (14 March): A1–A2.

Niebuhr, R. (1957) *The Social Sources of Denominationalism*, New York: Meridian Books.

Paris, E. (1985) 'Herbalife, anyone?' *Forbes* 135 (February): 46, 50.

Peven, D. (1968) 'The use of religious revival techniques to indoctrinate personnel: the home-party sales organizations', *The Sociological Quarterly* (Winter): 97–106

Roberts, K. (1990) *Religion in Sociological Perspective*, Homewood, IL: Dorsey Press.

Simon, D. and Eitzen, D.S. (1990) *Elite Deviance*. Boston: Allyn & Bacon.

Smith, R. (1984) *Multilevel Marketing: A Lawyer Looks at Amway, Shaklee, and Other Direct Sales Organizations*, Grand Rapids: Baker Book House.

Stacey, J. (1990) *Brave New Families: Stories of Domestic Upheaval in Late Twentieth Century America*, New York: Basic Books.

Stark, R. and Bainbridge, W.S. (1979) 'Of churches, sects and cults: preliminary concepts for a theory of religious movements', *Journal for the Scientific Study of Religion* 18 (June): 117–31.

Starker, S. (1989) *Oracle at the Supermarket: The American Preoccupation with Self-Help Books*, New Brunswick, NJ: Transaction Publishers.

Streiker, L. (1984) *The Gospel Time Bomb*, Buffalo, NY: Prometheus Books.

Taylor, R. (1978) 'Marilyn's friends and Rita's customers: a study of party-selling as play and work', *The Sociological Review* 26 (August): 573–94.

Trine, W. (1897) *In Tune with the Infinite*, Indianapolis: Bobbs-Merrill.

Troeltsch, E. (1961) *The Social Teaching of Christian Churches*, New York: Harper & Row.

Tunley, R. (1978) 'Mary Kay's sweet smell of success', *Reader's Digest* (November): 17–21.

Williams, M. (1991) 'The selling of the American Dream', *Washington Post* (30 July): C1–C3.

Willimon, W. (1982) 'The American Way', *Christian Century* (13 October): 1007–8.

8

AMERICA LOVES SWEDEN[1]

Prosperity theology and the cultures of capitalism

Simon M. Coleman

INTRODUCTION

The worldwide revival of conservative Protestantism at a time when capitalism has apparently been experiencing a global resurgence is a dramatic, but highly ambiguous, occurrence. If capitalism can be seen as much more than a mode of production, since it implies a cultural totality of political, social and symbolic elements (cf. Tomlinson 1991), we are perhaps justified in asking whether the religious revival can provide a means of re-sacralizing the assumptions on which it depends. This question is complicated by the fact that, just as there are many different ways to be a conservative Protestant, so capitalism can adopt a variety of guises. Thus, while both phenomena display expansionist tendencies in by-passing the geographical and cultural boundaries of nation-states, we have to examine the extent to which such apparently homogenizing and totalizing influences can be reinterpreted and transformed in the many cultural contexts they encounter.

I want to explore these issues through an examination of the spread of a particular branch of North American Protestantism, called the Faith Movement, to reputedly one of the most secular countries in the world – Sweden. This movement, consisting of media ministries and local congregations, propounds a Gospel of Prosperity, which stresses the notion that material blessings come to those who are faithful to God. Its leading members in the United States – including Kenneth Hagin, Kenneth and Gloria Copeland, Lester Sumrall, and Jerry Savelle – are dedicated to evangelizing throughout the world. The latter is achieved through the establishment of local offices, preaching-tours and the spreading of literature, cassettes, videos and television programmes. A newsletter produced by the Copeland's ministry includes reports from offices in South Africa, England, Canada, Hong Kong, Australia and the Philippines. In addition, it states:

> . . . the increased availability of satellite equipment across the continent should soon bring all of Europe within the reach of our broadcasts . . . . The videotape program . . . has reached thousands of people throughout the United Kingdom and is now filtering into Scandinavia and Germany.[2]

Of course, the international diffusion of Prosperity Theology should be seen in the context of the widespread resurgence of conservative Protestantism in general. David Martin's *Tongues of Fire* (1990) presents an up-to-date and wide-ranging analysis of this phenomenon, chiefly through tracing what can in crude terms be called the diffusion of a Western, Protestant ethic, via the medium of Anglo-Saxon revivalism, to the Catholic countries of Latin America.[3] He, like me, is therefore concerned to examine the tensions and resonances not only between religious and economic orientations, but also between national cultures. However, while Martin looks at conservative Protestantism as a factor in a modernizing *process*, I am going to be looking at its effects in a European country that is notable for *already* having modernized quickly and highly successfully. The issue thus becomes one of assessing religion as a possible means by which to embody – or at least illustrate – the possibility of a transition between two patterns or sub-types of developed capitalism.[4]

A striking aspect of much contemporary Protestantism is its attempt to run an ideological gauntlet between, on the one hand, the maintenance of sectarian purity, and on the other, a crude accommodation to mainstream institutions through redefining and indeed attempting to assimilate such institutions for its own purposes. This approach reveals a belief that political and cultural influence can be achieved through appropriating the symbols and resources of secular power-holders, and indicates a stance towards some aspects of modernity that is one of attraction and affinity rather than outraged opposition. It therefore has important implications for the Swedish situation.

SWEDEN: A TURNING-POINT FOR THE MIDDLE-WAY?

> In my dreams I have a plan
> If I got me a wealthy man
> I wouldn't have to work at all
> I'd fool around and have a ball

These words may seem familiar. In fact, they are a verse from a song called *Money, Money, Money* by one of the most successful exports Sweden has ever had, the pop-group Abba. Although the song is about a widespread human preoccupation – the lack of money – it is, according to the ethnologists Gaunt and Löfgren, an 'extraordinarily Swedish song' (1984: 99). By this they mean that the verses express the difficulty of attaining and retaining personal wealth by one's own efforts.[7] If the 'American Dream' is concerned with the achievement of success through the results of individual labour, skill and determination, the 'dreams' of this verse refer instead to an almost miraculous event – a marriage to money – and therefore the reliance on an *external* force to gain prosperity. Clearly, not too much should be read into the lines of a song, but Gaunt and Löfgren do at least illustrate an important feature of Swedish political and social discourse, albeit one that is hard to quantify – a notion of equality that recommends the organized and widespread diffusion of resources, and regards the accumulation of large amounts of personal wealth as exceptional. Such an ideal has been exemplified and implemented through a relatively punitive system of income tax which ensures the availability of resources for extensive welfare programmes. Ingvar Carlsson, the previous prime minister, expressed this aim of equality through economic and social solidarity in a speech given in 1987 to the Social Democratic Party Congress, when he stated: 'There is no winner unless we are all winners'.[8] To understand the historical and cultural roots of this stress on equality of *distribution* as well as opportunity, we must look at some important aspects of the political and economic development of contemporary Sweden.

Social democracy has exercised a voluntary hegemony in the country for most of the past 60 years, steering a path between *laissez-faire*, competitive capitalism and state socialism. Indeed, after the transformation of Eastern Europe, Sweden gained new significance as one of the few advanced, industrial states in which a largely dominant (albeit non-Marxist) socialist regime retained considerable legitimacy. In order to retain power almost unbrokenly from 1932, Social Democratic governments proved willing to enter into coalitions and alliances with other parties, resulting in a period of both political stability and relative consensus across party lines. Close co-operation between government and unions, low levels of income inequality and a well-developed welfare-state combined with a highly efficient economy that enabled internationally successful private accumulation. Sweden, indeed, has often been seen by economists and political scientists (see e.g. Rothstein 1991) as the model of a corporatist society, committed to both equality and efficiency, characterized by the state encouragement of social partnerships between political, bureaucratic and economic organizations.[9]

Simultaneously, Sweden has appeared to some scholars to provide a model for the future secularization of the West, since levels of organized religious practice are extremely low by international standards.[10] The Lutheran, State Church has remained established, but has in general become a symbol of national identity and provider of rites of passage rather than a centre of active faith. Its membership is decided by birth rather than voluntary association. Free Churches emerged, along with the Workers Movement, during the latter half of the nineteenth century, and originally defined themselves in opposition to what was perceived as a conservative church-state monopoly. However, they subsequently accepted a position of accommodation to the Social Democratic establishment, as well as the notion of a separation of powers between religion and government.[11] Overall, religion has had relatively little political resonance in Sweden in past decades. Although a Christian Democratic Party has existed since 1964, this has for most of its history been unable to gain enough votes to obtain visible representation in parliament.

Despite the alleged neutrality and consensus orientation of the Swedish 'middle-way',[12] it has ironically provoked some extreme reactions – both positive and negative. An example of the latter is provided by Huntford, who objects to its collectivist implications in his book *The New Totalitarians* (1971), and attempts to find parallels between Sweden and Huxley's *Brave New World*. However, it has become increasingly clear that the Swedish model – which has consisted in political and religious terms of a form of stable, even congealed, pluralism – is changing in significant ways. Many of the assumptions behind Sweden's development into a corporatist state are now being challenged. In effect, the country is experiencing processes of internal differentiation and competition. Milner (1988: 99) remarks:

> Swedes, remembering two-and-a-half decades when things worked smoothly and predictably, are troubled by a decade in which consensus needs to be frequently negotiated.

The last two decades generally have witnessed a reaction against the centralist planning model – in areas like urban planning, medical care and municipal administration – while experiments with submunicipal councils and other forms of local decision-making have been initiated. Increasing conflicts have occurred between private- and public-sector workers, and unions have experienced a general decline in membership levels.[13] In the 1970s, employers began more openly to attack the labour movement, and indeed the bourgeois opponents of the Social Democrats took power briefly in the late 1970s and early 1980s. During a governmental crisis of 1990, the Social Democratic government resigned after losing a parliamentary vote on its economic policy of austerity, but returned to power after the non-socialists could not form a government.

In early 1991, the electorate witnessed the emergence of a new, populist party, called New Democracy. Founded by two successful businessmen, this has been termed 'the *enfant terrible* of the non-socialist camp' (Wörlund: 135), and is explicitly designed as a proponent of radical *laissez-faire* principles in opposition to the bureaucratic apparatus of the state. According to one observer, quoted by Kelman in *The Guardian* (7 August 1991), it has a programme of supporting 'conservative politics and cheap liquor'. Certainly, it has adopted a populist style, opposing immigration, calling for lower taxes and arguing that ordinary citizens possess sufficient common sense to come to correct decisions, political or otherwise, without the heavy intervention of government. A graphic illustration of this argument was provided by the suggestion that traffic parking restrictions should be removed, on the grounds that drivers would naturally find the most efficient locations to park their cars.

What is striking about this party is not so much the fact that it exists, but that it has proved so popular in the polls. In the election of September 1991, just a few months after its inception, New Democracy secured 6.7 percent of the vote. At the same time the Christian Democrats (who after years of apparent neutrality had decided to support the conservative political bloc) gained far more than their usual 2 percent share of the electorate, by attracting 7.1 percent. Most significantly, of course, the election also saw the defeat of the Social Democrats in favour of a conservative coalition headed by the right-wing Moderate Party.[14]

An election campaign which had been dominated by debates over the size and growth of the public sector had therefore ended in two significant results (cf. Wörlund, 1992). First, a protest vote against the prevailing principles of Social Democracy, combined with the relative success of a conservative coalition whose slogan had been 'A New Start for Sweden' (involving privatization, tax reductions and aid for the small-scale entrepreneur). Second, the confirmation of a new volatility in voting patterns, indicated by the success of two minor parties whose policies, although very different, could be interpreted as representing dissatisfaction with the ethics of a long-established, seemingly moribund, political establishment.

Aside from such political developments, global developments in flows of people, commodities and information have also been affecting Sweden. The business sector has become more internationalized, aided by the elimination of foreign exchange restrictions. Over the past decades, ethnic and cultural pluralism have grown dramatically, both through the workings of the international media (in a country where the ability to speak fluent English is commonplace) and as a result of waves of immigrants from predominantly Yugoslavia, Greece, West Germany, Turkey, the United Kingdom, Poland and Italy, as well as other Nordic countries.[15] Minority voices are increasingly heard in a media apparatus that, on the local level at least, is becoming deregulated. From the late 1980s private companies have been able to broadcast television programmes via satellite and cable, while neighbourhood radio stations have increased in number. Over the past year, political and journalistic debates have discussed the issue of whether Sweden's self-ascribed role as an island of neutrality on the international scene will be irrevocably compromised by its decision finally to join the EC.[16] This position of neutrality on the world stage may also have been affected by the developments in Eastern Europe. Klas Eklund, one of the intellectual leaders of the Social Democratic party's right wing, is quoted by Kelman:

> For decades we saw ourselves as the third way, between the poles of *laissez-faire* capitalism and totalitarian communism. What do you do when one of the poles collapses?
>
> (*The Guardian*, 7 August 1991)

Taking the factors mentioned above into account, we can conclude that Petersson may be correct in predicting that the public sector decline, evident in the 1980s, is part of a deeper trend of the relative retreat of the state and a move away from a collectivist democratic ideal:

> The present period is characterized by individualization and internationalization. The fundamental problem of democracy, i.e., how to reconcile individual freedom with collective order, is now re-emerging in a partly new constellation.
>
> (1991: 199)

CONSERVATIVE PROTESTANTISM IN SWEDEN

In the following, I shall attempt to show that the emergence of American-influenced Prosperity Theology in Sweden has gained considerable significance

165

with regard to the developments mentioned above. In other words, it has acted as a catalyst for inspiring debates which, implicitly or explicitly, discuss issues relating to the future of the country as a social democratic, capitalist state. Although one might expect religious discourse to be pushed to the side of political discourse in a country that is so apparently secularized, in fact rather the reverse has occurred. The new wave of conservative Protestantism has taken on symbolic resonances which extend into both the political and economic realms, and indeed become a strikingly important object of public concern during the past ten years or so.[5] The following case study does not suggest that the spread of such theology from the United States to Sweden implies a situation of cultural imperialism in a crude sense, i.e. involving the direct imposition of a 'message' from power centre to periphery. Rather, the message is actively taken up and *adapted* for local purposes.[6]

The chief initiator (as well as object) of debate in Sweden has been an organization called the Word of Life (*Livets Ord*).[17] This is based in the university town of Uppsala, an hour's drive north of Stockholm, and was founded in 1983 by Ulf Ekman, a former priest within the Swedish Church. The Word of Life is now probably the largest Bible school in Europe, and trains around 800 pupils a year, from both Scandinavia and other parts of the world. It has also started up an English-speaking course to cater for non-Scandinavians from Europe and beyond. It attracts some 2,000 people to its Sunday morning services, although the members of its congregation number only around 1,500, and its extensive media business produces videos, cassettes, and books, as well as sending out a newsletter to over 20,000 addresses in Scandinavia and beyond.[18]

In the early years of the Word of Life, its leaders tended to deny connections with other Christian groups in Sweden, on the grounds that all were said to be appearing concurrently under the influence of the Holy Spirit. However, it has become clear that the group is simply the largest of a number of other, similar congregations or Bible schools – perhaps around 90 in number[19] – that have spread throughout the country during the 1980s and into the 1990s. Some of these, indeed, were started by ex-pupils of the Word of Life, and have tended to adopt similar names, such as Source of Life, Word of Faith, etc. In April 1991, the Scandinavian Faith Movement acknowledged its *de facto* status as an identifiable charismatic organization by forming a preachers' organization, with Ekman as its chairman.

As yet, it has not been possible to carry out extensive surveys of adherents of the Word of Life or the Faith Movement as a whole. Data on the class characteristics of members are therefore regrettably sparse and inconclusive. However, the movement does seem to attract a preponderance of people under 40, many of whom, rather than being new converts, were members of more traditional churches but see the new movement as the means to achieve a revival of Swedish Christianity.[20] It is also clear, in my own experience, that a large number of Christians attend the Word of Life regularly but choose to retain membership in an established congregation. A common reason for this 'division of labour' in allegiance was expressed most succinctly by a Pentecostalist missionary whom I regularly met at Word of Life meetings, who once remarked to me: 'I go to meetings in my own church to help other people, but I go to the Word of Life to help *myself*'. The element of self-realization implied in this statement reflects a frequent comment by supporters of Faith Teaching that it gives them *kraft* (force, or power) in their daily lives. It was illustrated well in a painting of Christ's crucifixion I once saw hanging up in the foyer of the group's offices. Rather than depicting an image of suffering, the artist, as he explained in comments accompanying the picture, had chosen to depict Jesus as a kind of bodybuilder, dwarfing the cross, and bulging with muscles of faith.

The connections between the Swedish Faith Movement and its counterpart in the United States are extensive.[21] Preachers from the American movement come to regular conferences put on by the Word of Life, and the latter's bookshop acts as the channel for the former's products in Sweden. Over half of the 200 or so videos available in the summer catalogue of 1987 featured Americans. Some Swedish preachers, including Ekman, received training at Kenneth Hagin's Bible school in Tulsa. Ekman's subsequent activity – i.e. the setting up of his own ministry in his native country – is common to other non-American Bible school students at Hagin's school.[22]

THE TEACHINGS OF PROSPERITY

Denis Hollinger, an American theologian, has traced some of the roots of the Prosperity Gospel to the notion of the Abrahamic covenant, and the idea of blessing coming to those who are faithful to God. Thus, he quotes an assertion of Kenneth Copeland:

> You are an heir to the blessing which God gave to Abraham. This blessing, found in the 28th chapter of Deuteronomy, covers every area of your existence: spirit, soul, body, financially, and socially.
>
> (Hollinger 1989: 4; Copeland 1979: 22)

In addition, this Gospel combines a stress on Pentecostal healing revivalism with elements of 'New Thought Metaphysics'. The latter, also known as the 'Science of the Mind', was an important element in the writings of E.W. Kenyon, a key theological influence on the movement who worked in late nineteenth and early twentieth century New England. Derived originally from the writings of P.P. Quimby, it stresses the primacy of mind as the cause in all effects as well as the role of incorrect thinking in misfortune, and appears also to have influenced Mary Baker Eddy, the founder of Christian Science. New Thought Metaphysics is expressed in Prosperity Theology partly through the notion of 'positive con-fession', the idea that the born-again Christian can make a statement in faith that appropriates the blessings of God. Critics of 'positive confession' parody it by branding it as a gospel which simply states: 'Name it and Claim it!' Adherents of the Faith Gospel, however, perceive it more as a means of self-realization through the possession of correct faith.

Thus, Prosperity Theology clearly parallels Calvinism in its stress on the connection between grace and material prosperity, but combines this with a notion that the benefits of grace are available to *all* who submit to the faith. (This emphasis, away from a strict doctrine of predestination towards a more 'Methodist' one of salvation by 'grace through faith', is in fact characteristic of American revivalism in general.) The stress on autonomy and personal responsibility for salvation is combined with the assurance of success, once correct faith has been attained. For instance, Ekman closely parallels Copeland's words, quoted above, when he writes in a book entitled *Financial Freedom* that God's 'blessings touch every area for those who are partakers of His covenant' (1990: 5), and it is further argued by him that human demands can be met by unlimited resources, provided by a deity that is entirely reliable. The possession of faith can also encourage high consumption patterns, aggressive investment and financial initiatives, since the Christian can be assured of enough divine assistance:

> Ever since I began to walk in faith, I have never seemed to have enough in the natural. My expenses are considerably larger than my income. But praise the Lord, He has always found a way to solve the problem. I do not walk by what I see, I walk by what God says.

> *(ibid.*: 67)

Clearly, this is a doctrine which advocates neither the virtues of conservation nor limitation of desire, but rather a belief in the infinite availability and renewal of resources as a reward for correct faith. Furthermore, the general good is made to depend on the premise of individual gain, since the prosperity of the Christian is seen not only as a means of self-realization, but also a form of empowerment, allowing him or her to help others towards salvation at a time when as many people as possible need to be saved before the presumed imminent return of Jesus. As a consequence, Prosperity Teachings stress that selfishness consists not in demanding *more* resources, but in being satisfied with *less*, since the best way to use resources is to cause the salvation of others.

This view has clear affinities with an ethic of efficiency and professionalism which is often expressed in the idiom of the business world. Ekman states of Jesus, for instance: 'Not a bank in the world will give you such a good return on your investment . . . ' *(ibid.*: 83). Money, therefore, is important:

> This teaching about money should be seen in the light of the fact that we are living in the last days and in a time in which God is restoring and equipping His army. Victors in this area will make it possible for us to spread the Gospel around the world.

> *(ibid.*: 7)

Ekman is aware of the apparent incongruity of such a message in Sweden:

When I returned from America in 1982 where I had been attending Bible school, the first thing the devil told me was, "You can preach faith and healing here but not finances because people will think you are Americanized so don't say anything about money!".

(*ibid.*: 26)

However, the Lord is said to reply that Prosperity Teaching is needed in Sweden more than anywhere else precisely because it has been ignored in the country for too long.

The essential elements of Peter Berger's characterization of capitalism in *The Capitalist Revolution* (1987) are present in this form of Protestantism: a stress on rational calculation, the pursuit of profit, the recommendation of a free market and the appropriation of technological resources. Individual initiative, expansion and competition take on a new morality, and the charismatic message becomes blended with a form of instrumental rationality.[23] The supernatural becomes a realm of perfect predictability, in which certain causes have given effects, and worship itself becomes an activity whose effects can be measured and assessed in terms of bodies healed or bank accounts increased. The task of evangelization, meanwhile, can be reduced to a number of codifiable principles, aided by the prudent use of communications technology. Jerry Savelle, an American preacher whose work is on sale at the Word of Life, describes the evangelization process in his book: *Sharing Jesus Effectively: A Handbook on Successful Soul Winning*:

I have too much to do to waste my time on things that don't produce results. That's the way we should approach witnessing. Sharing Jesus is something that is very effective. If you will take the principles outlined in this study and apply them to your witnessing, you will have success with every person with whom you have the opportunity to share.

(1982: 7)

A similarly pragmatic attitude is displayed towards attendance at the Word of Life Bible school. A publication of the group states:

The Word of Life has the aim of equipping men and women for the great revival of the Last Days . . .

while it is claimed that

. . . knowing how God's plan for the Last Days is looking, hearing the prophetic word through pastor Ulf Ekman, teachers and guest speakers, creates a forceful goal-orientation in your life. God wants you to know that he wishes to use you personally, and he wants you to know what weapons you have and how you should use them.

(*Word of Life Newsletter*, May 1991: 4–5)

It is a feature of adherents that they are very concerned with assessing the effects of faith in terms of people saved or the size and success of the congregation and its enterprises. This can take dramatic form, as one magazine sold by the Word of Life quotes a pastor claiming that: 'The Berlin wall fell because of goal-oriented and effective prayer in the Holy Spirit' (*Magazinet*, October 1990: 30).

The Word of Life itself is located in a purpose-built structure at the heart of the industrial zone of Uppsala (referred to sardonically as a 'sports hall' by its critics), far from any other congregation. The fact that the group succeeded in building a church large enough to incorporate some 5,500 people, as well as include offices, a cafe, television studio and shop, is seen by many as a literally concrete demonstration of what can happen if an initiative is taken 'in faith'. At the first meeting of the congregation in the new building, Ekman stated that the empty seats in the hall simply represented people who were about to be saved, and who were *already* claimed for God. Thus, within a short period of time, it was suggested, the group would have to move into an even larger building.

Prosperity teachings are clearly also taken to have implications for ordinary members. Christian success in what is conventionally described as the secular world is seen as a means of demonstrating the measurable benefits of possessing faith to others, and consequently the rationality of conversion.[24] Adherents of the Word of Life talk of the development of their 'spiritual careers', measured by their ability to advance in the organization, convert others or start up their own ministries elsewhere. On the one hand, activities such as preaching are seen as parallel to ordinary work. For instance, Per-Olof, the head of a computer company in Uppsala called K-Data (the 'K' stands for 'Christian') claims: [25]

Preaching the Gospel . . . is a profession, it's a kind of work . . . it's as serious as being president, or more serious . . . if you were prime minister of Sweden that's less serious than being Ulf Ekman, and having his job . . .

On the other hand, it is commonly stated that work within the so-called profane world is just as important to God's plan as more obviously spiritual occupations such as preaching or full-time evangelization. Activity 'in the world' can act, for instance, as a means of spreading the Christian message. These are the words of Peter, a lawyer:[26]

One is accused [by one's colleagues] of being out for a career and being out to earn money . . . It's very simple . . . God loves people who have careers . . . God loves people who have success. God wants you to have success, wants you to have a career.

As a consequence:

Instead of travelling to India . . . [one should] take a job . . . be a Christian at one's workplace . . . be a light, a witness for one's workmates . . . When they meet such a Christian, they are encountering the Holy Spirit.

Furthermore, such activity can release resources for entrepreneurial Christians. Stefan, who combines work as a part-time pastor in Stockholm and regular visitor to the Word of Life with a job as a business consultant, states: [27]

We need businesses in Sweden which are steered by the Holy Spirit. It's frightening to look at the Swedish business world – the most ungodly category in the whole of Swedish society. Sweden is one of the world's richest countries . . . and there sit a load of ungodly old men who keep hold of all that money . . . Think if God could take over Volvo, for example . . . That would be wonderful, wouldn't it? . . . [With] spiritually anointed people who led Volvo, and all their billions . . . we could send out Volvo missionaries to the whole world . . .

All forms of initiative, in the world of business or other areas of life, are ultimately guaranteed success by God, and thus a considerable amount of confidence is displayed by many adherents. Nils, a part-time preacher and journalist, told me for instance that he had decided to move into a new house (incidentally, in the same suburb as Ekman's home) at the same time as his wife was leaving her job to look after their children full-time. This might appear 'mad' in a worldly sense, he admitted, but he was sure that God's purpose and support lay behind the decision, since it would enable his family to live in more suitable conditions while he, the head of the family, discovered his true vocation.[28]

PROSPERITY THEOLOGY AND THE GLOBALIZATION OF CIVIL RELIGION

> God bless Sweden
> God bless Sweden
> Bless all countries . . .
> (Word of Life Song)

The kind of approach I have been outlining advocates the appropriation of worldly resources and institutions for Christian purposes. To some extent, this permits a tendency, noted by Steve Bruce (1990) with regard to conservative Protestantism in general, to set up subcultures within the wider social order, parallel to but insulated from mainstream institutions. The Word of Life, for instance, has set up its own primary and secondary schools as an alternative to secular, state-run education. In addition, it is argued by adherents that communications technology – including satellite or cable television, videos, cassettes and books – are as valid a means of evangelization as face-to-face contact, since 'the Word' is seen an autonomous, concrete, saving force, applicable in any cultural context, and separable from its medium of transmission. This 'hypodermic' model of evangelization, involving a one-way form of communication between sender and receiver, is especially suitable for groups committed to unambiguous and uncontested notions of biblical truth, since for much of the time the signifier – i.e. the message broadcast – is divorced from its signified, or context of reception (see also Coleman 1991). The group can simultaneously satisfy its desire for 'outreach' and, for much of the time, keep a distance from potentially

171

disruptive influences, as the saving message itself becomes a commodity, packaged and sold through cassettes, videos or books.[29]

At other times, however, the group's desire to assimilate the institutions of society to its own ends brings it into rather more explicit engagement with the secular world, and here it is necessary to re-examine its relationship with and parallels to activist, conservative American Protestantism. A number of authors have noted that some religious conservatives in the United States have developed a new ethic of civility which goes beyond a stress on purely personal salvation, as they have attempted to regain their hold on the institutional mainstream of society.[30] Thus, they have developed their own interpretation of the symbols of American civil religion in order to lay claim to widespread legitimacy far beyond the walls of the church or ministry. This is made easier because such symbols retain a strong Judaeo-Christian flavour, involving the acceptance of a missionary role in the world, the establishment of a covenant with God associated with the nation's foundation, and a Manichean division of other nations into forces for evil or good. As part of this package, American capitalism gains credence in contrast to Communism or Fascism, and free enterprise is seen as biblically prescribed. The state is urged to give a moral lead, but to avoid unnecessary meddling in the lives of its citizens. Both God and the market should be left free, it is argued, to reward correct behaviour and punish the evil or lazy. It may be the case, as Wuthnow argues (1989), that such a *laissèz-faire*, decentralized form of capitalism is increasingly giving way in the United States to a more regulated, centralized form of production. However, its contemporary resonance with much popular discourse in north American society cannot be denied, combining as it does a stress on individual autonomy and a strong sense of national identity.

It might appear as though a set of teachings which consciously and unashamedly incorporates a celebration of the exemplary calling of a single nation-state would be unsuitable for export. However, the Word of Life illustrates an effective resolution of this dilemma, a means of giving the American civil religious message *local* salience in terms of Swedish national identity (cf. Coleman 1993). Group leaders present the Word of Life as part of a worldwide revival, involving a global division of labour between nations, in which no single country has preeminence. At a conference, for instance, Ekman presented a vision of God's glory being spread from the four corners of the earth, and meeting in Israel.[31] These corners were represented by Sweden in the north, the United States in the west, South Africa in the south, and South Korea – the location of Yonggi Cho's congregation – in the east. At the same time, however, it is argued that the boundaries of the nation-state are God-given, and that each nation has its own special calling. This version of a kind of globalized, civil religious ethic, incorporating a global division of labour, is well illustrated on the cover of a Word of Life Newsletter from September 1985, which displays the preachers from a variety of countries respectively waving their national flags in front of the congregation. Ekman's book, *God, the State and the Individual*, is dedicated to

... the new generation of Swedes who will take the Gospel to every home in Sweden and reach far beyond Sweden's borders with the power of God.

(1988: 3)

Within the country, the group is placed in a tradition of revivalism, committed to restoring the country to its true spiritual status. Alphonso Belin, an occasional preacher at the Word of Life, writes:

Sweden needs you – yes, the country and, even more, its people. We have to stand up, like the revivalist pioneers of old . . . and transform the atmosphere in our nation.

(*Word of Life Newsletter*, January-February 1988: 7).

The country's potential is believed to be demonstrated by the fact that, historically, Sweden has had a far greater influence over other nations than its small population would seem to allow. Furthermore, it is said to be placed in a strategically important position, since it is located so close to the countries of Eastern Europe. Thus, adherents have been referred to in an idiom which appropriates but modifies the language of American preachers, since they are called by preachers 'pioneers' in their own land, who have to evangelize in what has been called the 'wild east' of the formerly Communist countries rather than the wild west of the United States.[32] At other times, language is more explicitly biblical, with born-again Christians in Sweden often being compared with the nation of Israel in Exodus from the Pharaoh in a spiritual desert.

The implication of such an attitude towards Sweden as a religious polity is that Swedish institutions are regarded as in need of transformation and redefinition, if the country is to reach its true potential in the divine plan for the world. Again, Ekman takes the lead in this respect (1988). Government, according to him, is an institution set up by God, but in practice Social Democracy in Sweden has lost its authority through its support of secular humanist principles. The achievements of the Swedish workers' movement are to be defended, not least their support of democracy, but not the spirit of socialism which has inspired many of its members. The prosperity of the country is a cause for rejoicing, but is threatened rather than reinforced by high taxes, monopoly TV and a social administration which has prevented the true exercise of initiative, and a state ' . . . which has its finger in the pie of every area of peoples' lives' (*ibid.*: 29). The message here focuses on some of the institutions which have formed the basis of Swedish corporatism – such as Social Democracy, a centralized mass media, and the funding of an extensive welfare system – and suggests that they are in need of both moral revitalization and organizational deregulation. Like its American counterparts, the Word of Life and Swedish Faith Movement as a whole adopt the characteristic contemporary fundamentalist pose of opposition to the mainstream, while asserting the right to come in from the sidelines of society in order to identify the true goals of the nation-state.

173

RESONANCES AND REACTIONS

The description of the Prosperity Gospel given above should make clear that, in Sweden, conservative, charismatic Christianity can act as a paradigm for a form of anti-institutionalization. The notion of the spirit is seen as important both in terms of providing personal empowerment and in the sense of breaking down institutional hindrances to the divine plan. Such a message, despite the inchoate success of New Democracy, cannot derive strength from possible parallels or affinities with a prevailing ethos of *laissez-faire*. However, somewhat paradoxically, it clearly gains significance from its lack of fit with the Social Democratic ethos of corporatist capitalism. In effect, it acts as a symbolic expression of and potential catalyst for the shift from *congealed* to *competitive* pluralism – particularly in the religious and economic spheres of society.

The extent to which the Swedish Faith Movement has struck a sensitive chord in Sweden is demonstrated by the quite enormous attention it and in particular the Word of Life have inspired. This has been evident in literally thousands of newspaper articles, numerous academic works, a conference involving the previous, Social Democratic, prime minister,[33] and heated television debates. Those who have criticised the movement have ranged from journalists, clergymen, mostly liberal theologians, local Social Democratic politicians, ex-members and parents of members.

As Beckford (1985) has noted, the social construction of controversies over religious movements reflects to a considerable extent the particular concerns and insecurities of the cultural context in which the movements appear. 'Deviant' religious organizations can be represented as embodiments of all that is most feared or least desired by a particular section of (or mutually reinforcing network within) society. Among the issues highlighted in the case discussed here are precisely those aspects of the message of Faith Teaching which challenge the institutional division of labour of the presently disintegrating religio-political establishment: the advocacy of a *laissez-faire* approach in religion and economics, the desire for institutional decentralization, and the refusal to confine religious influence to the private sphere of society. Thus, the Word of Life is accused of mixing religion with business, and Ekman has been referred to scornfully in the press as 'God's capitalist'.[34] Academic works on Prosperity Theology also reflect this concern, with Hellberg's (1987) book being entitled *God and Money: On Prosperity Theology in the USA and Sweden*, while Nilsson's (1988) has the subtitle *On Business and Prayer in Sweden*.[35] Faith Teaching is also said to advocate a bypassing of the welfare system in favour of survival of the fittest – a situation where, unlike the ideal put forward by Ingvar Carlsson at the beginning of this chapter, not all can be winners, but only those most adapted to the religious or economic market. In a programme made about the group by national television in 1985, scenes from the group were juxtaposed with extracts from an interview with a severely handicapped woman, who claimed that Word of Life pupils had taunted her with the suggestion that her problems were of her

own making, since she merely needed to gain faith in order to get better.[36] Both
the Lutheran (State) Church and the Free Church movement are said to be
suffering from the disruptive and competitive influence of the Faith Movement
which, unlike the Charismatic Movement of the 1970s, appears to challenge
rather than revive already existing congregations. The Archbishop of the State
Church, for instance, has been damning in his criticism: [37]

> . . . [new religious] movements are often foreign to our own Christian
> interpretation and tradition of faith. Among these movements there is one
> which is closer to our own Church than others. I refer to the tendency which
> is often called Prosperity Theology . . .

This is said to cause 'splits, confusion and arguments', and the argument that
'correct faith is always rewarded with economic success, bodily health and
earthly happiness' is seen as unbiblical. The desire to link the group with a
threatening, *external* force is also evident in the claims, made in a number of
newspapers, that the group may be part of a network of hidden right-wing
organizations which provide a channel for Americanism into the country. One
newspaper, *Expressen*, even speculated in a number of articles written in 1986
that an adherent of Faith Teaching may have been responsible for the murder of
Sweden's former prime minister, Olof Palme.

THE FUTURE: PROSPECTS FOR PROSPERITY TEACHING IN SWEDEN

In some ways, the future of the Faith Movement in Sweden does not look bright.
The fact that the Word of Life has gained so much negative attention in Sweden
clearly has the ironic consequence of strengthening the resolve of its opponents
in favour of the ideals of an apparently established pattern of economic, political
and religious relations. The extent to which opposition to Prosperity Theology
has united self-appointed representatives of the Swedish pattern of church–state
relations is perhaps best illustrated by the words of a local Communist politician
in Uppsala, expressing her willingness actually to co-operate with the local
Swedish Covenant Church in opposition to the group. Her argument states that
her party and the Church can make common cause in order to defend shared,
essential values: 'It's a question of the same morals, the same understanding of
the concept of democracy'.[38]

In addition, the Faith Movement is marked by a number of internal contradictions. It has not, for instance, resolved the apparent paradox of advocating an
ideal of free speech and democracy in its civil religious guise and yet on other
occasions – most notably those aimed for internal consumption – acting as the
proponent for a message of exclusive, fundamentalist certainty. Unlike the New
Christian Right in the United States, the Movement has not as yet formed an
alliance with any established political party, and this is hardly likely to be of
benefit to the latter in a country where militant evangelicalism still has little

175

grass-roots support. Meanwhile, the Word of Life's relation to elements of modernity is somewhat ambivalent. It is clear that the group is reacting consciously in opposition to the perceived advance of secularization and the divide between the public and private spheres of society. On the other hand, it appears to have adapted to an ethic of instrumental rationality through its businesslike and efficiency-oriented attempt to realize its original, charismatically legitimated, vision.

However, it would be premature to predict a standard sociological fate of imminent sectarianization, accommodation or disappearance for the Faith Movement, despite its seeming incongruity in Sweden. One of the interesting features of contemporary religious organizations such as the Word of Life is that, because they are linked up to a global network of ideologically similar groups, they are rendered less vulnerable to their immediate cultural, religious and political environment than most beleaguered religious groups. Resources as well as enthusiasm and even personnel can be transferred from strong to weak points in the network, and it is clear that explicit contacts with the United States and indeed South Africa (through Ray McCauley) are maintained by the group. Furthermore, as I have suggested, although the Faith Movement is extremely unlikely to transform Sweden into a theocracy, it is operating at a time of considerable change. If aspects of the media and the polity become simultaneously removed from the centralizing influences of Social Democracy and linked up to global developments in economic, religious and cultural spheres, the Swedish Faith Movement may be entering an era of increased competition, but also one of increased opportunity.

NOTES

1 The initial words of the title of this paper come from the preacher Sandy Brown, and express the close relationship that she and many of her colleagues within the north American 'Faith Movement' see as developing between charismatic organizations in the United States and Sweden.

2 In (1985) *Believer's Voice of Victory* 13, 12: 14.

3 Cf. also Stoll (1990).

4 My approach also invites comparison with work currently being carried out on Prosperity Theology in other contexts. See Gustafsson (1987, 1991) for data on the situation in South Africa. Hackett (Chapter 10, this volume), discussing the Gospel of Prosperity in Nigeria, raises the issue of the facilitation of Western-style capitalism, mediated through the capacity of local populations to appropriate religious signs and structures in terms of local experience.

5 For an extended discussion of this debate, see Coleman (1989).

6 As we shall see, this process is aided by the fact that, as Hunter (1990) has noted, fundamentalist ideology tends to posit the existence of an organic unity between religious and political authority that encourages it to resist the differentiation of institutional spheres.

7 Ironically, of course, the success of Abba illustrates the possibility of achieving great wealth, though admittedly this is attained through success in an international arena.

8 Also quoted in Milner (1989: 228).

9 With around 85 percent of the working population unionized, an implicit social

contract has emerged whereby labour minimizes its demands for wage increases and in return benefits from policies aimed at full employment. A universalistic principle of distribution of welfare services is applied as a method of achieving social integration by reducing the importance of boundaries between social classes.

10 According to the Swedish Institute fact sheet on religion, printed in 1991, somewhat fewer than 5 percent of the population go to church each week.

11 According to the fact sheet quoted in note 10, the largest Christian churches represented in Sweden apart from the Lutheran Church are (in a population of around 8.5 million): Roman Catholic (140,200); Pentecostal (97,300); Orthodox and Eastern Churches (91,000); Mission Covenant Church of Sweden (78,800); Salvation Army (26,600); Swedish Evangelical Missionary Society (23,000); Jehovah's Witnesses (21,900); Örebro Mission Society (22,400); Baptists (20,500). There are also around 16,000 Jews and some 45,000 Muslims.

12 The term 'middle way' was popularized by Childs (1936).

13 Petersson (1991) discusses the role of the unions and the issue of decentralization in some detail.

14 Social Democrats polled 37.6 percent, down from 43.2 percent in the 1988 election (making it their worst election result since 1928); the Moderates gained 21.95 percent, compared with 18.35 percent three years earlier. In parliament, the latter can usually expect the parliamentary support of the Folk, Centre, Christian Democrat (CDU) and New Democracy parties.

15 According to the Swedish Institute fact sheet on the Swedish population, printed in 1989, immigration accounted for nearly 45 percent of the population increase during the period 1944–80, and every eighth child now born in Sweden is of foreign extraction.

16 A similar debate occurred after the assassination of the prime minister, Olof Palme, in 1986, as this was seen by many as signalling the end of Sweden as a country where citizens could ignore the terrorism and massive security precautions prevalent in other Western countries.

17 I have carried out participant-observation within the Word of Life since 1986, chiefly between 1986 and 1987, with shorter visits in 1989 and 1991.

18 Skog (March 1993) estimates that the Faith Movement has attracted around 8,000 actual members to some 90 congregations in Sweden.

19 This is based on an estimate in Nilsson (1988).

20 For information on this issue, see Bjuvsjö et al. (1985); Engel (1987).

21 Although in recent years Ekman and his 'mentor', Kenneth Hagin, appear to have grown apart owing to some theological differences.

22 Ray McCauley, for instance, is a South African preacher who trained at Hagin's school in 1978–9, and who now heads the Rhema Church in Randburg, Johannesburg (cf. O. Gustafsson 1987). He has become a regular visitor to Word of Life conferences in Sweden.

23 Of course, it is the case that initiatives are first validated by a 'vision' or 'word' from God, but this is not to say that the process of gaining success in an enterprise is not seen as subject to codes of efficiency and rationality.

24 The most graphic illustration of success recently occurred when an ex-student of the Bible school, who has also made her name as a popular singer in Sweden under the name 'Carola', recently won the Eurovision Song Contest.

25 Testimony recorded at Kristen Student Front meeting, Tape Two, 1987.

26 Testimony recorded at Kristen Student Front meeting, Tape Four, 1987.

27 Testimony recorded at Kristen Student Front meeting, Tape Three, 1987.

28 Of course, for many adherents to the Gospel of Prosperity it was hard to relate such teachings to a life of conspicuous economic, physical or social hardship. In interviews with apostates from the Word of Life, many of whom left for this reason, I found that

such people had felt it to be difficult to discuss failure or self-doubt in a context where
to *speak* words of failure was believed to be a *cause* of such a condition.

29 The group's Russian Internal Mission placed 100 video machines throughout the
Soviet Union and Eastern Europe as part of its mission policy.

30 See for instance Capps (1990), Coleman (1992), Fields (1991), Hunter (1984),
Wuthnow (1988).

31 Discussed in Gustafsson (1987).

32 Quoted from Word of Life Sunday Morning meeting, May 1991.

33 Harpsund Conference, Autumn 1986.

34 In this context, it is perhaps significant that the Christian Democrats and New
Democracy, although both broadly supporting the conservative bloc, have retained
very separate identities. Little affinity is perceived between the morally and religiously conservative policies of the former and the *laissez-faire* ideals of the latter.

35 This concern appears, superficially at least, to contrast with the Nigerian case, since
Hackett (Chapter 10, this volume) reports that the association of faith and material
prosperity appears not to rouse such controversy.

36 Discussed in Engel (1987).

37 See his *Uttalande om Livets Ord* (Statement concerning the Word of Life), released
to the press in March 1986. This was followed by another statement in July 1987.

38 Minutes of meeting held at Uppsala Swedish Mission Covenant Church, October
1986.

REFERENCES

Beckford, J. (1985) *Cult Controversies: The Societal Response to the New Religious
Movements*, Tavistock: London.

Berger, P. (1987) *The Capitalist Revolution: Fifty Propositions about Prosperity, Equality
and Liberty*, Aldershot: Wildwood House.

Bjuvsjö, S. *et al.* (1985) *Framgångsteologi i Sverige: Lundarapporten om den nya
trosförkunnelsen*, Stockholm: EFS.

Bruce, S. (1990) *Pray TV: Televangelism in America*, London: Routledge.

Capps, W. (1990) *The New Religious Right: Piety, Patriotism and Politics*, Colombia:
University of South Carolina Press.

Childs, M. (1936) *Sweden: the Middle Way*, New Haven: Yale University Press.

Copeland, K. (1979) *Welcome to the Family*, Fort Worth: KCP Publications.

Coleman, S. (1989) 'Controversy and the Social Order: Responses to a Religious Group
in Sweden', Unpublished Ph.D. thesis, Cambridge University.

Coleman, S. (1991) '"Faith which conquers the world": Swedish fundamentalism and the
globalization of culture', *Ethnos* 56, I–II: 6–18.

Coleman, S. (1992) 'Konservativ protestantism, politik och civilreligion i USA, in D.
Westerlund (ed.) *Sekularism ifrågasatt*, Uppsala: Svenska kyrkans forskningsråd.

Coleman, S. (1993) 'Conservative Protestantism and the world order: the Faith Movement in Sweden', *Sociology of Religion* 54, 4: 353–73.

Ekman, U. (1988) *Gud, staten och individen*, Uppsala: Livets Ord.

Ekman, U. (1990) *Financial Freedom*, Uppsala: Livets Ord.

Engel, C. (1987) *Livets Ord, Livets Ordare: En rapport om Stiftelsen Livets Ord, dess
församlingsmedlemmar och bibelskolelever*, Stockholm: Sociology of Religion Institute.

Fields, E. (1991) 'Understanding activist fundamentalism: capitalist crisis and the colon-
ization of the lifeworld', *Sociological Analysis* 52, 2: 175–90.

Gaunt, D. and Löfgren, O. (1984) *Myter om svensken*, Stockholm: Liber.

Gustafsson, O. (1987) 'Örnen har landat – utkast till ett forskningsprojekt', *Svensk
Missionstidskrift* 3: 45–59

Gustafsson, O. (1991) 'A new religious political right', in C. Hallencreutz and M. Palmberg (eds) *Religion and Politics in Southern Africa*, Uppsala: Scandinavian Institute of African Studies.

Hellberg, C.-H. (1987) *Gud och pengar. Om framgångsteologi i USA och i Sverige*, Stockholm: Verbum.

Hollinger, D. (1989) 'Enjoying God forever: an historical/sociological profile of the health and wealth gospel', paper delivered to 1989 British Sociological Association, Sociology of Religion Group Meeting, London.

Hunter, J. (1984) 'Religion and political civility: the coming generation of American evangelicals', *Journal for the Scientific Study of Religion* 23, 4: 364–80.

Hunter, J. (1990) 'Fundamentalism in its global contours', in N. Cohen (ed.) *The Fundamentalist Phenomenon: A View from Within, A Response from Without*, Grand Rapids: Eerdmans.

Huntford, R. (1971) *The New Totalitarians*, London: Allen Lane.

Kelman, S. (1991) 'Swedish model on a diet', *The Guardian*, 7 August.

Martin, D. (1990) *Tongues of Fire: The Explosion of Protestantism in Latin America*, Oxford: Blackwell.

Milner, H. (1989) *Sweden: Social Democracy in Practice*, Oxford: Oxford University Press.

Nilsson, F. (1988) *Parakyrkligt: Om business och bön i Sverige*, Stockholm: Verbum.

Petersson, O. (1991) 'Democracy and power in Sweden', *Journal of Scandinavian Political Studies* 14, 2: 173–91.

Rothstein, B. (1991) 'State structure and variation in corporatism: the Swedish case', *Journal of Scandinavian Political Studies* 14, 2: 149–71.

Savelle, J. (1982) *Sharing Jesus Effectively: A Handbook on Successful Soul-Winning*, Tulsa: Harrison House.

Skog, M. (1993) 'The Mormons, Jehovah's Witnesses and the Faith Movement in Sweden', paper delivered at conference on New Religions and the New Europe, London School of Economics, 25–6 March.

Stoll, D. (1990) *Is Latin America Turning Protestant? The Politics of Evangelical Growth*, Berkeley: University of California Press.

Tomlinson, J. (1991) *Cultural Imperialism: A Critical Introduction*, London: Pinter.

Wuthnow, R. (1988) *The Restructuring of American Religion: Society and Faith Since World War II*, Princeton: Princeton University Press.

Wuthnow, R. (1989) *The Struggle for America's Soul: Evangelicals, Liberals, and Secularism*, Grand Rapids, MI: Eerdmans.

Wörlund, I. (1992) 'The Swedish parliamentary election of September 1991', *Journal of Scandinavian Political Studies* 15, 2: 135–43.

9

POWER AND EMPOWERMENT

New Age managers and the dialectics of modernity/post-modernity

Richard H. Roberts

INTRODUCTION AND CONTEXT

This chapter pertains to the research project entitled *Religion and the Resurgence of Capitalism* co-ordinated by the writer in the Department of Religious Studies at the University of Lancaster (1989–91).[1] The immediate socio-cultural context of the present argument is represented in a paper published early in 1992[2] in which I argued for an evolutionary and differentiated understanding of the 'Enterprise Culture'[3] and its religio-cultural dimensions in recent British experience.[4]

In summary, it was argued that the latter reveals the general patterns of a 'hard' Thatcherite '*lex*', a disciplinary and quasi-punitive view of society crystallized in the doctrine of 'rational expectations'. This was a kind of 'reality principle' characteristic of the early years of the Thatcher era which co-existed ideologically with a 'soft' understanding of the Enterprise Culture as the visionary goal of a new dynamic business-driven, enterprise-oriented society of free-ranging entrepreneurs, so thoroughly emancipated from dependency corruption that they could be motivated by reward rather than by the threat of punishment. The crucial difference between the 'Thatcher era' and subsequent 'Majorism' consists in the imposition of a managerial approach to many areas of society space and the virtual abandonment of high-profile, public rhetorical discourse in favour of context-related presentational and enforcement policies. On the one hand, the privatization of many potentially profitable state monopolies has taken place; on the other, the residual areas of state welfare, notably health, welfare and education, have been subjected to drastic reform in which the introduction of managers and managerialism has resulted in rapid social change and a crisis in the professions affected.

Metaphorically, the 'hard' side of the 'Enterprise Culture', designated the equivalent of the Roman '*lex*', was a structured, delimited existence which demanded obediential conformity to laws, transmitted, 'presented' and received through visible (and apparently universal) line-management structures.[5] These structures have gradually been extended as far as politically possible though the public sphere – indeed became co-terminous with society itself. Within this matrix

180

of differentiated enforcement there are degrees of severity and some exceptions: it is the highly significant rise of the manager as member of an elite (and the marked decline of other professionals)[6] which constitutes a key factor in the context addressed. In contradistinction to Harold Perkin's depiction of the 'rise' of professional society, we may now observe its 'decline'.[7] The role of this new managerial elite as key mediators, as a societal *Vermittlung*,[8] has yet fully to be evaluated.

Thus apparently opposed to the first 'hard' type of British enterprise, there is a second broad approach focused in the charismatic managerial elite of so-called 'core-workers',[9] potentially antinomian in character, which in terms of the parallel can be understood as the 'Montanist' or 'Gnostic' microcosm of those who are permitted and encouraged to maximize their performance and accumulation of economic and cultural capital through dynamic self-realization, rather than through conformity to rules.

On the theoretical level this juxtaposition of ideal types corresponds to a marked degree with a well-established (although much disputed and repeatedly defined and redefined) distinction between the 'modern'[10] and the 'post-modern condition'.[11] Particularly apposite for the purposes of this chapter is Anthony Giddens' articulation of the contrast between modernism and post-modernism. Modernism can be defined as:

cultural or aesthetic styles, visible in various realms such as architecture, the plastic and visual arts, poetry and literature, ... developed in conscious opposition to classicism; it emphasises experimentation and the aim of finding an inner truth behind surface appearances. Post-modernism, supposedly, is in some part a recovery of a classical romantic outlook. It is not a reversion to tradition, because tradition today is just as defunct as is the truth for which modernism strove. Post-modernism is decentred; there is a profusion of style of and orientation. Stylistic changes no longer "build on the past", or carry on a dialogue with it, but instead are autonomous and transient. Any attempt to penetrate to a "deeper" reality is abandoned and mimesis loses all meaning.[12]

As regards the particular context or the subject matter of this chapter, the broad distinction between the modern and the post-modern is expressed in the fundamental contrast that can be drawn for present purposes between a type A 'scientific management' as classically expressed by Frederick W. Taylor:

Under the old type of management, success depends almost entirely upon getting the "initiative" of the workman, and it is indeed a rare case in which this initiative is really attained. Under scientific management the "initiative" of the workmen (that is their hard work, their goodwill and their ingenuity) is obtained with absolute uniformity and to a greater extent than is possible under the old system; and in addition to this improvement on the part of the men, the managers assume new burdens, new duties and responsibilities never dreamed of in the past. The managers assume for instance, the burden of gathering together of the traditional knowledge which in the past has been possessed by the workman and then of classifying, tabulating and reducing this knowledge to rules, laws and formulae which are immensely helpful to the workman in doing their daily work.[13]

Opposed to this is a type B 'human resources management' which is open to far more open-ended depiction.[14] In other words, a whole array of 'post-modern' characteristics of fluidity and fragmentation are applicable[15] in the context of the death of metanarratives and the *disponibilité* of all cultural artifacts in a globalized marketplace in which global economic capital is the controlling factor in the production, distribution and acquisition of all cultural capital.[16]

The contrast between scientific and human resources (post-modern) management can be expressed in many ways, but one broad distinction can be drawn which is of some utility for this argument: *scientific management* is concerned above all with power and rational control of the total productive process through a transfer of reflexive agency from worker to management, quintessentially expressed in the ever extending application of British Standard 5750 in so-called 'Quality Audit':

A systematic and independent examination to determine whether quality activities and related results comply with planned arrangements, are implemented effectively and are suitable to achieve objectives.

This approach raises obvious, but little discussed ethical questions. *Human resources management*, by contrast, is concerned far more with understanding and then linking individual motivation with corporate goals through active *transformation* and *synergesis*. Management type A stresses overt power, obedience and conformity, in a low, or no trust environment;[17] management type B seeks to devolve power and enhance reflexivity and agency through 'empowerment'.[18]

Such a contrast drawn between type A 'low-trust' power and type B 'high-trust' empowerment approaches to the management of human resources is, of course, an extreme simplification of complex real situations, nonetheless it is representative enough to be employed for heuristic purposes in the present investigation.

The viability and appropriateness of type A and type B management approaches depend upon a number of factors, of which the following are important: (i) the historic 'culture' of any given organization; (ii) the type of task undertaken by the organization; (iii) the economic condition of the organization; (iv) the quality of the existing management. The crucial problem is the following: any given organization may fall primarily under a type A or type B category of management; but if *either* type A decides to change into type B; *or* if an organization wishes to combine *both* within a single (usually stratified) structure, then two problems occur with which the organization is often ill-equipped to cope. If change is to take place, then a level of reflexivity is usually required beyond the capacity of the extant organization; in other words a 'midwife',

182

'facilitator' or 'enabler' is needed. If, on the other hand, both type A and type B are to co-exist, then the transition points and fault lines have to be understood and managed effectively if staff are to cross the boundary without unproductive psycho-personal dysfunction.

In both instances organizational change takes place which precipitates crisis at the level of individual and corporate cultural identities and in root paradigms of the organizational or company 'culture'. In a shrinking economy and global recession it may prove a short term economy to terminate and discard staff whose cultural formation proves obsolescent.[19] If, however, change is to be attempted with existing human resources, then such change may well require facilitation by individual or teams of human resource specialists, whose identities and agency are, as it were, unpolluted by the environment into which they are to enter. It is interesting to note that the 'scientific' managerial type A approach would appear to be designed to safeguard a stable environment contructed for the implementation of policy, whereas the more flexible type B human resources approach equips a well-differentiated quality labour force with adaptive and innovatory skills.

Specialists in facilitating organizational change have a variety of designations, 'management consultant' and 'management trainer' being common collective terms that operate in a large market in which a wide range of niches open and close as the business climate changes. It is this sector ('group' is a misnomer, a constantly reworked 'network' is more apt) which provides specialist human resource services to business, industry and the residual public sector. Their trade is, as it were, personality and behavioural modification; or to resort to the discourse employed: 'empowerment', 'transformation', 'realization', 'facilitation', 'enabling', and so on. The human services thus provided are, however, very different from those traditionally associated with 'scientific (i.e. line-) management' and its specialisms. This is not a matter of a behaviourist approach involving a coherent scheme of punishments and rewards in the human equivalent of the maze – the changes involve self-willed transformations in consciousness and the opening up of the personality so that the selected employees will, through *self-discovery* and *self-development*,[20] uncover the sources of new dynamism in the context of the 'love'[21] that flows through the 'learning organization'.[22]

'JOINING FORCES': BUSINESS AND SPIRITUALITY IN A NEW AGE

This section consists in an ethnographic study, grounded in participant observation, of a large international conference of New Age management consultants and trainers.[23] This one event brought into a possibly unrepeatable conjunction a range of actors and factors. It took place in early 1990 when the second Thatcher government had reached a peak of self-confidence and the consumer boom had not yet broken; there was a sense that the sky was the limit and that a new world order was breaking in which human resources management would play a leading role in the process of social enlightenment; nothing less, indeed, than the evolution of a new cosmic and human order.[24]

The presentation and analysis is structured in terms which reflect the cycle of the event itself which was conceived as a totality, a large scale initiatory and transformatory ritual enacted by the whole conference. The event involved a sequential pattern of entry, psychic cleansing, illumination, transformation, collective reinforcement, bonding and a return to 'the world'. The diachronic structure that was relatively simple; the pattern of a ritual journey from where each individual was at, as it were, into the unknown, was clearly understood by most of those there (exceptions had a stressful time and had to integrate or 'migrate' very quickly). The synchronic structure was extremely complex; outside the plenary occasions a vast array of activities was taking place in a pattern which might be best described as an active post-modern cultural bazaar in which all were both customers and sellers. The vast majority of those present were adepts; those who were not appeared to do their utmost to enter the flow as soon as possible. There was no dissent or detectable discord throughout.

Entry qualifications and 'gate-keeping'

The event in question was co-organized by a team of management trainers based in the management school of a British university founded in the 1960s and a core team of independent consultants. As a researcher working in a university, it became apparent that gaining entry to the event was not going to be as easy as the writer initially anticipated. There was a definite psychic and intellectual security system in operation to filter out potentially disruptive attitudes. Thus it was that the only academic participants from the host university were a colleague (an anthropologist) and the present writer, and it became clear that access would be possible only on the basis of *active* participation; this was indeed to be a bazaar in which all were to be both sellers and tasters.

After a three month period of intermittent negotiation the colleague (an archetypal 'fly on the wall' anthropological observer) was admitted in order to present and comment upon some audio visual material, the writer was admitted as one of a small team of 'narrators'. The narrators' role was to crystallize and reflect back to the conference the evolution of the event itself as it took place. This involved considerable initial culture shock because, far from observing from the margins, it was necessary to take part in the plenary gatherings in a very exposed way as part of a small team of two women and two men (and two further part-timers). The team was under the direction of the women, both of whom were full-time partners in a leading independent consultancy specializing in transformatory techniques in 'learning organizations'. The initial briefing session made it apparent that the mode of control in the event was to be a through a virtuoso juxtaposition of leadership/orchestration (with group improvization) on the one hand, and the relative spontaneity of individuals on the other. This was no mean achievement in a highly diverse conference of some 150 participants, most of whom had a specific product to display, enact and sell, and who were in consequence in immediate competition for market attention. Indeed the 'market' was not only the target of effort but also, simultaneously, the *context* of human self-realization, interpersonal interaction and the arena of a variety of human relationships.[25]

The departure

The event proper began on two levels. First there was a briefing meeting on the opening morning of the event with the narrators during which all were presented with their collective role as narrators. The control of the group was pointedly non-hierarchical and woman-led, the emphasis being upon collective and affective planning along 'brain-storm' lines. The preparation consisted in the visual, oral and dramatic appraisal of the opening assembly. Having visited the site for performance and having some knowledge of rite and liturgy it was apparent that there was a considerable initial task to be faced which involved confronting and overcoming the grossly alienative environment (a massive early 1980s lecture theatre built for mass higher education on a windswept and decaying brick campus). On the spiritual level the problem of alienative modernity was tackled throughout the event by the deployment of two full-time women spiritual adepts/ counsellors, who, after an initial meditation over crystals with the narrators in a crowded university 'restaurant', provided spiritual support throughout the event through continual (and publicly announced) meditation.

The visual and affective deficiencies of the lecture theatre were confronted head-on in the first plenary session, once the spiritual power-base had as it were been set in action. It is not in this writer's judgement view possible to reduce or coordinate the opening 'ceremony' to a single dominant theme, but the ritual structure was obvious. The organizing motif and ruling metaphor was the representation of the conference itself as an organic entity with a 'spiritual life' of its own existing part-way between the source of the analogy, the 'spiritual life' and 'soul' of the individual, and a further 'target' *analogans*, the organization that was to be transformed. The often alluded to juxtaposition of narrative and work contexts constituted a consistent pattern of 'inter-spirituality'. Thus, in this instance, the first question posed in the opening plenary by one of the recognized leader-figures (an anthroposophist and follower of Rudolf Steiner) were: 'Does this Conference have a soul? And what is this soul like?'. Extensive discussion of the nature of this 'soul' followed.

It is important to record that the discourse of the conference specifically avoided (indeed excluded) all forms of traditional business or commercial discourse; such terms as 'money', 'finance management', even 'business', 'commerce' and their cognates were conspicious by their absence. The mediation of the transformatory process through discourses of enlightenment was rigorously (although apparently informally) enforced. This was an environment in which the refunctioned and relocated principle: 'Seek ye first the kingdom of heaven and all these things shall be added unto you' was throughly operationalized. Money and modernity did not transgress the perimeter of the exclusion zone in any overt form.

The opening collective act of the conference proper involved the aural and visual sanctification of the lecture theatre. After an hour of intense expressive activity with paint and paper the room was transformed by covering all the walls with pictures, declarations, poetry and slogans embodying the hopes and fears of the participants. The bare room had become an internally-differentiated sacred space with several focal points, including confessional, reflective and expressive wall spaces for the posting of spontaneous written utterance; the whole constituted a complete enclosure, a theatre of opportunity. There was, in addition, a specially arranged and dedicated computer network[26] available for individual and interpersonal spiritual communication. To venture into the lecture theatre was to depart from a mechanical and instrumental world and to enter into an affective realm of new possibilities in the sacred space. For the relatively successful initiate, stomach-churning embarrassment would turn into achievement as 'risk-taking' built confidence and mutual trust in the theatre of risk and opportunity.

At this juncture it is important to note that many of those present were advising senior management[27] in a series of reputable companies and on occasion given charge of complete cohorts of managerial trainees in order to 'transform' and enhance their human resources. Yet a suspension of belief in an external prescriptive modernity was seemingly central to what then took place.[28] It is also relevant to note that the economic conditions that underlaid the event in question may no longer apply.[29]

The narrators had conferred at length in preparatory meetings. It had become apparent that the only remotely organic image or artifact capable of functionalization in the hostile environment of the lecture theatre was the skeleton of a small whale about 5 metres in length which had been washed up dead on a local headland, buried and then exhumed and suspended from the ceiling. Thus it was that the narrators hit upon the key to resolve the problem set them, the instantaneous invention of a mythic narrative and particular ruling metaphor for the whole event. Thus the following declamatory narrative was formulated and pronounced in antiphonic form:

Once upon a time there was a baby whale.
That had the misfortune to float ashore not
far from here.
It's lost its mother
and lost its sense of direction
It ran aground
wriggled about
tried to escape
But it died.
And it began to smell – very bad
But some useful academics

186

found it and they brought it back
and buried it
And after two years they dug it up
and they thought
their students could learn something
from it.
And we may not be students of biology
But when we look at this
dead baby whale
We know and
the students know it once lived
It's got a head, flippers, tail.
But it's got no heart.
it's dead – very dead.
The question it poses
Is a universal one.
Can these dry bones live?
[Two teams alternating in unison]
No! No! No!
Yes! Yes! Yes!
How can we get some flesh on it?
How can we get it to move?
Is this once living organism
Like the organization known to you?[30]

In classic manner of Van Gennep and Victor Turner,[31] ritual and myth were functionalized in active interlocution. Thus in our instant rite of passage we moved a timeless primal origin in the sea, through a vulnerable existence full of ecological pathos, underwent the intervention of the critical instrumental intellect (and its failure!) to experience the latencies of the present moment of re-enfleshment. Thus a ritual act began in which pre-modern *arche* and the archaic, instrumental modernity and post-modern mythopoesis interflowed – the event was launched.

The New Age bazaar

The apparent synchronic complexity of the event was apparent in the great diversity of the individual programmes offered. Closer examination of the descriptions provided of each offering reveals a marked uniformity of discourse in which key commonplaces or *topoi* recur. It would be possible to draw a distinction between the discourse and form of the transformatory experiences on offer and the particular cultural and spiritual artifacts functionalized in the many individual rites of passage. Thus through meditation (coloured or styled from a variety of sources), dance, explicit ritual acts of, say, North American origin, psychodrama, experiential paths of self-discovery, voice discernment and therapy, and so on, the core terms took on flesh. Thus 'everyday spirituality', 'exploring the human spirit', 'connecting with your genius', the priority of the 'nourishment of the human spirit', 'spiritual common sense', seeking 'deeper Wisdom', 'resourcing the spirit', finding the 'soul of the business organization', 'learning networks', attaining 'wholeness', 'guided visualization', dealing with 'organizational angels and beasts', the 'organizational Dream', besides the whole panoply of now relatively traditional and widely disseminated New Age techniques.

One of the most striking 'disciplines' enacted was that of 'Warriors and Tyrants' demonstrated by a charismatic woman initiate of the Deer Tribe (from the West of Scotland) who outlined a cycle of conflict and resolution:

> It is not actually that difficult to stay happy and centred whilst sitting on a mountain top in India – commuting everyday to work in a large organiz-ation, or even living with your family or being with friends involves confronation with rather more tyrants. In this short session I will con-centrate on sharing[32] some of the Deer Tribe teachings on how to be a Warrior. We will talk about the tools of Reconnaissance, Tactics, Strategy, Forbearance, and timing to fight the enemies of Fear, Anger, Stress and Anxiety, and learn to transform them into the excitement of Stalking a Tyrant. The key to dealing with all tyrants is knowledge. Firstly to have enough self awareness to know yourself, especially your weak spots better than your tyrant. This knowledge will allow you to stay centred within yourself whilst tyrants try to push you off balance.

Exit and aggregation

The final plenary meeting, truly a congregational event, involved poetry, ecstatic utterance (including St Paul on love from 1 Corinthians), the recitation of personal myths, narratives, individual sagas of self-development and the enhanced expression of a sense of intense fervour, a spoken yearning for the regeneration of the organization as a salvific locus. The narrators tried to focus the event; the present writer composed and decalimed the following, which had the very useful purpose of isolating key terms used frequently throughout the conference:

A Deconstructive Prose Declamation (!)
(or)
Joining Forces – A Conference Alphabet
A is for avatar, aura, arrogant, act, for ally, angels . . .
and assertion
B is for beast, beauty, brute, baby, BMW, for birth . . .
and beginning
C is for colleagues and crystals, for calm, cause, for circles
and cycles, collision, collapse . . . and crisis!
D is for death, dance, delight, depths, decision,

188

and the definition
(we're always resisting)
E is for empathy, enlightenment (where?)
Exegesis (what's that?)
eggs and eggheads,
ENERGY!!! . . . and emergence
F is for failure, fear, for freak-out . . . and FUTURE
G is for goddess, gold, goodness . . . for gripes? . . .
for your god (if you have one)
H is for hell-hole (the company office?) . . . hugging and healing
I's for injustice, impotence . . . and incarnation
J is for justice, 'judicious' (the bishop?), jealous and jinxed
K is for Kill! . . . kerygma (the company message!) and karma
L is for lucidity, lust . . . link-up and love
M is for money and mind, for magic, meditation . . .
and the company mission
N is for neutral (participant observer)
O is for organ, organism, orgy, orgasm . . . the Organization!
P is for peace-pipe, for persons, persuasion . . . and PERFORMANCE!
Q is for quaking and quelling disturbance
R is for reach-out, rebellion, rights, revolution/resolution
S is sincerity, sex, spirit, and SPIRITUALITY!
T is for terror and tyrants . . . and for telling the story
U is for ultimate . . . and for use and utility
V is for voice, victim, values . . . and victor!
W is for WOMEN, for whales, work, weeping, and WARRIORS . . .
and wimps
X is for exact, excitement . . . and X the Unknown
Y is for youth, for yodels and Yuppies
Z is for zany, for zoo . . . and it's over to you!

INTERPRETATION: LUDIC RELIGION

The discourse employed at this fascinating conference was highly distinctive, and always *reflected* speech. Everything was *constructive*[33] and *complementary,* clearly one of the major reasons for excluding academics would appear to be the unrestrained critical and programmatic response to the play-led spontanteity and non-analytical, affective, goal-oriented style of all communications. No-one who could not 'become as a little child' could enter this particular kingdom. Huizinga's description of play as 'a free activity standing quite consciously outside "ordinary life" as being "not serious", but at the same time absorbing the player intensely and utterly . . . It proceeds within its own proper boundaries of time and space according to fixed rules and in an orderly manner'[34] would have some relevance at this juncture. The recirculation of experience was constant and aided by the systematic practice of 'reporting back'. The overall mythic and narrative structure of the event was informed by the pervasive use of organic metaphors and the ascription of consciousness to the collective dimension: the conference itself had a 'soul'.

Within the overall framework and orchestration of the main plenaries the open sessions were 'post-modern' in the purest sense of the power available to engage in the eclectic refunctioning of psychic cultural artifacts. Thus the spontaneous singing by a voice therapist of the hymn 'Amazing Grace' would follow a favourite poem, a dictum from Goethe, or a brief quasi-confessional narrative of a 'risk' taken. The general ocean of convergent feeling was filled as far as the eye could see with a myriad spiritual artifacts which gently rose and fell although sometimes this was disrupted when a primal scream rang out as the raw unconscious rose like a Polaris from the depths of a participant.

On the level of collective representations, it has become apparent in the material reviewed above how the extreme spiritual eclecticism is nevertheless informed by integrative themes. Central to the latter, and perhaps the most crucial, is the juxtaposition of 'being at cause' and 'being at effect'. The displacement of 'power' by 'empowerment' centres on the sustainability of social and network integration – it is a field worth further careful exploration.[35]

Observation of adepts in their capacity as management consultants and trainers indicates that a very close correlation between personal and work partnerships is sustained by 'switches' when one working relationship or partnership which has worked well for a period of perhaps several years is broken suddenly and apparently without explanation. The ready acceptance of such ruptures would appear to be a integral part of an attitude and life-world commitment which functions in terms of 'at-causality' and 'synchronicity'. Wide-ranging contact revealed little evidence of active involvement with children or other dependants. Indeed, forms of 'dependency' were not a feature of the many 'programmes' and initiations on offer.[36]

General goals were 'enhanced autonomy', increased self-awareness and systematic 'accessing' of undiscovered or lost parts of the person. The specific references made to William Blake by some participants were thoroughly representative of the general belief frequently expressed, that therapeutic and performance striving involved the rediscovery and actualization of a lost, primordial, empowering primal self.

On the level of the collective representations and 'metaphysics' of the event the discourse revealed a relative lack of concern with the past. Thus there was very little space given to regressive self-exploration: contact with the primal self appeared to be an encounter with forces tending to *empowerment* and not a judgemental *power*-holding authority to bind or loose the past. Life is *now* – and for *tomorrow*. The story begins where you want it to begin: the metanarrative no longer commands – your story frees. The informing motif of the event was a sense of discovering transcendental power in and within the mundane. For one leading woman participant this transfiguration of the mundane was best expressed by the poet Wallace Stevens:

Evade, this hot, dependent orator,
The spokesman at our bluntest barriers
Exponent by a form of speech, the speaker

Of a speech only a little of the tongue?
It is the gibberish of the vulgate that he seeks.
He tries by a peculiar speech to speak

The peculiarly potency of the general,
To compound the imagination's Latin with
The lingua franca et jocundissima.

Each encounter, each new decision, each task took on the character of an occasion of being, *my* being, *my self* in greater fulfilment. The ground swell of the event involved 'connecting with your genius' and an 'everyday spirituality' which identified self-realization with the flow, an unwilled because willed-from-the-cause identification which orchestrates reality and integrates *self-fulfilment* with *synchronicity* and *performance* in the at-causality of primordial being. The ethical implications of this expressivist conviction (despite the affective benevolence) are not risk free.[37]

CONCLUSION

The generation of a critique of the employment of 'New Age' techniques in management training involves many as yet inadequately explored areas of theoretical, methodological and ethical concern. As regards the latter, three obvious areas of concern arise. First, how far it is legitimate to oblige employees to submit themselves to training programmes which are (at the very least) mood-altering and may, if there is a predisposition, induce psychological disturbance or even health problems, both mental and physical.[38] Second, should the distribution of 'spiritual' and behavioural training be organized in ways which entrench and reinforce structural differentiation in the labour force, on the assumption that such training may be understood as a reward or benefit paid in kind. Third, the *spiritual* development of human resources implies the possibly problematic assimilation of religiosity as a human resource into a globalized capitalist world system. The latter might thereby assume unassailable control and management of *all* resources, material, economic, cultural – and now religion. Such an assimilation may well call into question basic convictions concerning the constitution and definition of the human and the nature of human development. Furthermore, we must now pose ourselves the question that if spirituality, religiosity and religion have been functionalized and commodified in the ways suggested above, then are we not bound to inquire as to whether aspects of human rights need to be reconstrued in 'post-modernity'? Do we not now need to recognize and chart the constitutive role of the production, distribution and exchange of cultural capital in the micro- and macroeconomies of local and and global religion?

191

NOTES

1 I wish to acknowledge the support of the Christendom Trust which funded the Reckitt Research Fellowship held by the writer in the Department of Religious Studies at Lancaster University from 1989–91. Many discussions with colleagues in Lancaster made this an extremely fruitful experience. Particular thanks are due to Adrian Cunningham, Paul Heelas and Paul Morris. In addition, I am indebted to James Good, Co-Director of the Centre for the History of the Human Sciences in the University of Durham with whom I have had many discussions concerning the nature of the human and social sciences and their interrelation. See Roberts and Good (1993).

2 Roberts (1992).

3 For background see Keat and Abercrombie (1991); Lord Young of Graffham (1990) and Heelas and Morris (1991).

4 In this paper I expand on the notion of 'enterprise religion' outlined in Roberts (1992). See also Sedgwick (1992).

5 'Structure' is a potentially misleading term. What is involved is not usually a visible and rigid system, unless the mode of visibility chosen for strategic managerial purposes requires this. Thus, for example, in organizational studies, the key terms are 'formations of power' and 'circuits of power' which recognize the dynamic, re-circulatory character of effective systems which maintain their stability through the constant incorporation or exclusion of real of threatened deviance. See Clegg (1989, 1990); Clegg and Dunkerley (1980).

6 See Perkin (1989) and Braverman (1974).

7 To what extent the instrumental religosity of this elite can be regarded as legitimatory rather than purely functional in increasing self-developed performance is an issue not directly confronted in this paper, but see Roberts (forthcoming).

8 'Mediator' is preferable to a term like 'hegemon' because it is in a sense unclear who is, as it were, in charge in contemporary British society. Often enough it is eccentric, but extremely powerful cliques of over-empowered 'Great and the Good/Bad' who appear to rule. Current (1993) enforcement of policy in secondary education is a case in point where professional judgement is ignored in the interests of total centralized control.

9 A key part of the rhetoric of policy presentation may involve the abandoment in hegemonic discourse of images of vertical hierarchy in favour of core–periphery models, in spite of actual political realities. For example, as regards higher education, see Sir Douglas Hague's model of the super-core and 'flexible labour force':

> What will the university be? The short answer is that it will become a base for a diverse set of people and activities . . . the 'shamrock' organization, which is now seen as typical of businesses in the 1990s, not least in the knowledge industries. The shamrock has three parts – hence its name: a professional core, a contractual fringe and a flexible labour force (Hague 1991: 57).

10 Bauman (1988a, b, 1989, 1991); Bellah (1970, 1976); Berger (1977); Davis (1990); Hartt et al. (1986); Poole (1991); Vattimo (1988); Whimster and Lash (1987).

11 Bernstein (1991); Foster (1985); Giddens (1990, 1991); Griffin (1989); Harvey (1989); Jencks (1989); Kroker and Cook (1988); Lawson (1985); Lyotard (1984).

12 Giddens (1992).

13 Taylor (1947: 357).

14 Adams (1986); Belasco (1990); Bennis (1989); Boyatzis (1982); Bradford and Cohen (1984); Brown (1988); Carmichael and Drummond (1989); Constable (1987); Deal and Kennedy (1988); Drucker (1985); Evans and Russell (1989); Handy (1985, 1987a, 1987b, 1989); Harvey-Jones (1987); Heider (1986); Kets and Miller (1985); Kotter (1982); Messing (1989); Moss Kanter (1984); Pascale and Athos (1982);

Peters (1989); Peters and Austin (1986); Peters and Waterman (1982); Sargent (1983); Schoef and Fassel (1988); Toffler (1989).

15 Lyotard (1979: xxiv):

> Incredulity towards metanarratives. This incredulity is undoubtedly a product of progress in the sciences: but that progress in turn presupposes it. To the obsolescence of the meta-narrative apparatus of legitimation corresponds, most notably, the crisis of metaphysical philosophy and of the university institution which in the past relied on it. The narrative function is losing its functors, its great hero, its great dangers, its great voyages, its great goal. It is being dispersed in clouds of language narrative elements – narrative, but also denotative, prescriptive, descriptive, and so on. Conveyed within each cloud are pragmatic valencies specific to its kind. Each of us lives at the intersection of many of these. However, we do not necessarily establish stable language combinations, and the properties of the ones we do establish are not necessarily communicable.

More critically, David Harvey maintains that:

> Post-modernism, with its emphasis upon the ephemerality of jouissance, its insistence upon the impenetrability of the other, its concentration on the text rather than the work, its penchant for deconstruction bordering on nihilism, its preference for aesthetics over ethics, takes matters too far. It takes them beyond the point where any coherent politics are left, while that wing of it seeks a shameless accommodation with the market puts it firmly in the tracks of an entrepreneurial culture that is the hallmark of reactionary neoconservatism. Post-modernist philosophers tell us not only to accept but even to revel in the fragmentations and the cacophony of voices through which the dilemmas of the modern world are understood. Obsessed with deonstructing and delegitimating every form of argument they encounter, they can end only in condemning their own validity claims to the point where nothing remains of any basis for reasoned action. Post-modernism has us accepting the reifications and partitionings, actually celebrating the activity of masking and cover-up, all the fetishisms of locality, place, or social grouping, while denying that kind of meta-theory which can grasp the political-economic processes (money flows, international divisions of labour, financial markets, and the like) that are becoming ever more universalizing in their depth, intensity, reach and power over daily life (Harvey 1989: 116–7).

16 This immensely complex set of issues will be explored in Roberts (forthcoming, 1994).

17 British Standard 5750. First encountered by the present writer as applied to universities in a presentation by Peter Williams, Director of National Academic Audit, to 'academic mangers' at the University of St Andrews in late 1992.

18 What is described in this paper is not exceptional, as Stewart Clegg reports, 'About one third of Japanese organisations give their employees "spiritual training", akin to techniques of religious conversion, therapy and initiation rites. These emphasise social cooperation, responsibility, reality acceptance and perseverence in tasks. Such techniques apply particularly to members of the internal labour market, incorporated by the benefits they receive as well as the sanctions that quitting would produce. Anyone who wanted to leave would be seen as untrustworthy by other employees and hence unemployable. It is a system which works well in securing loyal commitment by virtue of low turnover and dissent in the highly competitive core. Core labour market skill-formation is enhanced, compared to situations of much greater reliance on the external market as the source of recruitment' ('Postmodern management?', Inaugural Lecture, University of St Andrews, 11.3.92.: 16).

19 Given (following Bourdieu) the primacy of the circulation of cultural, informational and 'sapiential' capital, then it is in principle possible to mould social outcomes for very large groups (indeed through the 'education industry' to mould whole classes in the system of social stratification) through the choice and the manipulation of the management system imposed on any given sector.

20 Anthony (1977); Argyris (1957); Boydell (1988); Burgoyne et al. (1978); Burrell (1989); Harrison (1983); Holland (1970); Huxley (1946); Koestler (1975); Lyons (1988); Pedler and Boydell (1982); Pedler et al. (1978, 1986, 1990); Revans (1982); Schon'(1971); Stewart (1982).

21 Harrison (1987).

22 A Theory of Action Perspective, Reading, MA: Addison-Wesley; Boak and Stephenson (1987); Dearden (1989); Edmonstone (1990); Honey and Mumford (1986); Knowles (1975); Kolb (1976, 1984); Revans (1980).

23 Assagioli (1973); Bandler and Grinder (1982); Bannister and Franselle (1971); Bloom (1991); Bolen (1985); Dass (1985); Ferguson (1989); Gawain (1978); Greene (1986); Guzie and Guzie (1986); Jung (1952); Lao Tzu (1963); Ornstein (1975); Riddell (1992); Shone (1984); Spink (1991); Streiker (1990); Wilhelm (1983).

24 As it happens, by early 1991, with characteristic responsive agility and resourcefulness, respondents were rapidly shifting their activities into 'insolvency counselling'.

25 The 'personal' market as opposed to the so-called 'impersonality of the marketplace', a conception often deployed for political purposes, is an area worthy of further investigation.

26 'Networking' was not incidental, it was understood to have a specific 'spiritual' and developmental role. Once more specific research is required in order fully to understand their operation. Some unlikely interfaces are operationalized, for example between business interests and proponents of fairly 'deep' ecological thought.

27 Substantial remuneration was involved for the most successful, e.g. £650 per day plus VAT for individual counselling. In 1993, one respondent who had been present at the conference described in this chapter contacted the present writer to point out that his current fee was £3,000 per day plus expenses.

28 'Seemingly' because as T.M. Luhrmann argues the relation of instrumental rationality and affective 'irrationality' in the 'play' involved in the refunctionalization of the esoteric involves systemic ambiguity, see Luhrmann (1989: ch. 22).

29 Thus in his lecture 'Economics and business' delivered at the inauguration of the Centre for Research into Industry, Enterprise, Finance and the Firm (CRIEFF), University of St Andrews, Professor John Kay of the London Business School argued for a three-stage account of the evolution of microeconomics: corporate planning (1960s to 1970s), vision and mission (1970s to 1980s) and implementation (1980s to 1990s).

30 The whale's remains had in fact been carried by strong-stomached university staff from a local headland to the campus, buried, cleaned and then mounted for the benefit of biology students (and through fortuitous synchronicity, for the enablers).

31 For an introduction, see Turner's wide-ranging article 'Ritual' in Sills (1968), vol. 13: 520-6.

32 Description circulated in the conference notes.

33 Lyons (1988).

34 Huizinga (1951: 13).

35 Paul Heelas' pioneering work on 'Self-religion' is one indispensable source, see for example, Heelas (1991, 1992a).

36 This is in contrast with say Bruce Reed's early attempt to refunctionalize Christian church groups where a cycle of dependence is central to the enactment of the passage cycle. See Reed (1978) The Dynamics of Religion.

37 As Heelas has recently argued (1992b).

38 Some of the risks involved have been drawn to wide public attention by some striking television documentaries, not least that following the experience of a group of middle rank executives and managers on a particularly taxing leadership and team-building course in the Western Highlands of Scotland. A consultant based in Fife is now offering team-building expeditions which involve covering 200 miles over rough country and the climbing of thirty 'Munroes' (peaks over 3,000 feet) in *one week*.

REFERENCES

Adams, J. (ed.) (1986) *Transforming Leadership*, Alexandria, VA: Miles River Press.

Anthony, P.D. (1977) *The Ideology of Work*, London: Tavistock.

Argyris, C. (1957) *Personality and Organization*, New York: Harper & Row.

Assagioli, R. (1973) *Psychosynthesis*, London: Turnstone Books.

Bannister, D. and Fransella, F. (1971) *Inquiring Man*, Harmondsworth: Penguin.

Bauman, Z. (1988a), 'Viewpoint: sociology and post-modernity', *Sociological Review*, 36, 4: 790–813.

Bauman, Z. (1988b) 'Is there a postmodern sociology?', *Theory, Culture and Society*, 5: 217–37.

Bauman, Z. (1989) *Modernity and the Holocaust*, Cambridge: Polity.

Bauman, Z. (1991) *Modernity and Ambivalence*, Cambridge: Polity.

Belasco, J.A. (1990) *Teaching Elephants to Dance*, London: Hutchinson Business Books.

Bellah, R.N. (1970) 'Meaning and modernization', in *Beyond Belief*, Berkeley: California University Press, pp. 64–73.

Bellah, R.N. (1976) 'New religious consciousness and the crisis in modernity', in C.Y. Glock and R.N. Bellah (eds) *The New Religious Consciousness*, Berkeley: California University Press, pp. 333–52.

Bennis, W. (1989) *On Becoming Leader*, London: Hutchinson Business Books.

Berger, P.L. (1977) *Facing up to Modernity: Excursions in Society, Politics, and Religion*, New York: Basic Books.

Berman, M. (1982) *All that is Solid Melts into Air: the Experience of Modernity*, London: Verso.

Bernstein, R.J. (1991) *The New Constellation: The Ethical-Political Horizons of Modernity/Postmodernity*, Cambridge: Polity.

Bloom, W. (ed.) (1991) *The New Age: An Anthology of Essential Writings*, London: Rider.

Boak, G. and Stephenson, M. (1987) 'Management learning contracts: from theory to practice', *Journal of European Industrial Training*, 11, 4.

Bolen, J.S. (1985) *Goddesses in Everywoman: A New Psychology of Women*, London: Harper & Row.

Boyatzis, R. (1982) *The Competent Manager*, New York: Wiley.

Boydell, T.H. (1988) 'Transformations for men?' in M.J. Pedler, J.G. Burgoyne and T.H. Boydell (eds) *Applying Self-development in Organizations*, Hemel Hempstead: Prentice-Hall.

Bradford, D.L. and Cohen, A.E. (1984) *Managing for Excellence: The Guide to Developing High Performance in Contemporary Organizations*, New York: John Wiley & Sons.

Braverman, H. (1974) *Labor and Monopoly Capital: The Degradation of Work in the Twentieth Century*, New York: Monthly Review Press.

Brown, Mark (1988) *The Dinosaur Strain*, Dorset: Element Books.

Burgoyne, J.G. *et al.* (1978) *Self-Development*, London: Association of Teachers of Management.

Burrell, G. (1989) 'Post-modernism: threat or opportunity', in M.C. Jackson, P. Keys and S. Cropper, *Operational Research and the Social Sciences*, New York: Plenum Press, pp. 59–64.

Campbell, A. and Devine, M. (1990) *A Sense of Mission*, London: Business Books.

Carmichael, S. and Drummond, J. (1989) *Good Business*, London: Century Hutchinson.

Clegg, S. R. (1989) *Frameworks of Power*, London: Sage.

Clegg, S.R. (1990) *Modern Organizations: Organization Studies in the Post-modern World*, London: Sage.

Clegg, S.R. and Dunkerley, D. (1980) *Organization, Class and Control*, London: Routledge & Kegan Paul.

Constable, J. (1987) *The Making of British Managers*, Northants.: Stanley Hunt.

Dass, R. (1985) *Journey of Awakening*, London: Bantam.

Davis, C. (1990) 'Our modern identity: the formation of the self', *Modern Theology*, 6, 2: 159–71.

Deal, T. and Kennedy, A. (1988) *Corporate Cultures*, Harmondsworth: Penguin.

Dearden, G. (1989) *Learning While Earning*, Oxford: Learning from Experience Trust.

Drucker, P.F. (1985) *Innovation and Entrepreneurship*, London: Heinemann.

Edmonstone, J. (1990) 'What price the learning organization in the public sector?', in M. Pedler, J. Burgoyne, T. Boydell and G. Welshman, *Self-Development in Organizations*, New York: McGraw-Hill, pp. 252–78.

Evans, R. and Russell, P. (1989) *The Creative Manager*, London: Unwin.

Ferguson, M. (1989) *The Aquarian Conspiracy. Personal and Social Transformation in the 1980s*, London: Paladin.

Foster, H. (1985) *Postmodern Culture*, London: Pluto.

Gawain, S. (1978) *Creative Visualization*, Mill Valley, CA.: Whatever Publishing Inc.

Giddens, A. (1990) *The Consequences of Modernity*, Cambridge: Polity.

Giddens, A. (1991), *Modernity and Self-Identity: Self and Society in the Late Modern Age*, Cambridge: Polity.

Giddens, A. (1992) 'Uprooted signposts at century's end', *The Higher*, 17 January: 21–2.

Greene, L. (1986) *Relating – An Astrological Guide to Living With Others*, London: Aquarian Press.

Griffin, D.R. (1989) *God and Religion in the Postmodern World: Essays in Postmodern Theology*, Albany: State University of New York.

Guzie, T. and Guzie, N.M. (1986) *About Men and Women: How Your 'Great Story' Shapes Your Destiny*, New York: Paulist Press.

Hague, Sir Douglas (1991) *Beyond Universities: A New Republic of the Intellect*, London: Institute of Economic Affairs.

Handy, C. (1985) *Gods of Management*, London: Pan.

Handy, C. (1987a) *The Making of Managers*, London: HMSO.

Handy, C. (1987b) *Understanding Organizations*, Harmondsworth: Penguin.

Handy, C. (1989) *The Age of Unreason*, London: Business Books.

Harrison, R. (1983) 'Strategies for a new age', *Human Resource Management*, 22, 3: 209–35.

Harrison, R. (1987) *Organization Culture and the Quality of Service: A Strategy for Releasing Love in the Workplace*, London: Association for Management Education and Development Focus paper.

Hartt, J.N., Hart, R.L. and Scharlemann, R.P. (1986) *The Critique of Modernity: Theological Reflections on Contemporary Culture*, Charlottesville: University Press of Virginia.

Harvey, D. (1989) *The Condition of Post-modernity: An Enquiry into the Origins of Cultural Change*, Oxford: Blackwell.

Harvey-Jones, J. (1987) *Making It Happen*, London: Guild Publishing.

Heelas, P. (1991) 'Cults for capitalism? self religions, magic and the empowerment of business', in P. Gee and J. Fulton (eds) *Religion and Power*, London: British Sociological Association, Sociology of Religion Study Group: 27–41.

Heelas, P. (1992a) 'The sacralization of the self in new age capitalism', in N. Abercrombie and A. Ware (eds) *Social Change in Contemporary Britain*, Cambridge: Polity Press, pp. 139–66.

Heelas, P. (1992b) 'God's company: new age ethics and the Bank of Credit and Commerce International', *Religion Today*, 8, 1: 1–4.

Heelas, P. and Morris, P. (eds) (1991) *The Values of the Enterprise Culture*, London: Harper Collins Academic.

Heider, J. (1986) *The Tao of Leadership*, London: Wildwood House.

Holland, R. (1970) *Self and Social Context*, London: Macmillan.

Honey, P. and A. Mumford, A. (1986) *The Manual of Learning Styles*, Maidenhead: Honey.

Huizinga, J. (1949) *Homo Ludens*, London: Routledge and Kegan Paul.

Huxley, A. (1946) *The Perennial Philosophy*, London: Chatto & Windus.

Jencks, C. (1989) *What is Post-Modernism?* London: Academy Editions.

Jung, C.G. (1952) *Synchronicity: An Acausal Connecting Principle*, London: Routledge & Kegan Paul.

Keat, R. and Abercrombie, N. (eds) (1991) *Enterprise Culture*, London: Routledge.

Knowles, M. (1975) *Self Directed Learning*, Chicago: Follett.

Koestler, A. (1975) *The Ghost in the Machine*, London: Pan.

Kolb, D. (1976) *The Learning Style Inventory*, Boston: McBer & Co.

Kolb, D. (1984) *Experiential Learning*, New York: Prentice-Hall.

Kotter, J. (1982) *The General Managers*, New York: Free Press.

Kroker, A. and Cook, D. (1988) *The Postmodern Scene: Excremental Culture and Hyper-Aesthetics*, Basingstoke: Macmillan.

Lao Tzu (1963) *Tao Te Ching*, trans. D.C. Lau, Harmondsworth: Penguin.

Luhrmann, T.M. (1989) 'Serious play: the fantasy of truth', in *Persuasions of the Witch's Craft: Ritual Magic in Contemporary England*, Oxford: Blackwell.

Lyons, G. (1988) *Constructive Criticism*, California: Wingbow Press.

Lyotard, J.-F. (1984) *The Postmodern Condition: A Report on Knowledge*, Manchester: Manchester University Press.

Messing, R. (1989) *The Tao of Management*, London: Wildwood House.

Moss Kanter, R. (1984) *The Change Master*, London: Unwin Paperbacks.

Ornstein, R.E. (1975) *The Psychology of Consciousness*, Harmondsworth: Pelican.

Pascale, R.T. and Athos, A.G. (1982) *The Art of Japanese Management*, Harmondsworth: Penguin.

Pedler, M. and Boydell, T. (1982) *Managing Yourself*, London: Fontana.

Pedler, M.J., Burgoyne, J.H. and Boydell, T.H. (1978, 1986) *A Manager's Guide to Self-Development*, Maidenhead: McGraw-Hill.

Pedler, M., Burgoyne, J., Boydell, T. and Welshman, G. (1990) *Self-Development in Organizations*, New York: McGraw-Hill.

Perkin, H. (1989) *The Rise of Professional Society England since 1880*, London: Routledge.

Peters, T. (1989) *Thriving on Chaos*, London: Pan.

Peters, T. and Austin, N. (1986) *A Passion for Excellence*, London: Fontana/Collins.

Peters, T.J. and Waterman, Jr., R.H. (1982) *In Search of Excellence*, New York: Harper & Row.

Poole, R. (1991) *Morality and Modernity*, London: Routledge.

Reed, B. (1978) *The Dynamics of Religion*, London: Dartman, Longman & Todd.

Revans, R.W. (1980) *Action Learning*, London: Blond and Briggs.

Revans, R. W. (1982) *The Origins and Growth of Action Learning*, Bromley: Chartwell Bratt.

Riddell, C. (1992) *The Findhorn Community: Creating a Human Identity for the 21st Century*, Forres: Findhorn.

Roberts, R.H. (1992) 'Religion and the "enterprise culture": the British experience in the Thatcher era (1979–90)', *Social Compass*, 39, 1: 15–33.

197

Roberts, R.H. *Religion and the Resurgence of Capitalism*, London: Routledge (forthcoming).

Roberts, R. H. and Good, J.M.M. (1993) *The Recovery of Rhetoric: Persuasive Discourse and Disciplinarity in the Human Sciences*, Bristol: Classical Press/Duckworth and the University Press of Virginia.

Sargent, A.G. (1983) *The Androgynous Manager*, New York: American Management Organization.

Schoef, A.W. and Fassel, D. (1988) *The Addictive Organization*, London: Harper & Row.

Schon, D. A. (1971) *Beyond the Stable State*, New York: Random House.

Sedgwick, P. (1992) *The Enterprise Culture*, London: SPCK.

Shone, R. (1984), *Creative Visualization*, Wellingborough: Thorsons.

Sills, D.L. (1968) *International Encyclopaedia of the Social Sciences*, New York: Macmillan.

Spink, P. (1991) *A Christian in the New Age*, London: Darton, Longman & Todd.

Starhawk (1991) *Dreaming the Dark. Magic, Sex and Politics*, Boston: Beacon Press.

Stewart, R. (1982) *Choices for the Manager*, Maidenhead: McGraw-Hill.

Streiker, L.D. (1990) *New Age Comes to Main Street*, Nashville: Abingdon.

Taylor, F.W. (1947 [1911]) 'The principles of scientific management', in *Scientific Management*, London: Harper Collins, and in V.H. Vroom and E.L. Deci (1970) *Management and Motivation: Selected Readings*, Harmondsworth: Penguin.

Toffler, A. (1989) *The Third Wave*, London: Pan.

Vattimo, G. (1988) *The End of Modernity: Nihilism and Hermeneutics in Post-modern Culture*, Cambridge: Polity.

Whimster, S. and Lash, S. (1987) *Max Weber, Rationality and Modernity*, London: Allen & Unwin.

Wilhelm, R. (1983) *The I Ching*, London: Routledge & Kegan Paul.

Young of Graffham, Lord (1990) *The Enterprise Years: A Businessman in the Cabinet*, London: Headline.

10

THE GOSPEL OF PROSPERITY IN WEST AFRICA

Rosalind I.J. Hackett

Signboards, posters, tracts, newspapers, radio and television alike, proclaim to even the most disinterested observer in many parts of Africa that spiritual power and blessings are available and more necessary than ever before.[1] Such claims are to be effected through the blood of Jesus, the visitation of the Holy Spirit, the anointed words of a man of God, the power of prayer or the discipline of Bible study. To many this increase in evangelical and pentecostal discourse is a symptom of the difficult economic times being experienced by many African countries as people resort to religion as solace or source of income. I here examine the notion that a 'gospel of prosperity' is an increasingly marked characteristic of this Christian revival and discuss American involvement and African agency in the whole phenomenon.[2] I argue that there is a close affinity between the type of religious multi-nationalism, religious enterprise, values and competitive pluralism engendered by the charismatic revival in Africa and global, particularly Western, capitalist forces. I seek to account for such religious developments and examine notions of conspiracy, neo-dependency and hegemony. By focusing on such issues I do not wish to imply that the experiential dimension of these new movements, for example, is not a significant feature of their appeal.

Based on my fieldwork carried out over a number of years in Nigeria, Ghana, Liberia and Kenya, I argue that we are not only dealing with an immensely significant development in the religious history of Africa, but one which is highly complex with important political, social, economic and cultural ramifications. To that end I trace briefly the historical roots of the present-day quest for spiritual renewal, identify some of the key figures and movements and discuss their theological justifications for prosperity. I am also concerned to analyse the configuration of forces which seem to be underpinning this revival and address the interrelationship between global economic and religious trends, particularly as they affect the African context. In this essay I shall focus on the Nigerian and Ghanaian situations.

The current Christian revival in Africa is variously referred to as either charismatic, pentecostal, evangelical, fundamentalist or gospel. This is an indication of both the variety of theological orientations and popular terms and their tendency to interrelate and merge, particularly in the case of indigenous African movements. In my earlier writings I used the term 'revivalist' as it seemed more neutral and comprehensive, and identified an aspect which was common to the various groups involved. More recently, in the course of further research in Ghana and Nigeria this year, I noted the common usage of the term, 'pentecostal', as well as the growing predominance of pentecostalism more generally. However, given the fact that the renewal is being experienced at a number of levels and is not necessarily confined to pentecostal institutions, the term 'charismatic' seems more appropriate as a general label. It also reflects the finer doctrinal distinction now being made by those who believe the Holy Spirit is necessary for healing, deliverance and worship, but do not claim that speaking in tongues is an essential sign (as would do the older pentecostals). The former would be labelled 'neo-pentecostals' in other contexts.[3] The term 'fundamentalist', while common in the popular parlance of non-charismatic observers, is unhelpful since not all groups subscribe to biblical inerrancy and it is unfair to confuse militancy with enthusiasm and commitment.[4]

If we look briefly at Nigeria, for example, pentecostalism dates back to the 1930s, when British (the Apostolic Church) and American groups (Assemblies of God, Faith Tabernacle and the Apostolic Faith) began missionary work in the West and the East. (There is also evidence of pentecostal-type activity occurring in some parts before the arrival of Western pentecostal missionaries, some six decades after Christianity first was planted on Nigerian shores.) Around the same time prayer groups, that were later to become independent churches, began to emerge, either inspired or assisted by the overseas pentecostal agencies. In the 1950s, some American missionaries of the Latter Rain Movement in Los Angeles conducted a number of revivals in southern Nigeria at the invitation of a British missionary, Rev. S. G. Elton.[5] Around that time, the Student Christian Movement and the Scripture Union were establishing themselves in Nigeria's educational institutions, to be followed by the Christian Union. Evangelical revivals began in the south, particularly Yorubaland, from the 1960s onwards, with the visits of well-known American evangelists, such as Billy Graham, T.L. Osborn, Oral Roberts, Morris Cerullo and Brother Argemiro. Evangelical literature also began to circulate on a larger scale.

However, it was in 1970 that the emphasis on evangelical witness began to shift to the baptism of the Holy Spirit and the experiences of speaking in tongues and healing and miracles. This charismatic revival occurred principally on the campuses of Nigeria's educational institutions and so in effect unleashed and disseminated teachings, previously confined to specialist organizations. The revival was also linked (particularly in the east) to the reconstruction and rapid urban development after the Civil War (1967–70), as well as educational expansion (Ojo 1986: 225).

Indigenous pentecostal movements, such as the Deliverance Church in Kenya, the Church of God Mission in Nigeria and Christian Action Faith Ministries in Ghana began to emerge with increasing frequency in the 1970s and 1980s. Many areas of African Christianity have been affected in some way by the charismatic revival, engendering both enthusiasm and conflict. This is in part due to the challenge to ecclesiastical authority and time-honoured liturgies that a spirit-centred revival represents. But the controversy is also related to the message of blessings, miracles and prosperity propagated by a number of leading evangelists. Let us now turn to some of these proponents. My focus is on African, particularly West African, evangelists, although I do consider the nature and consequences of American religious activity later in the essay.

For many the name of Archbishop Professor Benson Idahosa is synonymous with conspicuous salvation and the building of religious empires. This highly successful evangelist and founder of the Church of God Mission International in Benin City, Nigeria is a protégé of several well-known American religious personalities and their theological schools.[6] He studied with Gordon Lindsay at the Church for Nations Institute in Texas in 1971, received funding from the PTL Club to set up his televangelism ministry and has close ties with Dr John L. Meares, founder and pastor of the Evangel Temple in Washington, DC[7] Idahosa presides over the Word of Faith group of schools, the child training arm of the church, the Faith Medical Centre, a modern medical unit established in conjunction with (and heavily subsidized by) the Oral Roberts Evangelist Association and the Oral Roberts University, the All Nations for Christ Bible Institute, which has students from forty nations pursuing accredited diplomas and degrees and taught by lecturers from the United States, India, England and Nigeria and the Idahosa World Outreach.[8] The latter is the international arm of the church which organizes international crusades and church growth. They claim to have taken the gospel to more than 20 million people in over eighty nations.

Idahosa is keen to cite his humble beginnings, from being a sickly, rejected child with limited education to securing a job as a store clerk with the shoe company, Bata. The combination of conversion, evangelism and hard work makes a good 'rags to riches' story. He espouses a flamboyant lifestyle (for example, driving through the streets of London before his crusade in an open-topped Rolls Royce). He is undeniably a gifted speaker and performer, able to relate successfully to both individuals and large gatherings of thousands of people.

Arguably Africa'a most famous (and infamous, due to some unpleasant incidents with former associates and his financial dealings) evangelist, Idahosa does not conceal his American connections nor his worldwide peregrinations. Beyond African shores he is frequently referred to as the 'Apostle of Africa'. Not only are American sources of funding visibly advertised (e.g. 'provided by the saints in Florida') on the back of his buses and gospel trains (vehicles which transport people to the headquarters and the more than 120 branches throughout Benin City), but he reportedly has declared in the media on a number of occasions that overseas bodies fund 30 percent of his activities. He is also known to say that in contrast to politicians, he earns money overseas and brings it back to Nigeria, whereas politicians earn money in Nigeria and send it abroad! When I asked him about whether this creates an image of an American church (in the course of a splendid lunch in the magnificent dining room of his palatial home), he recalled the fact that Nigeria's political and university educational systems are now structured according to the American model.[9] More personally, Idahosa replies to those who criticize his spiritual neo-colonialism by saying 'look where it got me'. Symbolic evidence of the Idahosa–American connection is displayed in the impressive Faith Miracle Centre auditorium where the Nigerian and American flags hang either side of a large painting of Christ.

The core of Idahosa's theology is his teaching on prosperity and possibilities (Ojo 1990: 10–12). He firmly believes in the power of faith, that God has the power to change circumstances (as evidenced by his own life) and dispel fear.[10] His theology seeks to free the Christian from failure, problems and satanic oppression and advocates the need to strive for success and not accept failure or poverty – 'A possibilitarian finds alternative courses of action in the face of obstacles, on his way to success'.[11] There are two dimensions to his theology of prosperity: the prosperity of the soul or salvation, followed by material prosperity ('God loves the poor, but hates poverty'). Wealth and well-being are assured by giving, in the form of tithes or offerings. Idahosa condemns ungenerous giving and has enshrined himself in popular memory by his refusal of coins at crusades and his call to people to empty their pockets. He claims to have introduced the concept of fund-raising in the Nigerian church from the United States in the early 1970s, arguing that there is a direct correlation between giving and receiving.[12]

Archbishop Idahosa's teachings on prosperity have been disseminated by a number of his associates and former students, such as Reverend Ayo Oritsejafor (Word of Life Bible Church – Warri), and Bishop David Oyedepo of the Living Faith Church, Kaduna in the north of Nigeria. The latter's book, *Power for Wealth*, is an unambiguous affirmation of the connection between anointing by the Holy Spirit and material abundance and an exposition of the religious qualifications for wealth ('sin breeds poverty') (Oyedepo 1988). Other noted prosperity preachers in Nigeria are Rev. Chris Okotie (Household of God Fellowship), Rev. O. Ezekiel (Christian Pentecostal Mission), Rev. Olubi Johnson (Scripture Pasture), and Bishop (Dr) Mike Okonkwo (The Redeemed Evangelical Mission).[13] All are well known to Nigerians through their broadcasts, publications, media coverage and newspaper features.

Further afield in Ghana, the highly successful Christian Faith Action Ministries in Accra was founded in 1980 by a former student of Idahosa's Bible college, Rev. Dr Nicholas Duncan-Williams. Duncan-Williams has pursued a policy of financial self-sufficiency, although he frequently welcomes overseas pastors and speakers, as well as those from other African countries, particularly Nigeria. While I was conducting research on the church in February this year, I heard a sermon preached by Rev. Gabriel Oduyemi of Bethel International Ministries (Lagos), a self-made multi-millionaire industrialist-turned-evangelist. The main thrust of his sermon was 'God can change your status as he changed mine', with a detailed account of how he had risen from hunger and homelessness in the

United States to wheeling and dealing in millions of dollars. Equally interesting was the introduction of this 'business sheik' by Pastor Duncan-Williams, who lauded Oduyemi's business skills and highlighted the symbols of his wealth, namely a Lincoln Mercury and a James Bond car at his palatial home on Lagos' Victoria Island. Oduyemi ended his sermon with prayers explicitly addressed to the needs of businessmen and businesswomen. They were invited to the front of the church and asked to declare their debts and financial needs, so that God could answer their prayers that very day.

The following week I encountered a leading executive of the Full Gospel Business Men's Fellowship International from the United States, Don Ostrom, who led a seminar in the church on 'Bible Economics: Faith and Finances'. In the Action Bookshop, books by Dr John Avanzini (Tulsa, Oklahoma) predominate, with titles ranging from *Powerful Principles of Increase, 30, 60, Hundredfold: Your Financial Harvest Released* (1989), *The Wealth of the Wicked: Yours for the Taking* (1986), *Always Abounding: the Way to Prosper in Good Times, Bad Times, Any Time* (1989). Pastor Nick's own recent book, *You are Destined to Succeed!*, not only draws on his own experience of deprivation and depravity, from drug hoodlum to successful evangelist, but also preaches of the covenant of wealth and success for born-again Christians (Duncan-Williams 1990). He speaks out forcefully against the message propagated by many of the older, 'orthodox' churches that 'poverty promotes humility'. In effect, he claims, 'to be poor means to be powerless' and is a ploy of Satan:

> You see, Satan knows that if he keeps the saints in hole-ridden shoes, in rented houses, with unpaid bundles of bills and hardly enough to eat, then he can effectively stop the spreading of the gospel through books, equipment, international crusades and by satellite, radio, television and other means.
>
> (Duncan-Williams 1990: 146)

His associate pastor, Leslie Buabasah, spoke to me of the need to view the concept of prosperity more holistically, citing 'Seek ye first the Kingdom of God and all other things shall be added unto you'.[14] He proudly recounted the gifts of cars he has personally received and given away as a sign of God's blessings during his time as a pastor. Other noted prosperity churches in Ghana are the Calvary Charismatic Church in Kimasi (the English church of the Assemblies of God) and a group of churches known as the Faith Convention Group. Pros-perity preaching may also feature in the context of prayer groups within the mainline churches, as in the case of the Friday Prayer Fellowship in the Wesley Methodist Church, Kumasi in Ghana.[15]

For some, the present 'war against poverty by the preaching of the prosperity message' is an integral feature of the pentecostal revival with its revelations and gifts of the spirit (hidden from previous generations) (Addo 1989: vi). Poverty and failure are seen by many as the work of the devil or as resulting from association with evil spirits (Taiwo 1988: 24–5). (It is on this point that the critics of the prosperity gospel deliver their strongest attack, claiming that it leads to psychological oppression and potential corruption.) In the words of a well-known exponent of the gospel of prosperity, Francis Wale Oke, founder of the Sword of the Spirit Ministries in Ibadan,

> We are also redeemed from poverty. One of the rods of destruction in the hands of the devil is poverty. God never made us poor. He made us in His image, put us in His garden and put the whole world and its resources at our disposal. But with the fall came poverty and the human race has been struggling with it ever since. Jesus Christ came, identified with our poverty and lifted us out of it. The Bible says: "For ye know the grace of our Lord Jesus Christ, that, though he was rich, yet for your sakes he became poor, that ye through his poverty might be rich".
>
> II Cor. 8: 9[16]

In a seminar he conducted on 'The Life of Prosperity', Rev. Oke examines the biblical basis for prosperity, viewing it as threefold: spiritual, physical and material. He seeks to demolish 'Satan's lies' (e.g. 'Money is the root of all evil') about the negative aspects of wealth.[17] He also offers advice on how to work towards material prosperity (the main emphasis of his presentation), such as putting God first, working diligently and being faithful and honest in business. The Christian Students' Social Movement of Nigeria, a charismatic organization directed to the social, political and economic affairs of the nation, believes that Satan, who had always been seen as an evil in the Christian life, has now manifested himself in the adverse economic and political situation of the country (Ojo 1986: 260–1).

Not all the key figures in the current religious revival are proponents of the gospel of prosperity. Many preach more generally of 'blessings', 'miracles' and 'deliverance' without advocating the importance of wealth and avoidance of failure. One example would be Evangelist M. B. Ojo's *The Secret of Success and Blessing*, which is more about a humble Christian perspective on our worldly possessions.[18] Rev. Dr S. G. A. Onibere, an Anglican priest and senior lecturer in Religious Studies who runs a nationwide student ministry, Amazing Grace Fellowship, claims that there are many such as himself and the well-known Rev. Dr T.O. Obadare of the World Soul Winning Evangelical Ministry (WOSEM). now expelled from the Christ Apostolic Church, who would not preach prosperity as a doctrine and would give it less emphasis than evangelism, salvation, healing, counselling and deliverance.[19] Rev. Dr David Olayiwola, founder of Christ's Trumpeters Church in Ilesha, has taken a stand in his church against the worship of wealth. One manifestation of this is that no collections are taken during the service. Assimeng reports a survey among pastors (not limited to pentecostals) in Ghana of attitudes towards selected socio-cultural issues where only 11.6 percent deemed capitalism favourable (out of sixty-three responses) with 49.2 percent against (Assimeng 1989: 204). In those churches or ministries founded or led by women their discourse is not generally centred on the gospel of prosperity – blessings are interpreted in a more holistic sense, with particular attention to healing and fruits of the womb.[20]

William F. Kumuyi, founder and General Superintendent of the rapidly growing Deeper Life Bible Church in Lagos, is renowned for the strict holiness orientation of his church and his disavowal of worldly excesses and signs of salvation. Yet even his writings are interspersed with the 'promise of prosperity' for true believers (Kumuyi 1990: ch. 3) – 'Unbelievers do not desire failure, they seek after success' and 'When you are part of the flock of God you will have superabundant supply' (*ibid.*: 84). He is also keen to emphasize that 'sinners, church-goers and misinformed believers have mixed up holiness with POVERTY' and that 'God wants you to switch over from the minimum to the maximum' (*ibid.*: 87). He continues, ' . . . God knows your need and whatever you ask for, be it pardon, peace, purity, power or prosperity – whatever the need in your life, if you are in true relationship with Him, all things are yours' (*ibid.*). The increasing attention given to prosperity and financial matters by many of the movements and the literature within the last decade in particular may be attributable to a number of factors which I shall outline below.

STRUCTURAL ADJUSTMENT AND 'SPIRITUAL ADJUSTMENT' PROGRAMMES

The first and perhaps the most important reason is the economic recession being experienced by the majority of African countries. Structural adjustment programmes have entailed real economic hardship for many Ghanaians and Nigerians, for example, as they have seen their currencies devalued and their salaries eroded. Given the this-worldly approach which stems from traditional beliefs, it is not surprising that many turn to religious organizations for support or source of income. Several even talk of economic minuses equalling spiritual pluses, or structural adjustment programmes leading to much-needed spiritual adjustment programmes. Idahosa, commenting on the difference between his American and African audiences, stated the following: 'Americans have money but do not know God, Africans know God but need money'.[21] Professor Martin Bestman rationalizes the Devil's grip on Africans and the resultant poverty as having a positive aspect as it leads people to accept Jesus – 'in affluent countries God is needed so much less'.[22]

Increased religious activity to some extent reflects political disillusionment (which is rife in both Ghana and Nigeria), and frustrations with the government's economic failures and shortcomings – a quest for alternative forms of power. But it more often signifies a belief in the transformative power of religion.[23] Given the emphasis on lifestyle changes for the born-again and sanctified Christian, it is not uncommon to encounter many individuals who would testify to a reversal in their fortunes. For the majority of believers, politics is a matter for prayer not involvement. Prayer groups (or at least prayer sessions) abound both in Africa and among[24] migrant Africans in Europe and the United States, driven by the conviction that conversion and prayer are the keys to national salvation.[25] There are indications, however, given the Muslim domination of politics in Nigeria and Christian fear of their continued expansion, that several evangelical and pentecostal groups are renouncing their apolitical and quietistic stance and supporting and lobbying selected candidates. For example, the Church of God Mission International, in its communiqué from the 1990 International Convention, resolved to '[e]ncourage the active mass participation of all Christians in the new political process and to engage more seriously in bringing to being a sound and stable social and economic order in the new dispensation'.[26]

Governments themselves are influential in nurturing a more pragmatic and materialistic orientation among religious groups by expressing a concern for the latter to demonstrate their utilitarian mettle. A Ghanaian government official is recorded as saying in his official welcome to the gospel ship M/V Anastasis at Tema port in February 1991, that 'the Church should not occupy herself with satisfying the spiritual needs of the people only but that all the areas of life must be catered for – spiritual, material, physical and emotional'.[27] Kenya's president, Daniel Arap Moi (who himself attends the Nairobi Pentecostal Church) praised the effects (reported healings and drop in crime rate) of Reinhard Bonnke's 1988 crusade and encouraged him to return for more outreaches in the future. Sierra Leone's president, Joseph Saidu Momoh, who was the guest at a Presidential State Dinner organized by the Full Gospel Business Men's Fellowship International, stated that: 'The answer to the needs of mankind and this nation is a personal faith in God.'[28]

GOD'S OWN COUNTRY

As alluded to by Idahosa earlier, Nigeria has since the 1970s increased its political, economic, cultural and educational links with the United States. This has had obvious repercussions in the religious domain. With references to the economic miracle of 'God's own country', it is not surprising that there has been a call in Nigeria to put a biblical quotation on the Naira as there is God on the American dollar bill.[29] It may also be influenced by one of the many American tracts which circulate, such as the 'cheque' that I encountered one day between the pages of someone's Bible:

> THE BANK OF ETERNAL LIFE
> (Resources Unlimited)
>
> Pay to the order of Whosoever believeth
>
> _____
>
> The Sum of Eternal Life
>
> _____
>
>   by Jesus Christ

Many African evangelists have emulated styles and techniques of their American counterparts. Journalists have a field day with these 'funky preachers' and 'flashy fishers of men [who] carve out an empire of money and souls'.[30] Their 'showbiz' evangelism draws thousands of young people to these 'happy churches'. American gospel music has been enthusiastically appropriated and adapted for African needs. Chris Okotie, a successful Nigerian musician before he founded his successful Household of God Fellowship in Lagos, is a good example of this new trend.

JESUS CHRIST AS SENIOR PARTNER

In the same way as the Scripture Union and the Student Christian Movement were influential in disseminating evangelical and later pentecostal ideas, para-church organizations such as Full Gospel Business Men's Fellowship International (FGBMFI) are now playing a major role in promoting the gospel of prosperity. FGBMFI is experiencing rapid growth in many parts of Africa, despite financial cutbacks and structural readjustments at its American Headquarters in Costa Mesa, California.[31] It has over sixty chapters in Ghana (since 1983), from where a lot of missionary work has been spearheaded and the largest number of chapters (280) in Nigeria (since 1972).[32] The organization is experiencing its most rapid growth in Zaire owing to a committed leadership and good strategy.[33] Twenty-nine African countries now have chapters and FGBMFI is close to the government in Liberia, Ghana, South Africa, Kenya and Nigeria.[34]

The current African president of FGBMFI, Kwabena Darko, is a highly successful businessman and poultry farmer – he is Managing Director of Darko Farms and Company, based in Kumasi. An epitome of the FGBMFI ethos, he sees entering business as 'a calling of the Lord' and that one should use God's methods, namely 'integrity' and 'uprightness'.[35] He attributes his business successes to being 'in partnership with God' (he noted that all his workers are 'born-again') and that 'any action or business decision which leads you to God is success'.[36] He is also a firm advocate of hard work and good business ethics. FGBMFI sees itself primarily as a fellowship to bring businessmen to Christ (in Ghana they have a separate fellowship for women – Women's Aglow, whereas in Nigeria, women are active in some of the FGBMFI chapters). FGBMFI in Africa lays much emphasis on training and to that end they co-operate with the Haggai Institute,[37] the Billy Graham Leadership Training Group and the Maurice Cerullo School of Ministry. The training focuses on evangelism, business skills and ethics. The Executive Secretary, who is a trained management consultant, describes this training as a means of 'encouraging people to move from a civil service to a private sector mentality'. Their successes in transcending ethnic, racial and national boundaries in Africa faster than the Organization of African Unity or ECOWAS (the Economic Community of West African States), particularly those between francophone and anglophone countries, have sparked government interest in and eventual association with FGBMFI. In South Africa, FGBMFI claims to have brought black and white businessmen together. A white South African is Vice President for the whole of Africa and Chief Buthelezi has attended several of their meetings.

FGBMFI is underwritten by the conviction that 'Jesus is the answer' to both individual and national business needs and problems. Their meetings are structured around talks and addresses and personal programmes such as on Ibadan television (Oyo State Broadcasting Corporation) early Sunday evening where they bill themselves as 'The Happiest People on Earth'. There are interviews with members or sympathizers and shots of spirit-filled breakfast and lunch revivals, with information on their Bible study programmes and meetings. The correlation between spiritual power and material success and the oral transmission of this successful blend through testimonies and personal evangelism, as well as the employment of proven American administrative and marketing techniques, are the obvious ingredients in FGBMFI's unsurpassed success in the African context,

A SIGN OF THE TIMES?

There is no denying the existence of a prosperity gospel in Nigeria and Ghana today. The debate centres more around its timing and provenance, and of course its merits. At one level one might argue that the preconditions were already there for a gospel of prosperity to develop. In traditional, pre-colonial societies, it was common for people to associate the deities with prosperity. Among the Yoruba of Nigeria, for example, the orisa were believed to bestow fortune on the devotees (Falola 1982: 29–30). The worshippers of Obatala would say, '*O gbe omo re, o soo daje*' (he stands by his children and makes them materially prosperous). It was believed that a harmonious relationship with the spiritual forces was necessary to ensure good health, long life and prosperity and to ensure that one's destiny was not altered for the worse. One could also argue that the emphasis of some early Christian missionaries on the links between Christianity, Commerce and Civilization (Livingstone, for example) sowed the seeds for the later prosperity tradition to flower. Notwithstanding the other-worldly riches emphasized by some missionary traditions, many Africans still linked religious, political and economic power in their perceptions and interpretations of colonialism. Similar beliefs may be found among the older spiritual churches who have frequently preached that joining the fold will bring about prosperity. Both the Celestial Church of Christ and the Christ Apostolic Church believe that if one's business is not thriving, then witches or powers of darkness are at work.[38] Also as stated earlier, miracles and blessings are an integral feature of the pentecostal tradition, which has been active in West Africa since the 1930s. Prayers are an important indicator of trends. For example, in Yoruba churches, references to the Supreme Being as 'Oluwa Alagbara' (God the Powerful One) have noticeably increased in difficult economic times, so has the prayer – '*Fun wa ni agbara*' (give us power), now heard in both spiritual and mainline churches.[39] People are supplicating God for the power to conquer their enemies, overcome trouble, be rich and be healthy.

However, it is the newer pentecostal and charismatic churches and ministries which are more obviously characterized by the message of prosperity. At one level this is due to the new breed of educated evangelists (several of them are [ex-]university lecturers with degrees) who bring professional and organizational skills into their calling. This in turn attracts a more literate, educated and prosperous clientele who see their religion as an affirmation of their (more Western) lifestyle while offering a moral and spiritual additive. It is popularly held that Christian Faith Action Ministries in Ghana is a home for 'portfolio businessmen', those who sell and buy out of their briefcases and shuttle between Accra and Mondon. Organizations such as Scripture Pasture in Ibadan venerate and symbolize success in modern, urban living.[40] They play on many people's concern to keep abreast of the latest developments, the newest trends and ideas and not be characterized as *'colo'*, as Ghanaians would call someone who has remained in colonial times.[41]

MASS MEDIA RELIGION

One of the major factors behind charismatic expansionism is the global mass communications revolution. The possibilities of mass evangelism opened up by technological innovation have been exploited to the full by many American evangelists. Several of their African counterparts, particularly those who have had exposure to American techniques, have availed themselves of radio, television, cassette and literature ministries. This diversity, overseas expertise and ability to attract large numbers of people are important variables of ritual power in the African context.

Several of the larger ministries and the well-known evangelists get drawn into the type of multi-national religious enterprise facilitated by the mass communications revolution. A good example of this is the 'Vision is Still Alive' international gospel music festival organized in October/November 1990 in Los Angeles, Lagos and Abeokuta, Accra and London by the Maranatha International Network (Los Angeles) and the Ebenezer Obey Music Ministries (based in Abeokuya, Nigeria).[42] The Maranatha International Network has worked in partnership with Chief Ebenezer Obey (one of Nigeria's leading musicians, in both highlife/juju and gospel music) to build the Rock New Life Centre, a resort and conference centre which will house the African headquarters of MIN and a school of music. There have been several co-operative ventures with regard to satellite evangelism. When visiting the Deliverance Church in Nairobi in 1987, I was informed that they were planning live broadcasts with the Morris Cerullo Ministries in California to be shown simultaneously in Britain, the United States and India. A similar project was attempted in Lagos in January 1988 by Rev. Ayo Oritsejafor and Evangelist Joseph Martins, President of the Intercontinental Broadcasting Network (ICBN) in Virginia Beach, with the support of over fifty churches from around Lagos State.[43] The revival was supposed to be a live satellite transmission to the United States, with Martins cajoling the crowd: 'God is going to use you today to minister to America' and 'We are going to worship God together for the first time in history'. Owing to technical problems the occasion was only recorded but nonetheless relayed to the Christian Broadcasting

Network for further transmission to over 3,000 churches and individual satellite subscribers in North America.

'THE BEST COMES FROM THE WEST'?
SPIRITUAL AUTONOMY OR NEO-DEPENDENCY?

There seems little doubt based upon the evidence adduced above, that the prosperity gospel is making inroads into strategic areas of African life. I have here addressed the Nigerian and Ghanaian situations principally.[44] Rapid growth, ambivalent attitudes and varying interpretations are justification enough for more research to be done on this important chapter of Africa's religious history and its economic, political and cultural ramifications. For example, those more interested in the workings of global capitalism would like information on whether there is evidence of direct corporate support being filtered through religious channels. Current economic and political developments will prove telling. As economic conditions remain difficult or even worsen, promises of spiritual and material prosperity will likely have a growing appeal for needy individuals and churches alike. In the climate of increased political participation and democratization, the pronouncements of the charismatic movements will prove revealing, and certainly influential in shaping the ideological stance and political action of their flocks. It remains to be seen whether political lobbying will replace passive prayerfulness (although the latter is arguably a form of political protest). The pervasive and uncontainable nature of charismatic discourse, more specifically the gospel of prosperity, suggests countless areas of confluence and conflict with other 'gospels' whether of liberalism, tradition or secularism. Music, marriage, morality are some of the areas of public and private life being affected by this burgeoning religious culture. The details and dynamics of this must form the subject of future research, especially if more generally we are witnessing a rejection of or at least a questioning of dominant values, namely materialism, and a nostalgia for a more integrated role for religion in everyday life.

My research thus far demonstrates that global capitalism thrives off and is nurturing religious independency in Africa, particularly of the charismatic variety. In other words, freedom of the spirit and the spirit of free enterprise seem to go hand in hand for many Africans. As people turn to religion as a source of income and support in difficult economic times, they sustain pre-existing groups and services or generate new ones. Despite the co-operative spirit of the soul-winning enterprise, it is ultimately a competitive situation, for members generate funds and funds facilitate expansion and success. Governments may challenge the ideology, overseas connections and funding of the charismatic movements from time to time and the media may call for greater accountability.[45] Radical African intellectuals view the movements despairingly, as evidence of continuing neo-colonial attitudes and dependency. Demonstrations of chauvinism and denials of external support occasionally sound forth from religious leaders, but for many observers ring somewhat hollow in the face of bookshops stocked with American materials, pulpits regularly filled with American evangelists, churches organized along American lines, choirs singing American gospel music and Bible colleges accredited by American institutions. Nor should we forget the predominantly American origins of the pentecostal and charismatic revival in Africa.[46] Yet in its present phase, the forces of appropriation and negotiation seem to be more active, with more evidence of agency by African evangelists. It is hard to resist gospel ships and their cargo, but indigenous inspirational literature is now beginning to proliferate and some African evangelists are becoming well known on the global circuit. At one level they appear to be content to reproduce the theological tenets of the movement (a skill much admired in certain cultural contexts), but it is in the process of selection that we find an African emphasis and creativity – in the importance attributed to deliverance, healing and experience, for example.[47]

For the participants themselves, they are generally unaware or unconcerned about the provenance of the literature they read or the videos they watch. If challenged, they deny the idea of the Bible as a culture-bound text or of their charismatic experience as being externally generated. As to the notion of a conspiracy on the part of the United States to effect political and economic dominance through religious means, many would reply that Africa (except South Africa) is too troubled and unstrategic for American interests (Bowman 1990: 18), and the whole impetus is too fragmented and diverse to suggest any conspicuous manipulation. Agreement would rather centre on a perceived conspiracy by Western churches to hide 'true Christianity' from Africans, to deny those aspects which were meaningful for African experience and brought material and spiritual wealth.[48]

Discussion is far more lively, both within and outside the charismatic movements, concerning their economic underpinnings and effects. The chief icon of success, the evangelist's car, is paraded, highlighted, praised or scorned. The wealthier the movement the more questions asked – is money or divine calling the objective? This raises the wider and challenging question (for both academics and members of the public) about the 'authenticity' of these movements – are they 'religious' or 'pseudo-religious'?[49] Are they 'consciously' religious, but 'subconsciously' self-justifications for status and wealth? As I have suggested earlier, the nature and complexity of the African context belies such distinctions and necessitates a phenomenological perspective which takes into account the perceptions, intentions and belief systems of the actors themselves. Such questioning and reservations aside, is it surprising that in a country such as Nigeria, with its conspicuous consumption and cult of the 'big man', or Ghana with its persistent economic problems, conspicuous salvation and material signs of anointing drown the voices of sceptics and critics and draw in the crowds?

NOTES

1 I am grateful to both Kofi E. Agovi and Douglas Sturm for their helpful comments on this essay.

2 See for example, Gifford (1990), who argues that Africa's current evangelical revival, particularly the prosperity gospel, is in large measure funded and directed from the United States.

3 I am grateful to Samuel B. Adubofuor for clarification of this distinction. Personal communication, 5 July 1991.

4 See Marsden (1991). Also the term 'fundamentalist' is generally viewed negatively by Nigerians and Ghanaians because of its association with Islam.

5 This section draws on the work of Ojo (1986) and (1990). He uses the term 'pentecostal' to refer to churches centred on the doctrine of the baptism of the Holy Spirit, and 'charismatic' for movements and fellowships which occur in the context of the mainline or other churches.

6 His initial contact, however, was with Rev. S.G. Elton, the British independent pentecostalist, mentioned above. See (1990) 'The Church of God Mission International', *Thelia* 3, 3: 6–7 [a special issue on Idahosa].

7 Information on Idahosa's early life is available from Garlock (1980). See also (1990) 'Archbishop Benson Idahosa: his early life', *Thelia* 3, 3: 4–5. Lyons, A. and Lyons, H. (1987) offer an excellent analysis of the rise of Idahosa's church and his television evangelism, and the effect of television on the message, audience and ritual.

8 See (1990) 'The ministries of the Church of God Mission', *Thelia*, 3, 3: 8–9.

9 Interview, Benin City, 30 April 1991.

10 'The Power of Faith' was the theme for the 1990 International Convention of the Church of God Mission. See (1990) *Redemption Faith* 5, 38.

11 (1990) *Redemption Faith* 5, 39: 6.

12 Bible study for ministers, Church of God Mission, Benin City, 28 April 1991. The concept of giving may now be part of Nigerian Christianity if the presence of a small booklet, 'Giving Your Way to Prosperity' by John R. Rice (1954) which I purchased in a small, family supermarket in Ibadan is anything to go by.

13 Information from Rev. S. G. Onibere.

14 Interview, Accra, 14 February 1991.

15 Information from Sam Adubofuor.

16 Francis Wale Oke (n.d.) *The Precious Blood of Jesus*, Ibadan: Victory Literature Crusade, p. 23.

17 Francis Wale Oke (n.d.) 'The Life of Prosperity', *1988 Convention Seminar Papers*, 23rd Annual Convention of the Gospel of Faith Mission International, Ibadan: p. 28–9.

18 Ojo (n.d.) *The Secret of Success and Blessings*, Ibadan: JEFAP Power Packed Books.

19 Interview, Ile-Ife, March 22, 1991.

20 Although I am informed by Dr Onibere that Lady Evangelist Odeleke of the Christ Message Ministry does belong to the prosperity group (but of the 'non-preaching' variety).

21 Interview, 30 March 1991.

22 Interview with Professor Martin Bestman, Ile-Ife, 21 March 1991.

23 For a more anthropologically oriented discussion of power in this connection, see Arens and Karp (1989).

24 This follows from the interpretation of the root cause of national problems (corruption, coups, economic recession) as individual sin, 'turning away from God' and hostile ('supernatural') forces. See Lyons and Lyons (1987: 117) who confirm this point for the early 1980s and who also note that Idahosa and his congregation prayed for peaceful elections in 1983. They also rightly point to the merits of a class analysis (taking into account, for example, the rise of a powerful bourgeoisie) in providing more insight into Nigeria's economic problems.

25 See for example, Olukolade (1988) – the proceedings of an all-Christian National Symposium on Nigeria's problems which determined the cause of these economic

and political problems as being due to spiritual warfare and as necessitating spiritual treatment through Jesus Christ. See also, Okonkwo (1989).

26 (1990) *Redemption Faith* 5, 38: 7.
27 '*Anastasis, Akwaaba!*' (1991) *The Watchman*, 2: 1 [Christian newspaper published in Accra].
28 (1988) *Vision*, second quarter: 20.
29 'Designer Turned Lady Evangelist' (n.d.) *The Nigerian Christian Journal* 1, 5: 22.
30 *Quality* (Nigeria), 1, 4 (September 1987).
31 Information from Martin Asamoah-Manu, Executive Secretary, FGBMFI, Pan-African Council Secretariat, Accra, 13 February 1991.
32 Interview with Kwabena Darko, International Director, FGBMFI and President of the Pan-African Council and Martin Asamoah-Manu, Pan African Council Secretariat, Accra, 13 February 1991.
33 In fact one of the major hotels in Kinshasa is now referred to as the 'Full Gospel' hotel because of the number of meetings they hold there. Information from Martin Asamoah-Manu.
34 Mr Darko was due to meet with the President of Gabon two days following our interview. The Vice President of Gabon is already a member.
35 '*Kwabena Darko: Secrets of His Success*' (1991) *Step Magazine* (Ghana edn) 3, 1: 12–16.
36 *Ibid.*: 13.
37 The role of the Haggai Institute, an American organization based in Singapore which trains third world Christian leaders in evangelism, in promoting American religious ideas and structures and in promoting African religious independency (i.e. creation of new groups) has yet to be investigated.
38 Olayiwola (1986: 271).
39 J. K. Olupona, personal communication, 5 October 1991.
40 See Ojo (n.d.) 'The Life of Prosperity', *1988 Convention Seminar Papers*, 23rd Annual Convention of the Gospel of Faith Mission International, Ibadan: 402.
41 Information from Sam Adubofuor.
42 In the programme the festival is billed as 'Bridging the gap between the Black Diaspora around the World through Gospel Music'.
43 *The Guardian Sunday Supplement*, 21 February 1988.
44 It is extremely difficult to be precise about membership statistics etc. As I have tried to suggest, the nature of the charismatic revival and its multi-media *modus operandi* challenge conventional categories of denomination, affiliation etc. For example, someone may claim membership of the Methodist Church, but belong to a charismatic fellowship or read charismatic literature. It is possible to say, however, that virtually no church of any variety has been unaffected by the charismatic revival in one way or another, whether through pressure from members or leaders to 'go charismatic' or through unrecognized *ecclesiolae in ecclesia* – potentially schismatic fellowship, or the public preaching of itinerant evangelists or televangelists.
45 A more recent and growing concern is the role of these movements in inciting religious conflict. The crusade and revival of the West German evangelist, Reinhard Bonnke, was reportedly at the centre of religious riots in the northern Nigerian Muslim city of Kano in mid-October 1991. While such issues are beyond the purview of this essay, it is however important and relevant to note persistent Christian fears in Nigeria about Muslim economic domination.
46 This point is made by Ojo (1986); Ranger (1987: 31), and Pillay (1983).
47 Lyons and Lyons (1987: 119f., 126) are also keen to dismiss the notion that Idahosa's and Oritsejafor's 'electronic churches' are simply and American phenomenon (in form perhaps but not in content).
48 This is an enduring theme, but one which has taken on a new impetus within the

context of the present 'spiritual revolution'. See Turner (1979: 271–88) where he describes how several 'primal' peoples viewed the Bible as the source of European power, particularly those parts held back from them.
49 The case for such a distinction has been put by Wach (1958: 37–9).

REFERENCES

Addo, F. (1989) *Supernatural Love: Your Key to the Release of Power*, Yola, Nigeria: Supernatural Love Publications.

Arens, W. and Karp, I. (eds) (1989) *Creativity of Power*, Washington, DC: Smithsonian Institution Press.

Assimeng, M. (1989) *Religion and Social Change in West Africa*, Accra: Ghana Universities Press.

Bowman, L. W. (1990) 'Government officials, academics, and the process of formulating U.S. national security toward Africa', *Issue: A Journal of Opinion* 19, 1: 18.

Duncan-Williams, N. (1990) *You Are Destined to Succeed!*, Accra: Action Faith Publications.

Falola, T. (1982) 'Religion, rituals and Yoruba pre-colonial domestic economy', *Ife Journal of Religions* 11: 29–30.

Garlock, R. (1980) *Fire in His Bones: the Story of Benson Idahosa*, Plainfield, NJ: Logos.

Gifford, P. (1990) 'Prosperity: a new and foreign element in African Christianity', *Religion* 20, 4: 373–88

Kumuyi, W. F. (1990) *The Lord is my Shepherd*, 3rd edn, Lagos: Zoe Publishing.

Lyons, A. and Lyons, H. (1987) 'Magical medicine on television: Benin City, Nigeria', *Journal of Ritual Studies* 1, 1.

Marsden, G.M. (1991) *Fundamentalists and Evangelicals*, Grand Rapids, MI: W. B. Eerdmans.

Ojo, M.A. (1986) 'The Growth of Campus Christianity and Charismatic Movements in Western Nigeria', Ph.D. thesis, University of London.

Ojo, M.A. (1990) 'The 1970 charismatic revival in Nigeria', *Thelia* 3, 2: 4–9.

Okonkwo, Ifeanyichukwu E.R. (1989) *Anambra State of Nigeria. The Crisis of Peace: What Can You Do To Help?* Enugu: International and Communication Ltd.

Olayiwola, D. O. (1986) 'The Aladura Movement in Ijesaland: 1930–1980', Ph.D. thesis, University of Ife.

Olukolade, Olushola Rev. (ed.) (1988) *Arise and Build: the Role of Christians in Nation-Building*, Yaba: Pentecostal Assembly Publishers.

Oyedepo, D. O. (1988) *Power for Wealth*, Kaduna: Dominion Publications.

Pillay, G. J. (1983) 'A historico-theological study of Pentecostalism as a phenomenon within a South African community', PhD thesis, Rhodes University.

Ranger, T. (1987) 'Religion, development and African Christian identity' in K.H. Peterson (ed.), *Religion, Development and African Identity*, Uppsala: Scandinavian Institute of African Studies.

Taiwo, B. (1988) *Power of the Cross over Human Problems*, Ibadan: The Truth Sowers Publications.

Turner, H. W. (1979) 'The hidden power of the whites: the secret religion withheld from the primal peoples', in *Religious Innovation in Africa*, Boston: G. K. Hall, pp. 271–88.

Wach, J. (1958) *The Comparative Study of Religions*, New York: Columbia University Press.

11

EVANGELICAL RELIGION AND CAPITALIST SOCIETY IN CHILE

Historical context, social trajectory and current political and economic ethos[1]

David Martin

Evangelical religion in Chile has been almost from the beginning authentically Chilean and always of the poor. The Anglicans, Presbyterians and Lutherans, who arrived first, existed initially only to serve foreign communities or, in the Anglican case, to work among the Mapuche. Even today they have small Chilean followings and pursue specialized ministries, though charismatic Anglicanism now finds a cordial response in the Santiago middle class.

Local Protestantism emerged in the early 1900s as a clear assertion of Chilean evangelical identity, free of missionary direction and external governance. It was autonomous, pietistic and revivalistic. So the question of American influence did not and does not arise in any serious way, and lacks even the superficial plausibility it possesses in some other Latin countries. Even the Electronic Church lacks an extensive audience, apart from popular transmissions entirely under Chilean control. Talking to Catholic and other non-evangelical observers the rhetorical move which attributes evangelical expansion to American influence is strikingly absent. Yet, clearly the expansion has been one of the most dramatic in Latin America.

Between 1920 and 1930 evangelicals remained static at about 1.5 percent. In the 1930s their number started to rise until in 1952 it stood at 4 percent. In the two decades between 1952 and 1973 their percentages doubled, and in the seventeen years following it more than doubled. There has, in short, been a gently rising curve in the increase of evangelicals relative to population. Within this overall trend, however, there was a steep rise between 1970 and 1973 from 5.5–8 percent, during the time of the left wing Popular Unity government, followed by a plateau in the first six years of military government.

Commentators attribute the initial increase in the 1930s as a response to urbanization, industrialization and the Great Depression, and the spurt in the early 1970s to serious political instability and social conflict. Throughout the whole period from 1930 till now, evangelical religion in Chile has avoided political entanglements of all kinds and many pastors have looked averse at political or union membership.

Evangelical religion in Chile is overwhelmingly Pentecostal, and the Methodist Pentecostal Church, set up in 1909, is much the largest body. For the most part, Chilean evangelical churches are in the umbrella organization of the Council of Pastors, which numbers forty-four denominations among its affiliates.

Apart from a few small evangelical bodies, the main instances of North American influence are the Jehovah's Witnesses and the Mormons. These faiths arrived respectively in 1930 and 1956 and employ many foreign missionaries. The Jehovah's Witnesses are most active in the very poorest areas, even more so perhaps than the evangelicals. The Mormons are more visible and perhaps also the more feared by Catholics and evangelicals alike. Many of their buildings are impressive and they offer all kinds of facilities to young people, such as tennis courts and swimming pools. Even so, perhaps only 3 percent of Chileans belong to these groups compared with 17 percent identifying in one way or another with evangelical churches. In Gran Santiago alone there are some 1,500 places of evangelical worship. Carmen Galilea, who has engaged in extensive study of evangelicals for the Catholic Church, comments (in personal conversation) on the growth of evangelical Pentecostal religion as part and parcel of popular culture and as authentically Chilean.

NEW LIFE? CONTINUITY AND CHANGE

Pentecostalism is one of the most vital of several popular movements carrying forward traditional elements in Chilean culture. Christian Parker, for example, has explored several movements active at the beginning of the century, despised equally by the leaders of workers' organizations and the official Church, and for a long time invisible to most historians (Parker 1987: 185–204) Parker sees everyday Catholicism as concerned with the management of ordinary problems. Nor is this true only of Chile and Latin America but even of cultures with a thicker veneer of rationality like the United States. Catholicism, and religion more generally, provide supernatural technology for getting by. In the United States, for example, St Jude (according to the advertisements of his devotees) will succour those who ask and engage in the prescribed rituals within nine days at the outside. Everyday Catholicism is not confined to Chile or Latin America.

Resort to supernatural technology is part of traditional religion the world over and in Chile it clusters not only around accepted saints and the Virgin but around shrines for people who simply suffered some tragic mishap which now offer sanctified succour to the living. Such 'saints' help in everyday problems, especially worries about health. Exactly the same coverage of everyday problems and of worries about health is provided by Pentecostalism, and by Pentecostal leaders, except that the spirits and saints are brought together under the single aegis of the Holy Spirit.

Most Chileans, living in rural areas or even long established in the towns, entertain a lively fear of the Evil Eye. They may well possess a television (and value its possession way above adequate food and clothing) but the old fears and folk explanations remain potent. After a first resort to the doctor, the next resort is to the healer. What in Santiago and in Valparaiso appears to be a rational culture, elegant and open on an obvious Parisian model, is in fact thoroughly inspirited and animated. The supernatural has ordinary unproblematic reality. The Pentecostal preacher who expels demons, confronts spirits and cures the ills of the flesh can be seen as a healer in another guise. He, or she, appeals to a variant of a deep code unobliterated by modernity.

The point is important because the psychical and physical aspects of living have not been split apart in Latin America to the same extent as in Europe or North America. The science of medicine merges into the practice of ancient cures and into the spirited expulsion of demons. What in Europe appears as secularization is, in Chile and in Latin America more generally, a recombination of elements of modernity with the deep code of tradition. Something parallel may be observed in Japan where devotees of 'new' religions receive medical reports surrounded by astrological predictions as part of their membership.

So Pentecostalism is a new variant within an old tradition, and runs parallel to other popular movements. One such movement described by Christian Parker arose in the early 1900s among workers in the North of Chile. They were much exploited by English or American companies, and experienced a great deal of crime, alcoholism and prostitution. They responded with an anti-clerical and radical rhetoric based on anarchist and socialist models, and with an equally anti-clerical rhetoric combining devotion to the Virgin with Andean rites and beliefs. People from the countryside or of Indian origin sang jubilant songs to the Virgin and danced in her honour. Naturally, the Catholic Church tried to head off both the secular and religious versions of protest, trying to moralize and incorporate the cult, and provide alternative workers' organizations.

What Parker stresses is precisely the way this religious 'exodus' in the North ran parallel to Pentecostalism in Valparaiso, a city which was at that time rapidly urbanizing and the centre of the export trade. Parker sees Pentecostalism alongside anarchism and socialism as part of the rapid transitions affecting agricultural workers in the Central Valley, pastoralists in the Andes, and the artisanate among mestizos in the ports (Parker 1987).

Carmen Galilea makes a supplementary point in the circumstances of today in a study for the Jesuits entitled 'Movimiento Pentecostal e Iglesia Catolica en Medios Populares' (1988). This time, however, the secular mode has been adopted, or at any rate shadowed, by the Catholic Church itself. Rather than trying to incorporate popular religious culture, some enthusiasts within the Catholic Church have actually attempted to jettison it. The situation is complicated, since at Puebla the assembled representatives of Latin American Catholicism showed themselves anxious to use popular culture and regarded much of it as positive. But in practice many pious traditional Catholics have seen their practices downgraded. Their priests have preached a different and so far alien message, with intellectual supports and social demands remote from their immediate concerns. Though the idea was to support the poor in their particular situation, the thrust appeared to

217

come mainly from above and many of the faithful lacked the means to interpret it. For that matter, many of those who could interpret it did not like it.

The main point is the partial displacement of the personal, tangible and spiritual by the rational and abstract. Even the face of the Redeemer blurs into some kind of generalized representation. Juan Escobar, a lay theologian professionally concerned with Catholic social responsibility, reinforces the point in a personal interview by regretting the way the political has taken up the space of the personal. The argument is hardly novel, but at a deeper level it has to do with the way religion achieves an imprint on the individual through the tangible, sensuous and familiar, including for many sonorous organs, chanting and incense.

The poor, argues Carmen Galilea, remain conversant with miracles. In Pentecostalism the miracle is immediate and palpable. A man gives up the worst aspects of machismo, ceases to drink or smoke, and 'supposedly has no other love' (Galilea 1988). This too is very traditional, and in two ways. First, '*Rerum Novarum*' itself recommends this particular 'miracle'. It argues that Christian morality properly practised 'conduces of itself to temporal prosperity' and "makes men supply by economy for the want of means, teaching them to be content with frugal living, and keeping them out of reach of those vices which eat up not merely small incomes but large fortunes'. And second, Pentecostalism attempts to restore the traditional family. Not merely is the father restored to the family in a kindlier, gentler atmosphere, but he exercises some of his traditional authority. Old teachings have been made good by another route.

In other ways, however, Pentecostalism has to be seen as a dramatic break with the past. It recommends itself as new life. How then might this be characterized? A good place to start is the lay preacher, the man who now speaks for God in his own voice. Carlyle called him in his English manifestation 'the speaking man'. The sacred canopy no longer closes above such a person, but he himself upholds it by his powerful words.

The lay preacher is an unpaid missionary imbued with boundless enthusiasm for something which has become his main source of self-realization. This is where he – and she – really matters. Lay preachers meet to divide up a territory and then gather together the signatures required for permission to build a chapel. After that it is a matter of collecting money and finding labour, most often among fellow-believers.

Like the self-taught anywhere, the lay preacher is a man of the dictionary. He consults the words to understand and expound the Word. In this way he acquires a vocabulary that is both amplified and archaic, pronounced oddly but used correctly.

The Bibles of lay preachers are thumbed and worn from Genesis to Revelation, and like all Pentecostals they are on easy and familiar terms with prophets and disciples. These are men of energy and probably of intelligence, and those who know them comment on their clean, neatly furnished houses. They belong wholly and completely to Chile and to the Chilean poor.

The pastors themselves, at least those in the more established churches, are burly people possessed of almost Edwardian confidence and unction. In face and figure they resemble Lech Walesa and are clearly determined to be master in their own 'household of faith'. The pastorate is often passed from father to son in a charismatic genealogy. Most of the chapels they serve are tiny gated dwellings, others are clearly chapels set apart from ordinary housing. Some are unexpectedly charming way-stations on the grid of roads, neatly painted and with twining flowers. At the top of the architectural scale is the Methodist Pentecostal 'cathedral' at Jotabeche, said to hold up to 6,000. (Some sources claim it holds 18,000 but this can only be true in the sense that the world's population could, if necessary, stand on the Isle of Wight.) It is a bare, airy and resonant hanger with a platform in one corner and a gallery facing.

The sense of a people closely knit is very clear as the congregation begin to respond with shouts of praise and jubilation, and when the tithe of gifts is expressly set aside for some named person, sick or in trouble. Above all it is manifest as the congregation breaks out in fervent singing, in tune or not. This gives Pentecostals their sense of power, and in some of their communities anyone can compose a tune or a lyric. Often the singing is accompanied by guitars or chimes, though in some churches singing is, in principle, unaccompanied. Pentecostal men and women quite frequently walk in the street, singing or preaching, unabashed by any absence of response or support.

Doorkeepers in chapels are always male, but otherwise women can do most things, even in a few denominations enter the pastorate. Women act as ushers, take collections, visit jails, and also visit the sick and 'lay hands' on them. In the street you can tell them by a certain severity of style. Evangelical women wear long skirts (never trousers), keep to dark colours, avoid cosmetics, and leave their hair long.

The presence of a cultural break is most clear in the way the Pentecostal people see themselves as set apart, and in the special language of salvation. Though the preacher is of the people and speaks their language, nevertheless, the group cherishes a distinctive speech and vocabulary. Though almost all belong to the poor they form an enclave within the poor, seeing themselves and regarded by others as separate. This means there is often a diminished sense of territorial or political responsibility. By contrast a new Catholic church in a poor suburb proclaims its social centrality in the choice of site and scale of construction. The priest has the social confidence to offer comment on affairs. The Church may also demonstrate its social responsibility by experiments in communal care, staffed by devoted and trained personnel, and offering a wide range of services, even including health. In other parts of Latin America many evangelical churches provide at least some of these services, such as the clinic, but in Chile their care and concern seems focused on the faithful. This social reality is mirrored in the law. The Catholic Church is a public corporation whereas all other churches are private corporations.

THE SPLIT AMONG PENTECOSTALS OVER SOCIAL ACTIVISM

Since the 1960s the Pentecostal churches have acquired a greater variety of approaches, politically and theologically. This variety reflects the political appeals made first by Christian Democracy, and then by the Popular Unity government and the opposition to General Pinochet's military government. It also reflects wider international contacts and the experience of a minority of Pentecostals in contact with higher education. Clearly this shift bears on any enquiry into social mobility.

Pentecostalism is, as has been suggested, a movement running parallel to modernization, yet indifferent to reason and progress as usually and humanistically conceived. It revives tradition, and it breaks with tradition. The heart of Pentecost is a drama in the soul which brings to birth a new self or a 'new creature', dead to the past with its loneliness, hate, shame and fear, and 'alive to God'. The Pentecostal has gained life, discovered meaning, and responded to the call of salvation. These are, of course, the terms used by Pentecostals themselves but they do tend to undermine the kind of external explanation based on loss of moral norms and anomie. Testimonies speak rather of a release of deep-seated and powerful moral feelings about the 'dirt' and 'shame' of previous existence, and of a desire to avoid moral failure. They deal in a fear of becoming lost, of 'dying', of 'not making out' or drifting into the degradation and hopelessness of alcoholism. Pentecostals are clearly aware from the outset of the duties of parenthood and neighbourliness. So their conversion is experienced as a shift from moral failure to personal empowerment.

This sense of power needs constantly to be replenished since the demand for their labour is intermittent, their hold on any contractual employment weak, and sickness may strike at any time. They are in insecure circumstances which they experience as a sea of vanities. Hence the search for new exemplars to replace models which seem no longer to work and the intense desire to rise out of a 'miserable individualism' rooted in envy, aggression and worthlessness.

The transition from failure to empowerment is cast in terms of mighty opposites: Spirit and Matter, Church and World, the Faithful and the Faithless, the Holy Spirit and the Demonic Powers. Such a transition can only be made by an almost physical struggle to throw off what is holding you down and cross to safety and graceful acceptance. The map of salvation as provided in the Bible is no longer sequestered in the sacred but provides an everyday manual eagerly scrutinized. It does not matter that the tight band of persons emerging from all this heart work is despised and rejected, and in Chile given the derisory title '*canutos*'. Experience of rejection strengthens assurance of salvation.

This is the kind of religion which expanded between 1909 and 1964, and it worked within strict religious boundaries amongst the small artisans, the casually employed and the rural migrants. Then in 1964 it encountered a Christian Democracy offering revolution with liberty. Christian Democracy sought a constituency precisely among such marginal people to balance to a socialist constituency of the organized workers. At roughly the same time, Pentecostal churches came into contact with wider currents of fundamentalism and the World Council of Churches. The earthquakes of 1960 and 1965 also challenged them to service. In any case, they were beginning to have a sense of being a large minority capable of attracting social recognition. The carefully patrolled boundary with the World seemed less necessary.

The result was a conflict between, on the one hand social service and political change, and on the other hand the belief that nothing much can be done outside the sphere of redemption. The military coup sharpened this conflict, because those opting for change saw the powers of evil not only in permanent array but historically present through the exercise of unjust power. For such people the crucial boundary was now no longer between Church and World but between all the poor and the military government. Their solidarity was not solely with their believing brethren but with all their neighbours, and their charisma was more the fruits of the spirit expressed in service than the gifts of the spirit expressed in jubilation.

This tendency among Pentecostals (and some other evangelicals) led in 1982 to the founding of the Christian Confraternity of Churches. The Confraternity probably represented some 15 percent of the Pentecostal community. A typical example of how this approach manifested itself was in an attempt to use the church to bring together the poor as poor in a semi-rural area of Bio-Bio in southern Chile. The local Catholic priest was rather inactive, and his Bishop a member of Opus Dei. Pentecostals felt sufficiently confident to galvanize three communities around a core of 1,000 families. This certainly broke with traditional Pentecostalism by fusing the people of God with the people.

An example of a parallel trend is the arrival of Pentecostal students at a major seminary in Santiago belonging to the 'historical' Protestants. This is important because an erosion of evangelical commitment has often come with educational advance. Most of the young Pentecostals come to study technical subjects but they also encountered the critical study of the Bible. This did not lead to any rift with their religious community, since that was probably their one focus of loyalty and belonging, but it may have brought about a rift in the mind. These young people already knew some of what they referred to as 'Blessings of the Lord', notably better things in the home. They were now in a familiar bind: how to acquire the technical benefits of capitalism without liberalism, and how to acquire education without succumbing to intellectuality.

The period of political change from 1958 to 1970 was not specially conducive to Pentecostal advance. After all, traditional Pentecostalism demanded a total commitment of time and talents whereas the call to political participation assumed other loyalties. 'Free time' for other interests had never been part of the Pentecostal way of life. Yet they were torn. The new political programme aimed to ease their conditions of life and the average Pentecostal was inclined to vote more or less as did his secular neighbours placed in similar circumstances. After

1970, the collapse of Christian Democracy and the advance of the left increased tension throughout Chile and inside the Pentecostal churches – and also brought increased growth. Pastors in particular expressed their fear of Marxism. Even democracy itself had a vague association with moral anarchy in some of their minds.

The most serious rifts occurred with the onset of military government. A day or two before the coup, evangelicals of all kinds met to express their grave concern. After the coup, however, there were some expressions of sympathy with the army, and the Council of Pastors representing most Pentecostals actually published its support. With one part of the Catholic Church more and more uneasy about the dictatorship, and in the end openly antagonistic, the military leadership sought alternative sponsorship from their rivals. This happened in spite of the fact that General Pinochet was himself aligned with the older style Catholicism and even assumed quasi-liturgical functions in the national devotion to the Virgin of Maipu. Pentecostals found themselves, for the first time ever, acknowledged by the state. They were even allowed to preach in the army, though the suggestion that they were disproportionately present in the army is not correct. When the new Methodist 'cathedral' was opened at Jotabeche in Alameda, Santiago, General Pinochet attended a celebratory *Te Deum*. The long-delayed and entirely proper recognition of the Pentecostal community had come about under unfortunate circumstances, and Pentecostal opponents quickly accused their brethren of 'selling their birthright for a mess of potage'.

What actually happened is not easily reconstructed, but even accounts given by Pentecostals and evangelical opponents stress the difficulty in which the pastors found themselves. Unlike the Catholic Church, all evangelical bodies had a 'juridical personality' open to immediate cancellation. Again, unlike the Catholic Church, Pentecostal pastors as individuals were internationally invisible. They represented people who had hitherto lacked a voice and had, in any case, preferred to live quietly within their own enclave. Certainly they were anti-Marxist. The government played on their fears of Marxism and presumably indicated the unfortunate consequences of non-compliance. Of course, the Catholic Church also celebrated a *Te Deum* in the presence of the head of state and the archbishop's sermon offered a chance to assert basic human rights which was increasingly used as time went on. In the event, the *Te Deum* was enlarged into an ecumenical occasion, with the Catholic Church playing the major role.

The position of Pentecostals looks very different, depending on what frame and what rhetoric you employ. Humberto Lagos (1988), for example, analysed Pentecostal discourse from a Gramscian point of view. In his view, such discourse exemplified unresolvable contradictions in the symbolic realm and supported an alien hegemony. The pastors who produced the discourse were, he claimed, a lower class version of the organic intelligentsia. On the other hand, ordinary Pentecostals were clearly just like other Chileans: not only did they vote just as others did in their class situation, but they shared a general scepticism about most political solutions. Political commitments are not central for most people in any society, certainly not in Chile, and it is highly likely that Pentecostals most of all wanted an end to violence, insecurity and social conflict. They flourished in times of violence and insecurity among those who most wanted security and peace.

POLITICAL AND ECONOMIC ATTITUDES: RECENT POLLS AND RECENT RESEARCH

A great deal of information has been collected since the late 1980s about religion in Chile and the varied attitudes of Catholics and evangelicals. Data available in late 1990 from the Centro de Estudios Publicos, Santiago (*Puntos de Referencia* 67) show that three out of four persons over 18 are Catholic and one out of five Protestant. The great majority of Protestants is evangelical, but there is a largish group of Jehovah's Witnesses (2 percent) and a smaller group of Mormons (less than 1 percent). Of those describing themselves as Catholic, over half are occasional attenders, with the rest equally divided among those who attend regularly and those who do not attend at all. As you might expect, evangelical Protestants are much more often regular attenders than Catholics, and it may well be that on a given Sunday, the number of evangelicals at worship is nearly half the number of Catholics. Among the poor the proportion of dormant evangelical Protestants is higher than that of Catholics. Either you go to your humble evangelical chapel or you do not. It looks as if over the several generations of evangelical adherence in Chile there has emerged a large number (28+ percent) who have ceased to be committed, and who are maybe drawn disproportionately from non-Pentecostal denominations. Both practising Catholics and evangelical Protestants are tilted towards the older age groups, with a noticeable concentration of evangelical Protestants in the age range of 45–54. Practising Catholics and practising evangelical Protestants are disproportionately female, and to about the same extent. Overall practice declines as you move down the status scale and as you move to the political left.

Reviewing the various enquiries, Catholics are overwhelmingly birth-right adherents, accepting their faith as part and parcel of their social existence and status, whereas evangelicals are frequently converts from Catholicism. That is just as expected. However, one might not expect to find most Catholics who never attend and most evangelicals, committed or not, to register benign approval of the Catholic Church. For that matter, some 15 percent of regular Catholic attenders register strong disapproval of their Church, which may have something to do with the irritation felt by traditionalists at changes since the Second Vatican Council. Some have clearly been irritated to the point of ceasing to attend.

Upper-class Catholics do not take much notice of their priests, deriving religious influences more from parental example and school. It is the left-wing Catholics who most clearly take a lead from their priests. As for lower-class evangelical Protestants, they are very respectful towards their pastors. Evangelical Protestants mostly register strong approval of their churches, especially (perhaps) those who never attend. This broad approval all round for churches as such is obviously compatible with a very high level of generalized belief.

It is quite clear that evangelical Protestants are overwhelmingly concentrated among the fairly poor, though not the very poorest. Evangelical churches may expect the bulk of their support from the better-off poor, and the Catholic Church from the worse-off members of the middle class. On an ascending income scale divided into eleven categories, nearly half of practising evangelical Protestants were in the low categories 2 and 3, and nearly half of practising Catholics in categories 4, 5 and 6. Only 1 percent of practising evangelical Protestants were classified as ABC1, and 5.8 percent were classified as C2, whereas the comparable figures for practising Catholics were 20.3 percent and 16.1 percent. These crude indicators almost certainly fail to show just how sharp is the ceiling cutting off evangelical Protestants from the social world of Catholics in terms of status, locality and contact, apart that is from evangelical Anglicans and Lutherans. Other indices reinforce the point. Practising evangelicals are primarily in unstable employment, whereas practising Catholics enjoy stable employment with contracts. Evangelical Protestants decrease in number as you ascend the scale of pay and education and provision of domestic amenities like warm water.

The political attachments and attitudes of evangelical Protestants reflect their class and status, whatever the support given to Pinochet in the mid-1970s by the Council of Pastors. When presented in 1990 with a list of possible candidates for the Presidency, 0.2 percent of practising evangelical Protestants chose Pinochet and 0.6 percent of practising Catholics. Both practising Catholics and evangelicals approved of President Alwyn and the performance of his government. Equally both groups contained a majority well disposed to the main Trade Union body (the CUT). Indeed, about a quarter of practising evangelical Protestants were very positive in their attitude towards the CUT, and a third considered it should prevail in any conflict with the government. In their party preferences, evangelical Protestants of all kinds and degrees of practice clustered on the centre and centre left, as they probably did in the period of Allende before the military take-over. Compared with practising Catholics, the evangelical Protestants were less well disposed to the National Renovation Party, or more inclined to identify with the Socialist Party, or else they retained their historic attachment to the masonic and (anti-clerical) Radical Party. Perhaps as a reflection of their social situation, evangelicals seemed marginally more pessimistic about the integrity of the judiciary and the efficacy of political action. They tended to stress employment and production somewhat more strongly than democracy and education. But both evangelicals and Catholics gave massive support for Christian Democracy and, in any case, it appears that Chileans as a whole expect little from politics or politicians. Only 15 percent declare a strong interest in politics, which is somewhat less than those who declare themselves strongly integrated in groups run by religious bodies. One person in six belongs to such a group. And one person in sixty belongs to a base community, giving base communities less than a tenth the numerical influence of evangelicals.

Chileans are, for the most part, morally and culturally conservative, approving of discipline for children and the exercise of authority. Many of them in a measured way respect the role of the armed forces. Opinions are about equally divided on the legalization of divorce, but a large majority are against abortion, even on the left. Practising evangelical Protestants are strongly against abortion, particularly the women and the lower class. Opinion among evangelicals about divorce is more evenly divided, with a small majority of the non-practising in favour. Young practising Catholics and evangelicals both tend to reject divorce, but their resolve apparently weakens with age.

A study conducted in Santiago in 1988 brought out some differences in economic attitude between evangelical Protestants and Catholics. The evangelicals expected more help from God in business whereas the Catholics were more inclined to believe in luck. The evangelicals put more trust in God than in personal initiative and were more inclined to place the burden of failure on the individual than on fate. This finding is important: personal responsibility and trust in God displace luck as arbiters of the future among evangelicals.

Enquiries also bring out the way religious practice and evangelical adherence vary in different localities and areas. Though in the country as a whole about three in four are Catholic and one in five 'Protestant', this varies a great deal. In Greater Santiago the Protestant population is perhaps around 10 percent, not much more than it was fifteen years ago, whereas in the mining areas of Lota-Coronel evangelicals may be almost in the majority, and in some rural areas and poor barrios at least 30 percent. In Antofagasta by contrast both evangelicals and Catholics show a depressed total, while disaffiliation is high and adherence to the Witnesses or the Mormons is above average. The crude figures thrown up by the kind of polls taken in the regions and in the capital indicate, once again, the kind of complex religious geography discussed by Christian Lalive D'Epinay (1975). Padahuel on one side of Santiago is honeycombed with evangelical churches, whereas elegant Providencia on the other side can show very few.

To these results may be added further data collected by the Centro de Estudios Publicos and made publicly available in November 1991 (*Puntos de Referencia* 90, and other material). In general, the data indicate that only 3 percent of Chileans account themselves atheists. For 84 percent God is very important in their lives, and 53 percent pray every day. With respect to evangelicals some fresh material emerged. Morally they were more inclined to the conservative positions advocated by the Roman Catholic hierarchy than practising Catholics! And politically they were relatively more inclined than their immediate social peers to be volatile and to offer support to independents.

At the same time, preliminary data became available on lifestyle, life histories, and economic ethos, among evangelicals in a poor suburb of Santiago following research directed by the author, in association with the Centro de Estudios Publicos. The data have, of course, to be treated with some caution. They show, first of all, how very frequently conversion is associated with healing. They also show that churches are built by local contributions, and sustained by sacrificial giving. Believers are morally rigorous, especially with regard to alcohol and drugs, and violence and promiscuity, and also with regard to activities that may be associated with such things, for example, football. But they mostly possess radio and television, and listen regularly to evangelical radio. Economically they are more likely than their social peers to be without work contracts. And they definitely see their faith as requiring an economic ethic of hard work, trustworthiness and fair dealing. In their view, God blesses hard work and moral discipline and financial foresight. They do not complain about their situation, and believe in personal independence and responsibility together with schemes for mutual help among the brethren, especially when sick. Their 'social work' is to change lives and priorities. They want to obviate the need for social workers.

Evangelicals often have plans for the future and hope to acquire small businesses of their own, for example in such activities as baking and upholstery. Few are well enough off to save. It is worth adding that they admire technology, science, and practical skills. The world of humanist education, including theology, is alien, threatening, and useless so far as their pragmatic needs are concerned. They want mastery and practicality not polish, therapy, and good conversation.

SUMMARY AND CONCLUDING COMMENT

Chilean evangelical religion, and Pentecostal religion in particular, is part of the Chilean world. Its resources in people and in money derive from the Chilean poor. It accompanied a first industrialization and urbanization in the early 1900s and has accompanied a second wave of industrial change since the mid-century. During the second phase it has expanded its constituency from one in twenty-five to nearly one in five. Yet the social status of evangelicals has not so far risen all that much, because they encounter an upper limit beyond which evangelicals hardly exist at all. In this they differ from evangelicals in Brazil who encounter no such limit. To some people securely in the middle class and living in their own kind of suburb, evangelicals are almost invisible. There is little doubt that evangelicals work hard, and that they exercise modest entrepreneurial initiative at the margin of the upper working class and lower middle class. They are adept at strategies for survival, and seek personal betterment in their priorities and the furnishing of their homes. But their further mobility has been limited by a clear ceiling. In this they resemble Methodists in nineteenth-century England: psychologically equipped to move but in practice able to move only short distances.

Perhaps that cautious assessment needs to be qualified. The post-Pinochet situation is one in which evangelicals are being recognized as a presence and in which new forms of evangelical initiative are weakening the class ceiling. Within the relatively narrow band where they have so far been mobile, they themselves will be conscious of what they have achieved. They are poised for further advance, and as economic opportunities occur they are the kind of people most likely to take them.

Politically they remain an enclave and (unlike Brazil) do not have a single representative at national level. They see politics as dirty business just as they regard 'the world' as a terrain of moral seduction and unsatisfying vanities, unlikely to respond to any political initiative. So they have eschewed politics, at least at the level of their official theology, though as far as ordinary voting is concerned, they vote much as their fellows in similar social circumstances. During the period of Christian Democracy, some of them were pulled towards the political arena, and over time that has led to the emergence of a socially active evangelical minority. After the military coup in the 1970s the leaders of the majority were successfully pressured by fear of the army, fear of Marxism and the promise of the first official recognition ever accorded to lend some support to General Pinochet.

Basically, Pentecostals in Chile (and elsewhere) would have emerged whatever strategy had been adopted by the Catholic Church. In terms of sociological theory they were part of a wide ranging differentiation of spheres. In ordinary language, they represent the break up of religious monopoly and the establishment of an open market in beliefs.

NOTES

1 This research was undertaken under the aegis of the Institute for the Study of Economic Culture, Boston University, director Peter Berger. Grateful thanks are due to the Institute and Peter Berger for continuing support and financial assistance. Thanks are also due to Carmen Galilea, Juan Escobar, Juan Sepulveda, Arturo Chacón and Christian Parker, who provided much of the material for this paper in the course of personal conversation. Much help and documentation was provided by Dr Arturo Fontaine and the Centro de Estudios Publicos.

REFERENCES

D'Epinay, C.L. (1975) *Religion, dynamique sociale et dépendence*, The Hague: Mouton.

Galilea, C. (1988) *Movimiento Pentecostal e Iglesia Catolica en Medios Populares*, Centro Bellarmino, Santiago: Mimeo.

Lagos, H. (1988) *Crisis de la Esperanza. Religión y Autoritarismo en Chile*, Santiago: Presor.

Parker, C. (1987) 'Anticlericalismo y religión popular en Chile (1900–1920)' *Revista Mexicana de Sociologia*, 49, 3: 185–204.

Part III

RELIGION AND MODERNITY/ POST-MODERNITY – CAPITALISM AND CULTURES EAST AND WEST

12

MODERNITY OR PSEUDO-MODERNITY? SECULARIZATION OR PSEUDO-SECULARIZATION?

Reflections on East–Central Europe

Ivan Varga

At first glance one is prompted to speak of *de*-secularization in East–Central Europe. With various degrees of intensity, religion and church-related activities seem to flourish. The churches have begun to move out of the stupor into which forty-plus years of totalitarian and authoritarian regimes[1] had forced them. Initially, after the recent system change, the prestige of the churches rose amongst significant parts of the population, as various public opinion surveys indicated.[2]

Why, then, do we speak of secularization? Indeed, can we? By now it is a truism in the sociology of religion that the phenomenon of secularization includes elements – mainly historical and cultural ones – that do not lend themselves to quantification even though certain aspects of them can be grasped in a quantifiable way (cf. among others, Dobbelaere 1981). This problem cannot be answered unless one tries to make sense of the structural and cultural changes that East–Central European societies have undergone in the past 45 years. Namely, after the historical changes in the late 1980s and in 1990s, when the return to a society based upon a parliamentary democracy and private property became the alternative to the Soviet type of society, the debate: 'return or renewal' flared up.

By 'return' it was understood that the system which existed prior to the Sovietization of society ought to be restored. The idea of 'renewal' did not mean the reform of a socialist society, but rather the creation of a modern society corresponding to the established institutional set-up of existing Western societies.

This alternative not only had far-reaching policy consequences but also required a reassessment of the changes that East–Central European societies had undergone since the end of the Second World War. One could state that the changes that occurred in those societies, at least the most salient ones, are irreversible. I am not suggesting this in a rhetorical manner. In fact, the structural changes, such as urbanization, industrialization, the extension of compulsory education until the age of 16 (or 18, depending on the given country), demographic and family changes, literacy, and so on, profoundly altered the face of East–Central European societies.

With the exception of the Czech lands (now the Czech Republic), the countries of this area were late in developing a bourgeois society with its characteristic institutional system. The remnants of a society based on the traditional estates and nobility were strong; democratic institutions were feeble. The end of the Second World War and the collapse of the old system opened up the possibility not only of physical but also of systemic (i.e. institutional and cultural) reconstruction. The first post-war years gave hope that the region would undertake decisive steps to embark on the road towards modernization. The brief period of hope, however, came to an end with the Sovietization of East–Central Europe by about 1948.

The seizure of power by the communist parties resulted in the establishment of a totalitarian system. This included the superimposition upon society of an ideology which claimed the status of what Jean-François Lyotard has called metanarrative (*grand récit*) that was capable of explaining nature, society and human beings alike.[3] Communist ideology considered religion its main opponent because religion could be looked upon as the only other metanarrative able to compete with it.

Needless to say in particular fields – as in economic theory, political theory, philosophy, ethics, logic, aesthetics, and so on – there were other trends, schools of thought and theories (e.g. liberalism, social democracy, existentialism, logical positivism, modern and non-Marxist economic theories, etc.) which were in opposition or contrary to the tenets of Marxism–Leninism. As such they were rejected and suppressed by the official ideology. None of them, however, claimed the status of universality as religion did. It was thus 'logical' – within the logic of the absurd – to target religion in the first place, the more so because religion as a system of beliefs, practices, meaning-giving and morally-regulating views cannot be presented as the world-view of any particular social class. Amongst workers and peasants, the alleged beneficiaries of the system, large groups followed the teachings of churches.

In spite of these factors, the Sovietization of East–Central Europe brought about a modernization process as well. This was, however, a distorted, quasi-modernization. For modernization means much more than merely industrialization and urbanization. It is a 'package'[4] insofar as it includes the structural transformation of the whole social system including its culture. Of course, the concept of modernization, as with all sociological categories, is equivocal and lends itself to different interpretations. In my view, modernization is the totality of inter-relating technological, economic, political and cultural processes within which each process happens not in a sychronic but rather in a diachronic way, that is to say the processes do not occur simultaneously and with the same intensity. Thus in societies we consider as modern there are elements of pre-modernity as well (e.g. prejudices, intolerance, bigotry, prevalence of vested interests over purposive rationality, just to mention a few).

Without claiming to give a comprehensive analysis of modernization and without ranking its elements according to their relative importance, the following basic criteria of modernization could be mentioned:

1 The creation of a type of technology which is self-generating in its own development.
2 Sustained modernization which cannot occur without the market taking over the main (though by no means all) economic regulatory functions.
3 The individual as such acquires a value. As a result, the idea of individual freedom and human rights as intrinsic to the essence of human beings has emerged.
4 Civil society and a system of institutions develop that allows the individual to arrange his or her life according to their own wishes, desires and interests. Economic, class, cultural, religious and racial constraints place a limit on absolute freedom of choice; needs can be manipulated but there is little or no state interference which might force the individual to accept a particular style of life or take up a defined ideological position.[5]
5 Individuals possess the possibility of associating themselves with other, like-minded individuals with similar concerns, thus promoting their common interests.
6 Purposive rationality takes over as the primary motivation of action.[6]
7 Technological developments lead to the emergence of mass culture and mass communication; folk culture declines and the divisions between so-called 'high culture' and 'low culture' become ever more relativized.
8 The pace of scientific and technological discoveries and innovations increases exponentially; this leads to rapid economic and cultural changes.
9 As a result of the emergence and acceptance of a pluralist system of ideas and politics, meaning-systems become fragmented and the maintenance of any universal discourse becomes impossible. (By universal discourse I mean one which is accepted and held plausible by the whole society.)
10 As a result of the acceptance of pluralism the idea of tolerance becomes, at least in principle, recognized.

Of course, industrialization and urbanization as well as the dominance of the nuclear family are part and parcel of the modernization process. If we compare the above criteria with the reality of modernization based upon Soviet ideology it becomes understandable why the latter can be regarded as flawed – a quasi- or pseudo-modernization. That is to say, the Soviet type of modernization contradicted each of the above-mentioned features, or at least it only managed to realise them in an incomplete form. Several historically determined conditions contributed to this.

There was, indeed, the necessity of re-shaping the structure of the economy. Pre-war East–Central European societies (with the exception of Bohemia and Moravia) were predominantly agricultural, although by the 1930s and 1940s a not negligible industrial development had taken place. True, this was the result of the economic and technological preparation for the Second World War and thus the structure of industrial development was heavily influenced by the needs of a war economy. The industrial plant, however, had largely been destroyed during the

Second World War. Since the East–Central European countries refused under pressure from the Soviet Union to participate in the Marshall Plan, they were forced to imitate the Soviet pattern of industrialization.

The Soviet model, however, is based upon the centralized, and centralizing, role of the totalitarian state. Historically the state had to, and indeed did, play a significant role in the development and modernization of the East–Central societies. Economic, fiscal, monetary and taxation measures; protectionism; preferential treatment of some branches of industry; state support of external trade, and so on, were necessary for the regulation and enhancement of the process of modernization. It should be noted that these measures are not unique to the development of East–Central Europe: Japan and the rapidly developing East Asian countries have applied much the same policy. Thus, without the active regulatory role of the state there was not, and could not be, modernization.[7] Modern economies cannot exist with the total passivity of the state. The state cannot play the role of *deus absconditus*.

The Soviet model was incapable of fostering modernization.[8] Its centralized structure, apart from being slow, arbitrary and thus ineffective, was based on the subordination of the economy to the political goals of the state. Such a model was, at best, capable promoting *extensive* development (i.e. that based on conventional, mostly labour-intensive, technology). The subordination of the economy to politics and the centralization of economic decisions remained dominant, even when some steps had been taken to introduce certain market elements. To put it simply, modern market relations cannot be created by decisions of the Central Committee of the Communist Party.

Modernization is a historical fact and not a value in itself; nor is it an unmitigated blessing. Modern societies put burdens on the shoulder of the individual that did not exist in pre-modern times (e.g. the possibility, nay, the necessity for the individual to make decisions and bear their consequences). Modern societies feel the effects of anomie and alienation. Nonetheless, modernity has brought about several features of society and institutions that, relatively speaking, ensure the highest standard of living for the largest number of their citizens. Modernity also developed institutions (particular legal and parliamentary systems, civil society, etc.) that defend the citizens from the unchecked domination of the state.

There are no societies which can be regarded as fully modern. It has been mentioned above that the process of modernization is a *diachronic* one. Thus, societies that can be considered as modern still carry elements of pre-modernity (e.g. prejudice, intolerance, bigotry and the prevalence of vested interests over purposive rationality, etc). Sociologically speaking, we ought to look at the dominant features of the modernization process and at the state of a particular type of society in order to assess the degree of modernity of any given society. Even with such reservations and restrictions one could state that the Soviet type of enforced modernization was, at best, a pseudo-modernization. This may also be seen if we explore the field of culture.

Certain achievements of communist societies ought to be acknowledged. Children of workers and peasants, who previously were excluded from access to certain types of education, especially higher education, were encouraged and helped to acquire it (although it has been well documented that the offspring of elites had better access to institutions leading to prestigious jobs, such as the foreign service). Illiteracy declined, adult education was extended and certain elements of 'high' culture were made accessible to wider circles of the population: radio and later television too, regularly broadcast theatre performances, concerts, and so on.

All this was based on the unspoken premise stemming from the Enlightenment, and taken over by Marx, that people can be improved. And, of course, there were the considerations of power: this required that all cultural activity could and should be tightly controlled. The nationalization (*étatization*) of culture was accomplished by the nationalization of *all* cultural institutions, including film distribution, the centralized consignment of printing paper to newspapers, magazines and publishing houses, and by the establishment of censorship offices. Cultural manifestations which escaped the control of the party-state were suppressed. Even permissible artistic styles and cultural forms of expression were defined by the party.[9]

All this was in crass contradiction to modern culture. It is certainly difficult to define unequivocally the characteristic features of modern consciousness. Nevertheless, one may point to purposive rationality, fragmentation, future-orientation, individualism, a basically critical attitude,[10] the demise of universal discourse (e.g. Lyotard 1984; Turner 1990; Bauman 1992) as parts of post-modern consciousness. The ideology of the Party represented diametrical opposition to these features. Its collectivist ideology was nothing other than the disguise of the practice of monolithic power and ideology.

The ideology of the Sovietized totalitarian system contained elements of the philosophy of Enlightenment. In addition to the progressivist view of history, Rousseau's ideas on the perfectability of human beings were theoretically declared (without reference to Rousseau but rather to Marx): these maintained that people by changing the social order change themselves as well, a view which found its simplified expression in Stalin's image of the 'new man'. Other Rousseauian ideas drawn from the *Social Contract* which found their application in the political practice of the party-state were the treatment of the masses and of the legislators. Rousseau espoused the idea that it is the legislator who has to create the people who deserve democracy. This is the source of the logical correspondence of Rousseau's reasoning with the theory and practice of *terror*: thus *revolutionary* terror is not problematic when in the form of bloody *popular mass action* it sweeps away the real enemies of the popular revolution. It is more problematic, however, when it turns to terrorizing the people who cannot match the holy principles of the democratic revolution which want to make an empirical people worthy of the ideal power of the people (Ludassy 1991: 23).

Indeed, the societies of East–Central Europe did not have a history of democratic social order. The brief period of parliamentary democracy in the inter-war Czechoslovakia was neither characteristic of the region, nor without problems, especially in dealing with the Czech and Slovak relationship. The absence of an earlier democratic tradition was used by the communists who claimed that it was not possible to establish democracy without democrats (and, moreover, liberal democracy was not considered a real, but rather a fake democracy.) Thus, it was the vanguard party's duty to lead the people to the real, proletarian democracy through a period of the dictatorship of the proletariat. This was deemed to be not only a political, but also a moral act. Here, again, reinterpretations of Rousseau's ideas on a positive system of morals based on selected concepts of virtue can be found. These concepts served as rationalizations for, amongst other things, the intro- duction of a biased curriculum in schools, the re-writing of history, and the promulgation of the 'correct' world view as the measuring rod of all intellectual and artistic activity, besides the suppression of views and ideas that the regime considered 'false' or 'hostile', and so on.

Since by its very nature communism is a totalitarian system which subordinates society to the state, modern institutions ensuring civil liberties and a functioning civil society could not develop. Instead, in correspondence with the ideology that socialist societies have to be highly centralized, a planning system was created, the task of which was bureaucratically to direct the process of industrialization according to set political goals. Thus the dynamism of industrial and technological development was stifled, individual initiatives and innovations were inhibited and the market was excluded from economic mechanisms. Money ceased to be the measure of value, and (purposive) rationality disappeared from the nationalized sphere of economic activity.[11] It was in the interests of the bureaucracy which planned and directed production not to innovate. Hence, the system was operating with an outdated technology (except in the area of military production) which was unable to satisfy even the elementary needs of the population.

Of course, all modernization processes introduce a different dynamic into all walks of social life. They fundamentally change the patterns of everyday life. All this, however, happens over an extended period of time as a result of historical development. The process does not exclude disruptions, disturbances and social upheaval. Nevertheless, it allows people and societal institutions to adapt themselves gradually to the changing circumstance. The enforced, Soviet-type modernization, however, required people to adapt themselves to rapid change. In other words, whilst Western development took place over many generations,[12] in East–Central Europe it happened within a few years. The methods of industrialization and urbanization were such that they tore apart traditionally established family forms and structures with an unprecedented suddenness. For example, the first generation of industrial workers had to live in factory dormitories, away from their families, whom they could see only once in a while.

The human and social costs of this misconceived modernization were enormous. It is no exaggeration to say that that society was fraught with anomie: no social group was an exception, save the bureaucrats of the Party and the state who were the only real beneficiaries of the new system. An especially destructive feature of the situation was that a general mistrust developed in the population because of the omnipresence of informers, secret police, and of Party and state personnel directors.

A general uncertainty set in. Words lost their meanings, for example, what was the meaning of the word 'peace' under the conditions of large-scale militarization of the economy and of broad areas of life? For instance, members of several organizations such as the trades unions' youth wing, or the communist youth organizations of several countries, at one time wore uniforms. The language of propaganda was full of militarily derived expressions such as 'the fight for peace'; 'we are fighting for the fulfilment of the five-year plan'; and 'we have won the battle for the harvest', and so on. Under these conditions, it would have been quite obvious and natural that people would turn to religion for stability of meaning, consolation, truth, hope and moral ideals. The oppressive policies of the party-state towards the churches, and the tremendous pressure to which believers and church-goers were subjected drastically reduced the number of people who dared to resist repression. There are indications that a certain type of 'bedroom religiosity', a private practising of faith, developed.[13] It would be impossible to measure how widespread this was. Probably more people maintained their religious beliefs than one could guess. An indirect indication of this was the sudden jump in the numbers involving themselves in religious activities when the totalitarian grip began to subside. But we can only surmise.

So far we have discussed mainly the negative aspects of the lop-sided modernization. It is clear that the conditions under which it was carried out either slowed down the process of secularization or hid the real picture. At least this could be assumed; but were there factors which still contributed to the advancement of the secularization process?

The concept of 'secularization' belongs to one of the most discussed and controversial areas in the sociology of religion. This is not the place to offer a critical discussion of the different views and ideas involved. For the purposes of this chapter, and as an indication of my general view, I understand by 'secularization' the Weberian concept of the 'disenchantment of the world' and the confinement of religion largely to the private sphere. This does not imply a rejection of the view, inspired by Durkheim's considerations, that emphasizes the functional differentiation in modern society (cf. Tomka 1991) with the result that religion becomes a separate sphere of the life of the individual. In fact, I consider the two processes to be complementary rather than antagonistic. In taking up this approach, and especially in order to understand the non-linear character of the secularization process, I shall now turn to the ideas of Hans Blumenberg.

Blumenberg, in his work *Secularization and Self-Assertion* (1983), regards secularization as a long-lasting process that involves a turning-away from religious bonds, form transcendental attitudes, from expectations directed to other-wordly life, and from cultic arrangements as well as from fixed, foreseeable changes in private and public everyday life. Blumenberg, however, goes beyond Weberian and Durkheimian *skepsis* concerning the negative sides of modernity and secularization.[14] He does this by a process of transcendence-containment (i.e. the Hegelian *Aufhebung*). Whilst Blumenberg is highly critical of the Enlightenment-inspired thesis of progress, he acknowledges that modernity brought about the self-realization and self-assertion of man, together with human beings' domination over nature and the creation of a universalized legal system. Moreover, he argues that secularization at the level of ideas began within theology, and specifically in philosophies which were still close to, and influenced by theological ideas (e.g. Descartes and Leibniz). He also cites the example of Pelagianism and the continuation of Epicurean ideas on the relationship between man and nature, and so on. It would be impossible to give here even a cursory review of Blumenberg's ideas. Suffice it to say that he stresses the incomplete character of the secularization and non-secularization processes in modernity and thus relativizes the concepts. This, in my view, helps us to understand better the complexity and ambiguity of secularization, both as a historical process and in its theoretical expression.[15]

In particular, it could be helpful to grasp theoretically the especially contradictory character of the process of secularization in communist societies. As I argued in my paper 'Opium made in East Europe' (Varga 1986), taking at face value the Marxian analysis of the factors that cause the endurance of religion in capitalist societies, the same factors were seen to be working in the East European societies because they reproduced the social, political, economic, cultural and moral conditions that, in Marx's view, necessarily originate, sustain and reproduce religion.

At the same time, a certain advance in secularization took place. Even though at the time of suppression of religion there was no possibility of being able to indicate empirically the level of secularization (an exercise which even under the best of conditions is imperfect and leaves many questions open), participation in church-oriented activities after the system-change, when freedom of religion has been constitutionally or legislatively established, is indicative. For example, the Central Statistical Office of Hungary, in its preliminary report, entitled *Religious Life in Hungary in 1992* (KSH 1992: 7), notes that of the Uniates about 50 percent, the Roman Catholics 38 percent, the Lutherans 32 percent and the Calvinists 28 percent of those baptized into the respective denomination practise religion within their churches. The gap is even wider according to the age groups: of those under 30 years of age only 24 percent practise, whilst in the group of over 60 close to 50 percent participate in church-directed religious practice. Also, the divergence in religious practice between men and women, and between city and village, is not much different from the available figures from Western Europe.

What then are the causes of the decline in religiosity? As has been mentioned above, religion and the churches commanded the respect of the people, first and foremost because until the last phase of the communist system the churches represented the only legally tolerated (albeit only grudgingly) sphere of civil society and opposition to the communist world view. The churches have their own metanarrative (universal discourse) which is diametrically opposed to the metanarrative of Marxism and thus the deepest source of the antagonism of Marxism to religion. Indeed their discourse, nay, their very presence could, and did, serve as a rallying point.

This can be best seen in the sphere of morality. Communism destroyed the web and spontaneity of social relations and allowed a relative autonomy of the individual in the private sphere alone, although fear and distrust penetrated even this. For example, parents in Hungary did not dare in general to tell their children their view of the 1956 uprising, if it differed from the official stand of the Party, because they did not want to jeopardize the advance and opportunities of their children. Communist ideology, with its denial of universal morality and its substitution with a class morality,[16] introduced a moral relativity which not only contrasted with the customary conception of morals but was also considered to be a cynical manifestation of power. Religious discourse was therefore seen as the only provider of consolation and support as well as countering relativism. Also, the churches declared the dignity of the person and the existence of human rights, even though it was from a religious point of view. This was especially prominent in the documents of the Second Vatican Council and its encyclicals, such as *Populorum progressio*. This is why individuals like Adam Michnik, himself a non-believer, discovered universal human values in Christian morality and the Church's stand on human rights (Michnik 1979).

Whence, then, secularization? There are several reasons for the decline of religiosity. First of all, one has to stress that even under the conditions of pseudo-modernization industrialization and urbanization did, indeed, happen. Millions of people became urban dwellers and industrial workers. This caused irreversible changes in the social structure and in culture, in particular in the culture of everyday life. Urban culture is different from the rural, and even if we assume that, at least at the beginning, people did not transform their lifestyle and their values, with time these too have undergone considerable changes. While urban culture *per se* does not necessarily do away with religiosity, the manifold cultural impacts and the possibilities that the city provides changes foci of interest and makes possible the abandonment of religious practices, and eventually even faith itself. Also, amongst the newcomers to the city there were many young people who for the first time in their lives escaped traditional forms of control by their family and smaller community.

Second, all this has been coupled with the elimination of religion from the everyday discourse and culture, with massive atheist propaganda, administrative restrictions of church activity (especially of pastoral work), a drastic reduction in the number of religious schools, a ban on teaching religion in public schools, and the re-writing of school textbooks and the curriculum in the spirit of dialectical and historical materialism. These actions were not without their effects. Those cohorts which began their schooling after 1949 were largely ignorant not only of the teachings of religion, but also of the Bible and those religious symbols which penetrated European culture and everyday life. Based on the Soviet model, the communist regimes substituted religious ceremonies marking transitions in life (baptism, confirmation, marriage and death) with secular ones (the 'name-giving ceremony', the festive handing-out of ID cards at the age of 16, the establishment of 'wedding halls' and the 'comradely funeral'). There is no doubt that a great many people went along with the new ceremonies not out of conviction but rather because of fear and pressure. And it happened quite often that a newborn baby would be secretly baptized after the public name-giving ceremony.[17]

On the other hand, it cannot also be excluded that there were people who sincerely welcomed the elimination of religious ceremonies from private and public life. As in Western Europe, so in East–Central Europe too, there were people who, whilst not necessarily Marxist or communist, did not want to belong to any denomination and were therefore pleased to have the opportunity not to do so. Before the communist take-over registration of one's denominational affiliation had been compulsory. One cannot even dismiss the possibility that the representation of religion as a remnant of the past embraced by old, ignorant or retrograde people alone impressed part of the youth. The pseudo-rationality and pseudo-scientism of the watered-down version of Marxian ideas as presented by 'Soviet Marxism' (Marcuse 1958) might well have had its effects as well.

There was a change in the value-system too. During the hay-days of Stalinism the severity of everyday life put the exigency of material survival in the forefront. The East–Central European countries were hermetically closed from the rest of the world (for a while even from each other) and the media were under strict control. People, however, soon understood that a gap existed between the rosy pictures drawn by the propaganda and their everyday life conditions. Their reaction was either defiance or withdrawal into their private life with a consequent de-politicization, resignation or even cynicism. Since up until the mid-1960s sociology has been considered by the Party a 'bourgeois pseudo-science', no serious sociological research or public opinion surveys could be conducted. The only permitted research projects were ones which were directed at the buttressing of the Party's claims, and the opinion surveys were classified information, available to the Central Committee only. Thus, the above considerations are rather impressionistic, and by necessity restricted to hindsight and re-thought experiences of the individual sociologist.[18]

A further factor contributing to the decrease in religiosity was, perhaps paradoxically, the change in exercise of power. In assessing this one has to take into consideration the different reactions of the ruling communist parties to the upheavals between the years of 1953 and 1968. By and large two types of reaction can be distinguished: that of the hardliners and that of the 'realists'. The hardliners' conclusion was that any softening of the grip over society would inevitably lead to dire consequences and could ultimately result in the loss of their power. This was the response of the leadership in the GDR, in Czechoslovakia after 1968, and in Bulgaria and Romania. The 'realists' in Poland and in Hungary concluded that in order to maintain the social system and the Party's leading role (i.e. its power) in society they would have to make some concessions both in improving the material standard of living and in allowing a somewhat greater cultural freedom.

Both strategies had unintended consequences. The hardliners' strategy managed to prolong the suppression of discontent and to maintain the status quo. Underneath, however, the tensions were growing and, as the example of the GDR (and to a lesser degree of Czechoslovakia) showed, it increased the prestige and influence of the churches.

The 'realist' direction was for a while successful in diffusing the discontent, but the price such regimes had to pay was the growth of oppositional forces and the greater articulation of the critique of the system (through the spread of *samizdat*, the existence of underground study groups like the flying university in Poland, and similar undertakings in Hungary, and so on).

That the prestige of a church does not entirely depend on the strategy of the Communist Party is illustrated by the different ways in which the Roman Catholic church in Poland and the Hungarian churches reacted to the 'realist' strategy. Both reactions were consequences of historical, cultural and political circumstances. In particular, the divergent political developments in Poland and Hungary after 1956 were important factors.

In Hungary, the Kadar regime cruelly suppressed all forces which stood up against the Sovietized system (including reform communists). By mid-1957 the backbone of the churches had been broken and a loyal leadership had been re-established (cf. Varga 1992: especially 66). The Kadar government, for instance, pressured the Calvinist church to re-establish in his functions Albert Bereczky, who had resigned from his position during the 1956 revolution. Calvinist Bishop Janos Peter was appointed in 1961 to the post of minister of foreign affairs. Similarly, the government insisted on exercising its right to vet candidates for Catholic bishoprics as it wanted to ensure their loyalty. To a degree the government was successful. For example, the Catholic bishops' conference issued a statement which condemned the conscientious objectors, and it thus defended the government's punitive policy against them (only the Nazarenes were exempt from prosecution). Also, the fact that Cardinal Mindszenty took refuge in the embassy of the USA in Budapest after the Soviet armed intervention, effectively excluded him from intervening in the policy of the Church.[19]

By contrast, the Polish church continued to enjoy the respect of the vast majority of population. The communist authorities had to take account of it as a major political force as well. In Poland the Church represented a counter-legitimating force (cf. Walaszek 1986). Cardinal Wyszynski projected the image of being 'the father of the nation'. When, in 1953, he was imprisoned, he was considered a hero and martyr. In 1956 he was freed, together with Gomulka who became the first secretary of the Communist Party and who, at least for a while, made concessions to the Church. Also, Poland had a significant, and partly progressive, Western-oriented Catholic *intelligentsia* organized into various clubs which also published their reviews. In Lublin, a Catholic university operated during the whole post-war period. Thus, in Poland both popular and intellectual

Catholicism co-existed. The election of Karol Wojtyla, the bishop of Cracow, as the 236th Pope, of course endowed the Polish Church with such an authority and prestige which perforce limited the state's power over the church. In no other country in the region did the Church enjoy as high a prestige as in Poland.

As the terror began to subside, information about Western societies started to seep into the East–Central European societies. Previously the official propaganda depicted the Western societies as decaying and morally bankrupt, as falling apart at their seams and ready to attack the peace-loving socialist societies. A large part of public opinion, however, perceived the Western societies as ones of material abundance where common people lived under conditions which were unattainable even for the elites, except for those who occupied the highest positions in the party and state hierarchy. Consequently, the value system turned towards materialism, the 'good life', and, in the 1960s when the supply of consumer goods somewhat improved, acquisition of money for their purchase came to the forefront of people's desires and in their system of values. The attraction of the Western mass and pop culture, fashion, fads, and so on, spread primarily (though not exclusively) amongst youth. This provided an outlet as well as a vehicle for – politically often indirect – protest against the restrictive practices of the system. It was, indeed, the political power that politicized originally non-political attitudes. A good example would be the persecution and subsequent ban of jazz clubs by the Czechoslovak authorities. Unintentionally or indirectly political protest against the regime, or at least against its excesses, became possible outside the political sphere, but also outside the churches.

In addition, the directly political protest movements, and the upheavals, uprisings, revolts and revolutions demanded extraordinary courage, solidarity, loyalty and altruism from the participants; this demonstrated that these virtues are not exclusively present within the domain of religion. A great number of people displayed such characteristics.

In this respect there was no difference between those who were led by religious motivations and those who were not. Moreover, even in cases where the churches were actively involved in leading the struggle for democracy and freedom (e.g. as with the Lutheran church in the GDR) and rallied a large numbers of people for the cause, it is highly questionable whether those who sided with it in mass protests, demonstrations, and so on, were doing so out of religious motivation. As a matter of fact, the post-reunification history of Eastern Germany shows a dramatic decrease in church affiliation. In Poland, as mentioned above, the efforts of the Church to clericalize the state and superimpose on society its often conservative, fundamentalist ideas and policies alienated many believers (as, among others, was shown by the spectacular defeat of Christian democracy in the latest parliamentary elections, despite the previously unheard of direct intervention by the clergy.) In Hungary, there is a slow increase in church-related religiosity but the historical churches face a strong competition by the strengthening sects and cults. In fact, the latter grow at a much faster pace than the established churches.

This development is not surprising. Since the collapse of the communist system brought about the autonomy of the political sphere, there is no need to resort to the religious field for political purposes. Moreover, the established churches, with their hierarchical organizational structures, are not attractive to a number of (mostly young) people. The latter seek in sects and cults an enhanced spirituality as well as a tightly knit community[20] which helps them to cope with the pressures of everyday post-communist life.

The East–Central European societies entered the period of a painful, and sometimes turbulent, transition to democracy and creation of a civil society. Their historical retardation has been compounded by a more than forty-year rule of communism which, in spite of its failure, managed to a large extent to destroy historically developed institutions and social bonds. Nonetheless, structural changes during the period of a lopsided modernization created a new situation, a new base from which the transition began. One should not, however, forget that even behind the pseudo-modernization long-lasting ideologies and practices survived, even if often disguised behind communist rhetoric. The tragic contradiction of the communist modernization was that it tried – with some success – to carry out the historical task of modernization, but did it with pre-modern means, in particular it did so by making the state the prime mover of modernization. Thus it entrenched, albeit against its declared goals, pre-modern structural elements and ideas (like the state as the supreme community) that have survived the demise of communism.[21]

As I have argued, the churches in East–Central Europe have survived, albeit not without scars, the period of communist rule. The past forty-five years have thoroughly changed the social basis on which they exist. The present situation is characterized by a mixture of contradictory trends. On the one hand, certain modernizing measures have, indeed, been carried out and the social structure of society has changed. On the surface, the East–Central European societies became urbanized and industrialized. What, on the other hand, did not change, or changed very little, was the consciousness of the population, partly because the modernizers operated within the frameworks of pre-modern institutions and consciousness (in particular, that of the all-encompassing party-state and of universal discourse.)

The impact of these contradictory developments is reflected in the intensity of secularization as well. In my view, the rigid juxtaposition of secularization and non-secularization is incorrect because it cannot take into account the complexity of the problem. Indeed, secularization did take place in East–Central Europe. However, if we take secularization to mean not simply an abandonment of religious practices, then this process was to a significant extent a pseudo-secularization. It was a pseudo-secularization because it was not prompted by the development of a modern consciousness, nor was it accompanied and sustained by a modern society with its emphasis on the individual and his or her rights and choice of world views. The very fact that from the time it became possible to do so numerous people returned to churches is evidence of the the problematic nature of secularization in the region.

East–Central European societies will eventually join the patterns of modernity and shed the ballast of pseudo-modernity. At present the favourite slogan in East–Central Europe is 'to catch up with Europe'. In order to realize this historical task and to make up for the centuries-long backwardness these societies face the task of accomplishing not only the economic turn-around but also – to use Norbert Elias' concept – the 'civilizing process'.

When this happens, they, too, will in all probability display the dynamics of secularization as it developed over a lengthy historical period in Western Europe. Then, and only then, will one be able to say that neither *ecclesia triumphans* nor *atheismus triumphans* would develop in the long run, but rather the pattern of secularization (and de-secularization) that we have seen in the history of the West.

NOTES

1 I make a distinction between totalitarian and authoritarian regimes. The first is characterized by the extension of the power of the state to *all spheres* of political, economic and cultural life. In a totalitarian regime society is subordinated to the state, and civil society is practically abolished. In an authoritarian regime the state keeps the political sphere under strict control and largely but not absolutely controls the cultural field, but it extends a relative autonomy to the economy.

   The Soviet type of society was characterized by totalitarianism at least until the last phase of its existence, that is when the centralized power could not maintain its grip over the whole of society. *Samizdat* and the growth of so-called second economy, as well as the enhanced interest in religion, were indications that the totalitarian system was gradually being transformed into an authoritarian one.

   This distinction does not prejudge the actual *form* of exercising power. An authoritarian regime can be more oppressive, bloody and dictatorial than a totalitarian one (cf. the Latin American military dictatorships).

2 However, with the increased political activity of the churches, their position on the questions of abortion, teaching of religion in public schools, their demand that the state take into consideration the interests of the churches in defining political issues, and so on, created opposition or even resentment amongst a large number of (mostly urban) women, liberal intellectuals (whether Christian or not), young people, and in general amongst significant segments of the population.

   In Poland, there was a public discussion in 1990–1 about the danger of an emerging political Catholicism in which among others such respected individuals as Leszek Kolakowski and the Nobel prizewinner Czeslaw Milosz took part. The aggressive eccelsiastical position resulted in a significant drop of popularity and confidence in the Roman Catholic church. Its position concerning abortion caused resentment amongst a large number of the urban population – men and women alike.

   This is just one example. One can say that in all post-Soviet societies there is opposition against the involvement of the churches in public, and in particular in political matters.

3 At least this was the Stalinist version of Marxism–Leninism. Efforts to 'return to the sources', especially to the ideas of the young Marx and the underlying humanistic elements in Marx's theory were accompanied by shifting the emphasis to the methodological (metatheoretical) character of Marx' theory. Early works of L. Kolakowski, Gy. Markus, K. Kosik, members of the Yugoslav 'Praxis' group, etc. aimed at this. The renewed interest in Lukacs' *History and Class Consciousness*, the discussion of

the problem whether alienation can exist under socialism, and similar attempts, belonged to the first phase of the so-called 'revisionism' which, still within the theoretical frameworks of Marxism, began to challenge a totalitarian ideology.

For the contemporary reader these efforts may seem naive or unimportant (occasionally they are even dismissed as quarrels amongst Marxists only). However, at the time they were the only theoretical–philosophical undertakings which could be expressed within the discourse that the Party claimed to be its legitimizing source. This is precisely why the powers that be perceived it as a most serious threat.

4 The terms stems from Peter L. Berger (cf. Berger *et al.* 1973: especially 17, 98–9).

5 One has to remark that even in modern, pluralist societies the influence of the state on civil society is growing. This can be explained partly by the civilizatory functions of the state: there is a need to curtail the impact of the selfish vested interests, to ensure competition, to maintain the welfare state and certain redistributive measures, to protect the environment, and so on. On the other hand there is an observable growth of state intervention in the private sphere of its citizens and an increase of measures (laws, by-laws and court decisions) regulating individual behaviour. This, of course, is also an expression of enhanced conflicts between individual and collective rights. Nevertheless the conflicts are largely being dealt with within the scope of civil society.

6 Here, again, we can indicate trends only. The 'iron cage of rationality', especially in post-modern societies, is different from the one assumed by Max Weber. Purposive rationality manifests itself in the first place in the development of technology and in the organization of production. It is, however, highly questionable whether the products are, indeed, satisfying in a rational way, or else, create needs. (The latest developments of computer technology, in the first place the non-scientific use of so-called virtual reality serve as an extreme but rather characteristic example.)

7 The only exception seems to be the United States which once was the largest *laissez-faire* country in the world. But even there, at least since the crash of 1929, the state has an active presence in regulating economic processes. Strictly speaking, since the introduction of taxation and centralization of issuing money, the state has always had an influence over the economy.

8 Perhaps the best example would be the underdevelopment, more accurately the late development, of the modern communication and information technology in the Soviet type of society. Thus if people can communicate directly with one another without state control then the channels of information cannot be centrally controlled; that, however, was one of the most important means of exercising totalitarian power over society. Another example would be that military technology (and military production – albeit we would probably never know its full scope – took up a significant part of GDP) did not trickle down to the sphere of civilian production. Thus, miniaturization, the application of the advances in microelectronics to civilian production, and so on, was virtually nonexistent.

9 It is indicative that in every East–Central European country the communist parties (following the Soviet practice, especially the infamous Central Committee decisions in 1948 denouncing the poetry of Akhmatova, the music of Prokofiev and Shosta-kovitch, etc.), organized conferences on the state of ideology, the arts, literature, even on particular works of individual artists. These conferences and the decisions arising from them defined the directions cultural activities had to take. Also, 'socialist realism' was declared the only literary and artistic style that expressed the ideals of socialism.

10 With the spread of mass culture and mass communication this feature is declining. The effects of 'simulacra' as analysed by Jean Baudrillard (which cannot be critically discussed here) coupled with, and partly caused by, the spread of mass media, increasingly restricts critical thinking to a relatively narrow circle of intellectuals and artists.

11 As a matter of fact, even the rationality in the organizations of the process of production, which Marx considered a characteristic feature of capitalism (and to be juxtaposed with the anarchy of the market) was not realized in the centrally planned economy.

12 The concept 'generation' is not taken here in its strict demographic definition (i.e., 33 years) but rather as cohorts of people who within an approximate age group share similar experience. Hence, my understanding of the concept of generation is closer to Mannheim's (1954: especially 242).

13 This 'bedroom religiosity' is different from what Thomas Luckmann called 'invisible religion' (1967). His idea of an 'invisible religion' is based on the transformations caused by the emergence of the industrial society where, however, there was a freedom of religion. In East–Central Europe, with the exception of Poland (and even here there was no unrestricted freedom), it was mainly the official repression which caused the privatization of religion.

14 Cf. Durkheim's idea of anomie and his writings on morality, as well as Weber's discussion of purposive and substantive rationality.

15 In a somewhat similar vein Marcel Gauchet, in his book *Le Désenchantement du Monde* (1985), argues that in spite of the disenchantment of the modern world, a fully fledged secularization did not, and cannot, take place.

16 The Leninist and Stalinist reinterpretations of Marxism suppressed Marx's views in which he acknowledged 'the simple laws of morality and justice' (Marx 1977). This is an indication that Marx implicitly acknowledges universal, and universally binding, ideas of morality, justice and truth.

17 Of course, we cannot know the precise number of secretly baptized children. As far as Hungary is concerned, Miklos Tomka calculated (1991: 7) that by 1991 more than 25 percent of young people under 25 years of age and about one third of youth under 10 had not been baptized or otherwise registered in a denomination. This means that a large proportion of parents defied the pressure. True, the pressure was somewhat relaxed after 1961 and it is thus no firm indication whether the same proportion of children had been baptized in the period between 1949–61. Other countries, for example Czechoslovakia, maintained a strong anti-religious and anti-clerical policy.

18 Actually, even the Party had no reliable information about the mood of the population. Hence, manifestations of dissatisfaction or outbreaks of revolts came as a surprise for the leadership.

19 Also, after the Vatican's change of its policy towards the East European regimes, and the substitution of negotiations for confrontations, the Vatican turned directly to the government and marginalized the role of the Hungarian Catholic church. Cardinal Casaroli negotiated with the government the conditions of free passage of Cardinal Mindszenty to Vienna; in return the Vatican committed him to refrain from any political activity or statements.

20 In the established churches the exceptions were the base, or small, religious communities (e.g. the *Regnum Marianum* or the 'shrub' movements in the Hungarian Catholic church – which meet the disapproval of the hierarchy – or other evangelical movements in Hungary and elsewhere).

21 Even most of the post-communist regimes have maintained the paternalistic role of the state. Also, it is not a matter of pure chance that in public opinion surveys ex-communist – or reformed communist – politicians are highly placed. The fact that ex-communists were re-elected to power (Lithuania or Poland) confirms the confusion stemming from ingrained ideas.

REFERENCES

Bauman, Z. (1992) *Intimations of Postmodernity*, London: Routledge.

Berger, P.L., Berger, B. and Kellner, H. (1973) *The Homeless Mind*, New York: Random House.

Blumenberg, H. (1983) *Sakulärisierunq and Selbstbehauptung* 2nd, enlarged and revised edn of the 1st and 2nd parts of *Die Legitimität der Neuzeit* (*The Legitimacy of the Modern Age*), Frankfurt: Suhrkamp.

Dobbelaere, K. (1981) 'Secularization: a multi-dimensional concept', in *Current Sociology* 29/2, London: Sage.

Gauchet, M. (1985) *Le Désenchentement du Monde*, Paris: Gallimard.

KSH (Central Statistical Bureau) (1992) *Vallasi elet Maqyarorszagon 1992* (*Religious Life in Hungary 1992*), Budapest (mimeo).

Luckmann, T. (1967) *The Invisible Religion: The Transformation of Symbols in Industrial Society*, New York: Macmillan.

Ludassy, M. (1991) *Teveszmeink eredete* (*The Origin of Our Fallacies*), Budapest.

Lyotard, J.-F. (1984) *The Postmodern Condition: A Report on Knowledge*, Minneapolis: University of Minnesota Press.

Mannheim, K. (1954) *Ideology and Utopia*, London: Routledge & Kegan Paul.

Marcuse, H. (1958) *Soviet Marxism: A Critical Analysis*, London: Routledge & Kegan Paul.

Marx, K. (1977) 'Inaugural address of the Working Men's International Association', in K. Marx and F. Engels, *Selected Works*, vol. II, Moscow: Progress Publishers,

Michnik, A. (1979) *L'Eglise et la Gauche*, Paris: Seuil.

Tomka, M. (1991) *Magyar katolicizmus 1991* (*Hungarian Catholicism in 1991*), Budapest.

Turner, B. S. (ed.) (1990) *Theories of Modernity and Postmodernity*, London: Sage.

Varga, I. (1986) 'Opium made in East Europe', paper presented at the XIth World Congress of Sociology, New Delhi (mimeo).

Varga, I. (1992) 'Société civile et la politique de la religion: Le cas hongrois', in P. Michel, (ed.) *Les Religions à l'Est*, Paris: Cerf.

Walaszek, Z. (1986) 'An open issue of legitimacy: the State and the Church in Poland', in *The Annals of the American Academy of Political and Social Science* 483, London: Sage.

13

GREEK ORTHODOXY AND MODERN SOCIO-ECONOMIC CHANGE

Nikos Kokosalakis

INTRODUCTION

There is now a general awareness that during the 1980s the world entered a new stage of development. With the collapse of the socialist regimes of Eastern Europe and the Soviet Union and with the Gulf War, recent global, political and economic developments have brought about 'a new order of things'. These specific events apart, however, social scientists have perceived for some time that, as the twentieth century draws to a close, all societies are involved in a process of transition towards new and as yet uncertain orientations.

The seminal characteristic of this development is that it is global; and, moreover, advanced capitalism is now the dominant economic force in the world and is clearly the locomotive of change in all local and nation-state societies. The concept of society itself as a bounded system (Parsons 1951; Shils 1975) can no longer fully describe socio-economic change anywhere in the world today. Indeed, one of the salient features of all societies is the tension which is produced at the level of interaction between global economic and social processes on the one hand and local cultures and situations on the other. Such tensions vary, of course, according to geopolitical locus and the history of specific cultures and societies. These tensions vary further according to the degree of affinity or contrast between the values of a given local culture and those of Western scientific culture and of capitalism. This is especially true over the last thirty years or so when advanced capitalism has undergone resurgence as the unchallenged economic system together with rapidly developing information technology and very effective and sophisticated media advertising.

In sociological terms, this development has been discussed within the modernity/ post-modernity and globalization conceptual framework. Certain authors (Bell 1976, 1980; Robertson 1986, 1987; Berger 1987; Beckford 1989; Beyer 1990) have maintained, from different analytical standpoints, that religion has a significant cultural role to play in this situation. The functions of religion are now of course multifarious. Beckford (1979: 170–1) has claimed that religion in advanced industrial society should be understood primarily as a form of cultural resource,

248

rather than as a social institution. This approach is helpful because traditional as well as new forms of religion respond as cultural forces in a variety of ways to contemporary socio-economic development. Each particular response depends on a variety of factors, but the response of major historical religions in their specific socio-cultural settings may still be of considerable significance, both as cultural and political factors.

Protestantism and capitalism were examined by Weber as related developments within Western society and culture. Eastern Orthodoxy is, however, a branch of Christianity which evolved outside the West, and as such it is substantially different from both Protestantism and Roman Catholicism. Deep cultural and theological differences divided Eastern and Western Christianity from the beginning, and thus their relationship to capitalism was also different. Historically, capitalism came relatively late to societies where Orthodoxy was the dominant religion, that is towards the end of the nineteenth and the beginning of the twentieth century.

With regard to the question as to why capitalism failed to develop in these societies initially, Weber did not produce a full comparative analysis of Orthodoxy and the economy on a scale comparable with his studies of Protestantism and other world religions. In several references to Orthodoxy, Weber argued that its culture was too mystically oriented and its concerns were too other-wordly to motivate engagement in capitalist enterprise (Weber 1978: 551, 561, 589, 1193). This view has been expanded by Muller-Armack (1959) and more recently by A. Buss (1989), mainly with reference to the Russian Orthodox Church. The resurgence of capitalism as global economic force over the last thirty years or so and its alliance with the mighty scientific and technological machine poses fundamental questions and presents new strains and new opportunities for Orthodoxy.

In a certain sense the economic and cultural hegemony of capitalism now threatens many, if not all, of the traditional functions of Orthodoxy. Over the centuries the Orthodox religion forged ethnic identities and provided means of social integration along with a cultural ethos, which, especially in Byzantium, coalesced with politics in a distinctive way. One of the main features of this cultural ethos is a specific form of popular religiosity which is deeply rooted in all societies where Orthodoxy has been the dominant religion. Capitalism now challenges this ethos by producing cultural strains and secular social orientations which are in direct conflict with the mystical and spiritual values of Orthodoxy. Yet, paradoxically, this very conflict seems to strengthen both the ethnic and the ecumenical role of Orthodoxy. However, Orthodoxy has never been a political religion in the sense of organizing itself as a political force, although the Greek Orthodox Church has in the past repeatedly engaged in armed struggles for ethnic liberation. There is also, I believe, a deep democratic ideal embedded in the Orthodox culture along with its pre-Enlightenment notions of truth and justice. Thus, in so far as market forces and the competitive capitalist spirit are compatible with the pursuit of democracy and justice, Orthodoxy will in principle have no difficulty in accommodating itself within an advanced capitalist system.

249

In connection with this last point Orthodoxy may have a direct or indirect social role to play in former socialist countries where totalitarian regimes attempted to eradicate both Orthodoxy and capitalism. Here I am referring particularly to Russia, Roumania, Bulgaria and Serbia, where Orthodoxy is the main religion and where the struggle to establish modern democratic institutions is now under way, inevitably within a capitalist economic framework. Needless to say, the full spectrum of these societies cannot be covered in this chapter even in the most schematic way.

I shall concentrate instead upon giving a brief account of the specific cultural and historical character of Orthodoxy as it relates to Greece, which was the sole country with a predominantly Orthodox population to remain outside the former socialist bloc. In addition, Greek Orthodoxy may also be regarded as the basis of the whole Orthodox world. The Slavs and the Russians received Orthodoxy from Byzantium at the end of the tenth century as a cultural tradition which had clothed itself with the Greek world from its very beginning. In this respect the fates of Orthodoxy and of Hellenism became inextricably intertwined over the centuries. Now, however, advanced capitalism poses special challenges to both religion and cultural identity in Greece, and this has created heightened tensions and opportunities, most notably when this country became a full member of the expanding capitalist socio-economic and political system of the European Community.

THE HISTORICAL CONTINUITY AND CULTURAL SPECIFICITY OF GREEK ORTHODOXY

The early period

The claims of the Orthodox Church to being the deposit and upholder of the authentic and true Christian faith (*orthodoxia*) rests on its claims to an unbroken continuity with the Apostolic Tradition. Many of the early Christian communities in the Eastern Church were established by the Apostles and St Paul. The latter's Hellenic education and the fact that the early Christian communities, including that of Rome, were mostly Greek-speaking, and, furthermore, that the books of the official canon of the New Testament were originally written in Greek, gave a Greek cultural character to the Eastern Church from the beginning. The terms 'orthodox' and *'orthodoxia'* evolved gradually, however, and their distinct theological meaning became explicit later during the fourth and fifth centuries (Stefanides 1959: 327). The causes of the emergence of this distinctive ethos were, of course, as much cultural and political as they were theological.

As regards theological factors, the two great heresies of Arianism and Nestorianism were condemned by the early Ecumenical Councils which produced the formal creeds of the Church and consolidated the notion of Orthodoxy. In this process the great theologians, and the Cappadocian Fathers especially, produced a complex theology based on an elaborate synthesis of Hellenism and Judaism within Christianity. This synthesis has been of crucial importance for the

Greeks ever since, but Parsons (1979) has also found it central for the evolution of the religious and economic symbolism of the Western world as a whole. It should be stressed here that the Hellenic rational element has not been always compatible with the religious element of Christian revelation which the Fathers placed at the core of the synthesis. This ambiguity has caused great tension both in the Orthodox Church and in Greek ethnic identity during modern times.

Along with the theological issues there were other developments which strengthened the cultural specificity of Greek Orthodoxy in the early period. As the moral and political disintegration of the Roman Empire was growing many devout Christians took to the desert. Some of these men of the desert acquired major reputations as holy men endowed with great spiritual and other powers. Gradually they became the prototype of the monastic life and an essential part of the Orthodox ethos, so much so, that before the bishops of the Church were allowed take up their duties in the world they had to have monastic experience outside it as monks, and they should remain celibate. This remains a prerequisite for bishops in the Orthodox Church to the present day. Parish and other clergy on the other hand need not be celibate. It should be emphasised that from the beginning monasticism and celibacy in the Eastern Church took on a very different meaning from that in the Western Church. Orthodox monasticism meant primarily a mystical spirituality and concern for transcendence and mystery which became a integral part of the Orthodox tradition. Weber (1978: 1173) found this especially relevant for the distinct types of economic ethics and the different forms of rationalization to be found in Eastern and Western Christianity.

On the political level, the Emperor Constantine did not merely grant religious freedom to Christians but also made Christianity the official religion of the state, and awarded it special privileges after the transfer of the capital of the Empire from Rome to Byzantium. Constantine thus established the model for church and state relations in the Orthodox Church which has remained in place in Greece up to the present day. This model involved a special relationship and fusion of religion and politics which is the hallmark of the Byzantine civilization.

The Byzantine and post-Byzantine periods

In Byzantium, Orthodoxy and culture were synonymous, and there was a total overlap between religion and society (Nicol 1979: 5). The Emperors exercised power over the Church and they had the last word in the election of the Patriarchs. They also convened the church Councils and presided over most of them. Many of the decisions of the Councils were turned into laws of the state and many of the Patriarchs were appointed and deposed, directly or indirectly, by the Emperor. This model of church and state relations, which has been called 'Caesaropapism', is now somewhat discredited (Geanakopoulos 1966: 57). The power of the state over the Church in Byzantium was in fact never absolute or arbitrary. This was a theocratic empire, in which religion was a matter of acute public concern; above all, the Patriarchs, many bishops, and even simple monks could – and did –

251

impose great pressure on the Emperor. Indeed, many Emperors were deposed or killed because of their religious politics (Nicol 1979: 8).

All the major and most of the minor political conflicts which divided Byzantine society, and at times shook it to its foundations, were theological in character. Much of the opposition usually came from the monasteries. The great iconoclastic controversies of the eight and ninth centuries, which involved extensive social upheaval and often persecution and martyrdom of opposing parties, were clearly political conflicts, but they were also struggles about the expression of Orthodoxy in visible material symbols: the icons. For Orthodoxy, icons, then as now, are not just religious symbols or religious art but the essential physical and spiritual expressions of Orthodox doctrine. 'Orthodoxia', that is right faith, was at the root of most social conflict in Byzantium, and its preservation has remained the objective of the Orthodox Church ever since.

The profoundly different expression of the Christian faith in the Greek East and the Latin West, together with the claims of the bishop of Rome for ecclesiastical and political supremacy, were also the principal causes of their eventual schism in 1054. Radical theological differences and the sack of Constantinople in the Fourth Crusade (1204) made it impossible for the mass of Byzantine clergy and laity to accept the union of the Churches declared by the Councils of Lyon (1274) and Florence (1439). The monks, whose role in the Orthodox Church has been always central (Savramis 1962), struggled vehemently against the proposed union and opposed any further contacts with the West.

During the last centuries of the Empire the Turkish threat was all too apparent, but the Byzantines preferred to regard this as punishment from God for deviations from Orthodox faith and thought that the Virgin Mary would save the City again as she had done repeatedly in the past. But Constantinople fell, and with it collapsed a distinctive civilization and a special age of faith that seemed to prefer the Turkish yoke to the contamination of Orthodoxy by the Franks and the Latins.

Yet, paradoxically, the Orthodox Church survived and even grew stronger during the post-Byzantine period. The end of the Empire and the Ottoman conquest meant the strengthening of both the ethnic and the ecumenical character of the Orthodox Church. Orthodoxy was all that had remained and it became the ideology, and in effect the only hope of the enslaved Greek nation. Its unity and integrity had therefore to be maintained at any price and this during the time when the West was torn apart by the Reformation and later transformed by the Enlightenment. It is important to emphasize that these latter movements scarcely affected Orthodoxy. The only institution which embodied both Orthodoxy and the ethnic idea was the Church, with the result that it became both the symbol and the reality of the ethno-religious identity of the Greeks and thus the bridge linking Byzantium to modern Greece.

Throughout the period of the Turkish occupation the Church performed this ethno-religious role to the full, not only on behalf of the Greeks but also for other enslaved Orthodox Christians in the Balkans. After the collapse of the Empire the Ecumenical Patriarchate felt responsible even more than before for the preservation of the ecumenical character of Orthodoxy. This awareness was enhanced by the fact that under Islamic rule besides its religious role the Patriarchate also exercised civil and political functions on behalf of all Orthodox Christians. The Sultans recognized the Patriarch as the chief (*millet-bashi*) of the Orthodox *millet* who were free to practise their religion, but in return the Patriarch guaranteed obedience of the Orthodox to the Sultan and the collection of taxes (Clogg 1979: 18–19). Apart from this political function the Church also exercised full juridical authority over Orthodox subjects in matters of marriage, divorce, dowry, property, inheritance and so on, along with an extensive programme of social welfare.

The Church became economically strong during this period. As its lands were not subject to confiscation, many Christians transmitted their lands to the Church and the monasteries, some of which became substantial land-owners. Social administration was almost exclusively in the hands of the *Phanariotes*, a wealthy, trading section of the Greek population, many of whom were educated and cultured. The Church did not seem to be against trading activity and even encouraged it in the Balkans, thus controlling the administration of these areas. Apart, however, from certain unscrupulous dealings of some of the high clergy, on the whole the Church remained a social and spiritual guide throughout the 400 years of Ottoman rule. At times the Church was also involved in revolutionary activity against Turkish oppression and it paid for this with more than its fair share of blood during the Greek war of liberation in the nineteenth century.

The modern period

After the Greek revolution in the 1820s, the ethnic character of the Church was more pronounced as it became a national church closely tied and subservient to the new-born state. This new development involved unusual arrangements in church and state relations. After the assassination of Kapodistrias, the first governor of Greece, the protecting powers of Britain, Russia and France invited Prince Otto of Wittelsbach, the seventeen-year-old son of King Ludwig of Bavaria, to serve as the monarch of Greece. This was a cultural and political anomaly, for not only was the young King a Catholic and a foreigner invited to rule over the Greek Orthodox Church and an Orthodox nation, but besides this, the three-man regency council which was in fact to rule was also Bavarian and Protestant. Georg Maurer, the head of the council, appointed a committee to draft a constitutional charter for the Church which would render it independent of the Ecumenical Patriarchate and subject to the King in conformity with the Bavarian prototype, where the monarch was also the 'supreme Bishop' (Frazee 1969: 106). According to the first constitution of the Church (passed in July 1833 without consultation or the consent of the Patriarchate) the Church of Greece was declared autocephalous, that is in communion with, but not under the jurisdiction of, the Patriarchate of Constantinople. The Church was to be administered by the 'Holy Synod' which was under the authority of the King.

The Church thus became subordinate to the state and this determined not

253

merely the relations between and church state up to the present day but it also had a crucial influence upon the Church's attitude towards modernization and social reform. The Bavarian regime had no understanding of the indigenous religious culture. As they attempted to adapt Western cultural norms to Greek society as a whole, and as these norms were imposed as it were from above, their original aims of modernization were compromised and ultimately failed (Legg 1969: 54). The transformation of society was attempted without the participation of the people. Thus, according to Svoronos (1975: 79), throughout the rule of Otto (1833–62), the impression is given that the Greeks were completely absent from formal political procedures. There was a Greek Westernized elite in the administration who along with some foreigners, believed that Greece should develop along the cultural path of ancient Hellenism. But these were rather romantic ideas and clearly out of touch with the realities of Greek society. In any case, as Frazee (1977: 134) pointed out, 'What they misjudged was the ability of their Greek countrymen to absorb both Hellenism and Orthodoxy, in fact, to identify them'.

Maurer's initial policies directed at the modernization and rationalization of church organization and resources involved a devasting attack on the monasteries. In the small Greek Kingdom at the time, out of 593 monasteries 412 were closed and their properties passed to the Crown. Such policies were politically inept and culturally out of place. Opposition to these measures was widespread but the Church, under the authority of the Crown, was not merely impotent to act but was obliged to support them.

By 1840 it was obvious that Greece was unlikely to develop along the cultural and economic patterns of modernization then prevalent in Western Europe. The traditional Orthodox ethos had revived and Greek nationalism was not underpinned by the ideas of the Enlightenment. Instead a strong irridentism was growing embodying 'the great idea' of recovering as much as possible of what had been lost to the Turks. This was the dominant ideology in Greece until the catastrophic expedition into Asia Minor in 1922. Furthermore, it should be emphasized that Greek nationalism was underpinned by the Orthodox religion throughout the nineteenth and the twentieth centuries, and as a result the secularization of Greek society was never deep or widespread. For the historical reasons already explained, the spirit of the Enlightenment and the Reformation had not penetrated into the structures of Greek society. Instead, a civil religion developed which involved a fusion of popular and official religion along with Hellenic and national ideals which have informed the dominant ideology of Greek society to the present day.

Despite the early efforts to modernize Greek society, industrialization was virtually absent and indeed the whole structure of the economy was clearly pre-capitalist well up until the 1870s. Interestingly, after the normalization of relations between the Greek Church and the Patriarchate in the 1850s, economic progress and modernization was significant. Banking and free enterprise became established, but mainly through the activities of Greek entrepreneurs who lived outside the boundaries of the small Greek state. For as Svoronos (1975: 91) points out, 'Constantinople and not Athens was the economic capital of Greece throughout the 19th century'. The Greeks of the Ottoman empire, sensing the various nationalist movements in the Balkans and aware of the emergent nationalism of the Young Turks, transferred substantial capital to Greece. Thus the foundations of industrial and banking activity were laid and commercial activity was increased, and this was followed by the emergence of an urban middle class. It must, however, be emphasized that capitalism as such was not an indigenous development in Greek society. In parallel with these developments, the state (which attempted to function on the lines similar to Western models) launched projects of modernization in communications, transport, ports, railways and other public works.

As I have argued elsewhere (Kokosalakis 1987a), the fusion of national aspirations with an Orthodox religious culture did not prevent a certain degree of modernization and capitalist development taking place in nineteenth century Greece. Because of its emphasis on tradition, the Orthodox religion is a naturally conservative culture. It is also a pre-Enlightenment culture, and as such it is not prone to Western rationalism and therefore not conducive to capitalism. But conversely, there is nothing in it which is intrinsically anti-modern that could set it against modern economic development. As a religious culture Orthodoxy is neither pro-modern nor anti-modern, neither pro-capitalist nor anti-capitalist; it is a transcendental ethos concerned primarily with spirituality, liturgy, the salvation of the soul, and the maintenance of what it considers it to be an unbroken continuity of the authenticity of Christian faith. As such, Orthodoxy does not possess either a political or an economic ethic which could be applied to the world, although in modern Greece and in pre-revolutionary Russia it has nonetheless been used to legitimize the politics of the state. In essence, the Orthodox ethos is other-wordly and unchanging, and these characteristics are evident in both Church architecture and Byzantine art which the Orthodox Church regards as unchangeable. Yet it is, perhaps, this timeless, mystical spirituality of Orthodoxy which gives it a special significance in the secular era of expanding, advanced capitalism.

THE RECENT ECONOMIC DEVELOPMENT OF GREECE

Compared with the West, Greece entered the twentieth century as an undifferentiated and underdeveloped society. Although it aspired to the Western type of economic development, its economic structures were hardly capitalist. The reasons for this have been elaborated very ably by several Greek sociologists (Filias 1974; Mouzelis 1978; Tsoukalas 1981; among others). Most of these writers, however, start out from a Marxist theoretical perspective, and if they pay any attention to culture and religion it is mere lip service.

Despite the neglect of the religio-cultural dimension, specific structural aspects of Greek society were elaborately analysed and the role of the state extensively discussed. Tsoukalas (1981) thus makes it clear that the reasons for the slow and locally distinctive development of capitalism in Greece has been the overdeveloped Greek state and the top-heavy structure of public administration. The bureaucratic features of Greek society established in the nineteenth century constitute to the present day an obstacle to economic development and modernization at a time when advanced capitalism requires a slim and efficient public sector.

Regardless of these structural factors, however, and despite the fact that up to the 1950s Greece was still an agricultural society, there has over the last forty years been a remarkable economic transformation, involving massive urbanization and significant industrialization. All economic indicators testify that Greece has entered into the rhythms of advanced capitalist development during this period. Thus agriculture became mechanized and rationalized and the mineral and chemical industries well established. Manufacturing industry (textiles especially) performed very well and by 1980 provided 35 percent of the GNP and half of the country's total exports. Greek shipping provided the world's largest merchant fleet and grew from 5 million tons in 1953 to 51 million tons in 1979, only to drop back to 42.5 million tons in 1984 because of the recession. Tourism also expanded greatly during that period to reach over 5 million visitors to the country annually, providing foreign exchange to the order of $1,300 million. The overall Gross National Income increased three-fold between 1955 and 1980 and there was an average growth of the economy of over 4 percent per annum. In 1978 the per capita income in Greece climbed to $3,430, with Denmark at $7,890 and Portugal at $1,730 being the highest and lowest in capitalist Europe respectively. Inflation in the 1960s was kept under 5 percent but climbed to 36 percent during the last year of the military dictatorship (1967–74). It was then brought down under 15 percent for the rest of the 1970s by the government of the New Democracy Party. There was also almost full employment during the 1970s, although this could in part be due to the fact that approximately 500,000 adults left Greece to seek work abroad during the 1960s. The ratio of industrial to agricultural exports had moved to 63:37, although investment in the private sector was, and has remained, very low compared to EC Countries.

It is because of this economic performance and for certain other political reasons that Greece's application to join the EC as a full member from January 1981 was accepted. High economic performance did not, however, mean a fair distribution of the national wealth within Greece. Indeed, if anything economic inequality and the gap between rich and poor increased during the period of economic growth under capitalist oriented goverments. So in 1981 PASOK, the socialist party, was elected on the basis of promises of a fairer distribution of national wealth and a reduction in economic inequalities along with various welfare policies for health, pensions, the support of the elderly and so on. PASOK, which was re-elected in 1985, put these policies into effect with a fair degree of success. Lower wages and salaries were raised and index-linked.

As regards economic growth and general economic performance PASOK did not do so well. Factors beyond the goverment's control affected the economy, but more seriously its policies and ideology did not inspire confidence on the part of capitalists. Public investment was weak, private investment worsened and on the international political level the Reagan administration and other conservative governments did not hide their dislike for PASOK. In the EC, however, Prime Minister Papandreou insisted on the idea of convergent development and as a result the EC agreed to support a series of Mediterranean Integrated Programmes (MIP) for the poorer countries of Southern Europe (Pantelouris 1987: 187). In overall terms the economic performance of PASOK was rather poor. In 1987 the per capita income stood at $3380, the same as it was ten years earlier, despite inflation which had risen to around 20 percent. Meanwhile, the per capita income of the rest of the EC countries had risen significantly, with Greece and Portugal at the bottom of the league. Through fairer distribution of incomes the standard of living of the great majority of the population rose during the 1980s, but it seems that this gain was made at the expense of the creation of a sizeable public debt.

In 1989 the New Democracy Party came to power pursuing liberal capitalist, almost Thatcherite, policies and an austerity programme of economic stabilization which primarily affected the lower and middle strata of the population. These policies, which are congruent with global capitalist developments, once more pose in an acute way the problem of social inequality and injustice for Greek society. Meanwhile the economy remains in a very weak and problematic position in the face of the abolition of all tariffs in the EC in 1992.

THE FUNCTIONS OF RELIGION IN GREEK SOCIETY

In discussing the functions of religion in any society one must distinguish between the functions of religious organizations or churches and the functions of religion as a cultural factor. In the Greek case this is especially so because of the character of church and state relations and the historical connections between Orthodoxy and Greek ethnic identity. As already explained, as an institution the Greek Orthodox Church was tied to the state from the 1830s onwards and because of this it has not been free even to elect its own leaders. In fact, throughout the twentieth century not a single archbishop was elected according to normal canonical procedures and the Hierarchical Synod itself was abolished and reinstated by the state several times.

Church administration has therefore followed the same turbulent political patterns as modern Greek political history and the Hierarchy has almost constantly been divided along the same party political lines as has Greek society at large. As modern Greece has been governed mostly by right wing governments, the institutional church acquired a conservative political outlook. Fear of communism and civil war strengthened this political conservatism, but even liberal social reform has been frowned upon and often opposed by the Church functionaries, especially when related to the family. Although the official Church has been anti-communist it has not been anti-capitalist, and has never intervened or commented on the economic policies of the state. In fact, as the Church is part of the state, it cannot really take an independent stance on the policies of any government. Nevertheless at an ethnic level the Church has always considered itself to be the conscience of the nation and as over 95 percent of the Greek population are Orthodox the Church has always claimed a cultural hegemony over Greek society. This explains its fear of pluralism and its opposition to Jehovah's Witnesses and other sects which have been growing rapidly lately.

On the other hand, the state also considers Orthodoxy inseparable from Greek identity and regards the Church as a central pillar of Greek society. Politicians of all persuasions and of all political parties make extensive use of both Church and religion when it suits them. President Karamanlis, for example, has stated on several state occasions that 'the concepts of Hellenism and Orthodoxy have been interwoven inseparably in the consciousness of the nation'. In most civil rituals the participation of the Church is very prominent and state officialdom is present in all major religious festivals. Yet, despite this close connection between church and state, or even perhaps because of it, the Church does not involve itself in the economic domain. There is also the central Orthodox ethos according to which this life is transient and we are here as transient visitors, as strangers and pilgrims in the world. According to this ethos, material concerns should be secondary.

On another level popular religion functions in the context of a wide variety of existential concerns. Questions of health and illness, birth, marriage and death and all kinds of personal problems are highly ritualized within a flexible personal faith and the cult of the Virgin (Dubisch 1990) and the Saints. It is interesting from a sociological point of view to observe that this popular religious ethos which was an integral part of agricultural society seems to continue and even show signs of revival in modern capitalist Greece without being limited to any particular section of the population. Certainly the religio-cultural ethos manages to coexist side by side with the frenzied activity of the market, high-profile advertising and extreme consumerism. It is also apparent that these two sets of activity seem to belong to two entirely different worlds. Nevertheless, it is not considered inappropriate for the President of the state (and a strong advocate of the free market) to wish that 'the Virgin Mary should protect the people and guide them in their efforts' (Feast of the Dormition, 15 August 1991). Thus although popular religion seems to function primarily in a privatized way, it also true that the Church and the state have in the past fused the former with official religion and politics to form an integrated whole (Kokosalakis 1987a; Dubisch 1990) which persists alongside and through social change.

RELIGION AND RECENT SOCIO-ECONOMIC CHANGE

The rapid socio-economic development that has taken place in Greece over the last forty years has brought about a radical change in the traditional relationship between religion and society. The social structure, that is the economy, polity and social organization, has become increasingly secularized. However, although the people's attachment to the Church weakened during the 1960s and 1970s and it looked as if secularization in Greece was going to follow the well-known patterns of other industrial capitalist societies, religion as a cultural agent has nevertheless maintained a strong presence and has even shown signs of revival during the 1980s. I would attribute this resistance to secularization in Greece to the cultural specificity of Orthodoxy and its special historical and ethnic connections with Hellenism and Greek ethnic identity.

One of the basic strengths of Orthodoxy is that it sanctions a tenuous relationship between private religiosity and the Church as an institution. The individual can thus privatize her or his religion and be very devout even without formal reference to the Church, and still be fully Orthodox. Thus, Campbell (1976: 321) has astutely observed that the highly religious Saracatsani shepherds could pay lip service to organized worship and had little connection with the official Church. Also, some of the greatest Orthodox virtuosi monks of Mount Athos live alone apart from the Church as a physical community. This ethos enables Orthodox believers to exercise their religion through the cult of the Saints and the Virgin in a highly personal way. The Saints and the Virgin are treated as real live persons in a spiritual sense and credited with having real power to affect personal circumstances. Here the icons are of great significance as mediating symbols. It is my view, based upon personal observation but without literature to support the claim, that over the last thirty years or so a great deal of privatization of religion in the form I have described it has occurred in Greece. Popular religion and the Orthodox ethos in general are conducive to such privatization. The individual can interpret his or her faith in the light of everyday experience without being obliged to sever relations with the Church or having to experience severe internal intellectual conflict. As a cultural practice Orthodoxy is not primarily an intellectualized religion and its adherents often have little or no formal knowledge of theological doctrine. Thus a person is never considered as 'lapsed' or 'non-religious' because he or she does not engage in formal religious practice.

The secularization of the social structure and the global impact of modernity further assist such processes of privatization (Luckmann 1967). Indeed, the more a social structure becomes secularized, the more the question of religion becomes a matter of personal choice. The interesting and significant feature of Orthodoxy in this instance is that it has always allowed a degree of choice in the realm of the personal exercise of faith, so long as this did not constitute a public deviation from doctrine, that is heresy. Even regarding the latter, however, the Church was permissive and flexible enough to allow deviants to come back to the faith through the principle of 'economy' (*oikonomia*). Whilst the impact of social change was felt, and advanced capitalism attenuated the Orthodox *Weltanschauung* people may have held, the privatization process is also facilitated. Such privatization does not conflict with either collective popular or official religiosity.

259

Thus, for example, the religious practice of the rights of passage continues on an almost total basis of participation (i.e. close to 100 percent of the population). All members of the Orthodox Church (95 percent of the Greek population) have their children baptized; over 93 percent of all marriages are solemnized in the Church; and there is a high participation of all the population (both rural and urban) in festivals and major holidays. But at another level, privatization and choice of faith imply indifference and pluralism, and this the official Church finds difficult to accept, as we shall see below.

At a collective and formal level, socio-economic change has brought about some very significant tensions and special social manifestations. Church and state relations during the 1960s and 1970s and the early 1980s became very strained and there was talk of separation. The policies of the state were deemed by the Church to accelerate secularization and the state considered the Church as an obstacle to modernization. But from 1983 onwards relations have become closer and there has not been further mention of separation either by the Church or by the state. This is despite some disagreement over ecclesiastical property which the Church had finally to cede to the state. The then Prime Minister Papandreou declared the Virgin Mary patron of the armed forces and engaged in religious acts himself. These included the religious solemnization of his controversial second marriage to a young woman, which was possibly one of the reasons for him losing the subsequent election.

In 1989, Prime Minister Mitsotakis, while announcing his liberal free market programme to Parliament, found it necessary to stress the importance of Church and religion in the context of global socio-economic change. He stated that,

> In our country religious freedom is constitutionally guaranteed and we Greeks have confirmed in our history that we respect all religious faiths. *Orthodoxia*, however, constitutes the support of the nation. *Orthodoxia* can and must play a significant role, especially today, in the context of cosmogonic changes which take place around us in the Balkans, in Eastern Europe, and in the Soviet Union. It is a spiritual force of global dimensions and surely supports the state in our ethnic concerns. The relations of church and state must be smooth and undisturbed.

(Minutes of Parliament, 24 April 1990)

Global socio-economic change thus seems to enhance the ethnic functions of the Greek Church. As elsewhere in the world, so in Greece, global socio-economic processes have also brought about a fundamentalist religious response during the 1980s. While the Church overall remained moderate, some bishops, clergy and certain lay movements displayed a rigorous conservatism and promoted an intransigent absolutization of Orthodoxy along with an almost paranoid xenophobia. A significant conservative element has always existed in both clergy and laity in the Orthodox Church, but the fundamentalism of the 1980s was strong and quite explicit. It took up a hostile stance towards the EC and was clearly anti-Semitic as it saw everywhere 'dark powers' and 'Zionist plots'. There was also extensive talk of the coming of the Antichrist, so much so that the government was obliged to put into abeyance an act (June 1986) concerned with new identity cards because the fundamentalists thought that the number '666' (the sign of the Beast) was somehow hidden in the new cards.

Such fundamentalism apart, however, socio-economic change brought to the surface a certain degree of theological conservatism in both mainstream theological circles and in the official Church itself. Thus the president of the Greek Theological Association (Mouratidis 1990: 73) told delegates at their 1990 annual conference:

> After the collapse of the Marxist–Leninist regimes and the complete failure of the capitalist system to form human communities, Orthodoxy is *the only possibility* for United Europe to become a community with a human face [italics added].

The Archbishop of Athens and all Greece also expressed his fears not only concerning the impact of socio-economic change on Greeek ethno-religious identity, but also about the influx of religious and ideological pluralism into Greek society. The relevant encyclical (15 August 1990) is worth quoting at length.

> It is not at all an exaggeration to say that from the time of the establishment of the Greek state in 1830 at no time has our nation faced a more serious crisis than today. Our problem is not located only in our weak economy. A cause of greater anxiety are the other aspects of our lives. Our problem is spiritual, ethical and cultural. Like Hercules, the mythical hero, our nation finds itself at the crossroads of choices and re-orientations. Our entry to the new world of a United Europe is connected with the agony and the struggle for the safeguarding of our national, cultural, and especially our spiritual and religious continuity . . . . Various propagandas from East and West flood our country and create tragic victims amongst those who have no foundation in the faith and the tradition of our fathers.
>
> Para-religions and heresies, various ideologies, and even magical cults imprison our brother Greeks ostensibly in the name of progress and freedom . . . . Let us then remain steadfast in our faith, our traditions, our ethics and customs, in everything which constitutes the specificity of Hellenism through the centuries.
>
> I, therefore, call you all to gather round the Church, the strength of unity and the antidote against the discoloration of our Greek Orthodox identity, our race itself. [my translation]

To any close observer of Greek society today statements like this sound hollow and a desperate plea for a bygone age. In one sense the Archbishop is right; there is a crisis of values and of tradition, and the influx of an exogenous pluralism does create havoc in the historic homogeneity of Greek culture. But the current of the river is too strong to swim against. Tradition has become relativized and religion privatized in everyday social experience. Global economic and powerful social forces are as deeply operative in Greek society as in any other and they cannot simply be averted by recourse to tradition. These forces can no longer be simply understood as exogenous invaders stemming from Western modernity. They are rather the ubiquitous agents of global culture; yet these very forces generate a religious response.

GREEK ORTHODOXY AND GLOBAL CAPITALISM

The question now arises as to the compatibility of Orthodoxy as a specific cultural idiom with the world of market forces and advanced global capitalism. An adequate answer to this question would require much space and so a few general remarks will have to suffice. It has been indicated earlier that in essence there is nothing incompatible between Orthodoxy and any economic system as such. What may be compatible or incompatible with Orthodoxy would be the ethical and salvationist implications of such a system. The Orthodox ethos is primarily concerned with the notion of *theosis* ('divinization'), that is the struggle of a person to reach ever so closer to the image of the Creator in the context of a sinful fallen world. This is made possible through the saving grace of the Church and the risen Christ. In so far as an economic or political system is conducive to this soteriological task the Orthodox ethos is compatible with it. Conversely, inasmuch as the system works against the soteriological objective, then the Orthodox ethos is incompatible with it. In this respect Orthodoxy exhibits a dual response.

There is of course substantial controversy as to whether advanced capitalism is compatible with Christian morality in general. I do not wish to engage with this problem, but it is true that in a certain sense the capitalist principle of free competition is inextricably linked with the pursuit and struggle for democracy globally. As Berger (1987) has argued the 'Capitalist Revolution' can contribute to liberty, equality, and prosperity in the Third World.

In so far as capitalism is conducive to democracy and as long as personal and political freedoms are enhanced, then Orthodoxy would welcome it. In this respect it is incidentally possible that Orthodoxy could itself contribute significantly towards the building of democracy in Russia, Bulgaria, Serbia and Roumania. It was in this spirit that the Ecumenical Patriarch recently remarked to the Patriarch of Moscow that 'there are now boundless opportunities for the Russian Orthodox Church'.

Nevertheless, capitalism, especially in its advanced forms, generates substantial cultural contradictions (Bell 1976). There cannot be much argument against the view that the overriding objective of advanced capitalism is the pursuit of money and economic power. As Sir William Ryrie (1991) has argued, 'Less developed countries will achieve faster growth and higher standards of living if they allow the market economy to work'. He also outlined four major defects of capitalism which need 'civilizing': inequality, unemployment, monopoly power, and the sacralization of the profit motive. These are all products of global capitalism which affect poorer countries more than the richer ones. But who is going to civilize these defects of advanced capitalism? The answer given by Ryrie and many others is the state. But even if we reject Habermas' (1976) argument that the state in advanced capitalism continues to undergo a 'legitimation crisis', it is increasingly evident that the state as a social actor is rapidly losing much of its traditional power and autonomy which it acquired during the period of industrial capitalism. More significantly, states do not have equal power when they seek to moderate the undesirable effects of global capitalism. Indeed, it is patently obvious that the weaker the economy of a country may be then the more impotent the state is in its attempts to 'civilize' capitalism.

The free market is normally subject to the morality of civil society, but as Tsoukalas (1981, 1986) has argued, in countries like Greece the rights of citizenship and the interests of social groups are not congruent with the organization of society and the structure of the market. In any case, global capitalism has become so powerful and generalized that it may be able to afford to disregard the morality of civil society. In short, global capitalism is an impersonal economic force with no substantive morality of its own, and no special human sensitivity to its effects on the human condition.

Paradoxically, it is at this juncture that religion becomes related to capitalism. Religion resurges as a cultural response to the secularizing ethos of capitalism and its dehumanizing impact on the human condition. Through advertising and information technology capitalism creates an ever increasing spectrum of consumer desires without ever addressing the existential and spiritual needs and propensities of the person. The fetishization of commodities does not meet such needs either. In its extreme form, as Heelas (1991) has shown, 'new age capitalism' tends to sacralize the self itself. Thus a proliferation of 'self-religions' has occurred during the 1980s in the context of the enterprise culture in Western societies from Canada to New Zealand. However, in societies less prone to Western individualism such self-religions seem odd and rather narcissistic. For Orthodoxy this is the worst of all forms of idolatry and religious alienation. Perhaps as a reaction to this tendency to sacralize the self there is a sense of religious quest becoming apparent along with the responses I have already alluded to.

One specifically Orthodox response to changing social conditions has been the manifest revival of monasticism, especially on Mount Athos. Thus the Athonian monastic community, which had been in severe decline in the 1950s and 1960s, has been growing rapidly of late. From 1972 to 1980 the number of monks rose from 1,146 to over 1,300 (Ware 1983: 223) and the increase has continued during the 1980s. Both male and female monasticism has also increased in monasteries throughout the country. These are young men and women in the age group 21–30, some of them professional and some intellectuals. Along with this there has been a neo-Orthodox lay intellectual movement which has attempted to relate Orthodox theology to contemporary social reality (Makrides 1989).

Taking to the desert and to monastic life in search of spiritual enrichment in periods of spiritual impoverishment is not new to Orthodoxy. The age of global capitalism is, perhaps, more spiritually impoverishing than any previous one, and thus a cultural response from within the spiritually rich Orthodox tradition is not unlikely in societies where Orthodoxy has been the major religion. Indeed, at this juncture it is arguable that the supranational, that is the catholic and ecumenical, character of Orthodoxy coincides with the global character of advanced capitalism. Several leaders from various Eastern Orthodox Churches have been of late concelebrating the liturgy at Athens cathedral every Sunday. The forms, of course, which such religious responses may take to globalized capitalism cannot yet be visualized and whilst they will vary from one society to another they will nevertheless carry with them direct political significance.

REFERENCES

Beckford, J. (1989) *Religion and Advanced Industrial Society*, London: Unwin Hyman.

Bell, D. (1976) *The Cultural Contradictions of Capitalism*, London: Heinemann.

Bell, D. 'The return of the sacred' in D. Bell, *The Winding Passage: Sociological Journeys 1960–1980*, London: Heinemann.

Berger, P. (1987) *The Capitalist Revolution*, New York: Basic Books.

Beyer, P. (1990) 'Privatization and the public influence of religion in global society', in M. Featherstone (ed.), *Global Culture: Nationalism Globalization and Society*, London: Sage, pp. 373–95.

Buss, A. (1989) 'The economic ethics of Russian-Orthodox Christianity part I', *International Sociology*, 4, 3: 235–58.

Campbell, J.K. (1976) *Honour, Family, and Patronage*, Oxford: Oxford University Press.

Clogg, R. (1979) *A Short History of Modern Greece*, Cambridge: Cambridge University Press.

Dubisch, J. (1990) 'Pilgrimage and popular religion in a Greek holy shrine', in E. Badone (ed.), *Religious Orthodoxy and Popular Faith in European Society*, Princeton: Princeton University Press.

Filias, V. (1974) *Society and Authority in Greece: the Illegitimate Embourgeoisement*, Athens (in Greek).

Frazee, C. (1969) *The Orthodox Church and Independent Greece 1821–1852*, Cambridge: Cambridge University Press.

Frazee, C. (1977) 'Church and state in Greece', in J. Koumoulides (ed.), *Greece in Transition*, London: Zeno.

Geanakopoulos, D. J. (1966) *Byzantine East and Latin West*, Oxford: Oxford University Press.

Habermas, J. (1976) *Legitimation Crisis*, London: Heinemann.

Heelas, P. (1991) 'The sacralization of the self in new age capitalism', in N. Abercrombie and A. Warde (eds), *Social Change in Contemporary Britain*, Cambridge: Polity Press.

Kokosalakis, N. (1987a) 'Religion and modernization in 19th century Greece', *Social Compass*, XXXIV, 2–3: 223–41.

Kokosalakis, N. (1987b) 'The political significance of popular religion in Greece', *Archives de Sciences Sociales des Religions*, 641: 37–52.

Legg, K. (1969) *Politics in Modern Greece*, Stanford: Stanford University Press.

Luckmann, T. (1967) *The Invisible Religion*, New York: MacMillan.

Makrides, V. (1989) 'Neo-orthodoxie: eine religiose Intellektuellenströmung im heutigen Griechenland', in P. Antes and D. Pahnke (eds) *Religion-Profession-Intellektualismus*, Marburg: Diagonal-Verlag.

Mouratides, K. (1990) *Orthodoxy in United Europe*, Athens (in Greek).

Mouzelis, N. (1978) *Modern Greece: Facets of Underdevelopment*, London: Macmillan.

Muller-Armack, A. (1959) *Religion und Wirtschaft: geistesgeschichtliche Hintergrund unserer europäischen Lebensform*, Stuttgart: Kohlhammer.

Nicol, D. (1979) *Church and Society in the Last Centuries of Byzantium*, Cambridge: Cambridge University Press.

Pantelouris, E.M. (1987) *Greece: An Introduction*, Scotland: Blueacre Books.

Parsons, T. (1951) *The Social System*, New York: Free Press.

Parsons, T. (1979) 'Religion and economic symbolism in the western world', in H.M. Johnson (ed.) *Religious Change and Continuity*, Washington: Jossey Buss Publishing Co.

Robertson, R. (1985) 'Humanity, globalization and worldwide religious resurgence', *Sociological Analysis*, 46, 3: 219–42.

Robertson R. (1986) 'Church–state relations and the world system', in T. Robbins and R. Robertson (eds), *Church–State Relations: Tensions and Transitions*, New Brunswick, NJ: Transaction Books.

Robertson, R. (1987) 'Bringing modernization back', *Contemporary Sociology*, 17 (6).

Ryrie, W. (1991) 'Capitalism and the Third World: the socio-economic and moral issues seen in a late twentieth century light'. Paper presented at the Conference *Religion and the Resurgence of Capitalism*, Lancaster University, 14–17 July 1991.

Savramis, D. (1962) *Zur Soziologie des Byzantinishen Monchtums*, Leiden: E.J. Brill.

Shils, E. (1975) *Center and Periphery*, Chicago: Chicago University Press.

Stefanides, B. (1959) *Ecclesiastical History*, Athens: Astir (in Greek).

Svoronos, N. (1975) *Review of Modern Greek History*, Athens: Themelio (in Greek).

Tsoukalas, K. (1981) *Social Development and the State: The Formation of Public Space in Greece*, Athens: Themelio (in Greek).

Tsoukalas, K. (1986) *The State, Society, and Work in post-War Greece*, Athens: Themelio (in Greek).

Ware, K. (1983) 'The church: a time of transition', in R. Clogg (ed.) *Greece in the 1980s*, London: Macmillan.

Weber, M. (1978) *Economy and Society*, Berkeley: University of California Press.

14

RELIGION AND THE DEMISE OF SOCIALISM IN ISRAELI SOCIETY

Stephen Sharot

FROM SOCIALIST ZIONISM TO NEW ZIONISM OR NEW CIVIL RELIGION

A widespread view among both the Israeli general public and Israeli social scientists is that religion has become more important in Israeli society in the last twenty years or so. In what ways religion is seen to have become more important has varied among commentators, but a number of analysts have suggested that the greater prominence of religion is related to the demise of socialism in Israeli society. The object of this paper is to consider critically such views and to introduce a number of qualifications and suggestions into the discussion of the relationship between developments in socialism and religion in Israel.

It has been suggested that developments in religion have contributed to the decline of socialist ideologies in Israel, but the more common view is that the decline in socialism preceded and provided a favourable condition for the upturn in religion. A number of observers have suggested that the demise or shrinkage of the Socialist Zionist ideology in Israel left an ideological vacuum that has been filled by a Religious Zionist ideology. Although this is a common claim, the tendency among Israeli social scientists has been to focus on either changes within the Labour movement or changes with respect to religion, and few have attempted to relate the two. Perhaps the most ambitious accounts that attempt to relate the two are a series of articles by Lilly Weissbrod (1981a, 1981b, 1983, 1985) and a book by Charles Liebman and Eliezer Don-Yehiya (1983; see also, Eisenstadt 1985; Kimmerling 1985; Davis 1987).

Weissbrod argues that there has been a fundamental shift in ideological allegiance within Israeli society from 'Labour Zionism' to 'New Zionism'. She begins with the assumption that every society coalesces around a core value system that provides it with a unique identity. In Jewish society, the messianic idea, promising national, social and individual redemption, has been at the centre of its value system. The success of Labour Zionism during the period of the *Yishuv* (the pre-state Jewish community in Palestine) in gaining widespread support of the Jewish population and power in the important Zionist organizations is attributed to its reinterpretation of all the components of the messianic message in a secular idiom: national redemption was to be achieved by immigration to Palestine, social redemption by setting up an egalitarian society, and individual redemption by tilling the soil of the Holy Land. Other secular Zionist movements achieved less support and power because they were less successful in reinterpreting the core value system. The most important secular alternative to the Labour movement, the Revisionist party, founded by Jabotinsky in 1925, only reinterpreted one component of the core value system, the national one, and lacked visions for social and individual changes.

Weissbrod writes that Labour Zionism has declined as the dominant ideology and has been replaced by New Zionism, best represented by the *Gush Emunim* (Bloc of the Faithful) movement, which fuses traditional messianism and modern nationalism. According to Weissbrod, Gush Emunim has incorporated the core values of Jewish society by its reinterpretation of the messianic idea. Recent historical events such as the foundation of the Israeli state, the ingathering of Jews from all over the world, and the conquest in 1967 of the historic heartland of ancient Israel, are interpreted as indications that the process of redemption of the Jewish people is well under way. In contrast with the more traditional forms of Jewish messianism that encouraged the Jews to wait patiently and passively for the coming of the messiah, Gush Emunim maintain that the Jews have an essential role to play in their redemption, and that the most important *mitzvah* (commandment) at this time is the settlement of the Land of Israel, especially the lands of 'Judea and Sumaria' (the West Bank). Setbacks, such as the war in 1973 and the internal confusion in Israel that followed it, are seen as 'birth pangs of the messiah', but it is believed that these can be reduced if Jews take their part in the process of redemption (for details of the beliefs of Gush Emunim see Sharot 1982; Aviad 1984; Lustick 1988).

Weissbrod contends further that the *Likud* party, which grew out of the Revisionist movement and came to power in 1977, has adopted the religiously influenced nationalism of Gush Emunim. This was demonstrated when, after the success of the Likud in the 1977 elections, its leader, Menachem Begin, visited one of the Gush Emunim settlements in the West Bank, and when, after forming a government, he visited the religious leader of Gush Emunim before going on to the Western Wall.

Other writers have also suggested that Gush Emunim has had a significant impact on Israeli society. Sprinzak (1985) writes that the political effectiveness of Gush Emunim can be explained, in part, by the fact that it is the extremist tip of a broader religious subculture that has grown considerably since the 1950s. The extent to which the particular messianic beliefs of Gush Emunim are shared by the broader subculture is not clarified by Sprinzak, but he emphasizes that the subculture of 'knitted skullcaps' shares the religious commitment to settlement in the whole of the Land of Israel, and that Gush Emunim is able to mobilize material and political support from the extensive organizations and institutions of this subculture. Of particular importance are the religious educational network, the *Bnei Akiva* religious youth movement, and *Mafdal*, the National Religious Party. Sprinzak and other writers recognize that the support for Gush Emunim is not limited to the national religious subculture, but comes also from secular groups, political parties, and the governments led by the Likud party. In an introduction to a book of articles on Gush Emunim, David Newman (1985) wrote that the movement has 'been responsible for a renewed debate concerning the nature of Zionism, Judaism and the state', and that it was, and remains, a 'major force' in the settlement of the West Bank. David Schnall (1985), a contributor to the volume, admits that it is not easy to assess the impact of Gush Emunim, but he claims nevertheless that it 'has fundamentally influenced the fabric of Israeli society'.

It is Weissbrod's contention that the success of Gush Emunim, like that of Labour Zionism before it, can be attributed to its comprehensive reinterpretation of core values, adapted to changing historical conditions, that enabled it to obtain support from people and groups with different outlooks. This argument rests on the assumption of the existence of, and the societal need for, a dominant ideology. A more nuanced formulation, that does not appear to require such an assumption, is provided by Charles Liebman and Eliezer Don-Yehiya in their book *Civil Religion in Israel* (1983). They argue that there have been three important civil religions in the recent history of the Jewish community in Palestine and Israel: Zionist-Socialism, which was the dominant civil religion of the Yishuv, Statism, which was the civil religion of the new state, and the New Civil Religion, the most recent civil religion.

Liebman and Don-Yehiya define civil religion as 'the ceremonials, myths, and creeds which legitimate the social order, unite the population, and mobilize the society's members in pursuit of its dominant political goals'. The civil religions of the Jews in Israel have differed from traditional Judaism in their beliefs, practices, and organization, and their historical forms are distinguished by their primary approaches in the reformulation of traditional symbols: confrontation, dissolution, and reinterpretation. The approach of Zionist-Socialism toward traditional Judaism was primarily one of confrontation, and socialist symbols and holidays, such as the red flag, the International, and May Day celebrations, were intended to replace those of the religious whose loyalties and solidarity were felt to compete with those of class. The Jewish immigrants of the second and third *aliyot* (waves of immigration from 1903 to 1914 and from 1919 to 1923) rejected the religious and 'petty bourgeois' character of their communities of origin in Eastern Europe, and they aimed to create a new Jewish society built on revolutionary socialist and secularist principles. They saw the 'Old Yishuv', a community of traditionalist Jews devoted to the study of the Torah or religious law and dependent economically on contributions from diaspora communities, as a deformed and parasitical society, and they were seen in turn by the Old Yishuv as the worst representatives of all that was evil and dangerous in the secular ideology of Zionism (cf. Knaani 1975; Friedman 1977).

The political circumstances of the Yishuv during the period of the British mandate led to a *modus vivendi* between the more moderate religious Jews, including an increasing number of religious Zionists, and the Zionist Socialists whose confrontational stance toward religion came to be mitigated. The Zionist-Socialists' claim that class and national Jewish loyalties complemented each other was challenged within the secular population of the Yishuv by the Revisionists who rejected any fusion of nationalism with another ideology, class or otherwise. Unlike their socialist opponents, however, the Revisionists failed to establish rituals and holidays, essential components of any successful civil religion. A high level of commitment to Zionist-Socialism may have been restricted to a political and cultural elite, but Liebman and Don-Yehiya maintain that the majority of the population of the Yishuv participated in its major symbols, ceremonies, and myths.

The decline of Zionist-Socialism after the foundation of the state was accompanied by the rise of Statism, the first major civil religion of the new state. In place of the notion of the class struggle or the correspondence of class and national aspirations, the state itself was equated with the highest moral order. The primary strategy of Statism toward traditional Judaism was dissolution, a selective affirmation of only some elements of the Jewish tradition. Its major exponent, David Ben-Gurion, saw modern Israel as a successor to the Jewish independent state of ancient times, and he tended to denigrate that part of the traditional culture that originated in the diaspora. Nevertheless, Statism represented a further moderation within the Labour movement of its stance toward religion, and it sought the political co-operation of the religious parties, especially the Zionist religious party which invariably joined the Labour-led coalition governments.

Statism may have strengthened Mapai, the dominant Labour party, for a period when many identified it with the new Israeli state, but Statism failed to generate long-term loyalties and it was followed by the 'New Civil Religion'. The strategy of this most recent Israeli civil religion has been to incorporate traditional religious symbols in a way that 'points the symbols away from God and toward the Jewish people, the Jewish state, and the particular needs of the state'. It emphasizes the unity of all Jews, Israelis or not, the sacred writings, the centrality of the Holocaust, and the Jews as an isolated nation confronting a hostile world. The New Civil Religion has its symbols, such as Masada, its rites, such as Holocaust Day and Memorial Day, and its sacred places, especially the Western Wall. Unlike previous civil religions, it grounds the values of the political system in a transcendental order.

Whereas Weissbrod suggests that one of the elements of New Zionism has been a greater religiosity among the population, Liebman and Don-Yehiya warn that the reliance on traditional religious symbols in the New Civil Religion should not be mistaken for a religious revival. There is, they argue, an inherent contradiction in adapting traditional religious symbols for a civil religion which is intended to serve a predominantly secular population. A coherent ideology has not been formulated for the New Civil Religion because an ideology would heighten the contradiction, and they argue further that its values, emphasizing national loyalty and patriotism, are likely to weaken as more inward, private systems of religion become more important.

Thus, Liebman and Don-Yehiya differ from Weissbrod in suggesting that, for the majority of the population, the changes from a Socialist or Labour Zionism to a religiously informed Zionism do not constitute a change to a new coherent dominant ideology. The new system of values and symbols is a rather low-key mixture of religious and nationalist elements, and should be distinguished from the Gush Emunim 'hotted up synthesis'. In Liebman's and Don-Yehiya's formulation, the New Civil Religion is understood as providing a congenial environment for Gush Emunim, but Gush Emunim is not seen to have played such an influential role in Israeli public life (Don-Yehiya 1987). Perhaps there are no clear ways of distinguishing to what extent Gush Emunim has been only part of general trends in Israeli society, and to what extent it has promoted those trends. The movement was founded in 1974 in response to the Yom Kippur War and the threat, as the leaders of the movement saw it, of territorial concessions which would reverse the process of redemption. Not only was the subculture of religious nationalism, from which Gush Emunim arose, well advanced at that stage, but in political and public life there had been an increasing penetration of symbols and legitimations that historically have been religiously grounded. The question remains of whether these changes have had the kind of widespread impact on the majority of Israeli Jews that it makes sense to refer to a religious renewal or a new civil religion that draws upon the traditional religion.

RELIGIOUS TRENDS

The widespread publicity given to *baalei teshuvah* (Jewish converts to ultra-Orthodox Judaism from secular backgrounds) appears to have contributed to the impression of a religious revival in Israel. However, surveys have shown that among most Israelis there is a decline in religiosity from one generation to another, and this decline is especially evident among Jews of North African and Asian origin whose immigrant generation had relatively high levels of religious observance (for a summary of the data, see Sharot 1990). The percentage of Israel Jews who identify themselves as 'religious' (meaning, in the Israeli context, Orthodox or a high level of observance of the religious law) has remained the same (about 15 percent) over the last twenty years; the percentage who identify themselves as 'traditional' (meaning partially religious in Hebrew parlance) has declined somewhat, and the proportion who identify themselves as 'secular' has risen slightly. The number of *haredim* or ultra-Orthodox Jews has grown in recent years (they constitute about 5 percent of the population) and they have spread into an increasing number of towns and neighbourhoods, especially in Jerusalem (Shilhav and Friedman 1985), but this growth is a consequence of a very high birth rate and increased wealth; the *baalei teshuvah* account for a very small part of it.

The relative size of the religious sector of the population does not appear to have grown, but opinion polls have shown that a large part of the population believes that the influence of the religious or Orthodox section of the population on the society is rising (Pollock 1989). The Orthodox religious parties have become more vocal and confident in pressing their demands in recent years. They have been in a strong bargaining position because the electoral parity in recent elections of the two largest secular parties, the *Ma'arach* (Labour Alignment, formed in 1968 from Mapai and other labour parties) and the Likud, has meant that neither could form a government and exclude the other without the support of the religious parties. The position of the religious parties was strengthened further in the election of 1988 when the percentage of their votes increased from 11 percent in 1984 to 15 percent, and their representation in the *Knesset* (Israeli Parliament) increased from thirteen to eighteen seats. This increase was, in part, a consequence of the unprecedented mobilization of the ultra-Orthodox electorate arising from the fierce competition among the ultra-Orthodox parties themselves. They also drew support from outside the ultra-Orthodox parties among lower stratum, religiously traditional Israelis of North African origin. The far-reaching demands of the religious parties after the 1988 elections produced an outcry among the secular population, but the religious parties joined the Likud-led coalition after modifying their demands.

If anything, recent changes in the fortunes of the religious parties run counter to the argument that a New Zionism, made up of a compound of religion and nationalism, has become dominant in recent years. The more successful religious parties have been the non-Zionist or even anti-Zionist ultra-Orthodox, and the largest religious party associated with ultra-nationalism, Mafdal or National Religious Party, has seen its electoral support shrink considerably. Up to the late 1960s Mafdal emphasized coexistence with secular Zionists that would safeguard the full participation of religious people in the mainstream of Israeli society, and it was also concerned to build and enlarge religious institutions that were intended for all Jewish citizens. These institutional concerns remain, but since 1967, and especially since 1973, they have increasingly taken second place to infusing the Jewish state with religious meaning and promoting Jewish settlement in the conquered territories. It is possible to argue that, even though it has not helped the electoral fortunes of Mafdal, the combination of religion and nationalism has become more pervasive, influencing secular parties including the Likud.

This takes us back to the discussion of the impact of Gush Emunim which began as a pressure group within the Mafdal. It can be admitted that the combination of religious and nationalist elements in the ideology of Gush Emunim has found it support among widely divergent groups. Its religious ideology has appealed to the 'knitted skullcaps', its nationalism has appealed to the political right-wing (including the Likud), its emphasis on the pioneering spirit has appealed to some supporters of the Labour party and members of kibbutzim, and its close-knit settlement communities have appealed to immigrants. The absence of ideological formulations produced by the movement, as well as its somewhat amorphous organization, have facilitated the wide support. This does not mean, however, that all its sympathizers and supporters share a world view. It would be more accurate to say that their world views overlap at significant points. For example, some Likud leaders share with Gush Emunim the view that Israel is 'a people that dwells alone facing the hostility of the rest of the world', but they do not appear to share the belief that settlement in the West Bank is hastening the messianic redemption.

Gush Emunim has co-operated with right-wing secular groups in advancing common political aims, but it failed to overcome the religious-secular division in its own settlements; some joint settlements failed and split apart, and a fully secular settlement remained an exception. Bauer (1985) notes also that the movement failed to attract Jews of North African and Asian origin despite their religiosity. Even among the religious settlers, there are a wide variety of viewpoints. Waxman's study of settlers from the United States, who are often regarded as among the extreme, religious fanatics, found that, only 11 percent were firmly convinced that these times are the period of the messiah. Less than 40 percent said that their primary reason for settling in the territories was ideological; most were motivated by economic and community factors. Many would have considered a similar type of community within the 'green line', and some would even have preferred it (see also, Weisburd and Waring 1985).

At the very least, these data require a considerable modification of the stronger versions of the 'New Zionism' thesis, such as that of Weissbrod, especially when they give centre stage to the importance of Gush Emunim ideology. The more qualified 'New Civil Religion' thesis may not have been refuted, but the evidence provided by Liebman and Don-Yehiya has not shown that its underlying tenets are shared among the majority of Israelis. Their emphasis on changes in the civil religion should also be qualified by noting elements of continuity in symbols and historical references. The New Civil Religion, like Zionist-Socialism and Statism before it, draws its symbols and references from the Bible rather than from the traditionalist talmudic society which is represented in Israel by the ultra-Orthodox, who remain quite distant from the tendencies in the civil religion to sacralize Zionism and territory. Continuities can also be traced between early Zionist-Socialism and Gush Emunim: both presented their aspirations and activism within a messianic mode of discourse, both drew inspiration from the Jewish Commonwealths of the ancient era, and members of Gush Emunim have themselves stated that their new settlements represent a continuation of the sacred mission of settlement that was formerly undertaken, albeit without a recognition of its divine source, by secular Zionists in the early decades of the twentieth century. This is not to detract from the enormous differences between the two movements: unlike the Socialist Zionists, members of Gush Emunim conform to the religious law, look forward to a state based on the religious law, and believe that the messianic redemption stems from the Godhead. In spite of these differences, the emphasis on pioneering settlements has persuaded some former

Socialist Zionists that Gush Emunim represents a renewal of the Zionist spirit that has been lost in the Labour movement.

Most Israelis have not been ideologically committed to either Socialism or Gush Emunim, and the changes that have occurred in the symbolic systems of the civil religions may have made little impression upon them; the majority participate infrequently in state-sponsored ceremonies and may take only a casual interest in their content. Nevertheless, the greater prominence in public life of religious symbols requires explanation, and most commentators have linked this development to the decline of Socialist Zionism and other secular interpretations of Jewishness. It is now time to consider the explanations for these changes. Three types of explanation will be examined: the demographic–cultural explanation, the historical–legitimation explanation, and explanations that point to contradictions within belief systems or between belief systems and institutional complexes.

Demographic–cultural explanation

The demographic–cultural explanation points to the consequences of the mass immigration of traditionally religious Jews from North Africa and Asia in the 1950s and 1960s. Socialist Zionism was expounded by Jews from Eastern Europe who were in revolt against the religious traditionalism of their communities of origin, but it held no appeal for 'Oriental' Jews who, far from being in revolt against religion, interpreted their migration in religious terms and wished to continue their religious heritage. Liebman and Don-Yehiya argue that the failures of both Zionist-Socialism and Statism were partly a consequence of their secularist orientations. Very few of the immigrants from other Middle Eastern countries had been members of, or had been familiar with, socialist movements in their countries of origin, and the association of socialism with an anti-religious stance was bound to alienate them from it. Statism represented an attempt by the political elite to overcome the incompatibility between Zionist-Socialism and the culture of the new immigrants, but it did not succeed in providing a lasting, meaningful symbolic system for the majority of the population: the state came increasingly to be taken for granted, and although Statism modified the antagonism toward religion, the continued negative attitudes toward religious patterns associated with the diaspora were upsetting to the immigrants.

Israelis from North African and Asian origins at first voted predominantly, like Israelis of European origin, for the major Labour party (Mapai, later Ma'arach), but from the late 1960s they increasingly transferred their support to the major 'right-wing' or 'hawkish' party, *Gahal* (formerly *Herut* and later Likud). A clear pattern of voting emerged with the Labour party receiving most of its support from *Ashkenazim* or European Israelis and the Likud receiving most of its support from the *Mizrachim* (Easterners or Middle Eastern Israelis). It has been argued that the Middle Eastern Israelis rejected the secular spirit of the Labour party

273

(Yishai 1982), and that the Israeli identity of the Middle Easterners was more congruent with the New Zionism represented politically by the Likud (Seliktar 1986). Nearly all the Likud leaders were of European origin and almost none were religious, but some of them emphasized their respect for religion and tradition.

The relative importance of different factors accounting for the voting pattern of Jewish Israelis of North African and Asian origins has been a subject of much dispute, but the transfer of political preference from Labour to Likud cannot be explained as a rejection of socialism in favour of religion. The Labour party made no attempt to socialize new immigrants into socialist values. Instead, it initially gained political support from the immigrants through a patronage system, receiving votes in exchange for employment, housing, and social services. The operation of this system produced a considerable amount of resentment and when, in the late 1960s, the development of more open markets reduced dependency on the Labour movement, its political support began to contract (Azmon 1985). Many Middle Eastern Israelis now accuse the Labour movement of blocking their mobility and of creating the socio-economic gaps between Israeli Jews of European and Middle Eastern origins. The higher levels of religiosity of Middle Easterners compared with Europeans appears to have been of little importance in prefering Likud to Labour. A survey that included samples of Israelis from Morocco and Iraq found that the supporters of the Likud and the Ma'arach in these groups were not differentiated significantly by levels of religiosity (Ben-Rafael and Sharot 1991).

The theses that there has been a change in Israel from Socialist Zionism to New Zionism or a New Civil Religion cannot point to a change within the population of Jews from North African and Asian origins because they were never socialists and they were always inclined to interpret the nation and the state in accord with their positive orientation toward their religious heritage. The Jewish communities from North Africa and Asia should not be categorized as a culturally homogeneous and traditionalistic category; some communities, such as the Iraqi Jewish community, had been influenced by Western and secular trends far more than others. There were very few, however, who came as socialists or became socialists in Israel, and the decline of socialist ideology could not, therefore, have left them with a void to be filled by New Zionism. The Israelis of North African and Asian origins can only be incorporated in the argument for ideological change by claiming that political leaders have had to take greater regard of their more religiously informed nationalism, but it should be noted that the majority of leaders and activists of the 'right-wing' or hawkish parties and movements, including Gush Emunim, have been Ashkenzim.

Historical–legitimation argument

The historical–legitimation argument emphasizes the problems of political and moral legitimation that arose as a consequence of the Six Day War in 1967.

Immediately after the war the conquest of territories was justified by many Israelis as a consequence of a defensive war and as something to bargain with in the pursuit of peace, but it is argued that the continued occupation of the territories posed problems of legitimation, especially for the secular ideology of the Labour movement. Weissbrod maintains that the political regime found itself in a 'legitimation crisis' after 1967, and Liebman and Don-Yehiya also contend that Statism's problem of legitimacy were heightened by the holding of newly acquired territories and the greater demands that this involved for Israelis, such as higher taxes and longer periods of military service. The victory in 1967 gave rise to widespread complacency, but the belief that military supremacy was so great that the Arabs could only inflict minimal losses was shown to be false by the war in 1973. The recognition of the hollowness of a complacency built on military strength generated a deeper crisis of legitimacy (Pollock 1989).

The economic expansion that followed the 1967 war has been seen by many as contributing to the decline of the idealistic visions that had been associated with Socialist Zionism. Values that had previously provided inspiration for building a new society became increasingly divorced from the reality of a society that appeared to be only imitating the norms and patterns of behaviour of Western, capitalist societies (see, for example, Rubinstein 1982). Amnon Rubinstein (1984) distinguishes between two separate social developments in Israeli society after 1967: extreme nationalism, and an emphasis on the 'good life', adopting Western fashions and patterns of consumption. He writes that, against the background of increasing materialism, hedonism and such phenomena as drugs and the decline of the family, it is possible to understand the sympathy of some secular circles for Gush Emunim with its claims of representing idealism and subordinating individual wants to the collective goal of settling the land. Gush Emunim met little serious opposition because its activities did not harm the daily pleasures of the secular majority.

The unambiguous justification of Israeli incorporation of the conquered territories by religious Zionists, that they are part of the historic homeland given to the Jews by God, has been echoed in part by 'rightwing' secular politicians who refer to historically given national rights, but the wide variety of views regarding the occupied territories among the Israeli public should not be ignored. Opinion polls report that about one-half of Israeli Jews are willing to make territorial compromises, and of those who say that they are opposed to territorial concessions, only about one in six justify their position by reference to religion as opposed to military or strategic justifications (Pollock 1989). It is by no means self-evident that secularly minded Israelis, who oppose territorial compromise, feel the need to draw upon the justifications provided by religious Zionists such as Gush Emunim. It was, after all, the secular Revisionist movement that was the most important forerunner in promoting the conception of an Israeli state on both sides of the Jordan. It may be that social scientists, who tend to be 'doveish' in their views, find it difficult to take at face value what appears to them to be simplistic justifications of secular 'hawks' and they seek, therefore, a deeper explanation by reference to the religiously informed legitimation of New Zionism. Acknowledging the existence of a pluralism of legitimations, varying in coherence, sophistication, and the extent to which they emphasize religious or secular factors, may be closer to reality.

Internal contradiction argument

The demographic–cultural and historical–legitimation arguments are rarely at the centre of accounts that suggest that there is a relationship between the demise of socialism and an increased role of religion in Israeli society. They are more commonly secondary points or part of a wider thesis that proposes a deep internal contradiction within an ideology or belief system that is both Jewish and secularist. One version of such a thesis is presented by Weissbrod, who suggests that Labour Zionism had the inherent weakness of any secular ideology that attempts to secularize a national identity that was historically anchored in religion. Religious symbols were given secular interpretations, but Jewish religious holidays were retained as national days of rest, the sacred language Hebrew was revived as the first language of the nation, the right to citizenship rested on the religious notion of a Jew, and the major symbols of the state, the Star of David and the Menorah, were adopted from the religious tradition. Many secular Zionists tried to interpret the Bible as a historical document that provided them with a national identity and tie to the land, but the pervasive religious content of the Bible made its adoption by secular Jews problematic. These contradictions were only made more evident by the conquest in 1967 of territories that were infused with historically religious meanings.

Luz (1988) makes similar points in his book on religion and nationalism in the early Zionist movement. He writes that many early Socialist Zionists conducted a war against the Jewish religion and believed that it would disappear, but that even the most secular among them could not deny that the Jewish past had a religious character. There was no Jewish cultural content upon which they could build that did not stem from religion, and in seeking historical legitimacy for their social message they appealed to 'Israelite' prophecy and represented modern socialism as a realization of Jewish messianism. Luz argues that the Jewish secularists were mistaken in their assumption that Jewish culture could be secularized like the cultures of other nations. Unlike non-Jewish nationalists, whose religions were not demonstratively national, Jewish nationalists had to confront the fact that their national tradition was a religious one and that total secularization was impossible.

Luz also points to the contradictions within early religious Zionism which emerged as a movement in the early years of the twentieth century. In contrast with the Socialist Zionists who were rebelling against their past, the religious Zionists presented themselves as a direct continuation of the past without appreciating that the nationalism that they were promoting was itself part of the process of secularization. Their failure to realize the true meaning of nationalism permitted

276

them to believe that, despite appearances, secular Zionism was the beginning of a return to the Jewish tradition.

The impression given by some interpretations is that the contradiction within Socialist Zionism, a secularist nationalism bound to a religious tradition, made its demise inevitable, or at least made it vulnerable to the challenge of the unambiguous combination of religion and nationalism in New Zionism. However, religious Zionism itself represented a combination of two ideological streams in Jewry, Orthodox Judaism and modern nationalism, that were for a long time fundamentally opposed to each other. The support by the religious Zionists of a pre-messianic state is condemned as a violation of the covenant by the anti-Zionist ultra-Orthodox, and although the majority of ultra-Orthodox Jews have came to accept the Jewish state, they still look with disfavour on the religious meanings attributed to it by the religious Zionists. For Gush Emunim believers, the tension between Jewish Orthodoxy and modern nationalism is removed by defining the entire Zionist movement and the Jewish state as sacred phenomena, regardless of the absence of religious observance among the majority. They expect that, in the future stage of the process of redemption, the whole of the Jewish people will return to the Torah, and the conception that all Jews are part of a sacred collectivity justifies the movement's co-operation with non-religious Jews who support their political aims (Raanan 1980; Aran 1990; Friedman 1990).

If religious Zionists have been successful in the appropriation of secular ideas and institutions, it should not be assumed that the secularist Zionist appropriation of religious symbols and ideas would inevitably fail. In fact, the process whereby religious symbols and holidays have become secularized and divorced from any supernatural or divine meaning by focusing on national and familial meanings is far advanced among large numbers of Jews, both in Israel and the diaspora. Secularized Jewishness is only a paradox or contradiction for those Jews who believe that anything Jewish has a religious essence which cannot finally be secularized. But religious origins or historically religious associations should not confused with religious essences. To paraphrase a classical sociological formula: if something is defined as secular (meaning here, divorced from supernaturalist assumptions), it will be secular in its consequences. Similarly, the sacralization of modern nationalism is only a paradox for those who define it as intrinsically secular. In short, the demise of Socialist Zionism cannot be explained in a social scientific perspective by an appeal to an intrinsic religiousness in anything Jewish.

The decline of Socialist Zionism is often interpreted as part of the failure of secular systems of symbols and values to replace traditional Judaism as an adequate source of integration and legitimation for the Israeli state and society. This failure is seen to have led to the tendency among formerly secularist Jews to turn to traditional Jewish values and symbols in order to invest their Jewish identity with content and meaning (Don-Yehiya 1987). Developments within the kibbutzim, collectivities built on socialist principles, might appear to demonstrate these tendencies. The early kibbutzim not only rejected religious rituals and symbols, they sought to reject any indication of routine and to express their sacred values of work, asceticism, equality, collectivism and pioneering in a free and spontaneous manner. They wanted to create the feeling of being born anew, without a past or a tradition, and at first the 'religion of pioneering' sanctified daily life to the point of obscuring the boundaries between the sacred and the profane, leaving little time for the observance of holidays or festivals. Once the kibbutz ceased to live as a youth movement camp and became a fixed, settled community, a need was felt for the ritual expression of their values and agricultural festivals were created. This involved adapting certain traditional festivals, such as *Shavuot*, emphasizing their agricultural elements or references to nature and disregarding or reducing in importance their references to God. As an ultimate reference, God was replaced by the land, nation, and social values. Thus, Passover emphasized the themes of national freedom and the coming of spring and *Purim* became a purely folk festival. New rituals were composed, although their texts tended to paraphrase the traditional religious texts.

Over the last two decades changes have occurred in the festivals and rituals of many kibbutzim. The festivals emphasizing agriculture have declined in importance as industry became an important component of the economic activities of the kibbutzim. Some of the more socially radical themes expressed in the rituals lost their relevance or ability to generate sentiment, and some of the more traditional symbols that had been discarded were reintroduced. The holidays of *Rosh Hashanah* (New Year) and *Yom Kippur* (Day of Atonement), which had no relation to nature or to important events in the nation's past, began to be revived. In most cases, however, these changes did not represent a return to Orthodox Judaism but rather a more tolerant combination of tradition and modernity. In the case of *Rosh Hashanah*, few kibbutz members are attracted to traditional prayer meetings; participation is in readings and songs drawn from ancient and contemporary Jewish literature (Lilker 1982; Rubin 1986).

The more extensive use of traditional symbols and rituals in the kibbutzim and among other sectors of the Israeli Jewish population does not represent a religious revival in the sense of a return to beliefs in God or to a concern to adhere to the complex system of Jewish religious law. What has changed is that the earlier militant secularism has almost disappeared. The early Socialist Zionists who settled in Palestine came from traditionally religious backgrounds and their rejection of religion was part of their rebellion against those '*petit bourgeois*' backgrounds. The sentiments of revolt waned and they had no affinity with the experiences of the generations born in Israel. The diaspora and its history was re-evaluated in a more positive light, and this removed the basis of the rejection of traditional symbols and rituals. The revolutionary goals of the founders were not achieved, but the secular way of life came to be taken for granted and this meant that traditional symbols and rituals, without their traditional supernaturalist premises and meanings, could be reintroduced. Thus, the decline of a radical secularism and the acceptance of some traditional practices are indications of the pervasiveness of secularization.

THE TRANSFORMATION OF SOCIALISM IN ISRAEL

Another version of the demise of socialism in Israel through internal contradiction emphasizes the Labour movement's own abandonment of its socialist principles and institutions in favour of nationalism and statism which, it is argued, created a favourable opening for New Zionism (Cohen 1987). The tensions in the socialist movement between advocating a class struggle and nationalism started early in the new Yishuv. In the 1920s two separate labour movements represented somewhat conflicting ideologies: *Ahdut Haavodah* put an emphasis on working class consciousness and class struggle, whereas the position of *Hapoel Hatzair* was that, although the working class had a central role in the nation-building process, the strategy of class struggle should be rejected. The two movements merged to form Mapai in 1930 and notions of revolutionary class struggle were abandoned in favour of building an economic sector under the control of the Labour movement. An important agency of this economic sector was the *Histadrut* (General Federation of Labour) which, in addition to being a federation of trades unions, developed a vast complex of industrial, commercial, and financial corporations. A stratum of bureaucrats and administrators working for the Histadrut presented themselves as self-sacrificing public workers who were devoting themselves to the good of the collectivity, but there developed among them a style of life which differentiated them from the majority of blue collar workers. At the same time, a private sector developed with an emphasis on achievement and individualist values. During the 1930s Mapai responded to these changes by cultivating national rather than class-based values, and in the 1940s it presented itself as a party of consensus, accepting a capitalist sector of the economy alongside the workers' sector, and advocating a policy of inter-class co-operation (Shapiro 1977; Horowitz and Lissack 1978; Liebman and Don-Yehiya 1983; Ben-Porat 1986; Cohen 1987).

Cohen writes that once the state was established with Mapai in power, the Labour movement subordinated its own institutions to those of the state. The party became statist, identifying itself with the state rather than with the working class, and its leader, David Ben-Gurion, proclaimed that Israel was neither capitalist nor socialist. The party sought to attract diverse socio-economic groups, it gave more attention to white collar and professional strata, the term 'socialist' was abandoned, and rituals such as May Day celebrations and the singing of the International became empty rituals or lost any meanings of working class solidarity. The new leaders presented an image of technocrats who discouraged ideological tendencies related to class. Shimon Peres declared, for example, that Israel was not a class society and that Mapai could not be classified as left, right, or centre. According to Cohen, the Labour movement dug its own grave by emptying its ideology and institutions of socialist content. It is a story of self-betrayal which left a void that was filled after 1967 by New Zionism.

If the argument that a Jewish movement that was both antireligious and

279

nationalist was bound to fail leaves little room for the influence of volantaristic action, Cohen's account of the Labour leaders' choice of statism over socialism gives little attention to the constraints under which those leaders made their decisions. Two important contraints in this context may be distinguished: the provision of the economic needs of members of the Labour movement, and the provision of capital in the context of the world capitalist system. Shafir (1989) emphasizes the first constraint in his account of developments prior to the First World War. He shows that the Jewish workers of the second *aliyah* (immigration wave) abandoned their attempt to compete with Arab workers by lowering their standard of living to the Arab level, and they sought instead to establish a sectoral economy, protected from the market economy, that would assure them a quasi-European standard of living. Thus, nationalist claims and state-building were conducive to the protection and advancement of the economic interests of Jewish workers. Shafir argues that the hegemony of the Labour movement in the Yishuv was not based on value consensus but on its success in providing for the interests, especially the attainment of employment, of Jewish workers.

The success of the Labour movement depended on the import and control of capital, and here the movement was subject to the contraints of the world capitalist system. Mapai's policy of 'constructionist socialism', the construction of an autonomous workers' economy by means of national funds, could only be achieved with imported capital, and this could only come from 'bourgeois' sources. Ben-Porat (1986) writes that, by the end of the 1920s, the Labour leaders had become convinced of the need to gain political influence in the World Zionist Organization, and this implied coalition with the bourgeois. Thus, the cost of the Labour movement's hegemony in the Yishuv was its economic and some political dependence on the World Zionist Organization and its co-operation with other bourgeois organizations in Europe and the United States. Hegemony was achieved by subjugating class to national interests: class struggle as a political instrument became an obstacle, and the very concept of 'working class' was replaced by the 'Labour Movement'. Those socialists who continued to empha-size class struggle were reduced to a marginal position in the political spectrum of the Yishuv and the Israeli state.

After the foundation of the state, the Labour-led governments both con-solidated the public sector of the economy that the Labour movement had established in the pre-state period and played an important part in the develop-ment of the private or capitalist economy. A large part of the imported capital was invested within the framework of public ownership (government and the Histadrut), but even most of the privately owned capital was originally imported and allocated by state agencies. The involvement of the government in the economy has continued to be greater than in Western capitalist societies; the percentage of investment financed by the public sector is higher than in any Western country, and most large private concerns are dependent on the govern-ment for various subsidies, tax exemptions, foreign currency allocations, and long-term loans. In comparison with the formerly socialist eastern European countries, the private sector of the Israeli economy is larger (about 40 percent) and the political centre does not run the economy according to detailed economic plans, but the governmental control over land and capital has been similar (Kimmerling 1983; Ben-Porat 1989).

The change in 1977 from a Labour-led to a Likud-led government was not followed by structural changes in the economy. The finance minister of the new government announced that an economic transformation would take place and he introduced an economic plan that was intended to remove various government-imposed controls, such as foreign currency regulations, and to encourage free enterprise, but the reforms proved unsuccessful and the transformation did not take place. The Likud government found that it could not combine its policies of Greater Israel with the advancement of a free market economy, and that government control of the economy had to play an essential part in the achievement of its political aims. There are, in fact, no serious ideological divisions along party lines concerning the nature of the state-directed economy, and no influential pressure groups have arisen to promote new conservatism or free markets (Ben-Porath 1986). The desire for change in the economy within the Likud party has not been directed against the notion of a large public sector, but rather against the importance of the Histadrut- or Labour-controlled part of that sector. For example, Likud has advocated a national health service and insurance scheme to replace the *Kupat Holim* (Sick Fund) controlled by the Histadrut.

Like the Likud, the religious ultra-nationalists such as Gush Emunim, have found that the centralized political economy, in which a private sector heavily dependent on the government coexists with a large public sector, could be adapted to serve their aims. In particular, settlements in the West Bank could only become economically viable communities if the government built the supporting infrastructure and allocated substantial economic resources. Thus, in contrast with the neo-conservatives in capitalist Western societies, the 'right-wing' in Israel, which includes the nationalist religious sector, has not fought for a more open capitalist or free market system.

CONCLUSION

The case of Israel demonstrates that theses linking a renewal of religion to the collapse of socialism should beware of oversimplifications based on assumptions of value consensus, dominant ideologies, or widespread changes in value systems. The Labour movement's achievement of hegemony during the British mandate and its continuation in the Israeli state until 1977 never represented the triumph of a socialist ideology among the majority of the population. Socialism and the rebellion against what was seen as the bourgeois nature of Jewish society in the diaspora were important for a large proportion of those immigrants who arrived in Palestine between 1904 and 1923, but the majority of immigrants thereafter, both from Europe and the Middle East, were not adherents of socialist doctrine. The message of class struggle and attacks on religion among certain sectors of the

Jewish labour movement were abandoned at an early stage in favour of a nation-building approach with an emphasis on the building of an economic structure under its control, and a political appeal, on the basis of national values, to all classes of the population. Thus, as an ideology that was widely shared or fervently held by a significant part of the Jewish population, socialism had declined long before the post-1967 period when religion purportedly became an important component of a New Zionism that took the place of Socialist Zionism.

The reasons for the loss of the Labour party's political hegemony are complex, but arguments that make a case for internal ideological contradictions or a 'legitimation crisis' over the occupied territories carry little conviction. Of greater importance was the resentment that accumulated, especially among immigrants from North African and Asia, under the system of patronage and dependency that was associated, in particular, with the Labour party. If there was a contradiction, it was between the Labour movement's claim that it represented the workers and its control of an economic sector in which relationships of employer and employee and income differentials were like those of the private sector. But whatever the reasons for the transfer of allegiance of Israelis of North African and Asian origins from the Labour party to Likud, this did not constitute a change in ideological allegiance from Socialist Zionism to New Zionism. In a sense, they had always been 'New Zionists', combining a nationalistic outlook with a positive orientation toward the religious tradition. Once the system of patronage had broken down, they could find a political party closer to their own outlook, but it should be emphasized that the process of secularization among them, in the sense of a decline in religiosity, continued during this period of changes in political support.

The majority of leaders and activists of the movement that has been seen as most representative of New Zionism, Gush Emunim, have been predominantly of European origin, but nearly all came from religious Zionist rather than Socialist Zionist backgrounds. A number of supporters or former supporters of the Labour party who believed in a 'Greater Israel' found, like the politicians of the Likud and smaller secular right-wing parties, an allegiance with Gush Emunim without changing their secular outlook. The few former socialists or Labour supporters who did adopt a religious way of life were more likely to convert to ultra-Orthodoxy rather than to religious Zionism. Israelis of European background who previously supported the Labour party appeared to have transferred their political allegiance to centralist or 'left-wing' parties with doveish foreign policies and secularist orientations. Thus, the majority of those who abandoned the Labour party, whether of Middle Eastern or European origin, have not been former socialists who, finding themselves in a void, became 'New Zionists' with a stronger religious orientation. It would be more accurate to characterize the change as one where the hegemony of the Labour movement (which, to stress again, was not an ideological hegemony) has been replaced by a more pluralistic and competitive political system in which the religious parties, both Zionist and non-Zionist, have been in a better position to promote their policies.

REFERENCES

Aran, G. (1990) 'Redemption as a catastrophe: the gospel of Gush Emunim', in E. Sivan and M. Friedman (eds) *Religious Radicalism and Politics in the Middle East*, Albany: State University of New York Press, pp. 157–75.

Aviad, J. (1984) 'The contemporary Israeli pursuit of the millennium', *Religion* 14: 199–222.

Azmon, Y. (1985) 'Urban patronage in Israel', in E. Cohen, M. Lissak and U. Almagor (eds) *Comparative Social Dynamics: Essays in Honor of S. N. Eisenstadt*, Boulder: Westview Press, pp. 284–94.

Bauer, J. (1985) 'A new approach to religious-secular relationships?' in D. Newman (ed.) *The Impact of Gush Emunim*, London: Croom Helm, pp. 91–110.

Ben-Porat, A. (1986) *Between Class and Nation: The Formation of the Jewish Working Class in the Period Before Israel's Statehood*, Westport, CT: Greenwood Press.

Ben-Porat, A. (1989) *Divided We Stand: Class Structure in Israel from 1948 to the 1980s*, Westport, CT: Greenwood Press.

Ben-Porath, Y. (1986) 'Patterns and peculiarities of economic growth and structure', *Jerusalem Quarterly* 38: 43–63.

Ben-Rafael, E. and Sharot, S. (1991) *Ethnicity, Religion, and Class in Israeli Society*, Cambridge: Cambridge University Press.

Cohen, M. (1987) *Zion and State: Nation, Class and the Shaping of Modern Israel*, Oxford: Basil Blackwell.

Davis, E. (1987) 'Religion against the state; a political economy of religious radicalism in Egypt and Israel', in R.T. Antoun and M.E. Hegland (eds) *Religious Resurgence; Contemporary Cases in Islam, Christianity, and Judaism*, Syracuse: Syracuse University Press, pp. 145–66.

Don-Yehiya, E. (1987) 'Jewish messianism, religious Zionism and Israeli politics: the impact and origins of Gush Emunim', *Middle Eastern Studies* 23: 215–34.

Eisenstadt, S.N. (1985) *The Transformation of Israeli Society*, London: Weidenfeld & Nicolson.

Friedman, M. (1977) *Society and Religion: The Non-Zionist Orthodox in Eretz Israel, 1918–1936*, [Hebrew] Jerusalem: Yad Izhak Ben-Zvi Publications.

Friedman, M. (1990) 'Jewish zealots: conservative versus innovative', in E. Sivan and M. Friedman (eds) *Religious Radicalism and Politics in the Middle East*, Albany: State University of New York Press, pp. 127–141.

Horowitz, D. and Lissack, M. (1978) *Origins of the Israeli Polity*, Chicago: University of Chicago Press.

Kimmerling, B. (1983) *Zionism and Economy*, Cambridge, MA: Schenkman Public Company.

Kimmerling, B. (1985) 'Between the primordial and the civil definitions of the collective identity, Eretz Israel or the State of Israel?' in E. Cohen, M. Lissak and U. Almagor (eds) *Comparative Social Dynamics: Essays in Honor of S. N. Eisenstadt*, Boulder: Westview.

Knaani, D. (1975) *The Labor Second Aliya and Its Attitude toward Religion and Tradition*, [Hebrew] Tel Aviv: Sifriat Po'alim.

Liebman, C.S., and Don-Yehiya, E. (1983) *Civil Religion in Israel: Traditional Judaism and Political Culture in the Jewish State*, Berkeley: University of California Press.

Lilker, S. (1982) *Kibbutz Judaism: A New Tradition in the Making*, New York: Cornwell Books.

Lustick, I.S. (1988) *For the Land and the Lord: Jewish Fundamentalism in Israel*, New York: Council on Foreign Relations.

Luz, E. (1988) *Parallels Meet; Religion and Nationalism in the Early Zionist Movement, 1882–1904*, Philadelphia: Jewish Publication Society.

Newman, D. (1985) *The Impact of Gush Emunim: Politics and Settlement in the West Bank*, London: Croom Helm.

Pollock, D. (1989) 'Political religion in Israel', *Studies in Contemporary Jewry* 5: 305–4.

Raanan, T. (1980) *Gush Emunim*, [Hebrew] Tel Aviv: Sifriat Po'alim.

Rubin, N. (1986) 'Death customs in a non-religious kibbutz: the case of sacred symbols in a secular society', *Journal for the Scientific Study of Religion* 25: 292–303.

Rubinstein, A. (1984) *The Zionist Dream Revisited: From Herzl to Gush Emunim and Back*, New York: Schocken.

Rubinstein, D. (1982) *On the Lord's Side: Gush Emunim*, [Hebrew] Tel Aviv: Hakibbutz Hameuchad.

Schnall, D. (1985) 'An impact assessment', in D. Newman (ed.) *The Impact of Gush Emunim: Politics and Settlement in the West Bank*, London: Croom Helm, pp. 13–26.

Seliktar, O. (1986) *New Zionism and the Foreign Policy System of Israel*, London: Croom Helm.

Shafir, G. (1989) *Land, Labor, and the Origins of the Israeli–Palestinian Conflict*, 1882–1914, Cambridge: Cambridge University Press.

Shapiro, Y. (1977) *Democracy in Israel* [Hebrew] Ramat-Gan: Misdah.

Sharot, S. (1982) *Messianism, Mysticism and Magic: A Sociological Analysis of Jewish Religious Movements*, Chapel Hill: University of North Carolina Press.

Sharot, S. (1990) 'Israel: sociological analyses of religion in the Jewish state', *Sociological Analysis* 51 (supplement): 63–76.

Shilhav, J. and Friedman, M. (1985) *Growth and Segregation – The Ultra-Orthodox Community of Jerusalem*, [Hebrew] Jerusalem: Jerusalem Institute for Israel Studies.

Sprinzak, E. (1985) 'The iceberg model of political extremism', in D. Newman (ed.) *The Impact of Gush Emunim*, London: Croom Helm, pp. 27–45.

Waxman, C. (1985) 'Political and social attitudes of Americans among the settlers in the territories', in D. Newman (ed.) *The Impact of Gush Emunim: Politics and Settlement in the West Bank*, London: Croom Helm, pp. 200–20.

Weisburd, D. and Waring, E. (1985) 'Settlement motivations in the Gush Emunim Movement; comparing bonds of altruism and self-interest', in D. Newman (ed.) *The Impact of Gush Emunim: Politics and Settlement in the West Bank*, London: Croom Helm, pp. 183–99.

Weissbrod, L. (1981a) 'From Labour Zionism to New Zionism; ideological change in Israel', *Theory and Society* 10: 777–803.

Weissbrod, L. (1981b) 'Deligitimation and legitimation as a continuous process: a case study of Israel', *The Middle East Journal* 35: 527–43.

Weissbrod, L. (1983) 'Religion as national identity in a secular society', *Review of Religious Research* 24: 188–05.

Weissbrod, L. (1985) 'Core values and revolutionary change', in D. Newman (ed.) *The Impact of Gush Emunim: Politics and Settlement in the West Bank*, London: Croom Helm, pp. 70–90.

Yishai, Y. (1982) 'Israel's right wing Jewish proletariat', *Jewish Journal of Sociology* 24: 87–97.

15

RELIGION AND CAPITALISM IN AUSTRALIA

Alan W. Black

If there is a date from which one can speak of a resurgence of capitalism in Australia, it would be November 11, 1975. This was the day on which Prime Minister Gough Whitlam was dismissed by the Governor-General in controversial circumstances. The Labor Party had been in power for only three years, having been in opposition for 23 years prior to that. In order to understand the significance of these events, one needs to view them from historical and sociological perspectives.

For reasons which have been analysed elsewhere (Hamilton 1958; Aitkin 1982) and which included the fact that a higher proportion of Roman Catholics than of Protestants in Australia at that time were from lower social strata, Roman Catholic influence was relatively strong in the Australian Labor Party from early in the twentieth century. The party's initial platform was more akin to that of the Christian and Fabian socialism of the English type than to the much more radical Marxist programme. Even prior to the emergence of the Labor Party, Australians had come to expect their governments to play an active role in general economic development. Thus, government-assisted immigration, public overseas borrowing and public capital formation constituted about half, respectively, of total immigration, total foreign borrowing and gross capital formation in Australia in the period from 1860 to 1890 (Butlin *et al.* 1982: 327–8). The governments of the various colonies in Australia were particularly active in the construction and operation of railways and telegraphs, to the virtual exclusion of private entrepreneurs. This was in marked contrast to the situation in Britain and the United States in particular.

Entrepreneurial activities by governments in Australia elicited the contemporary titles of 'colonial socialism', 'state socialism in the colonies' and '*socialisme sans doctrines*'. But it would be misleading to regard these titles as correctly characterizing the whole of the Australian economy at that time. Australia in the late nineteenth century was primarily an instance of what Denoon (1983) has termed 'settler capitalism'. The activities of the state in obtaining capital, labour and various manufactured items, including steel, from overseas (mainly from Britain) and in encouraging export commodity production in Australia strengthened

285

the linkage of the Australian economy into global capitalism. These and other state initiatives directly or indirectly subsidized various forms of capitalist activity. One could take farming as an example:

> By 1900 he [the farmer] had succeeded in getting the state to help him buy his land on the cheap, water it by irrigation, transport his crop at low rates by building uneconomic railways, protect his market by the tariff, provide him with cheap credit which he often refused to pay back, lend him money to help to destroy pests, like the rabbit or phylloxera, and help him to improve his technique by establishing agricultural colleges and research stations at the public expense.
>
> (Shaw 1972: 206)

Thus, although the Australian economy had a capitalist base, it involved a mixture of both public and private enterprise. In 1901, the ratio of public expenditure (including defence) to gross domestic product (GDP) was 20 percent in Australia, compared with 15 percent in Britain and 8 percent in the United States. The ratio of public sector employment (excluding defence) to total workforce was 8 percent, 3 percent and 4 percent respectively in these three countries (Butlin *et al.* 1982: 5–6).

In 1910 the Labor Party came to power at the federal level, and by mid-1915 it was also in office in all states except Victoria. This enabled it to implement many of its policies, such as the establishment of the Commonwealth Bank as a competitive savings and trading bank, the extension of provisions for compulsory arbitration of industrial disputes, and the expansion of governmental trading activities. New South Wales, Queensland and Western Australia developed state enterprises in insurance, coal mines, quarries, brick works, saw mills, bakeries, butchers' shops, even hotels and tobacco shops. The federal government developed woollen mills, clothing factories and a dockyard. Such activities were undertaken not so much as a step towards the nationalization of industry, but rather to provide a degree of competition to private operators, especially in the supply of goods and services to government departments, and to serve as model employers in the wages and working conditions they offered (Macintyre 1986: 105–6).

Partly as a result of pressure from the Labor Party, means-tested old-age pensions had been introduced in New South Wales in 1900, in Victoria in 1901 and then for the whole of Australia in 1908. In 1910, the federal Labor government began providing pensions for the permanently incapacitated and in 1912 it introduced a maternity allowance of £5 paid to the mother on the birth of her child (Macintyre 1986: 107–8). Without minimizing the significance of these social welfare initiatives, it is important to stress that the Labor movement in Australia has always accorded high priority to ensuring that workers receive wages adequate to support themselves and their families. This ideal was very similar to that enunciated in the 1891 papal encyclical *Rerum Novarum* and that adopted in the landmark decision of the Commonwealth of Australia Arbitration Court in 1907 on the meaning of the term 'fair and reasonable wages'. *Rerum Novarum* also declared that socialism, defined as the abolition of private property, was a false remedy for the plight of the working classes and must be utterly rejected.

In 1921, the Australian Labor Party (ALP) adopted as its official objective 'the socialization of industry, production, distribution and exchange'. The radical character of this objective alarmed Labor politicians at the time of its adoption. Interpretations were immediately appended to explain that the objective was to be obtained by constitutional means and that the Party 'does not seek to abolish private ownership even of any of the instruments of production where such instrument is utilized by its owner in a socially useful manner and without exploitation' (quoted in Rawson 1966: 66, 68; see also McKinlay 1979: 90–2). On the basis of this interpretation, the great majority of Catholics continued to vote for the ALP until the 1950s. Each Labor Prime Minister in the 1920s, 1930s, and 1940s was a Catholic, at least by birth and upbringing. Eleven of the nineteen members of the Chifley federal Labor Cabinet from 1946 to 1949 either were Catholics or had a Catholic background (Henderson 1982: 72). As Roman Catholics made up only about one-fifth of the Australian population, they were clearly over-represented within the ALP at that time.

By contrast, leaders and members of the Liberal and Country Parties were much more likely to be of Anglican or other Protestant background. Sir Robert Menzies, Australia's longest-serving Prime Minister (1949–66), was a Presbyterian. While he considered it prudent to include at least one Roman Catholic in his Cabinet, Catholics were markedly under-represented there. However, many Catholics had been upwardly mobile during the twentieth century and this helped to engender doubts on the part of some of them about the ALP's socialist objective. There were significant divisions of opinion among Catholics about the attempts by the Labor government in 1947 to nationalize the trading banks. Moreover, particularly after the Spanish Civil War, Catholic Action was increasingly directed toward the defeat of communists and those deemed to be communist sympathisers in the union movement and the ALP. After the 1955 split in the Labor movement over this issue, a substantial number of Catholics, especially in Victoria, transferred their loyalties to the Democratic Labor Party (DLP). The DLP's share of the national vote peaked at 9 percent in 1958 and 1961. Although this was never enough to win seats in the House of Representatives, it was sufficient to win a few seats in the Senate. Furthermore, nearly 90 percent of DLP voters followed that Party's recommendation to give their second preferences under the preferential voting system to Liberal or Country Party candidates. These preferences helped to maintain the Liberal–Country Party Coalition in power from the late 1950s until 1972, notwithstanding the election of Arthur Calwell, a devout Catholic, as federal parliamentary leader of the ALP from 1960 to 1967 (Bolton 1990: 142–5).

The 23 years of Liberal–Country Party rule which ended in 1972 were characterized by several important features that influenced the evolution of capitalism in Australia. Except for selling the government's majority shareholdings in

Commonwealth Oil Refineries and Amalgamated Wireless, the Coalition government did not privatize existing governmental enterprises. Trans Australia Airlines, Qantas and the Australian Broadcasting Commission (ABC) were maintained as a guard against monopoly and to set competitive standards. Likewise, the Coalition maintained existing prohibitions on foreign investment in some key areas of the Australian economy: banking, radio, television and civil aviation. With the advent of television, various provisions were enacted to prevent concentration of media ownership and to regulate content, including a requirement that some time on both ABC and commercial channels be allocated to religious programmes. On the whole, however, relatively few limitations were placed on the flow of capital both into and within Australia.

As Australia was seen as a safe and potentially profitable place for investment, many overseas firms established subsidiaries here during this period. This process was aided by the policies of the federal government, which continued the long-standing tariff protection for manufacturing in Australia, introduced incentives such as an investment allowance for taxation purposes of 20 percent of the cost of capital equipment (from 1962 onwards), imposed no capital gains taxes, and allowed freedom of remittance for dividends (Cuddy 1980). A 1967 study showed that of the 299 largest companies in Australia, 141 were foreign controlled (Wheelwright and Miskelly 1967: 53). Overseas ownership and control was particularly evident in the highly capitalized, most rapidly growing and technologically complex industries, such as motor vehicle manufacture, chemicals, petroleum refining and non-ferrous metals. In the late 1960s and early 1970s the inflow of foreign capital into mining, quarrying, oil exploration and production, large-scale pastoral enterprises, and tertiary industries such as finance, property and commerce also accelerated greatly (Simms 1982: 101–2).

The expansion of the Australian economy during the 1950s and 1960s was aided by a general growth in world trade and a stable international monetary system, both due largely to measures initiated by the United States to safeguard Western capitalism. Growth was also stimulated by a substantial and continuing inflow of migrants. Net intake over the period from 1947 to 1973 averaged nearly 0.9 percent of the population per annum, two-thirds of the new arrivals having their passage government-subsidized. As there were insufficient immigrants from Britain and Ireland to meet government targets, increasing numbers were drawn from elsewhere in Europe. This resulted in much greater ethnic and religious diversity in Australia than previously. Coupled with a higher birth-rate among Catholics than Protestants, it also resulted in an increase in the Roman Catholic proportion of the population from 20.7 percent in 1947 to 27.0 percent in 1971. In twenty years, the number of Catholics doubled. This in turn created financial difficulties for the Catholic school system, difficulties intensified by rising educational expectations in the community at large and by the Catholic teaching orders' inability to obtain sufficient recruits to keep pace with population growth. In the 1963 federal election, the Menzies government, which had lost some of its earlier popularity, promised to introduce financial aid for non-government schools throughout Australia. This promise was fulfilled when that government was re-elected. Although the relatively small number of Protestant schools shared in the benefits of this aid, most of it went to the much larger school system operated by the Catholic Church, which had been campaigning for such assistance for many years. Given the importance of the Catholic vote for its continuing hold on office, it is not altogether surprising that a predominantly Protestant Liberal–Country Party government undertook this initiative.

On the other hand, the Liberal–Country Party regime made few major innovations in social welfare. During the 1950s and 1960s, there were federal initiatives in hospital, medical and pharmaceutical benefits, in tertiary education, and in the provision of subsidies for homes for the aged. These and other programmes involved varying degrees of collaboration with state and local governments, voluntary organizations and commercial enterprises. In 1971, the year before the Whitlam Labor government came to power, the ratio of total government expenditure to GDP in Australia was 27.5 percent, which was well below the OECD average for that year (32.9 percent) and much lower than in Canada, Britain and most countries in Europe (see Table 1). It was also lower than in the United States. In short, although government expenditure as a proportion of GDP was relatively high in Australia compared with most other Western societies at the beginning of the twentieth century, this was no longer the case in 1971. During the long period of conservative rule, the activities of government had not expanded to the same extent in Australia as elsewhere.

Various factors contributed to the conservative parties' being voted out of office in 1972. One can point to the much less capable leadership of the Liberal Party after Menzies' retirement in 1966, and contrast this with the vigorous and articulate leadership of the ALP after Whitlam became parliamentary leader in 1967; to Whitlam's success in having the structure of the ALP changed and its policies rewritten so as to present a much less doctrinaire, more attractive image of the meaning of democratic socialism, or social democracy as he preferred to call it; to his success in having the ALP adopt a platform to give financial aid to government and non-government schools on a basis of needs and priorities; to the growing public disenchantment with Australia's involvement in the Viet Nam war, a disenchantment which was increasingly being voiced both within the churches and outside them; to mounting concern over the inadequacy of the conservative parties' policies in relation to health, social security, cities, housing, Aborigines, migrants, women and the increasing influence of multinational corporations in the Australian economy; and, in the light of the above, to a readiness on the part of some business interests and some of the mass media to advocate a change of government.

In a retrospective account of the aims and achievements of his government, Whitlam related the principal elements of his programme to what he called 'the doctrine of positive equality', of which he wrote:

289

Table 1 Total outlays of all levels of government as a percentage of GDP for various years

Nations	1971	1975	1982	1987	1992
G7 nations					
United States	31.6	33.5	33.9	33.4	35.4
Japan	20.9	26.8	33.0	32.2	32.2
Germany	40.1	48.4	49.0	46.7	49.4
France	38.1	43.4	50.3	50.9	52.0
Italy	36.6	41.6	47.6	50.2	53.2
United Kingdom	38.1	44.4	44.5	40.7	44.1
Canada	36.1	38.5	44.8	43.5	49.7
Total of above nations*	32.7	35.8	38.7	38.0	39.8
Smaller nations					
Australia	27.5	31.1	33.0	35.4	38.3
Austria	39.7	45.3	50.1	51.9	50.2
Belgium	38.0	45.7	56.3	52.6	50.8
Denmark	43.0	48.2	61.2	57.3	59.5
Finland	32.0	35.1	37.9	40.9	51.7
Greece	22.8	30.5	39.6	48.4	48.3
Ireland	40.5	45.7	55.1	52.0	43.9
Netherlands	45.0	51.2	58.7	58.6	54.7
Norway	43.0	45.4	47.5	50.5	57.5
Portugal	21.3	30.2	43.0	43.5	46.1
Spain	23.6	24.4	36.6	39.6	45.1
Sweden	45.3	48.4	64.8	57.8	67.3
Total of above smaller nations*	33.8	39.4	48.0	48.3	51.0
Total of above European nations*	37.4	43.7	48.7	48.1	50.7
Total of above OECD nations*	32.9	36.2	39.8	39.2	41.2

Note: Because the *OECD Economic Outlook* 53 (June 1993) presents figures only as far back as 1975 and uses a method of calculation which is slightly different from that used in previous editions, the figures for 1971 are not strictly comparable with those for subsequent years. They are, however, roughly comparable. The asterisked totals for 1975 and later years are based on 1987 GDP weights and exchange rates. Figures for the United States exclude deposit insurance outlays.

Sources: For 1971, *OECD Economic Outlook* 52 (December 1992) Table R15. For subsequent years, *OECD Economic Outlook* 53 (June 1993) Table R15.

This concept does not have as its primary goal equality of personal income. Its goal is greater equality of the services which the community provides. This approach not merely accepts the pluralistic nature of our system, with the private sector continuing to play the greater part in providing employment and growth; it positively requires private affluence to prevent public squalor.

The approach is based on this concept: increasingly, a citizen's real standard of living, the health of himself and his family, his children's opportunity for education and self-improvement, his access to employment opportunities, his ability to enjoy the nation's resources for recreation and cultural activity, his legacy from the national heritage, his scope to participate in the decisions and actions of the community, are determined not so much by his income but by the availability and accessibility of the services which the community alone can provide and ensure. The quality of life depends less and less on the things which individuals obtain for themselves and can purchase for themselves from their personal incomes and depends more and more on the things which the community provides for all its members from the combined resources of the community.

(Whitlam 1985: 3)

The Whitlam government proceeded as quickly as possible – some would say too quickly – to implement its policies but was hindered by a Senate in which it did not have a majority. For example, it introduced legislation for a system of recurrent grants to both government and non-government schools on the basis of their needs. This implied that poorer State and Catholic schools would receive more assistance than would other schools, whether State or Church-related, which were already better equipped and staffed. This legislation was initially blocked in the Senate by the conservative parties, but was eventually passed when the Country Party relented under pressure from some Catholic bishops (Whitlam 1985: 318). The legislation was scarcely a threat to the capitalist system, though it was a challenge to some existing inequalities.

The Whitlam government was nevertheless accused by many of its opponents, both within and outside Parliament, of being guilty of increased centralism and 'creeping socialism' because of its policy of seeking a more active role for the federal government, its efforts to provide equality of opportunity and social justice for all, including a universal system of health care (Medibank), and its attempts to ensure that Australian minerals and energy resources were harvested in a way which benefited the whole community. The government's problems were exacerbated not only by an obstructionist Senate, which rejected more government legislation in three years than it had in its entire previous history of seventy-two years, but also by the dislocations caused by a crisis in the international monetary system and by massive increases in oil prices. Around the world, the long post-war boom had ended and a period of stagflation had set in. Labor's programme was predicated on the Keynesian assumption that growth in government revenues generated by strong economic growth provides a platform from which a government can launch new expenditure programmes which, in turn, stimulate further growth in the economy (Whitlam 1985: 185). In the new situation of rising inflation coupled with rising unemployment, this simple formula would no longer work.

There is insufficient space here to detail the manoeuvrings whereby opponents sought to prevent initiatives proposed by the Labor government and to force it out of office prematurely. Nor can I deal in any detail with the particular circumstances which led to the Governor-General's dismissal of Whitlam from the office of Prime Minister. These matters have been examined extensively elsewhere (Horne 1976; Kelly 1976; Kerr 1978; Maddox 1978; Starr 1978; Whitlam 1979, 1985; St John 1982). For present purposes, it is sufficient to note that

Labor's downfall was brought about by a combination of factors: ineptness on the part of some of its ministers; adverse international economic conditions whose effects were exacerbated by large increases in government spending and the introduction of full wage indexation – i.e. wage increases geared to increases in the consumer price index; an inability to persuade the trade union movement of the notion of the 'social wage' which was central to ALP strategy; hostility from most sections of capital, especially those which felt that their interests were directly threatened by ALP policies; outrage among farmers and graziers at the removal of the superphosphate bounty; opposition from many sections of the medical profession over the introduction of Medibank; increasingly hostile editorial opinion within the press, a factor which was reinforced by the high concentration of newspaper ownership in Australia; and politicians on both sides of Parliament who were prepared to push the Australian Constitution to its limits – or, some would say, beyond its limits.

The return of a conservative government in 1975 resulted in the demise of many of the initiatives of the Labor government. Although the Liberal–Country Party Coalition claiming to stand for smaller government, lower taxation, tightened eligibility for social security payments, greater private incentive and other aspects of the neo-conservative agenda, the main effect of neo-conservatism in Australia during the Fraser government (1975–83) was not so much to cut the size of the public sector as to rearrange spending priorities. Expenditures were increased in some areas, such as defence and internal security, and cut in others, such as housing, education, and urban and regional development. In some fields, such as the policing of social security payments and the promotion of economic development through export incentives, state activity expanded rather than contracted (Head 1983: 10–11). In 1982, the last full year of the Fraser government, government spending in Australia represented 33.0 percent of GDP, compared with 31.1 percent in the last year of the Whitlam government and 27.5 percent in the year before Whitlam came to power. As the ratio of government spending to GDP was increasing in most OECD countries during the 1970s and early 1980s, Australia remained near the bottom of the league throughout the whole of this period (see Table 1).

When the ALP was returned to power in 1983 under Hawke, the growing influence of economic rationalists throughout the Western world was such that his government succumbed to much of the neo-conservative agenda. Although it reintroduced universal provisions for health care and instituted a capital gains tax on property other than motor vehicles and one's principal place of residence, the Hawke government went much further in deregulating the Australian economy than its conservative predecessors had dared. In particular, it deregulated financial markets and floated the Australian dollar on the international exchanges. At a time when the world's financial and securities markets were themselves becoming much more globally integrated, these actions intensified the impact of the global economy on the Australian economy. The federal government, along with most economists and financial journalists, believed that deregulation would accelerate the process of restructuring the Australian economy and make it more competitive (Dyster and Meredith 1990: 283).

In practice, most of the foreign capital brought into Australia after deregulation was invested in the finance, property, wholesale and retail sectors of the economy, including the financing of a spate of company takeovers. This intensified the process of monopolization but did little to improve Australia's productive capacity (Lougheed 1988: 54). It also resulted in a massive and growing foreign debt, so that whereas Australia's net foreign debt represented 6 percent of GDP in the early 1980s, by the early 1990s it represented 36 percent of GDP. About two-thirds of this debt was incurred in the private sector. Much of the inflow of capital was relatively short-term and able to be repatriated quickly. To avoid or offset capital flight, Australian governments during the 1980s and early 1990s adopted policies which maintained nominal and real interest rates much higher than in most OECD countries, not simply on foreign borrowing but throughout the whole economy. In short, deregulation resulted in a situation in which Australian governments had to assess nearly every major policy decision in terms of the likely reactions of international money markets (Stretton 1987: 43–7; Wells 1990: 11).

By the late 1980s, the financial empires created by many of Australia's most notable entrepreneurs who had taken advantage of deregulation were beginning to unravel. This was the start of a series of spectacular company crashes. Some of these involved losses exceeding $1 billion. Most notable of all was the collapse of Bond Corporation, which in its heyday had boasted assets worth $10 billion, with major operations in brewing, mining, media and property. In 1987, with the approval of the National Party government in Queensland, and in partnership with a Japanese company, the Bond Corporation had also established Australia's first private university.

In July–August 1990, the *Sydney Morning Herald* published a series of articles under the general title 'Greed Inc: Australia's Missing Millions.' These articles examined the tangled web of relationships and some of the methods used by various corporate high-fliers during the 'decade of greed'. After detailed investigation, the authors concluded that there were at least eight major networks of businessmen who had, during the 1980s, made secret deals with others in their network, helped one another with takeovers, cosmetically improved each other's balance sheets, and acted in ways which served their own interests rather than those of shareholders in their companies. Because many of these deals were undocumented and were on the fringe of the law or in some cases beyond it, the deal-makers often used an arbitrator, someone who could be trusted by all sides to remember the complicated details and adjudicate in any dispute. Within the networks, these arbitrators, who included several merchant bankers, lawyers and corporate executives, were referred to by various names: facilitator, intermediary or, in a profanation of religious titles, rabbi or archbishop.

Imprudent lending by State-owned banks in South Australia and Victoria after deregulation – especially to the tycoons mentioned above, often for projects outside those two States – left these banks with billions of dollars of bad debt. In this respect these State banks were not greatly different from the large private banks, except that the State banks had much smaller asset bases and their losses became part of the public debt. Massive losses were incurred in somewhat similar fashion by other State-owned financial institutions, such as the State Government Insurance Commission in South Australia, the Victorian Economic Development Corporation, and the State Government Insurance Commission in Western Australia. During this period, these three States had Labor governments which, at least initially, were rather starry-eyed about the possibilities of achieving benefits for their States through the activities of the State banks and corporations mentioned above. The results were just the opposite of what they had hoped for. To recoup some of its losses, the government of Victoria sold its State Bank to the Commonwealth Bank in 1991.

To finance this purchase, the Hawke government privatized 30 percent of the Commonwealth Bank. Then, in December 1991, Keating succeeded Hawke as Prime Minister in much the same way as John Major had displaced Margaret Thatcher in Britain a year earlier. On the grounds that it could not or should not be expected to provide needed injections of capital, the Keating Labor government decided in June 1922 to merge and privatize 100 percent of the two publicly owned airlines: Australian Airlines and Qantas. The main anti-Labor parties (the Liberal and National parties) stated that if elected to office they would privatize other public enterprises, such as the Australian and Overseas Telecommunications Corporation, the Australian Industry Development Corporation, the Snowy Mountains Engineering Corporation, the Australian National Line, the Commonwealth Serum Laboratories and the unprivatized 70 percent of the Commonwealth Bank. These parties were also critical of the Hawke and Keating governments' failure to deregulate the labour market. Both Hawke and Keating sought to establish and maintain a quasi-corporatist Accord with the Australian Council of Trade Unions in submissions to the Arbitration Commission, thus continuing the long-standing centralized system of determining minimum wages and conditions of employment. Under John Howard's and later John Hewson's leadership, the Liberal Party stated that it would deregulate the labour market if elected to office.

One writer has described recent Labor governments in Australia as being capitalist on wealth creation but socialist on wealth distribution (Suter 1990: 175). Democratic socialist critics, however, accused these governments of making too many concessions to the economic rationalists at the expense of the principles of democratic socialism (Stretton 1987; Maddox 1989). Although the Australian economy is, like all economies of the Western world, a mixed economy rather than a *laissez-faire* capitalist economy, it lies much more towards the capitalist than the socialist end of the spectrum. According to Maddox (1989: 180), Labor has never contested the capitalist base of the Australian economy; rather, it has sought to 'civilize capitalism' in the light of the socialist vision.

How has religion been related to political economy in Australia in recent decades? First, the acceptance by each of the main political parties of the legitimacy of government financial aid for denominational schools eliminated this as a major factor affecting voting patterns and thus helping to determine which political party is in office. The ending of the Viet Nam war, accompanied by a gradual thaw in East–West relationships, undercut much of the old anti-communist rhetoric and robbed the DLP of its main *raison d'être*. By 1975, the DLP was a spent force. It had, however, served as a bridge whereby some Catholics, especially those in the middle class, shifted their allegiance to the Liberal Party. In keeping with this shift, Philip Lynch, a Catholic, was deputy leader of the federal parliamentary Liberal Party and Treasurer during the first half of Fraser's term in office. Catholics nevertheless remained under-represented in the Fraser ministry. In his last Cabinet, for example, only three ministers in a total of twenty-six – Chaney, Hodgman and McVeigh – were Roman Catholics (Derriman 1983). On the other hand, Fraser tried not to alienate Catholic voters. On sensitive issues, he consulted Catholic leaders.

While the long-term trend from 1946 to about 1970 was for a decline in the proportion of Catholics voting for the ALP, this trend levelled off by the 1970s. Although the precise percentage fluctuates from one election to another, the trend line for the past two decades has been for about 55 percent of Catholics to vote for the ALP. The corresponding figure among Anglicans has been about 45 percent, among other Protestants about 40 percent, and among the growing number of people who profess no religion about 60 percent. There have been no long-term downward or upward trends in these figures in recent decades (Kemp 1978; Aitkin 1983; Graetz and McAllister 1988; Blombery 1991).

It is clear that Catholic influence within the Labor Party is now less than it once was. Catholics constituted no more than about 20–25 percent of the Whitlam, Hawke and Keating ministries. This proportion was similar to that which Roman Catholics made up of the Australian population but was much less than their proportion had been in the Chifley Labor ministry of the 1940s. Neither Whitlam nor Hawke professed religious beliefs, though Whitlam's father was a Presbyterian elder and Hawke's was a Congregational minister. Hawke's deputies, first Lionel Bowen and then Paul Keating, were each practising Catholics. They, along with others of Irish Catholic background such as Graham Richardson, Mick Young, Eric Walsh and Peter Barron, were key figures in the network within the ALP which engineered Hawke's rise to power (Kelly 1984).

With religious agnostics or atheists making up less than a quarter of the Australian population, they were over-represented in the Whitlam, Hawke and Keating ministries. About half of the members of the 1983 Hawke ministry and a similar proportion of the 1993 Keating ministry declined to take their oath of office on the Bible (Derriman 1983; Wright 1993). Several members of the Whitlam ministry had also declined to do so. Although one could undoubtedly have good religious reasons for refusing to take such an oath on the Bible, available evidence suggests that it was a lack of religious belief which lay behind the actions of most of these ministers on this matter.

A lack of personal religious belief is one reason why both Whitlam and Hawke, unlike Margaret Thatcher, Jimmy Carter, Ronald Reagan and George Bush, never invoked religious rhetoric in their public utterances; but it is not the only reason. Menzies, Fraser and Keating, despite holding some form of religious belief, did not invoke religious rhetoric either. Although religious denomination has at various times acted as an undercurrent in Australian politics, speaking about God has never been thought appropriate on the lips of political leaders here. The main form of civil religion in Australia is that associated with Anzac Day (see Black 1991), and this does not provide a basis for religious rhetoric outside the Anzac context. Nor is there an Established church in Australia. By contrast, civil religion in Britain is closely associated with the Church of England and to a lesser extent the Church of Scotland. It was in her clashes with leaders of these Established churches that much of Margaret Thatcher's religious rhetoric was generated. America lacks an Established church but has a form of civil religion which is explicit in many more areas of life, including the political process, than is civil religion in Australia. For example, the words 'In God We Trust' on coins and banknotes give civil religion a visibility and legitimacy in America not found in Australia. Consequently, whereas it would be thought odd for an Australian Prime Minister to invoke the name of God (other than as an expletive), it is not thought odd for an American President to do so.

Some religious bodies in Australia have, like their counterparts in Britain and North America, sought to influence community attitudes and government policy on social and economic matters. For example, in 1983 the Anglican Social Responsibilities Commission, the Catholic Commission for Justice and Peace, the Commission on Social Responsibility of the Uniting Church in Australia, and the Australian Council of Churches issued a booklet entitled *Changing Australia*. Amongst other things, this document noted the unequal distribution of wealth in Australia, argued that wealth and power go together, and called for 'more just participation and sharing of decision-making power in society' and 'fairer distribution of our national wealth and income' (p. 30). It also contended (p. 19) that 'Shared control enables fairer distribution. This requires increased co-operative ownership and control of resources and wealth-creating industries and increased worker-participation. It may also require increased ownership and control by the community as a whole.'

Changing Australia was publicly criticised by Senator Chaney, a Catholic layman who had been Minister for Social Security in the then recently defeated Fraser government. He noted that whereas the document dealt with the power of trans-national corporations, it said nothing about the power of the trade union movement or the determination of the employed to maintain their standards of living, even at the expense of the unemployed. In his view, 'the kind of society envisaged by *Changing Australia* would be less free than Australians would tolerate . . . The short term effect of wholesale redistribution of wealth may perhaps reduce the incidence of poverty but . . . it would in the longer term make us poorer as a nation and thus less able to care for the needy.' (*The Australian*, 28 October 1983).

296

Writers from the 'New Right' were most vociferous in their criticisms of *Changing Australia*. The fullest response was contained in a booklet entitled *Chaining Australia: Church Bureaucracies and Political Economy* edited by Geoffrey Brennan, a Professor of Economics who was also an active Anglican, and J. K. Williams, a minister within the Uniting Church. Other contributors to the booklet included Paul McGavin, who was both an economist and an Anglican deacon, Hugh Henry, a Catholic seminarian, and Greg Sheridan, a Catholic journalist. The booklet's subtitle was intended to indicate that the views expressed in *Changing Australia* were largely those of a small number of left-leaning church bureaucrats rather than being representative of views held by most church members. Certainly both at a scholarly level and among the rank-and-file within most denominations there was and is a greater diversity of viewpoints on these matters than is acknowledged in *Changing Australia*.

Because of misgivings over the process by which the Catholic Commission for Justice and Peace (CCJP) formulated its statements and over the content of some of those statements, the Australian Catholic Bishops' Conference abolished the CCJP in 1987, establishing in its place the Bishops' Committee for Justice, Development and Peace (BCJDP). The Bishops' Conference also decided that the first major task of the BCJDP would be to examine, from the perspective of Catholic social teaching, the distribution of wealth in Australia and that the Committee would use a modified version of the method which had been adopted in the United States by the National Conference of Catholic Bishops to produce *Economic Justice for All* (1986). About 700 submissions were received by the BCJDP in response to its initial call. After considering this and other material, the BCJDP prepared, and the Catholic Bishops of Australia issued, a draft statement, inviting further discussion and comment. This yielded approximately 600 written responses, which were considered before the final form of the pastoral statement, *Common Wealth for the Common Good*, was prepared and published in 1992.

Like the papal encyclical *Centesimus Annus* (1991), this document was critical of some aspects of contemporary capitalism. Nevertheless, discussion of the 'option for the poor' and of the blind spots inherent in economic rationalism was set in a framework of reforming rather than rejecting capitalism. Recognising that Australia is part of the global economy, *Common Wealth for the Common Good* dealt with issues of international trade and aid, as well as with matters of domestic policy such as the operation of the financial system, employment, housing, social security, taxation, health, education, families and Aboriginal people. Proponents of liberation theology, such as Leonardo and Clodovis Boff (1987), would probably argue that the Australian Bishops' statement, like that of their United States counterparts, was not sufficiently radical in its challenge to contemporary capitalism, whereas apologists for democratic capitalism, such as Michael Novak (1982) and Peter Berger (1986, 1990), would presumably contend that the Australian Bishops' statement was both economically and politically naive and likely to accentuate the politics of envy.

In conclusion, one can say that although there are still some differences in the religious composition of supporters of the various political parties in Australia, these differences are not as great as they once were, especially in terms of a Catholic/Protestant cleavage. In recent years there has also been an increasing convergence in the policies of the two main political parties – Liberal and Labor – and that convergence has been toward the operation of the market principle. The convergence has resulted partly from worldwide trends in that direction and partly from the desire of Labor leaders to avoid the fierce backlash of 1975.

There are nevertheless still some differences in the balance struck by the two parties between unfettered capitalism, government regulation, public enterprise and non-market methods of allocation, including the welfare-state. In the 1993 federal election, the Liberal/National Party coalition led by John Hewson stated that if it were elected it would deregulate the labour market, introduce a voucher scheme with a view to making higher education institutions more responsive to the student 'market', and go much further in the direction of privatizing existing public enterprises, reducing the size of government, cutting taxes and pruning welfare expenditure. As government spending in Australia already represented a lower proportion of GDP than in nearly all other OECD countries, the prospect of substantial reductions in social welfare provisions was viewed with alarm by the social justice agencies of the largest denominations – Catholic, Anglican and Uniting. In response to criticism from various church leaders, the Liberal/National Coalition eventually made relatively minor changes to its proposed policies. Despite this and despite an unemployment rate of 11 percent of the workforce, the Coalition failed to win the election. Had it done so, capitalism in Australia would have become even more unfettered than it had been under the Labor government.

In Wallerstein's (1979) terminology, Australia occupies a semi-peripheral position in the global economy. The deregulation of financial markets in Australia since 1985 has resulted in the fuller integration of the Australian economy into global capitalism. Within that system, Australia's relationship with countries in the Asia-Pacific region is becoming of increasing importance, not only for trading purposes but also because of migration and cultural exchanges. Although persons professing a non-Christian religion constituted only 1.36 per cent of the Australian population in 1981, by 1991 they constituted 2.64 per cent, and that upward trend is likely to continue for the foreseeable future. The impact of religious diversity on the further evolution of capitalism in Australia, and *vice versa*, merits continuing examination.

NOTE

1 This paper was written while I was on study leave from the University of New England and visiting the University of Exeter and Michigan State University. The assistance of each of these institutions is gratefully acknowledged. Michael Hogan kindly commented on a draft version.

REFERENCES

Aitkin, D. (1982) *Stability and Change in Australian Politics*, 2nd edn, Canberra: Australian National University Press.

Aitkin, D. (1983) 'The changing Australian electorate', in H.R. Penniman (ed.) *Australia at the Polls: The National Elections of 1980 and 1983*, Sydney: Allen & Unwin, pp. 11–34.

Anglican Social Responsibilities Commission, Catholic Commission for Justice and Peace, Commission on Social Responsibility of the Uniting Church in Australia, and Australian Council of Churches (1983) *Changing Australia*, Blackburn, Vic.: Dove Communications.

Australian Catholic Bishops' Conference (1992) *Common Wealth for the Common Good*, North Blackburn, Vic.: Collins Dove.

Berger, P.L. (1986) *The Capitalist Revolution: Fifty Propositions about Prosperity, Equality and Liberty*, New York: Basic Books.

Berger, P.L. (1990) *The Capitalist Spirit: Toward a Religious Ethic of Wealth Creation*, San Francisco: ICS Press.

Black, A.W. (ed.) (1991) *Religion in Australia: Sociological Perspectives*, Sydney: Allen & Unwin.

Blombery, T.L. (1991) 'Right-wing or radical? Australian churches today', *Pointers: Bulletin of the Christian Research Association* 1/4: 1–3.

Boff, L. and Boff, C. (1987) 'A Igreja perante a economia nos EUA – Un olhar a partir de periferia' *Revista Eclesiastica Brasileira* 47: 356–77.

Bolton, G. (1990) *The Oxford History of Australia*, vol. 5, 1942–1988, Melbourne: Oxford University Press.

Brennan, G. and Williams, J.K. (eds) (1984) *Chaining Australia: Church Bureaucracies and Political Economy*, Sydney: Centre for Independent Studies.

Butlin, N.G., Barnard, A. and Pincus, J.J. (1982) *Government and Capitalism: Public and Private Choice in Twentieth Century Australia*, Sydney: Allen & Unwin.

Cuddy, D.L. (1980) 'American business and private investment in Australia', *Australian Journal of Politics and History* 26: 45–56.

Denoon, D. (1983) *Settler Capitalism: The Dynamics of Dependent Development in the Southern Hemisphere*, Oxford: Clarendon Press.

Derriman, P. (1983) 'The barriers go down', *Sydney Morning Herald*, 16 May.

Dyster, B. and Meredith, D. (1990) *Australia in the International Economy in the Twentieth Century*, Cambridge: Cambridge University Press.

Graetz, B. and McAllister, I. (1988) *Dimensions of Australian Society*, South Melbourne: Macmillan.

Hamilton, C. (1958) 'Irish Catholics of New South Wales and the Labor Party, 1890–1910', *Historical Studies*, 8 (31): 254–67.

Head, B. (ed.) (1983) *State and Economy in Australia*, Melbourne: Oxford University Press.

Henderson, G. (1982) *Mr Santamaria and the Bishops*, Sydney: St Patrick's College.

Horne, D. (1976) *Death of the Lucky Country*, Ringwood, Vic.: Penguin.

Kelly, P (1976) *The Unmaking of Gough*, Sydney: Angus & Robertson.

Kelly, P. (1984) *The Hawke Ascendancy: A Definitive Account of its Origins and Climax 1975–1983*, Sydney: Angus & Robertson.

Kemp, D.A. (1978) *Society and Electoral Behaviour in Australia: A Study of Three Decades*, St Lucia: University of Queensland Press.

Kerr, J. (1978) *Matters for Judgment: An Autobiography*, South Melbourne: Macmillan.

Lougheed, A.L. (1988) *Australia and the World Economy*, Melbourne: McPhee Gribble.

Macintyre, S. (1986) *The Oxford History of Australia*, vol. 4, 1901–1942, Melbourne: Oxford University Press.

Maddox, G. (1978) 'The Australian Labor Party', in G. Starr, K. Richmond and G. Maddox (eds) *Political Parties in Australia*, Richmond, Vic.: Heinemann Education, pp. 159–316.

Maddox, G. (1989) *The Hawke Government and the Labor Tradition*, Ringwood, Vic.: Penguin.

McKinlay, B. (1979) *A Documentary History of the Australian Labor Movement 1850–1975*, Richmond, Vic.: Drummond.

National Conference of Catholic Bishops (1986) *Economic Justice for All: Pastoral Letter on Catholic Social Teaching and the U.S. Economy*, Washington, DC: U.S. Catholic Conference.

Novak, M. (1982) *The Spirit of Democratic Capitalism*, New York: Simon and Schuster.

Rawson, D.W. (1966) *Labor in Vain? A Survey of the Australian Labor Party*, Croydon, Vic.: Longmans.

Shaw, A.G.L. (1972) *The Story of Australia*, 4th edn, London: Faber & Faber.

Simms, M. (1982) *A Liberal Nation: The Liberal Party and Australian Politics*, Sydney: Hale & Iremonger.

St John, E. (1982) 'The dismissal of the Whitlam government' in R. Manne (ed.) *The New Conservatism in Australia*, Melbourne: Oxford University Press, pp. 161–79.

Starr, G. (1978) 'The Liberal Party of Australia', in G. Starr, K. Richmond and G. Maddox (eds) *Political Parties in Australia*, Richmond, Vic.: Heinemann Educational, pp. 11–101.

Stretton, H. (1987) *Political Essays*, Melbourne: Georgian House.

Suter, K.D. (1990) 'The Uniting Church in Australia and Economic Justice: The *Changing Australia* Controversy', unpublished M.A. (Hons) thesis, University of Sydney.

Wallerstein, I. (1979) *The Capitalist World Economy*, Cambridge: Cambridge University Press.

Wells, D. (1990) *In Defence of the Common Wealth: Reflections on Australian Politics*, Melbourne: Longman Cheshire.

Wheelwright, E.L. and Miskelly, J. (1967) *Anatomy of Australian Manufacturing Industry*, Sydney: Law Book Co.

Whitlam, E.G. (1979) *The Truth of the Matter*, Ringwood, Vic.: Penguin.

Whitlam, E.G. (1985) *The Whitlam Government 1972–1975*, Ringwood, Vic.: Viking.

16

RELIGION, POLITICS AND DEVELOPMENT IN MALAYSIA

Anne Eyre

INTRODUCTION

The theme of this paper is that religion – namely Islam – functions to both legitimize and check the Malaysian government's aim of continuing economic growth in order to make Malaysia a fully developed nation by 2020. Both Eastern and Western models of development are incorporated in this vision of the future, reflecting the concern that Malaysia's rich religious and cultural heritage will not be lost or replaced in view of the secular, modernistic and individualistic tendencies seen to be associated with contemporary developed societies.

The outline of the paper is as follows. First, the racial and ethnic constitution of the population will be described, highlighting the overlap between race, religion and socio-economic status. This is followed by an overview of Malaysia's development policies since independence and specifically since 1990 in 'Vision 2020'. The role of Islam as the national religion will be examined in this context leading to a consideration of the nature of Malaysia's civil religion and its effectiveness in unifying the various elements of this plural society in transition.

COMMUNALISM IN MALAYSIA

A recurrent theme throughout Malaysia's history has been division along racial and ethnic lines. These traditions have laid the grounds for today's plural society and the marked distinctions between its communal groups. During the nineteenth century large numbers of Chinese and Indian migrant labourers were introduced to Malaya to work in the tin mines and on the rubber-tapping estates, while the Malays tended to keep to their traditional subsistence economy based on fishing and growing rice. Ethnic boundaries became more marked between the Malays' rural lifestyle and the lifestyles of the Indians on the estates and the majority of the Chinese in the towns who became more economically active in their own businesses.

Islam came to be identified with the Malay community and eventually became a rallying symbol for their resistance to colonialism. At the same time Christianity became identified with colonial domination and economic exploitation. Northcott (1991) states that the identification of Christianity with the immigrant communities was to have important consequences for the development of Christian/Muslim relations later. Indeed, once political parties started to form and align themselves with these ethnic boundaries, religion became a significant banner for rallying support for and opposition to the different racial interest groups. This basic group identification in terms of race/ethnicity and religion is still an underlying feature of Malaysian politics today.

In the run-up to independence racial distinctions became marked in the political parties that evolved. This was despite British attempts to decrease them through the Malayan Union which proposed common citizenship for all. The Union represented a real threat to Malay political dominance: had it been implemented 83 percent of the Chinese and 75 percent of the Indians would have qualified for citizenship (Comber 1983: 32). The Malays also resented the planned introduction of a centralized scheme which would have had the effect of reducing the local Malay rulers to mere religious figureheads.

Thus, alongside the development of communal-based parties, came the establishment of the Federation of Malaya (1948) which forms the basis of the Malaysian Constitution today. This gave recognition to the 'special position' of the Malays which has, ever since, been expressed in the granting of rights and privileges to the *Bumiputeras* ('sons of the soil'), that is the indigenous Malays. The Federation also recognized first, the position of the Malay rulers as having the status of sovereign monarchs, and second, the 'legitimate interests' of the non-Malays, which was to be an important factor later in terms of the economic role of the Chinese.

In 1957 inter-communal tensions were managed through a series of concessions on different sides. Basically the non-Malays conceded the 'special rights' of the Malays in return for the liberalization of citizenship rights.

> The agreement conceded actual and symbolic Malay political predominance and a commitment to special policies to improve the socioeconomic position of the Malays. In return, non-Malays were given citizenship, a degree of protection for their cultural rights and freedom to pursue their economic activities. In crude terms, the agreement could be described as a 'quid pro quo': the institutionalization of Malay political dominance in exchange for continuing relative Chinese economic predominance. This communal 'bargain' became a central tenet of the political system.
>
> (Barraclough 1988: 16)

These issues and principles formed the backdrop to the foundation of the Constitution in 1963. This not only contained provision for the rights and privileges of the Malays, but also covered areas such as the national language and religion, all of which were, and remain, sensitive issues to this day. In many ways, the Constitution symbolizes features of Malaysian society – it gives the appearance of compromise, national values, integration and a positive approach to achieving long term racial harmony. In reality though, it is a front covering underlying conflict and communal tensions which simmer beneath the surface. It is significant that many of the non-Malays today feel that elements of the constitution originally guaranteeing their rights are gradually being eroded.

MALAYSIA'S POLICIES FOR DEVELOPMENT (1957–90)

This overview of Malaysia's history illustrates the socio-cultural tensions that bear on the government's attempts to develop and modernize the nation today. In terms of its economic policy, the government has, since independence, followed a strategy of central planning as oppposed to free market capitalism, believing that leaving the economy to the forces of the free market would be detrimental to the Malays.

Between 1957 and 1970 the government focused on building up the nation's basic infrastructure and emphasized economic growth but did not pay sufficient attention to the underlying tensions between the communities. The subsequent outbreak of violent and bloody riots in 1969 brought those tensions to the fore and jolted the authorities into rethinking plans for the concept and development of Malaysia. John (1986: 36) points out that one of the basic problems at this time was how to redistribute the wealth of the nation so as to benefit all parties fairly.

In 1970 the New Economic Policy was introduced in an attempt to overcome the marked separation of the communities along economic and social lines. At this time 64 percent of the Malays were in poverty as opposed to 26 percent of the Chinese and 39 percent of the Indians. The NEP adopted a two-pronged strategy:

> The first prong is to reduce and eventually eradicate poverty, by raising income levels and increasing employment opportunities for all Malaysians irrespective of race. The second prong aims at accelerating the process of restructuring Malaysian society to correct economic imbalance, so as to reduce and eventually eliminate the identification of race with economic function'.
>
> (*Second Malaysia Plan 1971–1975*, Kuala Lumpur: Government Printer, 1971: 1; reproduced in Barraclough 1988: 60)

This second prong meant, in effect, that the Bumiputeras received special privileges, for example quota system opportunities in education, employment, investment, etc. The aim was to raise Bumiputera sense of entrepreneurship and involvement in modern sectors of the economy. In setting out these plans the government claimed it would ensure that no particular group would experience any loss or feel any sense of deprivation.

(*ibid.*)

The Prime Minister, Mahathir, has summed up how he has tried to continue in this objective since coming to power in 1981:

My strategy has been to create growth and then to distribute the extra a little unequally in order to advantage the have-nots. It is racial discrimination yes, but unlike most racial discrimination it is in favour of the under-privileged. It should be called affirmative action.

(*The Independent on Sunday*, October 1990)

There can be no doubt that in purely economic terms Malaysia has seen great success, experiencing extraordinary economic growth – an average of between 7 and 8 percent a year in the 1970s and still high despite a period of recession. The leading economic sector is manufacturing, followed by the agricultural and mining sectors. Today Malaysia is the world's largest exporter of palm oil, natural rubber, tropical timber and a leading exporter of cocoa beans and pepper. It is also the world's largest exporter of microchips. One important factor in this spectacular growth has been oil, discovered in the late 1960s. All this has led some commentators to suggest that Malaysia is well on the way to becoming a 'newly industrialised country' (*Financial Times Survey*, 28 August 1992).

However the NEP's aims of restructuring society, eradicating hard-core poverty and creating a more just, united and integrated society were not achieved. Although some Malays have obviously benefited from the quota system, the Bumiputeras are still over-represented in the agricultural sector. Poverty remains highly concentrated in rural areas. Whilst Bumiputera ownership of equity in the corporate sector had increased from 2.5 percent in 1970 to 20 percent in 1990, the government had not achieved its 30 percent target. (Government figures as quoted in *The Star*, June 1991.) Meanwhile the preferential treatment of the Malays continued to reinforce ethnic distinctions and a sense of injustice amongst other groups.

VISION 2020

In early 1991 Mahathir outlined his hopes for the development of Malaysia over the next thirty years, stating that he hoped it would be a 'fully developed nation' by 2020. This is now commonly referred to as 'Vision 2020'. While referring to hopes of a mature and ethical society imbued with religious and spiritual values, critics have stressed that the main emphasis within 'Vision 2020' is on economic criteria of development at the expense of social and moral considerations. A few months after this publication, the NEP (having expired in 1990) was replaced by the new five-year plan – the NDP (New Development Policy) – which reinforced the emphasis on the economic basis of development. The NDP contains the same basic strategy of eradicating poverty and restructuring society to correct economic and social imbalances through affirmative action, i.e. positive discrimination to the Malays on the basis of their Bumiputera status. The government continues to legitimize these policies with reference to national harmony and stability in the name of progress. In June 1991 Mahathir said in Parliament:

> There should be no fear or doubts in the minds of any ethnic group that they would lose. Malaysia is rich in resources and there is enough for everyone to gain from the process of development. But it must be emphasised that if the bumiputeras gained more than others, this is because they began with a lower baseline and more needs to be done for them to bring them up to the level of development of other Malaysians. Only by doing this can we be assured of political and social stability as well as national unity, a pre-requisite of progress.

Resistance to the government's development policies comes, predictably, from non-Malay groups. But a second voice of resistance comes from groups within the Malay Muslim community concerned about the implications of emulating Western models of economic success. Sensitive to this, the government has made efforts to resist those elements of Western capitalist culture perceived to be a threat to positive Malaysian values. For example in his 'Look East' policy Mahathir has been concerned to encourage Malaysians to follow the work ethic, discipline, loyalty and economic success of the Japanese and South Koreans.

THE ROLE OF ISLAM

At the same time the government has made it its priority to introduce Islamic values as a check on the negative secularist tendencies seen to be associated with Western societies.

> Although we desire the success comparable to the developed countries in the world, this does not mean that we are prepared to accept those indecent tendencies which have engulfed the advanced societies in the West. We must preserve our honourable values and religious belief. We do not want to forget our roots.
> (speech by Dr Mahathir at UMNO General Assembly in Kuala Lumpur,
> 30 November 1991)

Here the government is attempting to walk a middle path in trying to satisfy the more extremist demands of the Muslim community while at the same time not wishing to alarm the majority of moderate Muslims and the non-Muslim communities.

In terms of incorporating Islamic values into economic policy, the government stresses that it interprets the Islamic concept of development as allowing for the pursuit of economic growth along Western lines as long as traditional religious values are not abandoned.

Happiness of life depends partly on material wealth. But material wealth

305

does not ensure peace of mind and happiness in the next world. It is due to this that the Government emphasises the assimilation of Islamic values. Islamic values are values that are not extreme. Islamic values also take into account contemporary situations.

(ibid.)

Consistent with the policy of Islamization have been the setting up of projects such as an Islamic University and Islamic Bank, the promotion of Islamic prayers in Parliament, Islamic-style architecture in new government buildings and anti-drug and anti-corruption campaigns.

From within an Islamic perspective, however, some have suggested that this is too moderate an approach. Ghazali, for example, suggests that continued reference to Western development models means Malaysia and other Muslim countries have yet to realize true Islamic ideals and free themselves from secular colonial domination.

In view of these sorts of criticisms, many non-Muslims fear that the government's Islamization policy will go further, especially in view of the Islamic revival that started in Malaysia in the 1970s in line with other Muslim countries and continued during the 1980s. Islamic resurgence was especially prominent among the urban Malay youth, though its influence has spread to the wider Malay community. As well as promoting greater attention to ritual and religious observance, revivalists aim to extend the role of Islam in everyday life. They work through *dakwah* organizations devoted to raising the level of Islamic consciousness in the Muslim community and beyond. Barraclough (1988: 23) points out that for some years the government has been concerned about the political potential of dakwah groups and has increasingly attempted to control their activities. As well as promoting its own Islamic Dakwah Foundation it has, since 1985, assumed responsibility for all dakwah groups.

There have however been signs of the government bowing to the demand to incorporate Islamic principles into the wider affairs of the state. For example, while the *Syariah* (Islamic law) has not been formally extended to cover the non-Muslims and religious courts remain distinct from the civil system, groups such as the Malaysian Consultative Council of Buddhism, Christianity, Hinduism and Sikhism (MCCBCHS) have expressed concern that the authority of the Syariah may be extended in future and have recorded many examples of discrimination against the rights of non-Muslims.

These tensions illustrate the difficulty for the government in trying to build a nation under the conflicting demands of, on the one hand, the drive to develop the country along the lines of a modern industrialized economy and, on the other hand, to legitimize those policies through the incorporation of Islamic principles, while at the same time accommodating the interests of the non-Muslims.

We want a balance between material advancement and spiritual development for we do not want a society which has achieved progress but has lost direction. This balance is an important factor influencing our efforts

306

towards progress. We hope that in this way our society will not decay as those progressive societies in the West, in the East and in the Middle East ... Moderation and balance between this world and the next is required by Islam and we should not forget this.

(speech by Dr Mahathir at UMNO General Assembly in Kuala Lumpur, 30 November 1991)

In this context it is easy to see why religion – namely Islam – becomes the bone of contention dividing the nation along communal lines and, at certain points, the Malay community.

CIVIL RELIGION IN MALAYSIA

The picture presented so far is clearly one of tension at various levels within Malaysian society, both between and within the various ethnic communities. While some see the prospect of multi-cultural harmony without the barriers of race and religion as remote, it is an essential prerequisite of successful development that social stability and unity are promoted through an over-arching civil religion. To this end the government has sought to achieve a sense of national identity and culture that overrides racial differences without threatening the identity of its citizens.

Our hope for this new decade is not merely economic growth and political stability but more importantly to forge a united progressive and dynamic Malaysian nation.

(Department of National Unity 1990: editorial)

This is a written assurance that there will be no cultural domination in the country.

(Department of National Unity 1990: 45)

However the government's various efforts to invoke a sense of nationalism through civic rituals, a national language and constant rhetoric referring to inter-ethnic co-operation has had limited appeal. This is because, despite assurances of freedom of religion and cultural practice, Malay culture and the Islamic religion predominate within the national culture.

The problem of inculcating nationalist sentiments among Malaysia's disparate ethnic groups has been compounded by the official policy of Islamization. The emphasis on Islamic elements in Malaysia's national identity and the hostility of some Islamic groups to the very notion of nationalism, has caused a degree of tension in reconciling universal Islamic values with those of nationalism.

(Barraclough 1988: 59)

A key institution symbolizing this Malay predominance is the monarchy and the system of hereditary rulers referred to above. Following on from their historical position as cultural and religious leaders of the community, the constitution states that the king must be both Malay and Muslim. However, recent controversy surrounding their role and behaviour serve to illustrate the tensions between the forces of tradition and modernity within the Malay community. Earlier this year (1993) resentment towards the rulers' extravagance, corruption and interference in politics led to an amendment in the constitution removing their legal immunity. Although disagreement between the (Malay-dominated) government and the rulers is not unprecedented, these recent developments highlight how intra-ethnic conflict remains bound up in the complex web of race, religion and politics in Malaysia.

CONCLUSION

Although Malaysia has partially achieved its goal of economic restructuring and development, it faces an uphill struggle as it strives to become a fully industrialized nation by 2020. It attempts to emulate the capitalistic processes adopted by Western and Japanese models of advance while at the same time retaining a sense of loyalty to its cultural heritage. The government is, however, aware that too strict adherence to Islamic principles would not be conducive to foreign investment or to its burgeoning tourist industry. Meanwhile its efforts to appease the Islamic sentiments of the Malays must be moderated by consideration of the other ethnic communities whose co-operation is required if a peaceful environment conducive to growth is to be achieved.

It is unlikely that in this context Malaysia will become secularized in the near future – religion still operates as an important brake on the pursuit of secular Western values and the government is aware of those elements of Western culture such as the break-up of the family, divorce rates, drug abuse and immoral values which it associates with the relentless pursuit of progress unchecked. Thus the Prime Minister has keenly urged the people to preserve the social fabric in their efforts to achieve progress and development. The price of the reference to the Islamic religion as a source of legitimation, however, is the retention of strong elements of communal identity and a people who, beneath the facade of peace, harmony, stability and economic growth, groan silently about the limits of their society.

REFERENCES

Barraclough, S. (1988) *A Dictionary of Malaysian Politics*, Singapore: Heinemann Asia.
Blomstrom, M. and Hettne, B. (1984) *Development Theory in Transition*, London: Zed Books.
Comber, L. (1983) *13 May 1969: A Historical Survey of Sino-Malay Relations in West Malaysia*, Singapore: Graham Brash Ltd.
Department of National Unity, [Setangah Tahun Pertama] (1990) *Negara*, Kuala Lumpur.
Fisk, E.K. and Osman-Rani, H. (eds.) (1982) *The Political Economy of Malaysia*, Kuala Lumpur: Oxford University Press.

Ghazali, A. (1990) *Development: An Islamic Perspective*, Selangor: Pelanduk Publications.

Goh Keat Peng (1986) 'The Christian and race relations in Malaysia', in *The Christian and Race Relations in Malaysia*, Selangor: Graduate Christian Fellowship.

Hwa Yung, (1985) 'The foundation of Christian Values', in *Christian Values in Building a Malaysian Society*, Malaysia: National Evangelical Christian Fellowship.

Hwa Yung (1989) 'Freedom, Government and Economics': Paper presented at South-East Asian Regional Consultation of the Oxford Conference on Christian Faith and Economics, Manila, 22 July 1989.

John, K.J. (1986) 'National Unity: The goal of government policies', in *The Christian and Race Relations in Malaysia*, Selangor: Graduate Christian Fellowship.

Kua Kia Soong (1990) *An Alternative Malaysian Economic Policy*, Kuala Lumpur: The Resource and Research Centre, Selangor Chinese Assembly Hall.

Lee Kam Hing (1986) 'From communities to nation', in *The Christian and Race Relations in Malaysia*, Selangor: Graduate Christian Fellowship.

Malaysian Consultative Council of Buddhism, Christianity, Hinduism and Sikhism (1989) *'Why MCCBCHS Rejects the Application of Syariah on Non-Muslims'*.

Northcott, M. (1991) 'Christian–Muslim relations in West Malaysia', in *The Muslim World*, Hartford, CT: Hartford Seminary Foundation.

Selvendran, M. (1986) 'The Christian model for racial integration', in *The Christian and Race Relations in Malaysia*, Selangor: Graduate Christian Fellowship.

Snodgrass, D.R. (1980) *Inequality and Economic Development in Malaysia*, Kuala Lumpur: Oxford University Press.

Sudhir, A. (1983) *Inequality and Poverty in Malaysia*, New York: Oxford University Press.

Sundaram, J.K. and Cheek, A.S. (1988) 'The politics of Malaysia's Islamic resurgences', *Third World Quarterly* 10, 2.

Zakaria, A. (1987) *Government and Politics in Malaysia*, Oxford: Oxford University Press.

17

THE POST-DENG ERA AND THE FUTURE OF RELIGION IN CHINA

Julian F. Pas

> China's present political system is an all-embracing totalitarianism with a superficial veneer of Marxism which forms a "unified entity" in which the Party-State dominates all spheres of society, including the economy, the military, and the field of ideology and culture.
>
> (Su Shaozhi 1991: 15)

PRELIMINARY DISCUSSION

On 19 July 1991, the London *Times* front page carried a news story titled 'Half of China affected in worst floods since 1930s'. Not only was there a heavy loss of lives (1,700 people killed) and property (4.5 billion pounds in economic losses), but infectious diseases and starvation threatened millions.

Have the Chinese people made a connection between this enormous catastrophe and their present political regime as they did in 1976? In July of that year, an unusually violent earthquake virtually destroyed the city of Tangshan, killing half a million people. In September of that year, Mao Zedong died. The ancient belief that natural disasters are Heaven's warnings about misrule is still a part of the belief system of the Chinese people.

As a matter of fact, in several recent publications the event of Deng Xiaoping's death has already been discussed: what will happen in China after Deng leaves the stage? Will the spirit of democracy, 'bottled up', since June 1989, liberate itself and turn into a new revolution? Or will it be a peaceful transition with a change of mind among the new leadership? Certainly drastic changes can be expected, but so many unexpected world events have taken place since 1989, especially in Europe, that any prediction is extremely hazardous.

Since the frame of reference of this volume is 'Religion and the Resurgence of Capitalism' (implying the 'Collapse of Socialism'), one is placed in a strange paradoxical situation with regard to China. There was no socialism to begin with, and today there is no capitalism. There has been since 1949 a rigid state dictatorship, while political power rests in the hands of the Chinese Communist Party (CCP)[1] and the Government of the People's Republic of China (PRC). The

310

Communist ideal of 'Dictatorship of the Proletariat' is meaningless and should be renamed 'Dictatorship over the Proletariat'.[2] Power was in fact centralized in a small group of elder octogenarian statesmen and party members with supreme power at the top, once with Mao Zedong, now with Deng Xiaoping.

It has been said of Mao that he made the Chinese people 'stand up'; it could equally be said of Deng, that he made the people 'walk'. But both leaders, after their great achievements, shot the people in the legs and it may hurt them a long time.

If one looks at the positive side of Deng's achievements, one is struck by the significant economic and social changes without, however, significant political changes which took place in China between 1978 and 1984. There have been incredible changes, very much in opposition with the situation during the Mao period. Described as China's 'Second Revolution', they are, in fact, a dismantling of some basic Marxist institutions, such as the commune system. In its place came the introduction of the responsibility system, accompanied by a decrease in state control over production both in urban and rural areas. Further changes were greater freedom for people to start prospering, although at one time they had been thought impossible. Harry Harding, in his book titled after Deng's expression 'China's Second Revolution', calls them 'moderate' reforms (which is probably an understatement if one looks at the detailed description):

> In the realm of domestic economics, the moderate reforms have expanded opportunities for private and collective ownership in both agriculture and urban services, offered greater autonomy to enterprise managers, given economic incentives to both peasants and workers, and assigned market forces a greater role in the production, circulation, and pricing of commodities. The moderate reforms have decentralized the management of foreign trade, allowed foreign investment within restricted organizational formats, and established special economic zones along the coast of southeast China to attract export-processing enterprises from abroad. Finally, in the political sphere, moderate reform has been characterized by an explicit repudiation of the principal ideological tenets of the Maoist period, greater freedom and predictability in the daily lives of ordinary Chinese citizens, greater creative latitude in scientific and academic pursuits, and greater pragmatism, institutionalization, and consultativeness in national policy making.

(Harding 1987: 3)

These changes were summarized in a new campaign slogan the 'Four Modernizations', which relate to advances in science and technology, agriculture, industry, and the military.

Is this still socialism? Yes and no. As stated before, there never was true socialism in China. Although the changes can be interpreted as borrowings from a capitalist system,[3] yet basically China has remained a state dictatorship in which the state still owns the majority of the means of production and in which the leadership insists on considering itself a socialist regime, as the PRC's 1982 Constitution points out:

> *Article 1.* The PRC is a socialist state under the people's democratic dictatorship led by the working class and based on the alliance of workers and peasants.
>
> (Ching 1990: 167)

The expression 'the people's democratic dictatorship' certainly shows a discrepancy between name and reality, but Article 1 points out that China's leaders consider their country a 'socialist' state, whatever the contradictions may be between words and realities. The Tiananman Massacre has certainly brought home the evidence that the PRC's present regime is a totalitarian system, a party dictatorship, which has nothing to do with democracy. The demands for democratic reforms have been brutally suppressed ('political power grows out of the barrel of the gun!') and the government scored a temporary victory. But the movement is not dead; there are even predictions that within ten years, drastic reforms will occur in China from within.

The situation of religion in the PRC has certainly been influenced by the June 1989 events, but how exactly is not easy to determine. Information gradually comes in bits and pieces. Putting these pieces together and drawing some careful conclusions will be one of the objectives of this chapter. But since the present in China is intimately linked with the past, we must review, albeit briefly, the historic relationships between the Chinese government and religion. The past throws much needed light on current events and sets trends for the future. Throughout China's past, politics and religion have been always intimately linked in various ways. The present situation is perhaps only a variation of a permanent theme. The discussion will break up into four parts or four periods:

1 Religion and political rule during imperial times;
2 Religion during the Republic (1912–49) and during the Communist regime (phase one: 1949–77);
3 Religion during the Communist regime (phase two: 1978–88);
4 Religion after Tiananmen (1989–).

RELIGION AND POLITICAL RULE DURING IMPERIAL TIMES

Religion and politics, the spiritual and the temporal, are two powerful forces in any society. They are often hopelessly mixed up; or they are combined or opposed to each other. In many cases, their rivalry can be intense; but if they are combined in the same leaders, it may lead to fearful consequences: intolerance of disbelief, persecution of heresy, punishment of perceived moral evil, revenge for blasphemy, and so on are some examples of religious–political totalitarianism.

Religion and politics are like two swords; if not handled by one body, then they are at odds; the one trying to control the other. In China 'religion belongs to the domain of politics' (Joseph Spae, in Pas 1989: 3). In trying to keep their autonomy, Chinese religion in fact often turned out to be handling the short sword. Facing the threat of total control by the long sword, it had to be flexible and skilful in manoeuvring in order to survive.

Since ancient times, political rule was legitimized by divine mandate (*Tian-ming*). This was probably the creation of the early Zhou kings[4] (*c.* 1000 BC) who claimed that Heaven appoints rulers. Because of the seriousness of the Mandate, the political and the religious spheres were one: as rulers 'held total power over the organization of society and the universe, and space and time, it was not possible for religion in China to be an autonomous power' (Gernet 1985: 105). If religion was a political matter, politics was likewise a religious matter.

When the voluntary religions, Taoism and Buddhism, arose they tried to remain independent, but failed. At the end of the Han period, Taoist millennarian movements arose in Eastern and Western parts of China. They set themselves up as theocratic states with political, military, and religious authority all combined in the same leaders. The Eastern movement became rebellious; they were called the Yellow Turbans and fought government forces in AD 184. Once the leaders were captured and executed, the movement barely survived. But in Western China, a smaller Taoist state established itself and ruled parts of Sichuan and Shenxi from *c.* AD 180 till 210. The third Heavenly Master, Zhang Lu, submitted to government attacks and was consequently officially recognized. But Taoism had capitulated to the state and only remained semi-autonomous.

Buddhism did not succeed either in its bid for independence from the state. In India, communities of monks had been autonomous; monks were respected by kings and even young novices received the homage of kowtow from their own parents. In China, this was unthinkable. During the period of North–South division, Southern monks resisted the imperial expectation to bow to the rulers in the same way as officials did. For some time they could maintain their position and one monk in particular, Hui-yuan, made the Buddhist viewpoint very clear. Monks, he wrote in an AD 402 treatise, are not like ordinary laymen. They have left the worldly life and are beyond the laws of the country which affect other citizens, even Buddhist lay believers.[5] In Northern China, however, which was ruled by non-Chinese dynasties, the situation was different. Due to political instability and constant warfare, the Buddhist community sought protection from the state. They were able to obtain it at the price of independence. Northern Wei rulers appointed Buddhist monks as official supervisors of the whole Buddhist establishment in their realm, and as state officials, these monks had to bow to their rulers. This system was adopted by the Tang and from then on became law all during imperial times.

As Buddhism and Taoism began to emerge as powerful movements, the state of balance between them and the state became precarious. Although the situation changed with each dynasty and even with individual rulers, religion remained subject to state control. The state, on the one hand, supported religion for various reasons of its own; on the other hand, it never gave religion a totally free hand. The religious communities also tried to exploit their good relationships with the government to obtain various privileges. As I have stated elsewhere, four different types of using religion for political goals can be spotted:

Firstly, religion was frequently used to establish royal or imperial authority, divine sanction, or divine legitimation of power. The "Mandate of Heaven" invoked by the Duke of Chou is the most eloquent example, but the adoption of Confucianism by Han Emperor Wu in 136 BC may have had the same purpose. Confucianism believed in the heavenly appointment of rulers, and thus played into the hands of Emperor Wu and his later successors to the throne. The performance of the Feng and Shan sacrifices by Ch'in Shih-huang-ti and Han Wu Ti served a similar purpose. Even the claims of the T'ang emperors to be descendants of Lao-tzu can be seen as a variation of the same theme. Their claimed religious and biological connection with the Taoist sage boosted the imperial family's prestige and political authority.

Secondly, religion occasionally provided an expedient escape from political disaster, as when the Sung Emperor Chen-tsung claimed to have received divine revelations from the Jade Emperor. These revelations countered the loss of prestige incurred through his defeat in war against the Northern barbarians.

Thirdly, religious organizations, especially Taoism and Buddhism, were frequently supported by rulers in order to ensure the sympathy and the co-operation of the masses. During the period of disunity, most Northern dynasties supported Buddhism (K'ou Ch'ien-chih's Taoist experience during the Northern Wei was rather a short interlude). The Sui and T'ang emperors favoured Buddhism and/or Taoism, depending upon each emperor's predilection. Yet most of them did not totally favour just one religion for fear of antagonizing the people. The Yüan emperors favoured Lamaism, although Genghis Khan had been impressed by Taoism, and gave it extreme support; he hoped that in Taoism, he would find a method to reach longevity or immortality.

The political, or rather diplomatic, use of religion has also had its modern applications. The Japanese occupying Manchuria in the 1930s, appealed to the people to rally around Buddhism as a common religious faith to ensure their collaboration. Chiang Kaishek's New Life Movement can also be seen as a quasi-political manoeuvre to rally public support for his regime. And in modern times, it is common practice in Taiwan for candidates in an election campaign to visit temples and offer incense as one way to gain votes.

Fourthly, and lastly, many Chinese emperors from T'ang through Ming times have summoned prominent Buddhist or Taoist masters to their palaces to serve as counsellors or to lecture to the imperial household. As a result, there have also been many cases of religious interference in matters of state, sometimes, as in the case of Taoist priest Lin Ling-su during the Northern Sung, with disastrous results for the dynasty.

All these are different types of interaction between the imperial government and the religious establishment. Also, it is obvious that in most of these relationships, the rulers used or exploited religion for their own advantage. Cases of persecution or proscription have not been uncommon and show that if religion was perceived to be a danger to the state, the government did not have the least hesitation to suppress it.

(Pas 1989: 3–5)

Besides and beyond these practical techniques of handling religious institutions, the state had its own way of fulfilling its religious functions. Because of the ancient belief in Heaven's Mandate, emperors felt they had the duty to sacrifice to Heaven. Throughout Chinese history, yearly sacrifices were performed by the ruling emperor to Heaven in order to pray for a bountiful harvest. If there was no rain, there would be no grain, and the multitudes of people would be threatened with starvation. Sacrifice to Heaven was the unique prerogative of the emperor. Anyone who dared to imitate this sacred act, was considered a rebel, and his performance was punished as high treason. During the early republic, China's president, Yuan Shikai, reinstated the yearly sacrifice, just once on 23 December 1914, and his action was clearly understood by all as an attempt to start a new imperial dynasty. He did not, however, succeed.

Sharing this imperial spiritual duty with his government, provincial and local officials had to perform seasonal sacrifices to the many deities in their own jurisdiction: mountain and river gods, city gods and apotheosed heroes all received official sacrifices in spring and autumn. These were sacrifices of thanksgiving as well as prayers for divine blessings for the people. In this way the temporal and spiritual realms were joined together; the imperial government felt responsible for the total happiness of the people. This total happiness implied economic well-being, resulting from seasonal rains and bountiful harvests.

Buddhism and Taoism, did, however, still have a reason for existence: to fulfil the personal spiritual needs of individuals which were not satisfied through imperial and official performances. In later times, probably starting with the Song Dynasty, the popular religion began to emerge as an almost independent religious system and, like Buddhism and Taoism, was often seen by officialdom as competing with the government's sole claim to orthodox religion. State codes clearly define the limits of non-official religious institutions. The common people, at least in theory, were only entitled to venerate their own ancestors and to worship the local spirits of the soil (Overmyer 1989–90). Other types of worship were forbidden and suppressed, again in theory. In fact, local officials were not always able (or willing) to stop further cult developments, as long as Buddhism, Taoism, or the popular religion did not become secret societies, which often were breeding grounds for uprisings and rebellion. In these cases, the bureaucracy was ruthless

315

in their efforts to stamp out all dangers of plots, so much so that de Groot wrote a monograph about 'religious persecution' by the Chinese government (de Groot 1901). The Chinese authorities never forgot the Yellow Turbans.

Within this context of an absolutist, totalistic world view according to which religion and the secular state were seen as one, it was unthinkable that any religion could be exempt from state control. Buddhism and Taoism failed to assert their independence; later Christianity did not fare any better. The only exceptions, perhaps, are the minority peoples in China, such as Muslims and Tibetans. For them, religion is part and parcel of their culture. Yet even here, the state tries to control their religious practices, just as it controls political, social and economic aspects of these minority peoples. One can, however, predict situations of deep tension here.

It is also to be expected that any political system that succeeds the imperial legacy will also inherit the imperial ways of handling religion.

RELIGION DURING THE REPUBLIC (1912–49) AND DURING THE COMMUNIST REGIME (PHASE ONE: 1949–77)

The early period of republican China, ending with the foundation of the People's Republic, was a time of many upheavals. Political instability was perhaps its most striking characteristic: the early struggles to set up a democratic government, followed by the foundation of the CCP (1921) and the May Fourth Movement for greater cultural and political independence, then the bloody struggle complicated by the power bases of warlords throughout the 1920s and 1930s, are just starters. Then came the war of aggression by Japan, which ended in 1945 after the USA exploded two atomic bombs, forcing Japan to surrender. The final episode was the renewed struggle between Communist and Nationalist armies, ending in favour of Mao Zedung's People's Liberation Army in 1949, while Chiang Kai-shek sought refuge in the newly recovered island of Formosa, or Taiwan.

In such a turbulent period, religion was put on the back burner: each contending political or military entity had its hands full with more immediate concerns. However, since the final decades of the nineteenth century, there were many voices calling for reform and religion played its modest role. Kang Youwei (1898) pushed for drastic and immediate reforms, in which he wished Confucianism to become the state religion. But the reaction was strong. In fact, Confucianism had been rejected by many intellectuals as a stumbling block toward reform, and as the cause of the corruption of the Qing dynasty.

Meanwhile, Buddhism and Taoism continued their precarious existence. There were efforts toward revival (Welch 1968) but time was running out. Also, the Nationalist government had plans to 'clean up' the superstitions of the folk religion. Here also, time ran out. All through the first part of the twentieth century, Christianity deployed enormous energy to evangelize China: both Catholics and Protestants participated in the campaign. But they operated with a serious handicap:

the Chinese government had been forced – because of their defeat in the Opium Wars of 1842 and especially 1857–8 – to allow foreign missionaries to operate freely in China.[6] Whereas thousands of missionaries, priests, nuns, and laypeople poured into China and started to build their own version of a Christian Church, they did perhaps not realize the serious resentment working against them, especially on the side of the elite. Christianity was forced upon them and in such a climate of prejudice and contempt, the evangelization of China was very slow and minimal: the cross behind the gun does not create a congenial atmosphere to preach the gospel! Later on, Christian missionaries were seen as agents of imperialism.

With the 'liberation' of China in 1949, the liberators had an enormous task ahead of them: to rebuild the nation. The new government was Marxist. It was rather ironic that they chose a system of Western inspiration when the people's mood was rather anti-Western – but perhaps there were no alternatives?

Marxism is professedly atheistic. Although the rule of the CCP, using Marxism as its ideology, is a political, social, and economic regime, it has not *per se* any particular view on religion. But historically, it was atheistic, since Marx saw religion as the 'opiate of the masses': it puts people to sleep, makes them focus their hope and efforts on a happy reward in the afterlife, rather than making them fight for a better world here and now. That attitude gives the capitalist elite a better chance to perpetuate their exploitation and privileges.

If Marx predicted the sponataneous demise of religion, once the social economic conditions were improved and the various alienations rectified, there should be no need to fight or persecute religion. Yet, in fact, the Marxist government, mostly on the local level, did assist and try to speed up the natural process of its disappearance. The period from 1949 to 1977 does not present a uniform or consistent pattern in the CCP's handling of the religious situation. Their politics fluctuated according to personalities and/or various circumstances. Even before Mao's armies swept the whole country, they had already occupied parts of the north and, although they did not persecute religion outright, religious personnel were often harassed, placed under house arrest, and boycotted in their activities.

Once China was solidly in the hands of the CCP, there was perhaps a more unified plan in dealing with religion. In the new government's view, religion was not only a waste, a useless luxury remaining from the feudal and imperialist past, but it could also become an obstacle for national reconstruction. Yet freedom of religious belief was inscribed in the first Communist constitution and this right should be respected unless there were other factors involved. The Communist leaders did in fact find other reasons for opposing religion.

First of all, Christianity was a major target of oppression. Because of the political and military protection already mentioned, Christianity was linked with imperialism. As soon as China stood on its own feet, the foreign missionaries were accused of being agents of foreign power. Many were thrown into jail, tortured, brainwashed, and forced to write confessions of guilt.[7]

The years from 1949 to 1951 saw a mass exodus of foreign missionaries. The reason for this was the CCP's goal of 'purg[ing] imperialist influences from within Christianity' (Bush 1970: 42). The statistics are as follows (Bush 1970: 60–1):

1948	5,496 Catholic foreign missionaries (priests 3,046; brothers 414; sisters 1,036)
1951 (Jan)	3,222
1952 (Jan)	1,848 – all Protestant missionaries had left
1953 (Jan)	750
1954 (Jan)	250 (or less)
1955 (Jan)	90 (or less)
1956	16 priests and 11 sisters remain (13 priests in prison)

One of the primary goals of the Communist government was to 'liberate' Christianity: to cut off its connections with imperial patronage, or, in other words, to make it fully independent. The Catholic Church was the prime target: it had to break its relationships with the Vatican.

All these happenings and policies did not, in the eyes of the CCP, violate the constitutional freedom of religious belief, for religion was not allowed to serve other, anti-socialist purposes and must, on the contrary, co-operate fully with the state to rebuild the country. One can imagine how easy it was to make totally false accusations to get rid of embarrassing personalities!

The fate of the indigenous religions has been treated in several scholarly volumes and does not need to be repeated.[8] Since Buddhism and Islam had diplomatic importance, their treatment had to be more carefully orchestrated. Taoism and the popular religion, on the other hand, did not find much grace with the new rulers, since the constitution guaranteed only freedom of religious belief, not freedom of superstition.

> [Taoism] was regarded as a superstition without ethical foundations, a barrier to raising the cultural level of the masses, and a political danger because the secret societies associated with it had been the source of past revolts. Taoists had no fellow believers outside of China whose cultivation might prove helpful in diplomatic relations, as was the case with Buddhists and Muslims.
>
> (Bush 1970: 383)

Popular places of worship and age-old festivals were under constant threat of being eliminated or transformed. The New Year Celebration is now commonly called Spring Festival. The Qing Ming Festival, a day for sweeping the ancestral graves, was changed into a National Memorial Day, commemorating the revolutionary martyrs (Bush 1970: 410).[9]

Up to the year 1966, we witness a multiple approach toward the 'problem of religion' in communist China: outright persecution, harassment, pressure, subtle manipulation, and strategic educational methods are used to remove the potential 'subversive' danger of the various religions. On the other hand, the state also 'protects' the freedom of religious belief by supporting the foundation of various national organizations, such as the Buddhist Association of China, the Taoist Association of China, etc. However, these bodies will also become instruments of government control.

The ups and downs of Chinese religion in the pre-1966 period, have been called the 'good years'; what happened from 1966 to 1977 are the 'bad years' (Ching 1990: 127). It is more accurate to call them the 'bad years' and the 'very bad or awful years'. (The 'good years' more appropriately refer to the time of 1978–88.)

The 'Ten Years of Chaos' the so-called 'Cultural Revolution' were a frightening experience for the Chinese people. After it was all over, the party leaders admitted the serious mistakes made during this chaotic period, which had nothing to do with 'culture' except for its destruction by the mob-like armies of Red Guards. The idealism of the younger generation was used by Mao and his then heir-apparent, Lin Biao, in order to unleash a power struggle. In the process Mao eliminated his rival Liu Shaoqi, but realized he had unleashed a storm that went out of control. The slogan of destroying the 'four olds' (old culture, old ideas, old customs, old habits) had disastrous consequences for *all* aspects of religious culture. It is a matter of speculation whether statistics have been made of the loss of lives (religious personnel), the destruction and/or closure of temples, churches, and mosques, the destruction of religious artifacts, paraphernalia, libraries, statuary, etc. But many facts have become known since 1978 and they are alarming.

It is perhaps unfair to blame the CCP for all the evil committed against religion during this period. Their blame is to certainly have caused the first spark that turned into a conflagration, but some of the leaders must have regretted it. Premier Zhou Enlai made great personal efforts to save at least some of the famous monumental temples. But the overall impression is one of terror and sadness: possibly the worst example of iconoclasm in human history, which not only caused material damage, but also great loss of life, and permanent wounds in the hearts and souls of those who survived.

While the storm lasted, religious life seemed to have expired. But the Chinese people are resilient: as soon as a storm was over, they started to rebuild.

RELIGION DURING THE COMMUNIST REGIME (PHASE TWO: 1978–88)

As was already mentioned, the period after 1977 (after the 'Gang of Four' had been arrested), when Deng Xiaoping assumed supreme control of the government, was a time of great changes: drastic economic and social reforms, but timid political changes were accompanied by a revival of religion. This was indeed a 'turning of the tide' in many respects and the people's mood started to become more cheerful, since greater economic prosperity was the result of the government's switch toward modernization. While keeping the economic–political changes in the background, our focus here will be on the changes in the area of religion. Three questions will be answered: first, are the Chinese people today religious?; second, how do the government and the scholarly world look at the 'problem of religion?'; and third, what is happening to religion among the people, usually called the 'masses' in government documents?

First of all, are the Chinese people today religious? Various answers have been given. One scholar states: 'The people of China are indifferent to religion because Confucian ideology, with its emphasis on ethics, has long been dominant' (Luo Zhufeng 1987, trans. 1991: 30). On the positive side, 'At present, quite a large number of people in China believe in religion' (MacInnis 1989: 40). Another voice states, '. . . it is interesting that communist Chinese scholarship has assisted us in identifying the presence of religious beliefs and sentiments, as well as the survival of religious communities in mainland China' (Ching 1990: 125). Julia Ching concludes, 'that the Hindu civilization is much more religious in character than the Chinese. On the other hand, when one sees the temples and churches, and witnesses the fervour of individuals and communities in worship, one cannot but admit that religion is also alive in China' (Ching 1990: 126).[10]

Of course, the educational impact of forty years of Marxist indoctrination should not be minimized; neither should the CCP's explicit demand that party members cannot be religious believers. Moreover, while the constitution grants freedom of religious belief, it does not extend this freedom to the practice of superstition. Several articles published in 1964 clarify what superstition means; listed as such are 'fortune-telling, physiognomy, casting of horoscopes, geomancy, and even the worship of local Chinese deities like the earth god and the dragon king' (Bush 1970: 26). Other popular traditions such as temple-oracles, the burning of spirit-money, and the recourse to mediums for advice and the cure of diseases were equally stamped as superstitious. However, strict standards to discriminate religious belief from superstition are hard to formulate, which leaves a great amount of opportunistic discretion in the hands of the government executives.

It appears that religious traditions have been better preserved in the rural areas than in the cities. The city people in general show little interest in religious worship, even though temples and churches are filled during Sunday services. But that only represents a minimal proportion of the total population. Most people are more concerned about improving their material life than about spiritual matters, and would take refuge in religion only when their material goals are not achieved or threatened. Yet, in view of the CCP's great concern for religion, indicated by institutions such as the Religious Affairs Bureau under the control of State Council, and the attention given the existence of religion in some detailed published directives, one must assume that in the eyes of the CCP, religion is still a strong force in today's society.

How do the government and party and the scholars today handle what they call 'the problem of religion in the socialist era?'[11] First of all, they go by the constitution itself, which has always contained an item guaranteeing freedom of religious belief (first PRC constitution in 1954; 1975 and 1978 revisions; latest revision in 1982). Other clauses have changed each time; the 1982 version, in power today, is as follows:

> *Article 36.* Citizens of the People's Republic of China enjoy freedom of religious belief.
> No state organization, public organization, or individual may compel citizens to believe in, or not to believe in, any religion; nor may they discriminate against citizens who believe in, or do not believe in, any religion.
> The state protects normal religious activities. No one may make use of religion to engage in activities that disrupt public order, impair the health of citizens or interfere with the educational system of the state.
> Religious bodies and religious affairs are not subject to any foreign domination.
>
> *(Beijing Review*: 20, 25, 52; 27 December 1982)

Several phrases in this short article are subject to interpretation. To clarify the many aspects of religion in a socialist era, the CCP published a detailed document for the guidance of its party members. This *Document No. 19*, as it is called, contains twelve sections (in twenty-one pages of Chinese text) and has received quite some attention in English publications.[12]

One can view this document in several ways: with scepticism, even cynicism, or with appreciation for the Party's true concern for religion. The optimist may be touched by the Party's concern to protect the freedom of religious believers and to support the right religious activities. He may be impressed by the Party's admission of the great wrongs afflicted upon religion during the Ten Years of Chaos (MacInnis 1989: 12–13). The cynic, however, would think that behind the expressed concern for the freedom of religion, there hides an intention to control religion more strictly than before. Besides, the document still maintains the basic Marxist belief that religion will disappear eventually. One could wonder why the official party line did not admit that Marx could have been wrong here as well as in some economic matters.

The document is, in fact, a two-sided sword: both protection and control of religion are emphasized. Religious believers are free to practise religion, but should co-operate with the socialist goals of modernization. They should not use religion as a pretext for sabotage or for imperialist purposes. One commentator views this new toleration of religious activities as 'aimed at placating the West and persuading Western countries to provide more aid to the modernization drive'. He adds the statement of a Taiwanese clergyman who believes this attitude of tolerance is 'to curry favour with the West, especially the United States' (Wang 1991: 126).

This latter statement points to an important recurring theme: the diplomatic value of religion. It was said earlier that during phase one after 1949, Buddhism and Islam were most favoured because of their diplomatic importance. Since 1978 the situation in China has changed, and the drive toward modernization needed a great influx of foreign investment. However, in a climate in which human rights are frequently violated, Western investors would not be inclined to assist an oppressive system. Therefore, it makes sense to say that Christianity was specially favoured to impress Western nations, which are perceived as followers of Christianity.

There is, however, one caution: in Chinese, there is no special term for 'Christianity': there are two terms, one – *Tianzhujiao* (teaching of God) or Roman Catholicism, and one – *Jidujiao* (teaching of Jesus) or Protestantism. In the eyes of most Chinese, these are two different religions. Therefore, when using the argument of diplomacy, one must be careful not to identify the two. It is quite possible that the Chinese view North America and the United Kingdom as dominantly *Jidujiao* (Protestant), while they view parts of Europe, Latin America, and especially the Vatican, as *Tianzhujiao*. It is to be expected that control of the religion identified with the Vatican is under stricter control than the Protestant churches. Of course, these hypotheses have to be verified if possible by factual evidence.

Among the Chinese scholars, one still finds an attitude of caution. As Jan Yün-hua said: 'The discussion of the place and the future of religion in a socialist society is a new development . . . ' (Jan Yün-hua, in Pas 1989: 39). The scholarly world admits that the study of religion has been affected by 'Leftism' in the past and that new approaches should be followed. Yet, the trauma of previous persecutions because of 'Rightism', and the deep wounds inflicted during the Ten Years of Chaos, have made scholars cautious. Academic freedom in the study of religion is still very weak. If one also considers the many years of isolation from the West, and more practically, the high prices of Western books for Chinese library budgets, and the inability of many scholars to read in Western languages, one can understand that Chinese scholarship in religious studies has lagged behind. Some Western scholars mention 'Chinese intellectual isolationism',[13] or complain that ' . . . Chinese scholars specializing in religion do not seem equipped yet, neither from methodological nor ideological viewpoints, to do justice to the spontaneous and exuberant renaissance of the traditional religions'.[14] Or they observe that even high ranking Chinese scholars 'when discussing the religious traditions of their own culture, do not refer to any Chinese voice, past or present, but exclusively to the foreigners Marx, Engels, and Feuerbach'.[15]

In order to obtain a correct understanding of how Marxist ideas (and party pressure) affect the quality of research, a broader study of modern publications on Chinese religions is necessary. One case study, however, is significant: a volume of articles published by a group of Chinese researchers and considered important enough to have it translated into English (Luo Zhufeng 1987, trans. 1991). The Afterword is symptomatic of the mentality of the researchers:

> Our basic methods for pursuing this research were to study and use Marxism, combine theory with practice, take reality as our starting point, and seek truth from facts. For three years, in numerous cities and villages, we carried

on broadscale field research, with guidance and support from party and government units in each locality (especially United Front and Religious Affairs work units), and received concern and help from each of the patriotic religious organizations.

(Luo 1987 and MacInnis 1991: 243)

Such an attitude does not leave much of a chance for the exercise of academic freedom, and unfortunately, it leaves its mark on important aspects of interpretation. A few examples will show this eloquently: 'The reactionary ruling class controlled and made use of religion' (ibid. 1991: 38).[16] The entire chapters 2 and 3 of the same volume mix up historical data with Marxist clichés and are unworthy of scholarly objectivity. Two examples: 'Christianity, both Protestant and Catholic, has been freed [in 1949] from the domination of colonialism and imperialism and is now run by Chinese religious believers themselves' (ibid.: 55). Likewise, 'Buddhism, Taoism, and Islam have freed themselves from being used and controlled by the domestic reactionary classes' (ibid.: 64). Such generalizations are suspiciously coloured by prejudice, even if the statements contain a partial truth.

The third question is about what is happening to religion among the people, leaving aside the question of the percentage of Chinese people who are believers (and not taking into account the post-1989 period).

There is no complete study available about the resurgence of religion during the period of liberalization 1978–88. But freedom of religious belief was reaffirmed by the constitution of 1982 and in party documents, and since 1978, there has been observed a modest revival of all religious bodies. Several authors have described their own partial observations.

Buildings for religious worship have been reopened, restored, even totally reconstructed. In many temples where the statuary had been destroyed, new images have been created. Some temples and churches, confiscated between 1966 and 1977 and used for secular or party purposes have been returned to the religious bodies who had owned them. In all these activities there was much co-operation between the individual associations (such as BAC, TAC, IAC, etc.) and the Religious Affairs Bureau, since without government assistance, these goals could not have been achieved.

But popular worship has also returned, and if not worship, at least visits to temples and other religious buildings have increased.

In the countryside, religious traditions have been revived: the resurgence of door-spirits (men-shen) during the Spring Festival has been noticed (Pas 1989: 175–80); there has been a return of magic charms (ibid: 181–2), but more importantly, religious rituals and festivals have been revived. Examples are the reinstatement of the Confucian birthday ritual in Qufu (Swart and Till in Pas 1989: 210–21); the celebration of the cosmic or community renewal festival (jiao), (Dean 1986: 191–209; Dean 1989: 51–78); the revival of funerals in Fujian province (Dean 1988: 19–77); the revitalization of Buddhist and Taoist monastic life (Jan Yün-hua 1984: 37–64; Sponberg 1984: 65–76; Powell 1984: 77–87; Hahn 1986: 211–17; Hahn 1989: 79–101). All these signs of renewal indicate that religious life is not extinct; moreover, the training of young personnel is of great concern for all religions in China; after forty years of disruption, the continuity of spiritual leadership was threatened and the revival of religion came in the nick of time. Even now there is a significant gap between the old and the new generation and continuity is still uncertain.

It has also been noticed that superstitious practices are on the upswing, once again, in rural areas more than in the cities. A recent research article[17] is a good sample of modern ideas and practices. Cited are cases of a return to old superstitions such as shamanism, in which talismans are used for curing disease (pp. 283–4). Results of an opinion poll indicate that only about 14 percent of the population believe in 'ghosts' and 'spirits', and that approximately 17 percent believe in the spiritual efficacy of temple oracles and fortune-telling. Whereas 84 percent of the population would consult a medical doctor in case of illness, 13 percent combine consultation with recourse to a shaman (or medium) (pp. 284–5). Belief in geomancy has not completely disappeared either: 7.5 percent of the people interviewed attribute illness to unfavourable geomantic influences (p. 285).

These are only a few glimpses of what is officially stamped as superstition. Much more information is needed, but an indirect indication of the comeback of superstition and its perceived dangers, can be found in a recent government campaign, mentioned by A. Seidel: it is a campaign against 'six evils', 'a campaign aimed at rooting out prostitution, pornography, drugs, gambling, the abduction of women and . . . "feudal superstitions"'.[18] Seidel justly observes that 'the confusion of some forms of Taoism (e.g. Cheng-i) with popular religion still lurks in the minds of the PRC officials. They are all indiscriminately labelled "feudal superstitions"'.[19] Mentioning this recent campaign brings us to the latest period to be considered: 1989 and beyond.

RELIGION AFTER TIANANMEN (1989–)

The contrast between the name 'Tiananmen Square' (The Gate of Heavenly Peace Square) and the events of June 1989 is very disturbing. The violent oppression of the pro-democracy demonstrations clearly indicated that the present Chinese government is anything but democratic. It showed that the leadership was scared and unwilling to give up power. The subsequent events in the USSR and in Eastern Europe must worry the CCP government even more. It can be presumed that they will entrench themselves in their barricades until the demise of Deng Xiaoping. What will happen then is unpredictable. For the time being, China painfully tries to build up once again its reputation and its relationship with the rest of the world.

In this 'post-socialist' era[20] (except for China, North Korea and Cuba), what are the chances for the CCP to survive? The people of China have obviously lost their trust in communism and in the CCP.[21] Does the party still hold the mandate?

If political power is only based on guns and tanks, it is doomed to collapse. What has happened in Europe, after the Tiananmen incident (and probably influenced by it), must give the Chinese people renewed hope and courage. But leaving once again speculation about the political aspects aside, we must focus on the consequences of the June 1989 events for religious culture. Information is slow to come in, but from scattered glimpses, one is able to form a fairly clear opinion.

The basic right of freedom of religious belief has not been abrogated. But is this just theory or is it true freedom? It seems that there has been a tightening of control on religion. Indeed, the party leaders are aware that adherents from all religious affiliations have either actively participated in the 1989 demonstrations or have supported it.

Moreover, the CCP is aware of Christian influences at work in the collapse of East-European Communism. They must, as a result, be very alert about the possibility of similar happenings in China. After the collapse of the Communist regimes in Europe, Christianity made increasing demands: Hungary and Poland introduced religious instruction in their school systems. 'Even in the Soviet Union, incredibly, there are now voices demanding the re-introduction of religion in the public schools – based on the claim that there can be no proper basis for morality without a religious framework' (Kurtz 1990–1: 24). Although education and government are two different enterprises in China, education is firmly under control of the Party. Within the present regime, it would be unthinkable to demand that the school curriculum include religious instruction.

The government's and Party's concerns for religion can be inferred from several recent activities. First, on 30 January 1991, Jiang Zemin, General Secretary of the CCP Central Committee, invited five leaders of China's religious organizations as his guests in Zhongnanhai. This seems to have been a shrewd diplomatic manoeuvre: to ensure the religious leaders' allegiance and support for the government in this period of great doubt and insecurity. Jiang expressed his hopes for support using the so often repeated party clichés:

> In religious work, we must unswervingly implement the policy of free religious belief, preserve the stability and continuity of the policy, and unite the many personages in religious circles and the broad masses of religious followers, so as to maintain social stability in our country and work together to accomplish economic development . . .

> . . . on the part of religious circles, they should firmly support the CCP leadership, support socialism, uphold the principle of an independently established church and insist on carrying out religious activities within the scope stipulated by the Constitution, laws, regulations, and policies.
>
> (*China Study Journal* 6, April 1991: 25–6).[22]

Is that not begging for the support of religion in the government's present state of uncertainty?

A second example. On 5 December 1990, Premier Li Peng (who together with

Deng Xiaoping was responsible for the gunning down of the students in June 1989), addressed a national conference on religious affairs in Beijing saying that the 'proper handling of religious affairs is significant to stability, unity, national reunification, and the fulfilment of goals set forth in . . . 1990 . . . in addition to safeguarding world peace' (*China Study Journal* 6, April 1991: 26).[23] In the same address, Li Peng added some notes about the progress achieved under the Party's protection: ' . . . about 2,000 national and regional affiliations and organizations have been restored or established. Currently about 40,000 temples, monasteries, mosques, and churches across the country are open to the public' (*ibid.*).[24]

In the third place, it appears that provincial governments and the provincial Religious Affairs Bureaus (RAB) have been given more autonomy to regulate religious activities within their own territories. This can be interpreted in different ways, either as an indication of a general policy to grant more independence to the provinces, or as a skilful way to control religion more effectively. As an example of provincial legislation concerning religion, there is a document issued by the Religious Affairs Bureau of Kunming (Yunnan Province) in August 1990,[25] entitled 'Provisional Regulations Concerning Places of Religious Activities in Kunming'. A preliminary editorial remark says that *China Heute* has already published a similar document issued by Xinjiang Province. The purpose of these provincial regulations is to adapt the central policies to the local circumstances, but it does not indicate a more liberal religious policy. The editor also states that, with regard to the Catholic Church, one can see this document as an attempt to outlaw even more strictly the underground church. In the preface to the document, issued by the city government of Kunming, there is a clause that resolves all doubts: the purpose of the document is ' . . . to sharpen the government's control over places of religious worship' (*ibid.*: 65). Some other details are interesting: 'only officially approved and registered religious personnel are entitled to exercise religious activities . . . ' (*ibid.*: 67, art. 23). As religious personnel are listed: 'Buddhist monks and nuns; Taoist priests and nuns; Muslim imams; Catholic bishops, priests and nuns; Protestant preachers, catechists; and those who exercise religion as their profession who have been approved by the Patriotic Association . . . and have been registered in the lists of the RAB' (*ibid.*: 67, art. 15).

However, Kunming was not the first province to formulate religious legislation: it appears that the Guangdong provincial RAB published a set of 'Regulations on the Administrative Management of Religious Venues in Guangdong Province' in March 1988.[26]

Following the example of the national leaders, provincial governments have also started to invite religious leaders for discussion meetings. The Shandong party secretary addressed religious leaders on 11 February 1991; in Xinjiang on 12 February 1991; in Liaoning a religious work conference was held on 3 March 1991.[27] An interesting sample of party 'diplomacy' is found in the address of the party secretary at the Fuzhou meeting (Fujian):

The religious personages in our province have always carried on their fine tradition of patriotism, solidarity and innovation . . . Especially, during the June 4 turmoil [another euphemism!] of 1989, the religious circle and various religious colleges of our province, together with the people of the whole province, withstood a grave test. Practice has attested that the broad masses of religious personages in our province are our party's friends who can be fully trusted.

(*China Study Journal* 6, April 1991: 30)

Legislating religion in China is not an easy matter; it has too many complications. One angle of the problem is the multiplicity of religions. In official documents, some of which we have quoted, there is a standard order of listing the officially recognized religions: Buddhism, Taoism, Islam, Roman Catholicism, Protestantism.[28] The same order is implied when documents mention religious buildings: temples, monasteries, mosques, churches. Today's government has to balance various forces at work in the area of religion: some religions have overtones of nationalism (in the sense of minority populations), such as the Muslims and the Tibetan Buddhists; other religions, the two Christian denominations, have an importance internationally. Even if the Chinese leaders insist that the churches must be totally independent from foreign intervention, they would not curtail their basic freedom too much. Christianity today has become diplomatically useful.

The leadership has also come to the realization that religion in China is there to stay, at least for a long time. 'Reasons for the persistence of religion' during this growing stage of socialism are carefully discussed in scholarly works.[29] One lesson the party has learned is that to persecute religion is counter-productive. The alternative is two-fold: legislate religion so as to control it. The party has been successful in following this policy, but one can never be absolutely certain that it will work. The other alternative is to find a substitute for religion. There has been a period when 'Maoism' became a surrogate religion (1966–9 especially) but it did not last. In a more recent period, the government made efforts to create a 'spiritual civilization'. The Chinese term *jingshen* for 'spiritual' is misleading and has no connection with a religious world view. This campaign seems to be doomed to failure: its goal is to establish a socialist foundation for morality, but when the people are confronted with the lack of morality in their own leaders (political oppression, privileges, corruption, etc.), how can their words be effective?

Are there other alternatives? The multiplicity of religions in China is somehow an obstacle. It seems that there is no winner, one religion which could unify the majority. Buddhism and Taoism have become active again, but do not attract great numbers. (Recruitment is also heavily controlled by government regulations.) Islam is not a religion of the Han people and is not likely to become so, although in past centuries Muslims in Asia have won (converted) significant segments of populations.

What about Christianity? Again, for the Chinese people, Roman Catholicism and Protestantism are two separate groups, not one single entity. If they were united into one body, their attraction would be much greater. Even so, Christianity has become a focus of interest since Tiananmen. One author, Zhou Derong, suggests that there is in China a 'Christian fever'; he even speaks of a 'renaissance of Christianity'. Quoting a *China Spring* (1990/9: 92–4)[30] article by Zheng Hanyi, he quotes the title: 'The Christian Renaissance on the Chinese Mainland. An astonishing phenomenon in most recent Chinese history: ten thousands of intellectuals and young students give up Marxism–Leninism and turn to Christianity' (Zhou Derong 1991: 76). Further on he says: 'Unfortunately Marxism has not helped China. After seventy years we are still facing the same problems, even worse perhaps: a dictatorial system and technological and economic backwardness. In some heads the idea plays around whether perhaps Christianity could help us. They plead for a Christianization of China' (*ibid.*: 77).

Christianity, as the religious background of the West, is seen as conducive to democracy and to respect for the individual. Moreover, it has gained extra points (in Chinese eyes) for its contribution to the collapse of socialism in Eastern Europe. In the absence of any other compelling world view which includes spiritual values, Christianity may have a chance in the near future.

One possible alternative is humanism. Confucianism, once freed from the historical paraphernalia of elitism and class privileges, could become attractive again as a world view. In fact, the Confucian emphasis on ethics, which has influenced many generations of people, is probably still an (unconscious) part of the Chinese ethical sense. Is there no way that it could be revitalized?

One final alternative is the people's recourse to physical exercises, such as *taiqichuan* and *qigong*. The latter has known a great revival since Tiananmen, and one author speculates on this phenomenon and interprets it as a silent popular protest against government tyranny. *Qigong* has been popular for several decennia already and modern authors try to divest it of its religious background, but that is perhaps not what the people take it for:

> What emerges on the cultural level is an alternative ideological value system. Its strength is in its ability to coexist without directly contradicting official dogmas and in its roots in supportable folk-science tradition. Beneath the surface, belief in a "higher realm" shelters and thrives.
>
> (Kelly 1992: 17)

CONCLUSION

With the downfall of Communism in Europe, sooner or later China will be affected. Economic improvements and social changes in the period 1978–88 awakened the need for political reforms. But the CCP and government are so far unwilling to give up their power. Yet the people will overcome. The political system must change and the advent of a new (Post-Deng) era will be accompanied by a greater valorization of spiritual values.

One final observation needs to be made: after re-reading my chapter I cannot escape the impression that I have painted a gloomy and almost cynical picture of the religious scene in contemporary China. But is there any other way to do it? Should one rejoice in the CCP's tolerance *vis-à-vis* the religious experience? Their tolerance must be taken for what it really is: expediency. And this tolerance is in fact another, more subtle kind of enslavement. A bird in a cage is free to move about . . . somehow. If it is put in a larger cage, it can move about even more. But is that still freedom?

In view of what has happened in China during the Communist regime, I can better understand why de Groot wrote his book on *Sectarianism and Religious Persecution in China*. Some scholars have wondered why de Groot would have done that; it seems to be a complete reversal of his sympathetic attitude in previous publications. But if one considers that he published this book in 1901, a year after the Boxer Rebellion during which many Western missionaries and Chinese Christians had been tortured and killed, one can appreciate his change of mind. Although de Groot was not a missionary and was a non-believer, he still must have felt hurt at the indignities to which European missionaries were subjected. It is a matter of human rights violated by a violent crowd. That would explain why the book was dedicated 'to all missionaries of every Christian creed labouring in China'.

As I write my conclusion, I also have a feeling of uneasiness and inadequacy, almost of shame. Scholars do their research in libraries and write in the safety and comfort of their home study. We are so far away from the live stage where the various acts are performed. The people involved suffer and we try to explain their suffering and pain from a safe distance. Our analyses perhaps satisfy our thirst for knowledge and information, but do they contribute to alleviate the pain of those who are pressured and persecuted?

NOTES

1 The 1985 party membership was estimated to be forty-two million, which is less than 4 percent of the total population. I am indebted to my colleague, Man-Kam Leung for this and other relevant information and for his many suggestions and corrections.

2 I believe that if Confucius would return to China today, one of the first tasks he would undertake would be the 'rectification of names'. Indeed, the CCP has a weird sense of language; one cannot call it 'euphemism' any more for it is rather a perverse use of terminology. Examples are 'The Great Proletarian Cultural Revolution', which had nothing to do with culture except for its destruction and should be renamed 'Ten Years of Chaos'; the 'People's Liberation Army' is another abuse of language, especially if one remembers how the army 'liberated' the Tiananmen Square in Beijing in June 1989.

3 From Harding (1987: 128):

Confronted with changes such as these, some observers have concluded that China has abandoned socialism to follow a capitalist course. Writing in the *New York Times* at the end of 1984, for example, William Safire declared that the "biggest event" of the past year had been the "embrace of capitalism" by the CCP. In a similar vein, *Business Week* published a cover story on the Chinese economic reforms entitled "Capitalism in China". Others, unwilling to jump to extreme conclusions, have suggested that China is engaged in an experiment with market socialism.

4 It is very likely that a similar concept of divine legitimation of power already existed during the Shang Dynasty. The title of Shang-ti, Supreme Lord, or Lord-on-High, may have been the elaboration of 'First Ancestor' (of the ruling house) into a Supreme Being needed when the Shang area had been expanded and a new symbol of divine authority was felt to be necessary.

5 See E. Zürcher (1959: 231–9).

6 The Anglo-Chinese Tianjin treaty, signed on 26 June 1858, contained six main provisions. The third was: 'Freedom of travel and missionary activity' (McAleavy 1968: 94). In 1860 some additions were made including that priests were allowed to buy land and build churches in every province (*ibid.*: 99).

7 There is an extensive bibliography concerning this aspect of early CCP rule: witness reports of missionaries expelled from China, mostly on trumped-up charges. In recent times, there is a great scholarly effort going on to identify and study archives of missionary societies, especially in North America. A useful resource book is that by Richard Bush (1970), which covers the first twenty years of Communist rule.

8 For Buddhism, see Welch (1972); for Confucianism and the status of Confucius, see Louie Kam (1980); for all three, including Taoism, see Bush (1970); moreover for Islam, see also Bush (1970).

9 The trend to invest old customs and festivals in China with new meaning is not a unique phenomenon. The Christian Church in Europe had made similar adaptations centuries before, transforming pagan festivals into more appropriate Christian celebrations.

10 One is easily reminded of C.K. Yang's conclusion about the same question a generation ago: 'The temples and shrines dotting the entire landscape were a visible indication of the strong and pervasive influence of religion in Chinese society, for they stood as symbols of a social reality' (Yang 1961: 6).

11 The Chinese expression *zongjiao wenti* can be translated in two different ways: 'the religious question' ('religious questions') or 'the problem of religion'. In this context, the latter translation is more accurate.

12 For a discussion and some highlights, see Pas (1989: 7–12); a complete translation is found in MacInnis (1989: 10–26); and for a summary plus comments on the twelve sections, see Wang (1991: 122–6).

13 D. Overmyer (1988) in a book review of Yu Song-qing, *Ming Qing bai-lian jiao yan-jiu* [A Study of Ming and Qing White Lotus Sects], *Cahiers d'Extrême-Asie* 4: 247.

14 J. Lagerwey (1988) in 'Point de Vue', *Cahiers d'Extrême-Asie* 4: 189.

15 A. Seidel, also in 'Point de Vue', *ibid.*: 189.

16 The author seems to forget that the CCP, since liberation, controlled religion even more strictly than any previous Chinese administration.

17 Mi Youlu and Chen Shi (1989) *Zhongguo nongcun jiating de bianqian* [The Transformation of the Chinese Rural Family], Beijing: Nongcun duwu. See ch. 13: 'The revival of religious culture', pp. 276–305. I am indebted to my colleague, Professor Man-Kam Leung, for bringing this to my attention.

18 Seidel (1989–90) in *Cahiers d'Extrême-Asie* 5: 286. She refers to *Japan Times*, 22 February and 18 July 1990.

19 *ibid.*: 285.

20 'Red is Dead' is printed in large letters on the cover of *Macleans* magazine (2 September 1991), and a cartoon from Taiwan shows two large tombstones with 'Marx' engraved on the surface and 'USSR' and 'Eastern Europe' on the sides. In the

back, the bust of Marx is still standing firm on a stone socket with two Chinese leaders, holding desperately on to the base, but with desperation on their faces, almost sinking in the abyss (*Free China Journal*, 5 July 1991).

21 'What was less frequently reported until recently was the degeneration of the Rural Party: the depletion of potential leaders, . . . the failure to recruit new members . . . More than anything else, this is the most ominous sign that the CCP is facing the loss [of] its last bastion of support, the rural population' (*China Review* 3, 16).

22 This is based on *Xinhua*, Beijing (Chinese text), 30 January 1991.

23 Such a talk reminds me of a Flemish proverb: 'When the fox preaches the passion, farmers, watch your geese!'

24 The number 40,000 means a significant increase as compared with the figure of 30,000, quoted in Document 19 (Luo Zhufeng 1987, trans. 1991: 17).

25 For the text of this document, translated from Chinese into German, see *China Heute* 10 (1991), 3: 65–8.

26 See *China Study Journal* 6 (1991), 1: 28.

27 *China Study Journal* 6 (1991), 1: 29–34.

28 It is interesting that Buddhism is listed first, above Taoism, which is a native tradition. In imperial times, Buddhism was usually downgraded as foreign, unsuited to Chinese culture. Obviously Confucianism is not even considered to be a religion.

29 See Luo Zhufeng (1987, trans. 1991: 85–112).

30 A journal published by the Chinese opposition party in exile in the USA.

REFERENCES

Ahern, E.M. (1981) *Chinese Ritual and Politics*, Cambridge, London & New York: Cambridge University Press.

Büro für religiöse Angelegenheiten (1991) 'Vorläufige Bestimmungen für Stätten religiöser Aktivitäten in Kunming' [Temporary Regulations Concerning Places of Religious Activity in Kunming], *China Heute*, 10, 3: 65–8.

Bush, R.C., Jr (1970) *Religion in Communist China*, Nashville & New York: Abingdon Press.

Ching, J. (1990) *Probing China's Soul. Religion, Politics, and Protest in the People's Republic*, San Francisco & New York: Harper & Row.

Dean, K. (1986) 'Field notes on two Taoist *Jiao* observed in Zhangzhou, December 1985', *Cahiers d'Extrême-Asie* 2: 191–209.

Dean, K. (1988) 'Funerals in Fujian', *Cahiers d'Extrême-Asie* 4: 19–78.

Dean, K. (1989) 'Revival of religious practices in Fujian: a case study', in J. Pas, (ed.) *Turning of the Tide. Religion in China Today*, Hong Kong: Hong Kong Branch of the Royal Asiatic Society in association with Hong Kong Oxford University Press.

de Groot, J.J.M. (1901) *Sectarianism and Religious Persecution in China*, Taipei: Ch'eng-wen (reprinted 1976).

Gernet, J. (1985) 'Religion and politics', in *China and the Christian Impact*, trans. J. Lloyd, Cambridge: Cambridge University Press, pp. 105–40.

Hahn, T. (1986) 'Fieldwork in Daoist studies in the People's Republic', *Cahiers d'Extrême-Asie* 2: 211–17.

Hahn, T. (1989) 'New developments concerning Buddhist and Taoist monasteries', in J. Pas (ed.) *Turning of the Tide. Religion in China Today*, Hong Kong: Hong Kong Branch of the Royal Asiatic Society in association with Hong Kong Oxford University Press, pp. 79–101.

Harding, H. (1987) *China's Second Revolution. Reform After Mao*, Washington, DC: The Brookings Institution.

Jan Yün-hua (1984) 'The religious situation and the studies of Buddhism and Taoism in

China: an incomplete and imbalanced picture', *Journal of Chinese Religions* 12: 37–64.

Kelly, D. (1992) 'Representative culture: official and unofficial values in tension', in *China Review 1991*, Hong Kong, pp. 1–26.

Kurtz, P. (1990–1) 'Europe '92: secularization and religion in conflict', *Free Inquiry* 11, 1: 23–8.

Louie, Kam (1980) *Critique of Confucius in Contemporary China*, Hong Kong: Chinese University of Hong Kong & New York: St Martin's Press.

Luo Zhufeng (ed.) (1987) *Zhongguo shehui zhuyi shigi de zongjiao wenti*, Shanghai: Shehui kexue yuan, trans. D. MacInnis and Zheng Xi'an (1991) *Religion Under Socialism in China*, New York & London: M.E. Sharpe.

MacInnis, D. (1972) *Religious Policy and Practice in Communist China*, New York: Macmillan Co.

MacInnis, D. (1989) *Religion in China Today. Policy and Practice*, Maryknoll, NY: Orbis Books.

McAleavy, H. (1968) *The Modern History of China*, London: Weidenfeld & Nicolson.

Mitrokhin, L.W. (1990–1) 'Religion and secularization under Perestroika in the USSR', *Free Inquiry* 11, 1: 38–42.

Overmyer, D.L. (1989–90) 'Attitudes toward popular religion in ritual texts of the Chinese State: *The Collected Statutes of the Great Ming*'. *Cahiers d'Extrême-Asie* 5: 191–221.

Pas, J. (ed.) (1989) *The Turning of the Tide. Religion in China Today*, Hong Kong: Hong Kong Branch of the Royal Asiatic Society in association with Hong Kong Oxford University Press.

Powell, W. (1984) 'More laughter at Tiger Creek: impressions of Buddhism in modern China', *JCR* 12: 77–87.

Shambaugh, D. (1991) 'China in 1990. The year of damage control', *Asian Survey* 31 (January): 36–49.

Sponberg, A. (1984) 'The study of Buddhism in China: some observations on the Chinese Buddhist Association and its seminary', *Journal of Chinese Religions* 12: 65–76.

Su Shaozhi (1991) 'Rethinking socialism in the light of China's reforms', *China Information* 6, 10–21.

Swart, P. and Till, B. (1989) 'A revival of Confucian ceremonies in China', in J. Pas (ed.) *Turning of the Tide. Religion in China Today*, Hong Kong: Hong Kong Branch of the Royal Asiatic Society in association with Hong Kong Oxford University Press.

Van Xuyet, Ngo (1976) *Divination, Magie et Politique dans la Chine Ancienne*, Paris: Presses Universitaires de France.

Wang, Hsüeh-wen (1991) 'Tolerance and control. Peking's attitude toward religion', *Issues and Studies* 27, 1: 118–29.

Welch, H. (1972) *Buddhism Under Mao*, Cambridge, MA: Harvard University Press.

Welch, H. (1968) *The Buddhist Revival in China*, Cambridge, MA: Harvard University Press.

Yang, C.K. (1961) *Religion in Chinese Society*, Berkeley & London: University of California Press (reprinted 1970).

Zhou Derong (1991) 'Christentum und die Demokratisierung Chinas' [Christianity and the Democratization of China], *China Heute* 10, 3: 76–8.

Zürcher, E. (1959) *The Buddhist Conquest of China. The Spread and Adaptation of Buddhism in Early Medieval China*, Leiden: E.J. Brill.

INDEX